MODERN CRIMINOLOGY

CRIME, CRIMINAL BEHAVIOR, AND ITS CONTROL

McGraw-Hill Series in Criminology and Criminal Justice

MODERN CRIMINOLOGY

CRIME, CRIMINAL BEHAVIOR, AND ITS CONTROL

JOHN HAGAN

University of Toronto

McGRAW-HILL BOOK COMPANY
New York   St. Louis   San Francisco   Auckland   Bogotá   Hamburg
Johannesburg   London   Madrid   Mexico   Montreal   New Delhi
Panama   Paris   São Paulo   Singapore   Sydney   Tokyo   Toronto

MODERN CRIMINOLOGY
Crime, Criminal Behavior, and Its Control

1 2 3 4 5 6 7 8 9 0 D O C D O C 8 9 8 7 6 5 4

ISBN 0-07-025450-8

This book was set in Times Roman by Black Dot, Inc. (ECU).
The editors were David V. Serbun and Barry Benjamin;
the designer was Janice Noto;
the production supervisor was Diane Renda.
The drawings were supplied by the author.
R. R. Donnelley & Sons Company was printer and binder.

Library of Congress Cataloging in Publication Data

Hagan, John, date
    Modern criminology.

    (McGraw-Hill series in criminology and criminal
justice)
    Bibliography: p.
    Includes index.
    1. Crime and criminals. 2. Criminal justice,
Administration of. I. Title. II. Series.
HV6025.H27 1985   364   84-10049
ISBN 0-07-025450-8

CONTENTS

PREFACE

There are important questions modern criminology must address:

- Who and what should be called criminal?
- Who makes criminal law?
- Are crime rates increasing?
- Are there class differences in criminal behavior?
- Are men more criminal than women?
- How criminal are the corporations?
- Why do some people commit crimes that nearly all of us condemn?
- Why do some people challenge the criminal law?
- Why do we react to crime the way we do?
- Do the poor and minorities receive discriminatory treatment from the criminal-justice system?
- Can the old theories explain the new crimes of class and gender?
- How could we and should we best respond to crime?

This book answers such questions. The answers are not final: they are open to debate. You are invited to join this debate, a debate that is fascinating for more than what it can tell us about crime. Think about what follows. It could change the way you think about the society in which you live.

ACKNOWLEDGMENTS

Although I alone assume responsibility for this book, others have contributed to it. Ron Akers, John Clark, Michael Gottfredson, David Greenberg, Martha Myers, Ruth Peterson, and James Short commented at various stages on the development of the book. Writing such a book is an expression of the excitement others have generated for me in the study of crime. These others include collaborators and teachers, such as Celesta Albonetti, David Bordua, Ron Gillis, Jeff Leon, Ilene Nagel, Gwynn Nettler, Alberto Palloni, John Simpson, Austin Turk, Marjorie Zatz, and Patricia Parker. All have made my work more interesting. I wrote this book while teaching at the University of Toronto and the University of Wisconsin–Madison. I thank both institutions for the support they provided.

JOHN HAGAN

STUDYING CRIMINOLOGY: WHY CRIMINOLOGY?

1

THE ISSUE: WHY CRIMINOLOGY?

"A criminologist," writes one of the most prominent practitioners of the craft, "is one whose professional training, occupational role, and fiduciary reward are concentrated toward a scientific approach, study and analysis of the phenomena of crime and criminal behavior" (Wolfgang, 1963, p. 160). Crime may or may not pay, then, but studying it does! You understandably may ask why: why do people get paid to study crime and criminal behavior, and why, beyond reasons of remuneration, do people engage in this area of study?

There are a variety of answers to these questions, built around the following kinds of concerns: the anxiety, anger, and fear that are common responses to crime; the desire to predict and control crime; the hope of preventing crime through individual and social reform; the wish to understand and explain crime and societal reactions to it; and the simple desire to learn more about crime and what it can tell us about our society. Criminologists disagree, sometimes violently, about which of these kinds of concerns are most legitimate and important. For example, I am most impressed with the last two concerns. However, let us consider the others first.

ANXIETY, ANGER, AND THE FEAR OF CRIME

Anxiety and anger are probably the most easily understood, if not the most widely accepted, motivations to study crime. Many people fear crime and react with apprehension to it. In recent years pollsters and criminologists have taken to measuring this fear. One reason for studying crime, then, is because people wish to know more about what they fear, the conditions under which this fear rises and falls, and the types of persons who fear crime more and less. This research has established that it is not the experience of crime alone that determines the fear of it. In fact, there is a tendency for those who fear crime (e.g., the elderly and women) to restrict their exposure to the risk of crime and therefore to reduce their likelihood of being victimized (Balkin, 1979). However, the fear of crime is undeniably real. It is a perennial concern of voters in English-speaking democracies (see Erskine, 1974; Courtis, 1970; McDonald, 1976, chap. 7), who rank crime among their nation's most serious problems, and who vote with their money and lives as well, buying arms for their own protection (Seidman, 1975. Lizotte and Bordua, 1980). With such concerns in mind, one important North American textbook on crime (Nettler, 1978) concentrates its attention nearly exclusively on those crimes that people fear most, the "predatory crimes," and this concentration is seconded by at least one other important "thinker about crime" (Wilson, 1975).

THE ATTEMPT TO CONTROL CRIME THROUGH PREDICTION

Criminologists have also sought to predict and thereby make possible the control of criminal behavior. The assumption is that characteristics of individuals (e.g., age, sex, work history, seriousness and frequency of earlier infractions) can be used to make predictions about their future involvement in crime. Research based on this assumption has been used to develop prediction tables, which in turn have been used to make predictions about the likelihood of future criminal behavior by specific individuals (e.g., Mannheim and Wilkins, 1955; Glueck and Glueck, 1950), and to make decisions about the treatment they will therefore receive. A goal of this type of criminological work, then, is to improve the capacity for the prediction and control of criminal behavior. Indeed, it has been argued that "research into prediction . . . has produced what is probably criminology's most distinctive contribution to knowledge in the social sciences" (Morris and Hawkins, 1969, p. 242). The case made for this conclusion includes the observation that prediction tables have been used with some success in making parole decisions and in reducing prison costs by releasing those with high probability of success earlier than originally intended. However, it is also acknowledged that the predictive capacity of existing prediction tables is low, and that methodological and ethical issues complicate their evaluation and use. Methodologically, an issue that confronts the use of these tables is the means of determining the rate at which they can be expected to generate false positive predictions (i.e., future noncriminals identified as criminals) and false negative predictions (i.e., future criminals identified as noncriminals) (Hirschi and Selvin, 1967, pp. 244–252; Reiss, 1951). Ethically, an issue presented by the use of prediction tables is the prospect of making legal decisions less on the basis of what persons are legally convicted of having done, and more on the basis of what they are *expected* to do (cf. Banfield, 1968). Notwithstanding these concerns, and for better or worse, "control through prediction" has been a recurring theme in modern criminology.

THE DESIRE TO PREVENT CRIME THROUGH REFORM

Related to prediction and control is the prospect of prevention. Criminologists have gone about crime prevention in decidedly different ways. Their chosen methods have varied from attempts to rehabilitate individual offenders to efforts to restructure society. It cannot be said that either approach has demonstrated great success. This is true in spite of the fact that efforts to reform offenders and the societies in which they live are as old as the field of criminology itself. In fact, one of the most persistent and important debates in criminology has involved a dispute about the proper role, if any, of reform work in this field of study. To understand why the issue of reform has loomed so large in criminology, it may be helpful to note that much that is current in American, Canadian, and British criminology has its roots in the first part of this century among sociologists in the United States (see Gibbons, 1979; Downes, 1978), and that many of the persons involved at this stage had religious and later social work backgrounds (Mills, 1943). Thus many, possibly most, of the early criminologists believed that the primary purpose of criminology was to reform criminals. In this sense, the early criminologists were meliorists, seeking to improve society by rehabilitating criminals. A latter-day expression of this view is that "criminology is basic preparation (or should be) for persons entering various types of social work as well as for the probation and parole officer who is engaged actively in helping the offender become readjusted (or stay adjusted) to his community life" (Elliott, 1952, p. 3).

Yet, from the beginning, there was disagreement among criminologists about the wisdom and appropriateness of becoming professionally identified with attempts to solve social problems, including the crime problem. Indeed, Maurice Parmelee (1918), the author of the first American textbook on crime, "spearheaded the campaign against contamination of 'the scientific character and objectivity of sociology' by social welfare considerations" (Geis, 1960; cited in Gibbons, 1974, p. 407). Parmelee took the position that if criminology was to be an objective, scientific part of the field of sociology, it must forgo an active commitment to a social welfare, melioristic approach. Thus even the early American criminologists quarreled about the purposes of criminology.

This quarrel has become more pronounced in recent years with the emergence of a much more militant attitude toward issues of prevention and reform. This attitude is reflected in a school of thought known as the "new" or "critical" criminology (Taylor, 1975). This school of thought seeks to redefine what is called "criminal" and to "actively participate in militant movements for social justice" (Schauffler, 1974, p. 58). The proposed method for doing this is to define social problems like racism and sexism as crimes (Schwendiger and Schwendiger, 1970), and to encourage militant action, aimed at restructuring the very bases of our society, to deal with them. We will have more to say in Chapter 2 about changing definitions of crime, and in the last part of this chapter we will discuss some of the consequences of this militancy. Here we simply note that militant forms of social action have been encouraged by this school of thought.

EXPLAINING CRIME AND REACTIONS TO IT

We come now to the concerns that I see as most important to modern criminology. The first of these involves efforts to understand and explain crime and societal reactions to it. These efforts begin with the definition and measurement of crime, proceeding from this base to attempts to account theoretically for criminal behavior, its recognition as such, and the reactions of society to it. In this book we will consider a variety of theories that address these issues. Very generally, we categorize these explanations as theories of undercontrol; culture, opportunity, and status; and over-control. The sequencing of these theory groups is intentional, for today the greatest interest is generated by the last group of theories, which see official attempts to control crime as an important topic for study in modern criminology. This is not at all to say that other types of theories are untrue or unimportant. Indeed, we will see that the evidence supporting some of them is impressive. Nonetheless, we submit that the most prominent explanations of crime today are what we will call the theories of "over-control."

WHAT CRIME CAN TELL US ABOUT SOCIETY

The final concern that characterizes modern criminology is the one I think deserves greatest emphasis. This concern is for *what the study of crime can tell us about the society in which we live.* Thus the way in which a society responds to crime can tell us much about what that society values and disvalues and about where that society sets its priorities; for example, between the achievement of social order and the pursuit of personal freedom. As well, the rise and decline of particular kinds of crime can tell us much about the way a society is changing, and with what consequences. Similarly, the social location and distribution of different types of crime, and the strategies used in their control, can reveal a great deal about how a society is organized, and about whose interests its mode of organization serves. Thus the purpose of criminology is not simply to solve the problems of crime but to learn from them. Indeed, one of the things we may have learned from the study of crime is that many crime problems have no simple solutions. Certainly the record of successful problem-solving so far is unimpressive. Nonetheless, this is one of the features of criminology that makes it a fascinating and valuable field of study, for it is in this field that some of the most important theoretical ideas we have about our society and its workings are put to very concrete and important tests. Furthermore, we will demonstrate in this book that notwithstanding the failure to solve the problems of crime, much has been learned about crime and about societal attempts to control it. It will be the results of the scientific study of crime and criminals that will be of greatest concern to us. As you will soon learn, the result of this work is a wide and varied body of knowledge.

CRIMINOLOGY DEFINED

Thus far, we have indicated what a criminologist is, in large part, by discussing what criminologists do. We have also speculated as to why criminologists do what they do. Now we should add to this discussion a formal definition of criminology. Following Webster (1959, p. 197), we take criminology to be "the scientific study of crime and criminals." However, we must also acknowledge that this definition is as inadequate as it is succinct. This is so because many criminologists disagree about what constitutes science, about what methods and investigative techniques should be used in the study of crime, and indeed about what a crime is and who is a criminal. Each of these issues will be addressed in considerable detail in later chapters. In other words, for the moment, we will leave these issues aside! The more pressing need here is to give some comparative and historical sense of how societal conceptions of crime and its control have emerged. Thus in following parts of this chapter we will talk first about historical and comparative aspects of the emergence of crime. The importance of this discussion is to make and emphasize the point that crime is a *social* as well as a *legal* conception—something to be studied rather than assumed. We will then talk briefly about the emergence of criminology in Europe, and finally about the development of North American and British criminology.

THE EMERGENCE OF CRIME

Crime and Culture

What is called a "crime" depends in large part on the culture considered. Therefore, what is called a "crime" in your culture and mine, may not be in another (see, for example, Black, 1983). Many examples could be chosen to make this point. The example we choose is that of the Inuit—or Eskimo—people of Alaska and the Northwest Territories of Canada. What makes this group a particularly interesting example is that "we" are a part of their "crime problem."

It will be useful to begin consideration of this cultural group by noting that crime is a type of social deviance, or in other words variation from a social norm, that is singled out for public punishment. Many noncriminal forms of deviance—for example, many forms of mental illness and some of the sexual pleasures of consenting adults—are neither a matter of public scrutiny nor the subject of punishment. Thus the public scrutiny and punishment of criminal deviance is a part of what makes it uniquely interesting and important—not only in our culture, but in others as well. The question to be asked here is, What is it about particular types of deviance that results in public scrutiny and punishment of those who are involved? In other words, why do some cultural groups designate particular kinds of deviance as criminal?

An important part of the answer to this question involves the central themes of the culture considered. Cavan (1968), Vallee (1962), and Clairmont (1963) offer vivid descriptions of Inuit culture. The very basic problem of physical survival in an intemperate climate is the dominant theme of this culture. Cavan goes on to note that there are two types of deviance in Inuit communities, "private wrongs" and "public crimes," with the distinction based on the perceived threat to community survival. Both categories reflect striking differences from European and American conceptions of crime and deviance.

For example, one of the best-known aspects of Inuit culture involved the acceptability of extramarital sexual relations. However, these encounters only remained accepted, and in this sense normal, so long as they were authorized by the wife-lending husband. When not so arranged, these liaisons could be considered instances of deviant behavior, and therefore subjects of dispute. Nonetheless, such disputes were thought to be a private matter to be resolved between the parties involved. It is also interesting to note that in these unauthorized encounters, it was the "other man," rather than the "seduced" wife, who was considered accountable. Furthermore, the adulterous husband was not considered to have wronged his *own* wife. Revenge, to the point of death, remained the sole prerogative of the offended husband. A significant restraint on the use of this privilege, however, was that the man who avenged himself by killing the offender was held responsible for the care of the widow and her children.

Thus far we have considered an example of "noncriminal" deviance in Inuit culture. "Private wrongs" only became "public crimes" in Inuit culture when the behaviors involved were conceived of as a threat to the welfare or survival of the group itself. Thus a person considered to have caused conditions of starvation was regarded much as we would a murderer. Pursuing this theme, Cavan (1968) summarizes several differences between Inuit and Anglo-American conceptions of criminality.

> Killing another person was not necessarily a crime. The destruction of an old parent or a newborn baby . . . was not a crime. Nor was it a crime to kill the seducer of . . . [one's] wife. But unprovoked killing or a chain of murders that threatened the supply of men in a community and therefore endangered the food supply was a serious crime and called for community action (p. 25).

Thus many acts we hold criminal were not so regarded by the Inuit. More interesting still, however, is a partial reversal in the conceptualization of theft. Hoarding food and possessions beyond one's needs was considered a form of stealing by the Inuit, and, during periods of scarcity, this form of theft was regarded as quite serious. On the other hand, Vallee (1962) points out that what we would be more likely to regard as theft rarely occurred or was rarely regarded as such in Inuit communities. As a result, there were no public or formal sanctions available when it did occur. Instead, "If someone took something which did not belong to him, it was assumed that he must be in dire need and that he would replace it quietly whenever he could do so" (p. 190).

A final word should be said about responses to crime and deviance in Inuit culture. Sanctions in Inuit communities were predominantly informal. Typical measures included ridicule, gossip, and ostracism (Birket-Smith, 1959). However, in extreme cases threatening the survival of the group, a redefinition of "private wrongs" as "public crimes" took place, and exile or execution was invoked. Such measures often followed from a process in which heads of families in the community reached agreement on the threat posed to the group by the offending member. Obviously, the judgments reached by such a process in Inuit communities could be quite different from those reached in American or Canadian courts of law. To note only one source of disagreement, where the Inuit were, and perhaps still are, much more concerned with survival, Americans and Canadians are more concerned with property and its protection. As the Inuit and the American and Canadian cultures have come into contact, and sometimes collision, these differences in cultural conceptions have come into conflict. Some of the results of this conflict are reflected in the writing of the previous paragraphs in the past tense.

In this conflict, American and Canadian courts have played a sometimes confusing, and often coercive, role in imposing foreign conceptions of crime and punishment on the members of Inuit communities. An example may help to make this point.

> Matthew Koonungnak . . . of Baker Lake, Northwest Territories, was charged with hunting musk-ox contrary to the Game Ordinance. Koonungnak had never before seen a musk-ox, and the animal was approaching his camp. In order to protect the camp, and on the advice of another Eskimo, Koonungnak shot it. He subsequently came to the police department . . . to advise the police what had happened, took the police to his camp, and was then charged with the offense. When he appeared before the Justice of the Peace, he readily admitted shooting the animal, and further stated that if he ever saw another musk-ox and it came towards him he would shoot it. The Justice of the Peace interpreted these statements as a plea of guilty, and imposed a fine of $200.00 or four months in jail in default of the payment (4).

This decision was reversed on appeal. One reason for the reversal was that the guilty plea was judged invalid. The problem, it seems, is that the Inuit people have no corresponding word in their culture for the term "guilty." Beyond this, the appellate judge found that the defendant acted in self-defense, noting that "it is notorious in the north . . . that an outcast bull musk-ox driven from the herd and wandering in the barrens alone and homeless is a dangerous animal" (Schmeiser, 1972, p. 4).

The lesson of this episode is that conceptions of crime and deviance are relative to culture and circumstance. These divergent conceptions can become particularly problematic when cultures come into close and continued contact. The results of such contacts include compromise, conflict, and coercion, and inevitably change. Furthermore, we should not be lulled into thinking that it is always *other* cultures that are subject to change. Our own culture, with its corresponding conceptions of crime, changes as well. One way of making this apparent is to consider next the emergence of crime, and particularly the changing character of its control, in Anglo-American societies.

Crime in Time

Much that will have seemed foreign in the Inuit conception of crime may seem less so when we look back over time for the roots of our own ways of dealing with what we have called "crime." We will begin this discussion by considering the early societies that preceded what we recognize now as the emergence of English society. These early societies were organized around kinship groups and tribes. No centralized system of criminal justice existed. Instead, a prominent role in resolving disputes was assigned to the victims of "crime" themselves. Victims and their kin were expected to put things right by avenging what they perceived as crimes against them: "All crime was against the family; it was the family that was regarded as having committed the crimes of its members; it was the family that had to atone, or carry out the blood-feud" (Traill, 1899, p. 5). We should make clear that the reference to "blood" in these feuds refers to the base of the conflicts in family units, rather than to their common consequences. Nonetheless, Schafer (1977, p. 6) writes that "in that primitive period the criminal-victim relationship . . . was hardly anything more than a mutually opposed effort to secure power." The image is of a social condition in which, as the famous English philosopher Thomas Hobbes put it, "Life is nasty, brutish and short."

Several features made this period unique. First, there were no effective laws, or for that matter a centralized state, to protect the rights of the accused or the victim. In this situation, the assignment of moral guilt was largely irrelevant; what was relevant was the initiative taken by victims and their kin in the form of retaliation. Thus Ziegenhagen (1977, p. 36) notes that "contrary to modern conceptions of punishment, the injury inflicted upon the perpetrator reflected the damage sustained by the victim as well as the context in which the offender was apprehended; and, contrary to contemporary Western conceptions, the moral guilt of the perpetrator was not of concern."

The rise of feudalism and Christianity were accompanied by a gradual elimination of blood-feuding and an emerging system of financial compensations involving the *wer, wite,* and *bot* (Jeffrey, 1957). The *wer* or *wergild* was a payment made to the victim's family following a killing or injury; the *bot* was a payment for injuries less than death; and the *wite* was a fine payable to a lord or king. By the seventh century, and the reign of King Ethelbert, the amounts of compensation involved were indicated in written laws and were related very explicitly to the statuses of the victims and accused involved. A variety of crimes and their literal costs were spelled out. For example,

A man who "lays with a maiden belonging to the king," . . . had to pay fifty shillings compensation, but if she was "a grinding slave" the compensation was halved. Compensation for lying with a nobleman's serving maid was assessed still lower at twelve shillings and with a commoner's serving maid at six shillings. If a freeman raped the slave of a commoner he had to pay more than five shillings' compensation, but if a slave raped this same girl he was castrated (Hibbert, 1963, p. 4).

The crimes covered in this elaborate system ranged from murder to fornication, with the compensation for each carefully stipulated and graded.

The church played a prominent role in some aspects of this system. Harding (1966, p. 13) notes that "the foreign clergy, venturing into a rough and pagan society, had to be given an appropriate status and protection for the property they would acquire from noble patrons." During this period the church was entitled to receive as compensation twelve times the value of goods stolen from a consecrated place; a bishop's compensation was sometimes greater than the king's; and large shares of some payments made by the accused were passed on to the clergy (Hibbert, 1963, p. 4). What is significant in this is that as feudalism developed in England, between 700 and 1066, lords and bishops gradually replaced kinship groups as recipients of compensatory payments (Jeffrey, 1957). This was a very significant beginning of the movement of victims out of a position of prominence in an emerging system of criminal justice that was developing its own increasingly independent ways of dealing with crime; independent, that is, at least from the demands of individual victims.

Two other important developments during this period involved what ultimately became the king's peace (i.e., areas under royal jurisdiction) and the king's courts. While both institutions took many centuries to develop, the seeds of each were present in the written laws of King Ethelbert. In this period, England was not a land of a single peace, but of many, one belonging to each great lord and one to the church. As well, proceedings began to emerge in which the king received a part of the compensation to be paid. This reflects the fact that "the king's court was already acquiring special authority" (Harding, 1966, p. 15). Schafer (1977, p. 14) notes that "before long the injured person's right to restitution began to shrink, and . . . the fine that went to the state gradually replaced it entirely." Significantly, it was now not only the church, but also the state, that was replacing the victim as a central actor in the criminal-justice process.

Whitelock (1952, pp. 139–142) provides a useful description of court proceedings in the feudal period, and of the role of defendants and victims in them.

> The procedure in law-suits was strictly formal. . . . The plaintiff summoned the defendant to appear to answer his charge, and if the defendant failed to appear, after a due number of lawfully given summonses, adequately witnessed, he lost his suit by default. . . .
>
> If the defendant appeared in court to answer the charge, it was

normal for the plaintiff to make a preliminary oath. . . . In most cases the defendant was then allowed to bring forward an oath to prove his innocence. . . . He could do this with the aid of compurgators, or oath-helpers, whose number was conditioned by the nature and severity of the charge involved. . . .

If on the appointed day the defendant came to court and performed the oath in full, the suit was ended and he was clear. But there could be circumstances that cut the defendant off from the right to produce an oath. If he were a man of suspicious character who had been frequently accused, or if he had ever been convicted of perjury, he was no longer "oath worthy." . . . In such cases, the court awarded the right of bringing an oath to the plaintiff, who then brought forward his compurgators to swear to the defendant's guilt. Similarly, the plaintiff, instead of the defendant, was awarded the oath if he had witnesses of the crime. . . . When the plaintiff had in this way produced his oath, or when the oath had been granted to the defendant and he had proved unable to give it, the defendant might then go to the ordeal, the judgment of God, the church then took control of the proceedings.

The court proceedings described represent a tradition of *private* prosecution in the sense that the responsibility for initiating a trial still resided with the injured party.

The transition in England to a more modern form of criminal justice occurred during the reign of Henry II (1154–1189). During this period the feudal system of law, with its monetary sanctions, disappeared. In its place, a system of common law emerged. The common law is a set of traditions formed out of judicial decisions rather than legislative statutes. Its importance is reflected in part by the fact that it remains to this day a basis for interpreting contemporary criminal statutes, which are often quite vague in their content. Included among what are still called "common law crimes" are murder, rape, robbery, assault, burglary, larceny, and arson (see Blackstone, 1965; Clark and Marshall, 1967). With the end of the feudal system, the punishments imposed for these crimes and others moved from the financial to the physical, including such practices as branding, mutilation, and the removal of limbs, not to mention execution. For a variety of reasons, then, this period of transition is of great importance. Jeffrey (1957, p. 660) observes that "a comparison of the laws of Henry I and Henry II reveals that a revolution occurred in the legal field. The former described a system of *wer, bot,* and *wite;* the latter described a system of writs, procedures, and common law.

Two significant aspects of the legal revolution that Jeffrey describes were the growing separation of the church and state in criminal matters, and the exclusive jurisdiction of the state in the imposition of public punishments. Thus by 1226 Jeffrey notes that an agreement between the criminal and the relatives of a slain person could no longer save the murderer from indictment and a death sentence: the state no longer allowed private settlements of criminal cases. As well, although the church continued to punish offenders of canon law through excommunication and a system of penances, the church finally lost its right to punish crime through the use of force. In other words, both the victim of crime and the church continued to be supplanted by the state.

Nonetheless, a system of private prosecutions based on the initiative taken by victims of crime remained in effect in England well into the nineteenth century. In fact, the final decline of the victim's role in the criminal-justice system did not begin until the Enlightenment, with the work of some of the first recognized criminologists, particularly Cesare Beccaria and Jeremy Bentham. A primary contribution made by these early criminologists was to draw the link between crime and society, and to insist on the role of the state in monitoring this link. We therefore will now turn to a discussion of the emergence of criminology in Europe, and to a consideration of the impact of the early criminologists on our cultural conceptions of crime and punishment.

THE EMERGENCE OF EUROPEAN CRIMINOLOGY

The Classical School

Modern criminology has its roots in what is known as the classical school of criminology. The classical criminologists were distinguished by the fact that they rebelled strongly against the methods used to control crime in their time, urging a new kind of criminal law in its place; and by the fact that they anticipated many of the most important reforms in criminal law that have occurred since that time, including the general understanding that crimes represent injuries to society as much or more than to the individuals who experience them. We will discuss these ideas as they were expressed by two classical thinkers, Cesare Beccaria and Jeremy Bentham.

Cesare Beccaria

It is doubtful that Cesare Beccaria (1738–1794) expected, or even aspired to, the position he has achieved in the history of criminology. He is known to have been an undistinguished student, and his interest in issues of crime was transient (Sylvester, 1972, p. 9). Nonetheless, he was a man who expressed his ideas clearly, and they were ideas whose time clearly had come.

Beccaria wrote in a time when the criminal law and its enforcement were, in a word, barbarous. Secret accusations, brutal executions, torture, arbitrary and inconsistent punishments, and class-linked disparities in punishments were the order of the day. Beccaria was not alone in his objections to these practices, and it is doubtful that he ever would have rallied fellow thinkers against them were it not for the fact that he came into the company of a group called the "Academy of Fists." This group was concerned with a variety of social problems of the day, and Beccaria took it as his contribution to learn and write about the problems of crime and its punishment. The resulting book, *Dei Delitti e delle Pene* (*On Crimes and Punishments*), was originally published (in 1764) anonymously, when Beccaria was only 26 years of age. Although he wrote little else of significance, this work was an immediate success, with profound consequences (Monachesi, 1960, chap. 2).

In terms of our cultural conception of crime, Beccaria's most important contribution was to consider crime as an injury to society. It was the injury to society, rather than to the immediate individual(s) who experienced it, that was to direct and determine the degree of punishment. Behind this thinking was the utilitarian assumption that all social action should be guided by the goal of achieving "the greatest happiness for the greatest number." From this viewpoint, the punishment of an individual for a crime was justified, and justifiable only, for its contribution to the prevention of future infringements on the happiness and well-being of others. While in today's world these ideas may seem common enough, their implications for the world of Beccaria were dramatic.

For one thing, Beccaria reasoned that certain and quick, rather than severe, punishments would best accomplish the above goals. Indeed, he argued (p. 99) that "in order for punishment not to be . . . an act of violence of one or many against a private citizen, it must be . . . public, prompt, . . . the least possible in the given circumstances, proportionate to the crimes, [and] dictated by the laws." This meant that torture, execution, and other barbarities must be abolished; in their place, there were to be quick and certain trials and, in the case of convictions, carefully calculated punishments. Beccaria went beyond this to propose that accused persons be treated humanely before trial, with every right and facility extended to enable them to bring evidence in their own behalf. The significance of this is that in Beccaria's day accused and convicted persons were detained in the same institutions, and subjected to the same inhumane punishments. In place of this, Beccaria argued for swift and sure punishments, to be imposed on only those found guilty, with the punishments determined strictly in accordance with the damage to *society* caused by the crime.

In many other respects, Beccaria was a modern thinker. McDonald (1976, p. 41) notes that Beccaria focused on two primary causes of crime—economic conditions and bad laws. On the one hand, he suggested that property crimes were committed mainly by the poor, and mainly out of necessity. On the other hand, he argued that too severe a punishment for a particular crime could deter someone from committing it, but at the same time make another crime attractive by comparison. As well, he argued that cruel laws could promote crime by diminishing the human spirit. What was needed, argued Beccaria, was a careful matching of the crime and its punishment, in keeping with the general interests of society. The classical thinker we consider next, Jeremy Bentham, went beyond this in attempting to create a "calculus" for realizing these interests.

Jeremy Bentham

If Beccaria was a reluctant writer, Jeremy Bentham (1748–1832) clearly was not. He wrote with abandon. However, a sense of the oddness of this second major figure in the classical school of criminology is found in the facts that he suffered from retarded physical growth during his early years, that he had "the colossal temerity to attempt to catalogue and to label all varieties of human behavior and the motivations giving rise to them," and that he is said to have formed a close relationship with only one woman in his life, to whom he proposed marriage at the age of 57 (Geis, 1960, p. 52). Bentham was an eccentric. However, it is also said, with somewhat greater significance, that Bentham was to the field of law reform what Adam Smith was to the world of economics (see Radzinowicz, 1948, p. 361n; Halevy, 1955).

Bentham began with Beccaria's concern for achieving "the greatest happiness of the greatest number." His interest was in giving precision to this idea, in part, through a pseudomathematical concept he called "felicity calculus." This "calculus" was intended as a means of estimating the goodness or badness of acts. Although not taken seriously today, these efforts were important in that they encouraged Bentham and other reformers to make explicit the intended logic of the criminal law and its enforcement. At this time, the law remained not only barbarous but also highly disorganized and contradictory. Against this, Bentham meant to make the law an efficient, indeed *economical,* means of *preventing* crime. Like Beccaria, Bentham insisted that prevention was the only justifiable purpose of punishment, and furthermore that punishment was too "expensive" when it produced more evil than good, or when the same good could be obtained at the "price" of less suffering. His recommendation was that penalties be fixed so as to impose an amount of pain in excess of the pleasure that might be derived from the criminal act. It was this calculation of pain compared to pleasure that Bentham believed would deter crime.

These ideas were formulated most clearly in his *Introduction to the Principles of Morals and Legislation,* first published in 1789.

It was part of the contradictions of Bentham's character that he was at least as calculating as he was humane. For example, Bentham argued that capital punishment should be restricted to offenses "which in the highest degree shock the public feeling." He went on to argue that if the hanging of a man's effigy could produce the same preventive effect as the hanging of the man himself, it would be a folly and a cruelty not to do so (Radzinowicz, 1948, pp. 381–382). However, he also suggested, with his penchant for calculation, that capital punishments might nonetheless be used to maximum effect as follows:

> A scaffold painted black, the livery of grief—the officers of justice dressed in crepe—the executioner covered with a mask, which would serve at once to augment the terror of his appearance, and to shield him from ill-founded indignation—emblems of his crime placed above the head of the criminal, to the end that the witnesses of his sufferings may know for what crimes he undergoes them: these might form a part of the principal decorations of these legal tragedies. . . . Whilst all the actors in this terrible drama might move in solemn procession—serious and religious music preparing the hearts of the spectators for the important lesson they were about to receive. . . . The judges need not consider it beneath their dignity to preside over this public scene (Bentham, quoted in Radzinowicz, 1948, pp. 383–384).

Bentham also had unusual ideas about imprisonment, an idea that was then in its infancy. He spent much of his life trying to convince authorities that an institution of his design, called the "Panopticon prison," would solve the problems of correction.

> Architecturally, the Panopticon was to be a circular building with a glass roof and containing cells on every story of the circumference. It was to be so arranged that every cell could be visible from a central point. The omniscient prison inspector would be kept from the sight of the prisoners by a system of "blinds unless . . . he thinks fit to show himself" (Geis, 1960, p. 64).

The suggested administration of this utopian prison is a further illustration of Bentham's utilitarian style of thought. The central figure in the prison was to be a manager who would employ the inmates in contract labor. The manager was to receive a share of the money earned by the inmates, but he was to be financially liable if inmates who were later released reoffended, or if an excessive number of inmates died during imprisonment. For Bentham, calculation was always the key to successful control. Two prisons of the Panopticon design were actually built in the United States: the Western State Penitentiary in Pennsylvania and the Statesville Prison in Illinois. However, the first was rebuilt seven years after construction, and the second was redesigned before it was finished.

Other of Bentham's ideas have fared better. He argued strongly for the establishment of the office of public prosecutor, and he furthered the notion that crimes are committed against society rather than against individuals. Beyond this, he argued that many victimless crimes were imaginary rather than real offenses, suggesting, for example, that "offenses which originate in the sexual appetite, when there is neither violence, fraud, nor interference with the rights of others, and also offenses aginst one's self, may be arranged under this head" (Bentham, quoted in Geis, 1960, p. 61). And, for better or worse, he anticipated the role that official crime statistics were later to play in advanced societies, noting that "they may be compared to the bills of mortality published annually in London; indicating the moral health of the country . . . as these latter do the physical" (Bowring, 1843, vol. 4, p. 29).

Karl Marx later said of all this that "in no time and in no country has the most homespun commonplace ever strutted about in so self-satisfied a way" (Geis, 1960, p. 51), while Sir Henry Maine concluded that "I do not know of a single law reform effected since Bentham's time which cannot be traced to his influence." Even with this brief introduction to Bentham, it probably is not difficult to understand this division of views. Nonetheless, Bentham's writings, and those of other classical criminologists, had a profound effect on the way we think about and respond to crime today.

From Crime to Science

Observation, description, and measurement are among the building blocks of science. In these respects, the roots of modern criminology are European as well, building, for example, on the pioneering works of the Belgian Adolphe Jacques Quételet and the Englishman Henry Mayhew. These two very different personalities developed methods for the study of crime that continue to have important analogues today. Quételet introduced the use of quantitative techniques in criminological research, while Mayhew provides an early example of a long tradition built on the use of observational research strategies. Both represent early contributions to the study of crime as a science.

Adolphe Jacques Quételet

The study of crime was only a part-time avocation of Adolphe Jacques Quételet (1796–1874). His early training was in mathematics, and by the age of 23 he had discovered a curve that earned him a professorial chair and established his reputation for life. This enabled Quételet to turn to applied areas of interest, including astronomy, meteorology, and sociology (McDonald, 1976, p. 63). What Quételet brought to these fields was a belief that scientific laws could be observed only within certain degrees of probability, resulting from, and reflected in, large numbers of observations rather than in individual occurrences (Sylvester, 1972, p. 25). In the realm of sociology, and more specifically in the study of crime, Quételet used what he called "moral statistics" to try to establish these scientific laws, or regularities.

In doing this, Quételet called attention to a basic problem with crime statistics that criminologists ever since have sought to resolve: the gap that exists between "known and judged offenses" and what the statistics are intended to measure, "committed offenses." The problem, he noted, was that "our observations can only refer to a certain number of known and tried offenses, out of the unknown sum total of crimes committed" (Quételet, 1842, p. 82). Quételet saw the problem as one of establishing the ratio that exists between the two kinds of offenses. However, he also noted that this ratio is susceptible to a variety of influences.

> Thus the greatness of this ratio, which will generally be different for different crimes and offenses, will chiefly depend on the activity of justice in reaching the guilty, on the care with which the latter conceal themselves, on the repugnance which the individuals injured may have to complain, or perhaps on their not knowing that any injury has been committed against them.

Nonetheless, Quételet observed that this ratio, at least in well-organized societies, should be closer to unity for serious crimes, and further from unity for less serious crimes. On the basis of this premise and others, Quételet undertook his study of the "moral statistics of crime." Some of his early findings have stood the test of time.

For example, Quételet observed that men have what he called a greater "propensity" for crime than women, and that the young have a greater propensity than the old. The persistence of these kinds of findings, over a large number of observations and in a variety of times and places, led Quételet to the conclusion that "we can enumerate in advance how many individuals will soil their hands in the blood of their fellows, how many will be frauds, how many prisoners; almost as one can enumerate in advance the births and deaths that will take place" (ibid., p. 97). However, Quételet also concluded that while these patterns were resistant to change, sustained efforts could nonetheless bring their gradual improvement, and that the failure to make such efforts would have its own cost. Thus there was a moral to the moral statistics:

I cannot repeat too often, to all men who sincerely desire the well-being and honour of their kind, and who would blush to consider a few francs more or less paid to the treasury as equivalent to a few heads more or less submitted to the axe of the executioner, that there is a budget which we pay with a frightful regularity—it is that of prisons, chains, and the scaffold: it is that which, above all, we ought to endeavor to abate (p. 96).

Henry Mayhew

While Quételet relied on enumeration and estimation as the means of answering questions about crime, Henry Mayhew (1812–1887) relied on observation and description. The result was a four-volume classic, *London Labour and the London Poor*, that provided a detailed account of the growing masses who made up the backwash of Victorian capitalism. Passages like the following made the problems of this period difficult to ignore.

There are thousands of neglected children loitering about the low neighborhoods of the metropolis, and prowling about the streets, begging and stealing for their daily bread. They are to be found in Westminster, Whitechapel, Shoreditch, St. Gile's, New Cut, Lambeth, the Borough and other localities. Hundreds of them may be seen leaving their parents' homes and low lodging-houses every morning sallying forth in search of food and plunder (Mayhew, 1862, p. 273).

Yet there was also an ambivalence in Mayhew's work. As he described in detail the varieties of crime and degradation that characterized this period, he tended to focus as much on the weaknesses of his subjects as on the circumstances to which they were subjected. Still, Mayhew brought the problems of crime forcibly into the consciousness of his readers. And, in doing so, he called his readers to action, arguing,

It is far easier to train the young in virtuous and industrious habits, than to reform the grown-up felon who has become callous in crime, and it is besides far more profitable to the state. To neglect them or inadequately to attend to their welfare gives encouragement to the growth of this dangerous class (ibid., p. 275).

Although this was clearly a plea for reform based on fear and self-interest, it nonetheless was a call for action, and, for its time, it was based on a systematic and literate survey of the problems of crime.

The Positivist School

The positivist school of criminology takes its name from the positive philosophy of the nineteenth century, which applied the scientific method to the study of social problems. The group of thinkers we consider from this school—Cesare Lombroso, Raffaele Garofalo, and Enrico Ferri—made the study of *criminals* self-consciously scientific. They did this by emphasizing the importance of the *controlled* investigation of criminals and noncriminals. This is *not* the same as saying that their investigations *were* well-controlled or, in this and other ways, scientific. Indeed, it seems that they often were not. However, the positivist school of criminology had provocative things to say about the causes of criminal behavior, and by saying them with at least a claim to scientific standards, this group of thinkers initiated a whole new tradition of criminological work that today prides itself on its scientific standing. In this sense, the positivist school of criminology may have been more significantly an aspiration than an achievement. Nonetheless, the aspiration proved to be important.

Cesare Lombroso

"In the history of criminology," writes Marvin Wolfgang (1960, p. 168), "probably no name has been eulogized or attacked so much as that of Cesare Lombroso." Thus while Lombroso (1835–1909) frequently is called "the father of modern criminology," it is also the case that most modern criminologists regard his ideas about the causes of crime as almost entirely erroneous. To understand how Lombroso could be both so revered and so wrong, it is necessary to appreciate his ideas as well as his methods of research.

The most significant aspect of Lombroso's work involved his application of the concept of atavism, and the principles of evolution, to the study of crime. Lombroso's thesis was that criminals could be distinguished from noncriminals by the presence of physical anomalies that represented a reversion to a primitive or subhuman type of person. In other words, Lombroso saw criminals as biological "throwbacks" to a primitive, or "atavistic," stage of evolution.

Lombroso developed these ideas during the course of his work as a prison physician. One particular offender, a famous inmate by the name of Vilella, attracted Lombroso's special interest. Lombroso conducted a postmortem examination of Vilella and discovered a depression in the interior back part of his skull that he called the "median occipital fossa." Lombroso (ibid., p. 184) recognized this feature as a characteristic found in inferior animals and excitedly concluded the following:

This was not merely an idea, but a revelation. At the sight of that skull, I seemed to see all of a sudden, lighted up as a vast plain under a flaming sky, the problem of the nature of the criminal—an atavistic being who reproduces in his person the ferocious instincts of primitive humanity and the inferior animals. Thus were explained anatomically the enormous jaws, high cheek-bones, prominent superciliary arches, solitary lines in the palms, extreme size of the orbits, handle-shaped or sessile ears found in criminals, savages, and apes, insensibility to pain, extremely acute sight, tattooing, excessive idleness, love of orgies, and the irresistable craving for evil for its own sake, the desire not only to extinguish life in the victim, but to mutilate the corpse, tear its flesh, and drink its blood.

Lombroso himself conducted thousands of postmortem examinations and anthropometric studies of criminals and noncriminals, leading him to the conclusion that the criminal was, in effect, a human subspecies, with very distinct physical and mental characteristics. In the beginning this led to a simple dichotomous scheme including two types of criminals, the true or born criminal, who was thought to make up about one-third of the criminal population, and occasional criminals, who presumably made up the rest. Lombroso later added additional categories that involved a greater attention to the influence of social factors. In these categories of criminals, Lombroso increasingly speculated about the interaction of genetic and environmental influences. Still, he maintained to the end his conviction that the true or born criminal was responsible for a large amount of criminal behavior. These ideas were expressed most fully in the several editions of *L'Uomo delinquente,* the first of which was published in 1876 (see also Lombroso, 1918). It is some testimony to his faith in these ideas and research methods that Lombroso made it a part of his will that on his death his own body was to be taken to his laboratory of legal medicine, where an autopsy was to be performed. His brain was preserved in the Institute of Anatomy (Wolfgang, 1960, p. 177n).

In 1913, only four years following Lombroso's death, Charles Goring published *The English Convict,* the most important refutation of Lombroso's theory. In this and other critiques it is convincingly demonstrated that Lombroso's work suffered from poor research design and measurement. His hypotheses simply were not well-supported by his own or others' data (see, for example, Lindesmith and Levin, 1937). Even Wolfgang (1960), a sympathetic assessor of Lombroso's contributions, notes that his "rash and easy generalizations about atavism and degeneracy deduced from biological anomalies left a vulnerable hiatus between theory and fact." The question that remains, then, is why Lombroso has been considered a founder of modern criminology. The answer lies in the fact that Lombroso's provocative assertions reoriented modern thinking about crime from a focus on the *offense* to a focus on the *offender*. Sellin (1937, pp. 898–899) made this point long ago by noting that "whether Lombroso was right or wrong is perhaps in the last analysis not so important as the unquestionable fact that his ideas proved so challenging that they gave an unprecedented impetus to the study of the offender." Similarly, Wolfgang (1960, p. 224) concludes that "Lombroso served to redirect emphasis from the crime to the criminal, not from social to individual factors." In doing so, Lombroso initiated a whole new era of criminological research.

Raffaele Garofalo

One indirect legacy of Lombroso's work is seen in the thinking of a second member of the positivist school of criminology, Raffaele Garofalo (1852–1934). Garofalo was born a member of the Italian nobility and went on to become a magistrate, a professor of criminal law, and a prominent member of government. It therefore is not surprising that Garofalo took a great interest in the criminal law and its reform. Drawing indirectly on the work of Lombroso, Garofalo came to a set of conclusions that provide a fascinating contrast with the ideas of the classical thinkers considered earlier.

Garofalo began with the assumption that to understand the criminal it is necessary to have a meaningful definition of crime. This definition is based on a distinction between "natural crime," to which Garofalo attaches great importance, and "police crime," a residual category to which Garofalo attaches less importance (see Allen, 1960, p. 275). "Natural crimes" are those which violate two basic "altruistic sentiments," pity (revulsion against the voluntary infliction of suffering on others) and probity (respect for the property rights of others). "Police offenses" are behaviors which do not offend these altruistic sentiments but are nonetheless called "criminal" by law. Garofalo was more concerned with the former category because he regarded the crimes in it as more serious, because he believed the category itself to be based on a unifying principle, and because he regarded this as the area in which criminal law played its most important role. It is to the latter ideas about criminal law that we turn next.

Although Garofalo found Lombroso's theories inadequate as an explanation for the "natural crimes" of "true criminals," he still wound up concluding that criminals have "regressive characteristics" indicating a "lower degree of advancement," and this premise was essential to Garofalo's ideas about criminal law. These ideas are most clearly presented in

Garofalo's *Criminology,* originally published in 1885 and translated into English in 1914. The key to the arguments presented in this volume is the assumption that true criminals, lacking in the basic altruistic sentiments, are unfit for the society in which they live. The solution to this evolutionary problem, Garofalo (1914, pp. 219–220) argued, was elimination of the unfit.

> In this way, the social power will effect an artificial selection similar to that which nature effects by the death of individuals inassimilable to the particular conditions of the environment in which they are born or to which they have been removed. Herein the state will be simply following the example of nature.

Thus where the classical theorists focused on the symbolic value of punishments as a means of *deterring* crime in the general population, Garofalo and the positivists were constrained by their belief in evolutionary principles to focus more specifically on the *incapacitory* function of punishments—including life imprisonment and the death penalty. In other words, the positivists were led to conceive of the relationship between crime and law in a quite different way from the classical criminologists. As we will see, both sets of ideas have analogues in modern criminology.

Enrico Ferri

It is appropriate that the last of the European founders of modern criminology we will discuss is Enrico Ferri (1856–1929), for Ferri was possibly the most interesting, and certainly the most eclectic, of the criminologists of his time. Ferri developed his ideas in the course of his work as a university professor, trial lawyer, member of parliament, newspaper editor, public lecturer, and author. Along the way, Ferri spent a year studying with Lombroso and became his lifelong friend.

Ferri's first contact with Lombroso occurred when he sent the latter a copy of his dissertation. It is said that although Lombroso's response was generally favorable, he also remarked that "Ferri isn't positivist enough." Indignantly, Ferri responded to a mutual friend, "What! Does Lombroso suggest that I, a lawyer, should go and measure the heads of criminals in order to be positivist enough?!" (cited in Sellin, 1960, pp. 280–281). Ferri eventually did just that, but not before he developed his ideas in a variety of other ways, including a study of crime in France patterned after the earlier work of Quételet.

In organizing his work, Ferri departed from Lombroso's example by giving social factors prominence. In doing this, Ferri insisted that crime "is the effect of multiple causes" that include a large number of anthropological, physical, and social factors. These factors were productive of criminals who were classified as: (1) born or instinctive, (2) insane, (3) passional, (4) occasional, (5) habitual. These ideas were expressed most significantly in Ferri's *Criminal Sociology,* with the title demarcating what Ferri called "the science of criminality and of social defense against it." Ferri (1917, p. 36) was not modest in distinguishing this positivistic approach from the classical tradition.

> The science of crimes and punishments was formerly a doctrinal exposition of the syllogisms brought forth by the sole force of logical phantasy. Our School has made it a science of positive observation, which, based on anthropology, psychology, and criminal statistics as well as on criminal law and studies relative to imprisonment, becomes the synthetic science to which I myself gave the name "criminal sociology."

However, what is most fascinating, and equally disturbing, is the unexpected political twist that Ferri's thought gave to his career. He was a tireless orator who was received enthusiastically by lay and academic audiences alike. Through much of his life, Ferri was a committed Marxist, and he attempted the difficult (impossible?) task in his work of bringing together Marxian and Darwinian principles. At one point, Ferri lost a professorship because of his Marxist leanings. However, the results of his thinking also included conclusions that today seem ludicrous, including arguments like the following (1917, p. 118):

> The Marxian doctrine of historical materialism . . . according to which the economic conditions . . . determine . . . both the moral sentiments and the political and legal institutions of the same group, is profoundly true. It is the fundamental law of positivist sociology. Yet I think that this theory should be supplemented by admitting in the first place that the economic conditions of each people are in turn the natural resultant of its racial energies.

Views like the above eventually allowed Ferri to turn from socialism to fascism as the system most likely to implement the type of reforms he thought necessary. Thus in the fifth edition of *Criminal Sociology* (1929, pp. 11–12) he noted in a footnote that,

> While in the fourth edition (1900) I alluded hopefully to socialist trends—to which I have given my fervid enthusiasm, especially by the propaganda I have carried on for the moral and social education of the Italian masses—now in the fifth edition (1929) I have to note with regard to Italy that since the influence of the Socialist

Party disappeared after the war, because it neither knew how to make a revolution nor wanted to assume the responsibility of power, the task of the social prevention of criminality was assumed and has begun to be realized by the Fascist Government.

It was a sad conclusion to a productive career that is perhaps most important for the encouragement it gave to the scientific study of the social causes of criminal behavior.

Looking Back

Looking back over this discussion of the emergence of European criminology, we can see good evidence for the contention that conceptions of crime are changeable, and that the way in which we conceive of crime influences the way we respond to it. In particular, the classical and positivist schools of European criminology represent very different approaches to the topic of crime, and these alternative approaches have had a continuing impact on the development of American criminology. We will see in the following pages that the positivist perspective prevailed in the early phases of American criminology, while the classical approach has reemerged as an influential viewpoint in more recent years. The American sociologist David Matza has played the roles of participant and observer in the renewed awareness of the contributions of the classical school, and it is therefore of interest to note the distinctions he draws between the two approaches.

Matza (1964, pp. 3–12) notes first and foremost that positivist criminology gives primacy to the criminal *actor* rather than to the criminal *law* as the focus for study. Second, Matza observes that while the classical school adopted the assumption that people exercise free will in the choice among alternative actions (i.e., through the process of human reasoning), the positivist school follows the assumption that human actions are determined in a scientifically ascertainable way (i.e., by physical and/or social causes). Third, Matza suggests that positivists see the criminal as fundamentally different from the noncriminal, and that the search for such differences is the positivist's preoccupation.

It is important to keep in mind that the differences between these schools of thought are in large part a product of the very different times and conditions in which they emerged (Jeffrey, 1957). The classical school developed in the eighteenth century as part of an attempt to reform a barbarous legal system, and as an effort to protect accused persons against harsh and arbitrary actions on the part of the state. Thus the classical school was anxious to make "the punishment fit the crime" by providing a definite and calculated penalty for each and every crime, regardless of the person committing it. In contrast, the positivist school developed in the nineteenth century as an attempt to apply scientific methods to the study of the criminal. In doing this, the positivists encouraged individual treatment tailored to the particular *kind* of criminal involved, with an emphasis as well on protecting society *from* the criminal. As we will now see, it was the positivist perspective that exercised the greater influence in the early stages of American criminology.

THE EMERGENCE OF NORTH AMERICAN CRIMINOLOGY

A Beginning

The positivist roots of American criminology are reflected in the fact that some of the earliest work done in the United States was centered around "child-guidance" clinics (Reckless, 1973, appendix B). The first of these clinics was established in 1909 in Chicago by Dr. William Healy. The work of the clinics was organized on a case-study approach, using a team of clinicians (a psychiatrist, physician, psychologist, and social worker) to collect information on the "multiple causes" of individual cases of juvenile delinquency. Healy published an account of his methods and findings in 1914, under the appropriately positivist title, *The Individual Delinquent.* Healy's work became a model for the establishment of such clinics in a number of major cities.

The organization of American criminology as a profession also began during this period. A National Conference of Criminal Law and Criminology was held in 1909 at the Law School of Northwestern University. Leaders from the fields of medicine, psychiatry, sociology, penology, and the criminal courts attended, and the American Institute of Criminal Law and Criminology was established. Beginning in 1910, the institute assumed responsibility for the publication of a journal, now called the *Journal of Criminal Law and Criminology,* which has maintained consecutive publication over seventy years. As well, a committee was formed that eventually took responsibility for translating and publishing the work of European criminologists, including Lombroso and Ferri (Elliott, 1952).

From the beginning, the fields of sociology and criminology were closely linked in North America (Clinard, 1951), and both were products of what is called the "progressive era" in American history (Gibbons, 1979, chap. 2). The progressive era was characterized by a growing awareness of the harsh social consequences of America's rapid industrialization and urbanization. This awareness was particularly pronounced among midwestern sociologists and was reflected in the concentration of attention on the "defective, dependent and delinquent classes." For example, Charles Henderson, a founding member of the sociology department at the

University of Chicago, authored an influential book titled *Introduction to the Study of the Dependent, Neglected and Delinquent Classes.* The assumption of the progressives (including middle-class farm-owners, store-keepers, clergymen, lawyers, doctors, as well as academics) was that hard work and the right laws could remedy these problems. In Chapter 3 of this volume we will consider the social background of some of these laws.

The first American textbook on crime written for academic use was authored by Maurice Parmelee in 1918. Although Richard Quinney (1975, p. 4) credits Parmelee's *Criminology* with focusing attention more clearly on sociological aspects of crime, Gibbons (1979, p. 29) notes that "it is difficult to know quite how to evaluate Parmelee's *Criminology* 60 years after it originally appeared in print." Indeed, the most interesting thing Gibbons (1974) can find to say about Parmelee is that he was a practicing nudist! This does distinguish Parmelee from what was otherwise a rather austere and somber group of colleagues in the field.

The midwestern roots of American criminology are reflected in two important texts that followed: Edwin Sutherland's *Criminology,* first published in 1924, and John Gillin's *Criminology and Penology,* published in 1926. Gillin spent most of his career in the sociology department at the University of Wisconsin, and the introduction to his text was written by another famous Wisconsin sociologist, E. A. Ross, the second president of the American Sociological Association. Sutherland received his doctorate from the University of Chicago and spent most of his career at Indiana University. Of the two volumes, Sutherland's had, and continues to have, through its many editions, a much greater impact. It was this text that made criminology distinctively sociological, beginning with a major critique of the work of Lombroso, and leading eventually to a social theory of crime—differential association theory—that we will consider later in this volume.

The Chicago School

American criminology found its first real coherence and sustained development in research done in Chicago in the 1920s. Much of the background for this work is found in the writings of the University of Chicago sociologists Robert Park, Ernest Burgess, and later W. I. Thomas. Park and Burgess stimulated an early interest in the development of cities, and Thomas established the use of life histories as an important research tool. Burgess (1928) went on to do important work on the prediction of parole outcomes, which was followed by similar kinds of research by the Gluecks (1930). These studies in particular carried on the positivist interest in the differentiation of criminals from noncriminals.

However, it was in the 1930s that criminological research came into full flourish in Chicago. Two giants of this period were Clifford Shaw and Henry McKay, who did their work at a state-funded child-guidance clinic, the Institute for Juvenile Research. Shaw and McKay's research consisted primarily of ecological area studies and the collection of life histories. Both approaches placed a great emphasis on the social disorganization that characterized particular areas of rapidly growing cities. Thus Shaw and McKay began with a premise found in the work of Park and Burgess: that cities grow outward from the center, in a series of concentric zones, each with specialized activities and distinctive populations.

> Broadly, the first zone at the city center is a business and industrial zone. Around the perimeter of these establishments is a zone in transition, where deteriorated housing is held for speculation in anticipation of commercial and industrial expansion. Regardless of the probability of expansion, housing in this area is undesirable, and therefore cheap, because of its proximity to industry and business. Its slums harbor the first immigrant settlement, the poor and dispossessed of all types, and vice industries. Zone three is an area of second immigrant settlement and workingmen's homes; zone four is a better residential area; the fifth and last is the commuter zone (Kornhauser, 1978, p. 62).

Shaw and McKay (1931, 1942) found that juvenile-court referral rates followed a gradient through the zones; that is, the rates were highest in the inner-city or core areas and declined with distance outward from the city center. A principal cause, it seemed, was the social disorganization of these areas. These points and others were made by Shaw and his colleagues (Shaw, 1930; in collaboration with Moore, 1931; Shaw et al., 1938) in a series of life history studies as well. Here it will be enough to say that the research of Shaw and McKay influenced, and eventually was influenced by, the theories of undercontrol and the theories of opportunity and status that we will discuss in greater detail in later chapters.

No discussion of early Chicago criminology is complete without at least some mention of Frederic Thrasher's *The Gang* (1937). This study recounts in detail the daily activities of 1,313 boys' gangs located and studied in Chicago by Thrasher. This research established the importance of in-depth fieldwork and clearly established the point, frequently forgotten but underlined by Bordua (1961), that crime and delinquency can be fun and rewarding to those involved. Thrasher's work provided (provides?) an important antidote to an increasingly grim portrayal of the urban criminal and delinquent.

OLD AND NEW CRIMINOLOGISTS

From Consensus to Conflict in the Study of Crime

We have spent a great deal of time in this chapter discussing the roots of modern criminology. One cannot examine these roots, even in the rather superficial way that we have had to do here, without being struck by how much the study of crime, criminals, and criminal law has changed over time. In turn, our conceptions and responses to crime, both as individuals and as members of a society, have changed as well. We will see much more evidence of these changes in the chapters that follow. We will see, for example, that while the beginnings of North American criminology were positivist in character—focusing on criminal behavior more than criminal law, on the determining causes of such behavior, and on the differentiation of criminals from noncriminals—more recent events have seen a return of criminological interest to its classical roots, with a particular focus on the role of criminal law in generating legal labels that may constitute the clearest distinctions that exist between criminals and noncriminals. Our consideration of the theories of overcontrol will make this transition and its importance a subject of extended discussion in a later chapter. Here we will start with the more basic point, central to the theme of this book, that criminology is a field of study that is continually changing. An important source of contemporary change in criminological work has been a disagreement about the role that processes of consensus and conflict play in our society, particularly in the definition of crime, and in the role that criminologists should play in influencing these events.

Many of the early criminological theories were premised on the implicit assumption that there is a consensus of values and interests in the definition of crime. Recall, for example, that Garofalo spoke of "natural crimes" that violated two basic "altruistic sentiments." The assumption was that these sentiments were widely shared and reflective of mutual interests in all parts of society. In recent years this assumption has been questioned in a variety of ways, and often replaced by the assumption that values and interests, particularly between social and economic classes, are in conflict (e.g., Turk, 1969; Quinney, 1975b; Chambliss and Seidman, 1971). This has led to a renewed interest in the criminal law, and to a questioning of the social and economic purposes to which the criminal law is put. As indicated at the outset of the chapter, this questioning, in one of its more extreme forms, has led to the demand that social problems like racism and sexism be considered crimes, and dealt with as such (Schwendiger and Schwendiger, 1975). This approach to the definition and study of crime, often called the "new," "critical," or "conflict" criminology, will be considered more extensively in the next chapter. Meanwhile, however, we can note that this type of demand has led to some very serious conflicts among academic criminologists themselves, particularly involving the roles they should play in modern society. One way of understanding these conflicts is to note how they developed in the United States, particularly in the School of Criminology at Berkeley, and more generally in Britain.

The Battles of Berkeley and Britain

The School of Criminology at Berkeley opened in 1949, with no anticipation of the turbulence that would eventually follow. During the first decade of its existence it offered a strong vocational emphasis, with most of its program directed to the training of persons to work, particularly at the administrative levels, in law-enforcement and correction agencies. Criminology was expected here to influence government policy by influencing the very people who would carry it out. However, by 1961 the school came under attack from the university for being too vocational. The eventual outcome was a reorganization of the school on an interdisciplinary basis that was to be more theoretical and academic in character.

The new orientation that persisted for much of the second decade of the school's existence focused on social, scientific, and legal approaches to the study of crime. As well, the emphasis of the school's program now shifted from undergraduate to graduate instruction. The products of this new phase of the school's history tended to be trained researchers, college and university teachers, and professional policy-makers. In this period, the contribution of the school to government policy seems to have been more in the generation and dissemination of ideas than in the actual implementation of them.

The final phase of the school's history brought a radicalization of its program content and activity. During this period, a faction of the Berkeley school adopted as its primary purposes to initiate, organize, and participate in militant movements dealing with issues like racism and sexism in the United States (Schauffler, 1974, p. 58). The very meaning of the study of criminology changed, as did the everyday activities criminologists were expected to be involved in. The call was for direct involvement and militant action. In the spring of 1972, with at least tacit support from other factions within the school, the administration of the university responded to these developments by announcing its intention to close the school and to release untenured members of its faculty. Two participants (Schauffler and Hannigan, 1974, p. 42) offer this description of the events that followed:

> The final weeks of the spring quarter at the University of California, Berkeley, saw a student struggle, the scale and intensity of which had not been matched since the demonstrations against the

invasion of Cambodia in 1970. At the height of the struggle . . . as many as 4000 people participated in marches, rallies, and building occupations. The first occupation resulted in the banning from campus of 159 students who refused to leave when ordered. In the final occupation, nearly 300 were removed by campus police who were backed up by more than 150 riot equipped police who had been called in from three other departments.

The principal demand in this confrontation was the continuation of the School of Criminology. Nonetheless, the school eventually was closed, and a new program was begun in the Law School.

A not-so-different chain of events unfolded in Britain (Cohen, 1974). A rather applied type of criminology characterized work in the late 1950s at the Cambridge Institute of Criminology and the government-based Home Office Research Unit. As more academically inclined criminologists, mainly trained in sociology, grew dissatisfied with this applied and vocational orientation, a new national organization, the National Deviance Conference, was formed. As in the early 1960s at Berkeley, the focus of this annual conference was on the development of new, sociologically based ideas about crime and its control. And, in the 1970s, Britain like Berkeley was faced with a new call for militant action: three British criminologists—Ian Taylor, Paul Walton, and Jock Young—authored a book titled *The New Criminology* (1973) which again called upon criminologists to assume a more activist role, this time in ending the part played by the state in defining "human diversity" as crime. In its place, the new criminologists called for a "crime-free society" based on "socialist diversity." Although we can point to no specific events associated with the new criminology as dramatic as the Berkeley riots, the advocates of the new criminology did encourage (see Taylor et al., 1973, p. 281) alliances with militant prison groups and other activist movements. Thus both in Britain and Berkeley, the expected role of criminologists in influencing social policy varied, from an applied vocational emphasis, to a more detached focus on sociological observation, training, and commentary, to the call for militant action. Criminologists today work in the aftermath of these events.

Greatly Exaggerated Rumors about the Death of "That Old-Time Criminology"

One can be justifiably suspicious of any scholarly movement that claims to be entirely "new." Ironically, even the appellation taken by Britain's "new criminology" has a rather startling precursor. In 1928, the Americans Max Schlapp and E. H. Smith published a volume titled *The New Criminology* which sought to show that children born malformed thorugh chemical imbalances exhibited gross defects making them the "typical criminals of Lombroso" (see Wolfgang, 1960, p. 220). Obviously, the British new criminologists had something quite different in mind.

Some of what the new criminologists had in mind has actually also been with us for some time. Gibbons (1979, pp. 75–76) points out that by 1927, Sutherland was suggesting that "[crime] is a part of a process of conflict of which law and punishment are other parts," and by 1938, Sellin was arguing that "the social values which receive the protection of the criminal law are ultimately those which are treasured by the dominant interest groups." What the new criminologies have done, then, is to insist on a shift in emphasis, providing, in part, a focus that resurrects some of the older concerns with the criminal law that, in a somewhat different way, characterized the classical school of criminology. The new approaches do other important things as well, and, as we will see in later chapters, there are crucial insights that go with these approaches. Nonetheless, there is much that is crucial and important about the "older criminologies" as well. Both contribute to the understanding and explanation of crime and our societial reactions to it; both, through their focus on criminality, can tell us much about the society in which we live. In other words, both the old and the new criminologies will be important to the purposes of this book.

DEFINING CRIME: AN ISSUE OF MORALITY

2

THE ISSUE: WHAT SHOULD BE CALLED "CRIMINAL"?

The act of defining crime is often, but not always, a step toward controlling it. That is, the ostensible purpose of defining some behaviors as criminal is to make them liable to public prosecution and punishment. However, being *liable* to prosecution and punishment is clearly not the same as actually *being* prosecuted and punished. During the twilight of the prohibition era in America there was little attempt to enforce temperance legislation and, when arrests and convictions did occur, the sentences imposed were light. Eventually, the production and distribution of alcohol was decriminalized. Attempts to prosecute and punish Selective Service violators produced similar problems during the last stages of the Vietnamese war. This law was never repealed, and it undoubtedly will be used again in the future. Meanwhile, there are many statutes that define white-collar crimes, but they are only infrequently enforced. This is not to say that such laws have no use; their mere existence at least serves the purpose of condemning certain unethical business practices. Thus each of the above laws serves (or served) the purpose of making a moral statement; a statement about how citizens *should* behave. Yet each of these laws has proved problematic, making explicit the issue of how the criminal law can and should be used to legislate morality. In one sense, this issue is moot because the criminal law is always and everywhere used to legislate morality. However, in another sense, the issue is very much alive, because the *way* in which the criminal law is used to legislate morality is constantly changing. And, in the process of changing, the criminal law expands and contracts, forcing us regularly and concretely to answer the question: what should be called a crime? Should the criminal law contract and make homosexuality and some kinds of drug use legal? Should the criminal law expand and make acts of racism and sexism crimes? These are the kinds of questions this chapter is about.

THE LINK BETWEEN LAW AND MORALITY

The lengths to which the law should go in officially defining and enforcing morality has been the subject of philosophical debate for centuries. In the nineteenth century, the noted participants in this debate were John Stuart Mill and Sir James Fitzjames Stephen. In the twentieth century, the principals have been H.L.A. Hart and Lord Patrick Devlin. It is important that we begin by grounding ourselves in the opposing premises of this debate.

On one side, Mill argued (1859, p. 263) in his famous essay *On Liberty* that the primary function of criminal law was to prevent individuals from doing harm to *others*.

> . . . the only purpose for which power can be rightfully exercised over any member of a civilized community against his will, is to prevent harm to others. His own good, either physical, or moral, is not sufficient warrant, he cannot rightfully be compelled to do or forbear because it would be better for him to do so, because it will make him happier, because, in the opinion of others, to do so would be wise or even right.

In other words, Mill regarded the criminal law as an improper instrument for regulating the private moral conduct of individuals that caused no direct harm to others. In contrast, Stephen (1883, vol. II, p. 183) saw the criminal law as serving a much broader function in the cultivation of personal responsibility, arguing that "the meaning of responsibility is liability to punishment." Thus Stephen regarded the criminal law as a fundamental means for developing a sense of individual responsibility, and he considered the use of criminal law as essential for this purpose.

The debate has been focused most clearly in this century in Britain around the work of the British Governmental Committee on Homosexual Offences and Prostitution. This body, known for its chairman as the Wolfenden Committee, issued a report in 1957 that renewed the classic debate by recommending that private and consensual homosexual behavior on the part of adults no longer be considered a criminal offense. Behind this recommendation lay a broader assumption, explicitly acknowledged by the committee, that the criminal law should not intrude on the private lives of individual citizens beyond what is absolutely necessary to maintain public order and decency, to protect individuals from offensive and injurious behavior, and to prevent exploitation and corruption— particularly of those unable to protect themselves. The committee (1957, pp. 9–10) put the matter succinctly when it concluded that "there must remain a realm of private morality and immorality which is, in brief and crude terms, not the law's business." The committee was quick to emphasize that it did not condone these forms of behavior, but neither did it see it as the proper role of the law to condemn them. These were simply not matters for legal control.

Lord Devlin (1965, p. 7), a prominent British jurist, objected to the committee's position. Devlin argued that "the criminal law as we know it is based upon moral principle," and furthermore that "in a number of crimes its function is simply to enforce a moral principle and nothing else." Thus Devlin's position (ibid., pp. 13–14) was that "the suppression of vice is as much the law's business as the suppression of subversive activities." In other words Devlin, like Stephen, believed that it was a proper and necessary function of the law to regulate private morality.

Another prominent British philosopher of law, H. L. A. Hart, defended the committee's work against Devlin's critique. Like Mill before him, Hart (1963, pp. 46–47) based his defense on principles of individual liberty, arguing that

> a right to be protected from the distress which is inseparable from the bare knowledge that others are acting in ways you think wrong, cannot be acknowledged by anyone who recognizes individual liberty as a value. For the extension of the utilitarian principle that coercion may be used to protect men from harm, so as to include their protection from this form of distress, cannot stop here. If distress incident to the belief that others are doing wrong is harm, so also is the distress incident to the belief that others are doing what you do not want them to do. To punish people for causing this form of distress would be tantamount to punishing them simply because others object to what they do; and the only liberty that could coexist with this extension of the utilitarian principle is liberty to do those things to which no one seriously objects.

To read the debate as it has been presented thus far, one might think the issue involved is one of simple and absolute principle: whether the criminal law should be used to control private morality. However, things are seldom so simple in law, and this debate is no exception. First, each side of the debate we have presented involves rather different assumptions about the sources and purposes of law. That is, rather different assumptions are made about where law comes from, about how law evolves and develops in primitive and modern societies, and about the purposes to which law is put. Second, the line between private morality and the concerns of the surrounding society is not a clear one. For example, it can be argued that while drug use imposes its most direct consequences on drug-taking individuals, there are consequences (e.g., lost productivity) for society as well. Third, part of what is at issue is not only the *propriety* of using the criminal law to control individual morality, but also the *efficacy* of trying to do so. In other words, can the criminal law be used *effectively* to control individual morality? Fourth, there is a concern with the costs and harms involved for those who are subject to control. One concern here is that such laws may have the effect of creating a permanent class of criminals; that is, a class of persons whose options for leaving a lifestyle defined as criminal are few. To fully understand the Hart-Devlin debate and the link between law and morality, it is necessary to address these several dimensions of the problem. We turn next, then, to a discussion of the sources of law, followed by a discussion of each of the additional concerns raised above.

THE ORIGINS OF LAWS

Anthropologists, philosophers, political scientists, as well as sociologists, have pondered the question of where laws come from. Although this question is raised and addressed in a variety of ways, and will be discussed in greater detail in the following chapter, two discernible kinds of answers can be considered briefly here. The first kind of answer sees the law largely as a source of social order that resolves and prevents disputes, thereby allowing individuals to live more harmoniously together. The law is seen here as a product of consensus, evolving as a means of maintaining this consensus. The second kind of answer sees the law primarily as an instrument of social conflict that is used to maintain the power and privileges of one group over another. The law is seen here as having evolved out of a conflict between interest groups. These two different kinds of answers can be understood best as they have been offered by their various proponents.

Law as a Product of Consensus

According to the consensus point of view, law is a natural product of the informal rules of interaction of a society. For example, William Seagle (1941, p. 33), a lawyer, argues that the law is simply a product of custom. Indeed, for Seagle "custom is king," and "while there is no automatic *submission* to custom, there is an automatic *sway* of custom." Similarly, Frederick von Savigny (cited in Friedmann, 1967, p. 160) asserts "that all law . . . is first developed by custom and popular faith," and Julius Stone (1950, p. 337) concludes that laws "are generalized statements of the tendencies actually operating, of the presuppositions on which a particular civilization is based." From this viewpoint, then, there is no easy division between morality and law: customary morality is the very source of law.

With Devlin, it is assumed that to deny this would be to deny the very foundations of law. "The folkways are the 'right' ways," wrote William Sumner (1959, p. 28), and these customs or folkways are seen as giving law both its force and its purpose. From this perspective, any separation of the law from this foundation would be both artificial and perilous.

Law as a Product of Conflict

In contrast, there is another point of view that sees the emergence of law as a very selective process. This view argues that there are many moralities representing a variety of group interests in a society. The issue, then, is whose morality will get expressed in law, and with what consequences? The answer given from this perspective is that the law is a "weapon" (Turk, 1976a), and that it will be used as such by any group that can do so to its advantage. Chambliss and Seidman (1971) argue that this is particularly the case in complex, highly stratified societies like our own. They note that as societies become more complex in their economic division of labor, it becomes necessary to have rules, and ultimately laws, that regulate the encounters of individuals who occupy different roles. At the same time, as societies become more stratified, it is argued that it becomes necessary for those who are economically advantaged to use the law as a means of maintaining and protecting their position. In Chambliss and Seidman's terms, "The more economically stratified a society becomes, the more it becomes necessary for the dominant groups in the society to enforce through coercion the norms of conduct which guarantee their supremacy." From this viewpoint, the connection between law and morality is partial, both in the sense that the enforcement of morality is selective, and in the sense that the morality enforced will be to the advantage of one group over another. In particular, this viewpoint notes that it is the alleged immorality of the poor that is much more likely to be called "criminal" than the presumed immorality of the rich. "What this means in modern times," writes Richard Quinney (1974, p. 141), "is that there is a moral basis to capitalism, a morality that supports the interests of the ruling class and, at the same time, underlies the legal system that maintains the prevailing social and economic order." Like Mill, then, those who see law as a product of conflict are usually wary of the attempt to link conventional morality closely to the law. When the closeness of this tie is preserved, they note, it is usually to the disadvantage of the less advantaged. We will have much more to say about this perspective in later parts of this chapter and in following chapters. Our purpose here is simply to present these viewpoints, not to arbitrate between them.

PRIVATE MORALITY AND THE PUBLIC INTEREST

A second dimension of the debated link between law and morality involves the thin line that may divide considerations of private morality and the societal interest. The problem is that while many matters that could be considered only issues of private morality, including some kinds of drug use, prostitution, and pornography, may have their most direct and immediate effects on the individuals who pursue them, there may nonetheless be less direct but no less significant effects on surrounding communities and their members. A particularly poignant illustration of this point is provided by Donald Clairmont (1974) in his description of the development of a "deviance service center"—a whole community adjacent to Halifax, Nova Scotia, that was given the "functional autonomy" to provide a whole range of illicit services to the adjoining city.

Clairmont notes that this community, called "Africville" by its residents, was founded around 1850 by the descendants of refugee blacks who fled slavery in the United States during the War of 1812. Initially, Africville was a viable community with a few fine houses, some small-scale businesses, plenty of space, and a strong community spirit based on a stable kinship system. However, Africville soon began to experience the problems of a sluggish surrounding economy, and this, combined with two other factors, led to its development as a deviance service center. The first of these factors was that Africville was located close to the adjoining city's dockyards and port activity. The second factor was that the city's ruling circles gave the community the "functional autonomy" to develop an alternative economy: "that is, not sharing fairly in society's wealth, they . . . [were] allowed by the authorities a range of behavior, that would not be countenanced elsewhere" (Clairmont, 1974, p. 36). These two factors came together during the First World War when visiting seamen added to the clientele of an expanding bootlegging trade. Fearing growing crime problems and the ultimate demise of their community, residents of Africville petitioned the city council of Halifax in 1919 requesting police surveillance and protection. However, no police assistance was provided, and in the period that followed the First World War, Africville continued to grow as a deviance service center. Gradually bootlegging gave way to more hazardous forms of deviance, and, as the younger and better-educated members of the community began to leave, the fears of the petitioners of 1919 eventually were confirmed. The entire community was finally designated for harbor development and urban renewal nearly a half-century later. This meant that the problems of the community finally were "solved," literally, through demolition, while the few remaining residents were "relocated."

It can be argued that the problems residents of Africville experienced would not have existed if the deviant services provided were not illegal elsewhere and therefore concentrated in that particular community. There is no clear way of evaluating how valid this argument may be. Nonetheless, this example makes clear that the pursuit of "disreputable pleasures" can have consequences beyond the individuals who are immediately involved.

THE (IN)EFFECTIVENESS OF LAW AS AN INSTRUMENT OF MORALITY

Aside from the issue of whether the law *should* try to control private morality, there is additionally the question of whether the law *can* do so. Social scientists and students of the law have long been skeptical about what the law itself can do. Sumner (1960, p. 89) asserts that the mores of a society always take precedence over the law, and that it is impossible to change the mores "by any artifice or device, to a great extent, or suddenly, or in any essential element." Similarly, Sutherland and Cressey (1966, p. 11) argue that "when the mores are adequate, laws are unnecessary; when the mores are inadequate the laws are ineffective." In other words, laws that are unsupported by widely shared moral beliefs are unlikely to accomplish what their legal architects would wish. This is particularly true of crimes of private morality. In addition, it is difficult to get the information and evidence necessary to control such behaviors, not only because the behaviors are not widely and/or harshly enough condemned to generate public cooperation, but also because they customarily take place with some measure of privacy, and because they are often only known to the persons whose behavior is involved. These problems are most notable at the level of police enforcement.

Skolnick (1975) makes this point in his study of a police department on the west coast of the United States. Skolnick notes that the narcotics officers of a police force often play a very central, although often corrupting, role in departmental operations. This is because the character of their work makes narcotics officers an important source of information and influence. To begin, narcotics offenses, like other crimes of private morality, rarely involve victim-complainants. As a result, information and evidence must be obtained in other ways, including the use of informers, entrapment techniques, and undercover work. Each of these techniques is potentially corrupting: the use of informers involves questionable use of cash and drugs as inducements; entrapment techniques can encourage crimes that might otherwise never occur; and undercover work provokes tempting possibilities for bribery and collusion. Nonetheless, in the course of these types of activities, narcotics officers develop sources of information that are important not only to the prosecution of narcotics cases but for other kinds of cases as well. Thus narcotics officers become central actors in police departments, valuable not only to prosecutors but also to other officers. Among the results of this type of law enforcement are ineffective efforts to control drug use and the corruption of narcotics and related areas of policing. In sum, crimes without complainants are difficult, if not impossible, to control. Worse still, however, efforts to control such crimes often corrupt the controllers.

LAW, MORALITY, AND THE CREATION OF CRIME

A final concern about using the law to control private morality involves the implications for persons whose behaviors are controlled. There are some alarming indications that attempts to legally control private morality have the unfortunate tendency of creating permanent classes of deviants (Mead, 1918), who must organize their lives around criminal roles (Lemert, 1967). The best example of this involves the problems of drug addicts. Well into the second decade of this century, addicts in America were able to buy most opiates across the drug counter. One result was that "our grandmothers used many home remedies and patent medicines whose ingredients would shock us today" (Cuskey et al., 1979, p. 226). Coincidentally, early surveys of opiate drug addicts in America reveal that the majority of addicts were white women. The watershed event that changed this pattern was the passage of the Harrison Act in 1914. We will discuss this law in greater detail in the following chapter. Here it is enough to note that although it was originally only a tax measure, the effect of this law and its enforcement by the federal Bureau of Narcotics was gradually to make opiate addiction a crime. The result was the emergence of a black market in drugs and the development of a whole new sector of the criminal underworld. Opiate addiction, therefore, shifted from being acceptable and respectable to being criminal and disreputable in a rather brief period of time, and the involvement of individuals in this world shifted as well. Cuskey et al. (ibid., p. 225) note that "in many ways the period from pre-Civil War to immediate post-World War I was like a film negative of the present." White American women substituted the use of various legal pain-killers, barbiturates, and amphetamines for the newly illegal opium. At the same time, black American men, gradually, and in increasing numbers, were pulled into this criminal underworld, a world that proved extremely difficult to leave. Access to the drug required increasing amounts of money, which usually could only be obtained through crime, and access to medical treatment became very difficult to obtain. Drug addiction became stereotyped as a black American problem that was to be the subject of policing more than treatment. The persistence of this crime problem and the scale of the other kinds of criminal activities associated with it are ominous indications that making a form of behavior criminal can create as many, and sometimes more, problems than it can solve.

VICTIMLESS CRIME AND THE LIMITS OF LAW

Because of the above kinds of concerns, social scientists and students of law have spent considerable time and effort trying to draw an effective line between the aspects of private morality that should and should not be made a part of the criminal law. One of the best-known of these efforts involves Edwin Schur's discussion of "victimless crimes." "Crimes without victims," Schur (1965, p. 170) writes, "may be limited to those situations in which one person obtains from another in a fairly direct exchange, a commodity or personal service which is socially disapproved and legally proscribed." After considering several victimless crimes (e.g., abortion, homosexuality, and drug addiction) in detail, and after weighing a number of the dimensions of the link between law and morality, Schur argues that public education about the problems of enforcing these laws, and the possibility of reforming them, is needed. Schur does *not* argue that all criminal laws relating to these crimes should immediately be abolished. In fact, he concludes (ibid., p. 177) that "legalization is not automatically or invariably to be preferred to criminalization."

A more provocative position is taken by Morris and Hawkins in their book, *The Honest Politician's Guide to Crime Control.* Morris and Hawkins (1969, pp. 5–6; see also Allen, 1964; Packer, 1968) argue that there is an "overreach of the criminal law" that contributes to the larger "crime problem" in the following ways that echo and extend our earlier discussion:

1 Where the supply of goods or services is concerned, such as narcotics, gambling, and prostitution, the criminal law operates as a "crime tariff" which makes the supply of such goods and services profitable for the criminal by driving up prices and at the same time discourages competition by those who might enter the market were it legal.

2 This leads to the development of large-scale organized criminal groups which, as in the field of legitimate business, tend to extend and diversify their operations, thus financing and promoting other criminal activities.

3 The high prices which criminal prohibition and law enforcement help to maintain have a secondary criminogenic effect in cases where demand is inelastic, as for narcotics, by causing persons to resort to crime in order to obtain the money to pay the prices.

4 The proscription of a particular form of behavior (e.g., homosexuality, prostitution, drug addiction) by the criminal law drives those who engage or participate in it into association with those engaged in other criminal activities and leads to the growth of an extensive criminal subculture which is subversive of social order generally. It also leads, in the case of drug addiction, to endowing a pathological condition with the romantic glamour of a rebellion against authority or some sort of elitist enterprise.

5 The expenditure of police and criminal-justice resources involved in attempting to enforce statutes in relation to sexual behavior, drug taking, gambling, and other matters of private morality seriously depletes the time, energy, and number of personnel available for dealing with the types of crime involving violence and stealing which are the primary concern of the criminal-justice system. This diversion and overextension of resources results both in failure to deal adequately with current serious crime and, because of the increased chances of impunity, in encouraging further crime.

6 These crimes lack victims, in the sense of complainants asking for the protection of the criminal law. Where such complainants are absent it is particularly difficult for the police to enforce the law. Bribery tends to flourish; political corruption of the police is invited. It is peculiarly with reference to the victimless crimes that the police are led to employ illegal means of law enforcement.

Based on these arguments, Morris and Hawkins conclude that a range of behaviors should be decriminalized. They suggest that public drunkenness should cease to be a crime; that neither the acquisition, purchase, possession, nor use of any drug should be a criminal offense; that no form of gambling should be prohibited by criminal law; that vaguely stated disorderly conduct and vagrancy laws should be replaced; that private sexual activities between consenting adults should not be subject to criminal law; and that juvenile courts should only retain jurisdiction over adolescents for conduct that would be criminal if committed by adults. This is obviously a sweeping set of changes. We offer these proposals here not because we believe they should all necessarily be adopted, but because they illustrate the point that what is to be called "criminal" is open to review and reform.

Thus the significance of the debates and proposals we have been considering is the possibility they represent for contraction and expansion in conceptions of the proper content of criminal law. It is precisely this potential for variable content that poses problems for social scientists who wish to define crime for the purposes of identifying the subject matter of their work. On the one hand, it might seem desirable to simply confine our attention, and therefore our definition of crime, to what is called "criminal" in any particular jurisdiction. On the other hand, and as we argue below, it is desirable that we remain sensitive within and between jurisdictions to the shifting divisions between what is called "criminal" and what is not, and why. This may be more apparent when it is noted that thus far in this chapter we have only considered this problem as it relates to our own culture, conveniently even ignoring the fact that each American state has its own criminal code, with significant variation between states in what is called "criminal." Our view is that the only effective way of responding to the problem of variability is to conceptualize crime as a specific instance of a broader range of deviant behavior. Before developing our particular version of this approach, however, we need to consider the ways in which others have addressed these issues.

SEVEN APPROACHES TO THE DEFINITION OF CRIME AND DEVIANCE

The responses of social scientists to the problems of variation in what is called "criminal" are seen in seven approaches to the definition of our subject matter. The seven approaches include: (1) a legal-consensus definition; (2) a socio-legal definition; (3) a cross-cultural definition; (4) a statistical definition; (5) a labeling definition; (6) a utopian-anarchist definition; and (7) a human rights definition. A critical review of the seven viewpoints follows. Then, elements of the seven viewpoints are combined in a new definition. We will argue that this last approach is best suited to the task of explaining crime, criminal behavior, and its control.

The Legal-Consensus Approach

The most articulate advocate of a legalistic definition of crime was the lawyer-sociologist Paul Tappan. Tappan (1947, p. 100) insisted that we should limit our study to criminality as it is legally construed: "Crime is an intentional action in violation of the criminal law . . . committed without defence or excuse, and penalized by the state." He insisted further that persons studied as criminals must be adjudicated (i.e., convicted) as such. Acknowledging that there is variation over time and across cultures in what is called "criminal," Tappan argued that governing statutes provide the

"It so happens, Gregory, that your Grandfather Sloan was detained by an agency of our government over an honest misunderstanding concerning certain anti-trust matters! He was not 'busted by the Feds'!"
Drawing by W. Miller; © 1971
The New Yorker Magazine, Inc.

only clear and definitive indication as to what any specific cultural group holds so seriously deviant as to be called "criminal": "Here we find *norms* of conduct, comparable to mores, but considerably more distinct, precise and detailed" (ibid.). In short, Tappan is suggesting that the criminal law provides a reliable guide to what is consensually defined as "criminal" in any given society.

A salient difficulty with Tappan's approach is that it systematically ignores much of what many criminologists today wish to study: behaviors that are on the margins of the criminal law and rarely prosecuted, including such things as unethical business practices and pollution of the environment. At the same time, the legal-consensus approach neglects the basic issue of why some acts are legislated as criminal, while others remain only informally the subject of disrepute. Further, this approach misinforms us in suggesting that legal definitions clearly reflect societal consensus about what is criminal. This is conspicuously the case when we note that the federal criminal code in the United States is widely regarded as being remarkably outdated but nonetheless is stubbornly resistant to change. As of this writing, Congress is on record as seeing the need for a new code, but unable to agree on what exactly that code should contain. Finally, being legally called a "criminal" depends on getting caught and convicted. This approach requires a sampling process for research that results in a collection of subjects (more correctly called "captives") that is not only narrowly defined but also nonrepresentative.

The Socio-Legal Approach

Edwin Sutherland (1945) suggested a relaxation of legal criteria so as to allow an expansion of attention to various "antisocial behaviors." Retained, however, was an emphasis on legally defined criminality, as designated by two explicit criteria (ibid., p. 132): "legal description of acts as socially injurious and legal provision of a penalty for the act." Sutherland demonstrated with the use of these criteria that it is possible to consider "criminal" many unethical business practices handled in the civil courts. The demonstration consisted of a comparative analysis of the procedures and punishments used in the prosecution of corporate interests in the civil and criminal courts. The conclusion (ibid., p. 135) is that "the criteria which have been used in defining white-collar crimes are not categorically different from the criteria used in defining other crimes."

Sutherland's redefinition of the field of study facilitated a new and important emphasis in criminological research on the economic crimes of "upperworld offenders." However, his reluctance to widen the scope of attention beyond statutory matters leaves this definition open to two earlier criticisms of the legalistic approach: first, little attention is yet given to the process by which behaviors come to be defined as criminal or civil wrongs; second, like the criminal courts, the civil courts undoubtedly yield a biased sample of actors and activities for study. Significantly, it should also be noted that Sutherland's emphasis on white-collar crime neglects undetected occupational indiscretions among workers of lesser social status (Horning, 1970).

A Cross-Cultural Approach

Thorsten Sellin (1938) proposed a definition of our subject matter that extends attention beyond the realm of law. His argument is that every group has its own standards of behavior, called "conduct norms," and that these standards are not necessarily embodied in law. "For every person, then, there is from the point of view of a given group of which he is a member, a normal (right) and an abnormal (wrong) way of reacting, the norm depending upon the social values of the group which formulated it" (ibid., p. 30). Beyond this, however, Sellin argued that there are some conduct norms that are *invariant* across *all* cultural groups. Further, he insisted (ibid.) that these norms were the appropriate focus for research: "Such study would involve the isolation and classification of norms into *universal categories* transcending political and other boundaries, a necessity imposed by the logic of science."

Unfortunately, Sellin did not specify what the universal conduct norms might be. The weakness of his strategy is the dubious proposition that such norms can be found either inside or outside of the law. The lesson of a large body of anthropological research is that norms of conduct are remarkably varied, with the universals of human behavior, if any, limited primarily to the trivial necessities of everyday life. Conduct norms that are universal *and* nontrivial probably cannot be found.

A Statistical Approach

Wilkins suggests a very different approach to our subject matter that is nonetheless attentive to the problem of cultural variation. He begins with the assumption (1964, p. 46) that "at some time or another, some form of society . . . has defined almost all forms of behavior that we now call 'criminal' as desirable for the functioning of that form of society." Wilkins then focuses on the frequency with which various forms of behavior occur in any particular society. The result is a continuum of behaviors, with high-frequency behaviors considered normal, and low-frequency behaviors deviant. Wilkins represents this approach in the form of a normal bell-shaped curve (see Fig. 2-1). "It may be supposed that the model given by the normal frequency distribution shown in this chart represents the distribution of ethical content of human action" (ibid., p. 47). Serious crimes and saintly acts form the two extremes in this definition. One of the most interesting features of Wilkins's approach is its accommodation of the variable character of crime and deviance. For example, the range of deviant behaviors included within legal definitions or considered worthy of police notification is recognized as indefinite, and as well the range of additional acts to be considered deviant remains at the discretion of researchers.

Nevertheless, one weakness of this approach lies in its simplicity. While infrequency of behavior is one way of identifying deviant behavior, a purely statistical approach underestimates the role of societal groups in selecting from infrequent acts those that are considered criminal. Obvious-

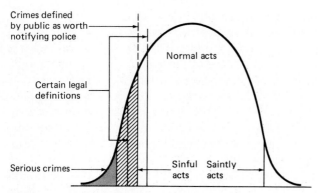

FIGURE 2-1 A statistical approach to the definition of crime and deviance. *(Source: Wilkins, 1964:47)*

ly, not all infrequent occurrences are designated "criminal" or even "deviant." What is required, then, is the addition of analytical content to the quantitative framework.

The Labeling Approach

If the statistical approach underestimates the importance of the societal response, the labeling approach clearly does not. Howard Becker (1963, p. 9) provides a concise statement of this viewpoint: "The deviant is one to whom that label has successfully been applied; deviant behavior is behavior that people so label." Becker's point is that behaviors are not recognized as deviant, or criminal, unless others, as members of cultural groups, react to them as such. This approach is important in making us aware of the significance of the ways in which we respond to crime and deviance. However, as a way of defining our field of study, the labeling approach also creates problems.

Bordua (1969) observes that the labeling definition tends to make crime and deviance "all societal response, and no deviant stimulus." His point is that the labeling approach characteristically assumes a passive subject who plays little or no part in eliciting a response (Hagan, 1973). In some cases this will be true, but often it will not. Thus, a more useful definition of crime and deviance will incorporate both possibilities.

A Human Rights Approach

We spent much time in the early part of this chapter talking about the efforts of social scientists and lawyers to justify the *deletion* of crimes of private morality from the criminal law. At the same time, there have been efforts by others to *add* to our conception and definition of crime a set of concerns having to do with violations of human rights. The most notable of these efforts involves the work of Herman and Julia Schwendinger. They begin with the assumption (1975, p. 145) that "all persons must be guaranteed the fundamental prerequisites for well-being, including food, shelter, clothing, medical services, challenging work and recreational experiences, as well as security from predatory individuals or repressive and imperialistic social elites." The Schwendingers regard these as rights (rather than rewards or privileges) that the criminal law should guarantee and protect.

The Schwendingers (ibid., p. 147) then go on to argue that it is the *conditions* that result in the denial of these rights that should be called criminal: "the *social conditions* themselves must become the *object* of social policy: . . . it is not an individual or a loose collection of atomistic individuals which is to be controlled, but rather the social relationships between individuals which give rise to criminal behavior" (emphasis in original). The importance of this shift in focus is that it allows the Schwendingers (ibid., p. 148) to recommend a radical change in what should be called "criminal," for "if the terms imperialism, racism, sexism, and poverty are abbreviated signs for theories of social relationships or social systems which cause the systematic abrogation of basic rights, then imperialism, racism, sexism, and poverty can be called crimes according to the logic of our argument." The final piece of this argument is essentially a plea that the resulting definition would be more just than existing definitions, in the sense that it would address some obvious inequities in the way our society works. The Schwendingers ultimately put their case in the form of a question:

> Isn't it time to raise serious questions about the assumptions underlying the definition of the field of criminology while agents of the state can, with impunity, legally reward men who destroy food so that price levels can be maintained while a sizable portion of the population suffers from malnutrition?

While many, if not most, criminologists might agree with the moral position taken in asking this question, it may nonetheless be the case that this approach to the definition of crime confuses more than it clarifies. A basic problem is that in its anxiousness to condemn imperialism, racism, sexism, and poverty, this approach confuses presumed *causes* of criminal behavior with the behavior we wish to study. It is not that we wish to ignore or neglect these conditions, but rather that we wish to study their presumed role in the causation of behaviors the state calls "criminal," explicitly or implicitly, in practice and in theory. This does not require that we morally endorse what the state defines as criminal (Turk, 1975). Indeed, one of the things our definition must make problematic is decisions about what the state does and does not consider criminal.

A Utopian-Anarchist Approach

A final and equally provocative approach to the definition of crime and deviance is found in the work of the "new criminologists" Ian Taylor, Paul Walton, and Jock Young (1973). The new criminologists ask that we redefine crime and deviance as "human diversity." Their argument is that deviance represents a normal and purposeful attempt to correct or protest social injustice. In response, society seeks to repress this challenge by criminalizing (i.e., arresting, prosecuting, and incarcerating) the actors involved. In short, crime is born of the conflict between the oppressed and the oppressors. The solution proposed (ibid., p. 282) demands a reversal of this situation: "For us . . . deviance is normal. . . . The task is to create a society in which the facts of human diversity . . . are not subject to the power to criminalize." More recently, Tifft (1979, p. 400; see also Black, 1976) has argued that this state of preferred anarchy is actually coming to pass: "We have been moving to preserve diversity of language, belief and life style, recognizing that diversity is critical to earth's survival and to human survival. As these continue, appropriation, crime, and prospective legality will diminish, and in their place will be a continuous process of anarchy and justice."

This approach is both useful and utopian. On the one hand, it alerts us to the possibility that some behaviors (e.g., disorder offenses, political crimes, and some property offenses) may be called "deviant" or "criminal" because they are offensive or threatening to privileged segments of society. On the other hand, to assume that all acts of crime and deviance, particularly the most serious (e.g., murder, rape, and child abuse), are justifiable consequences of a politically meaningful lifestyle is to invite a utopian form of anarchy. As students *and* potential victims of crime, the issue is one of how far we can go, while still wishing to live in the society of our design. In sum, there is a crucial difference between ranting and raping, and it is essential that our definition of crime and deviance, however imperfectly, make this type of distinction.

What, then, is the appropriate definition of crime and deviance to be used in our work? Our approach follows.

DEFINING CRIME AND DEVIANCE AS A CONTINUOUS VARIABLE

A basic assumption that we will make in developing the approach to be used in this book is that it is necessary to have a definition that takes into account not only what is formally considered criminal by law, but also a range of behaviors that for all practical purposes are treated as crimes (e.g., Sutherland's white-collar crimes), as well as those behaviors that across time and place vary in their location in and outside the boundaries of criminal law. In other words, we need a definition that considers behaviors that are both actually and potentially liable to criminal law. In this sense we will follow Sellin's (1937) dictum that as social scientists, criminologists cannot afford to permit nonscientists—in this case legislators and other agents of the law who make and enforce the criminal law—to fix the terms and boundaries of the scientific study of crime. Rather, our approach must recognize that the separation of crime from other kinds of deviance is a social and political phenomenon.

Our basic definition is simple: crime is a kind of deviance, which in turn consists of variation from a social norm, that is proscribed by criminal law. More generally, our argument is that there are many varieties of crime and deviance which can be divided and subdivided into several categories, and that these categories in turn can be conceived theoretically as ranging from those considered least to most serious in any given society. This can be said more concretely. There is an obvious difference in our society between multiple murder and adolescent marijuana use. We are saying further that most deviant acts can be located empirically on a continuum of seriousness between these two extremes. It is true that not all persons or groups, in any given societal context, will agree or have strong feelings about the wrongfulness of each act. For example, most persons will have no strong feelings about whether it is "decent" or "indecent" to dress in "erotic clothing," or, even more to the point, about what "public indecency" or "erotic clothing" is. However, this in itself is our first measure of seriousness: the degree of agreement about the wrongfulness of an act. This assessment can vary from confusion and apathy, through levels of disagreement, to conditions of general agreement. We will regard this as an index of agreement about the norm.

Our second measure of seriousness is the severity of the social response elicited by the act. Social penalties vary from public execution to polite avoidance, with a range of responses in between. The more severe the penalty prescribed, and the more extensive the support for this sanction, the more serious is the societal evaluation of the act.

Our third measure of seriousness involves a societal evaluation of the harm inflicted by the act. As we noted earlier, some possibly harmful acts, for example drug abuse, seem largely personal in their consequences, and therefore are increasingly regarded as "victimless." Other acts, like gambling, are "victimless" in the sense that the persons involved are frequently willing and anxious participants. Finally, some acts, for example most crimes of violence, are more clearly interpersonal, or social, in their consequences. Here there is also a more definite sense of victimization, although the issue is sometimes resolved by nothing more than who first had access to the most effective weapon. Thus, much of the debate that goes into an evaluation of harmfulness is concerned with the degree of victimization and the personal or social harm that a set of acts may involve.

Our argument is that in most modern societies, including our own, the three measures of seriousness are closely associated. In other words, the more serious acts of deviance, which are most likely to be called "criminal," are likely to involve (1) broad agreement about the wrongfulness of such acts, (2) a severe social response, and (3) an evaluation as being very harmful. However, the correlation between these three dimensions certainly is not perfect, and furthermore, as we will see, in regard to many acts that are defined as crimes, there is disagreement as to their wrongfulness, an equivocal social response, and uncertainty in perceptions of their harmfulness. It is precisely this kind of ambivalence that our approach attempts to capture. Thus the form of our approach can be visualized as a pyramid (see Fig. 2-2), with the less serious forms of deviance rarely called "criminal" at the base, the more serious forms of deviance usually called "criminal" at the peak, and a range of uncertain behaviors in between. Each vertical axis of this pyramid represents one of our measures of seriousness. The form of the pyramid purposefully suggests that the most

FIGURE 2-2 Kinds of crime and deviance. *(Source: Hagan, 1977:14)*

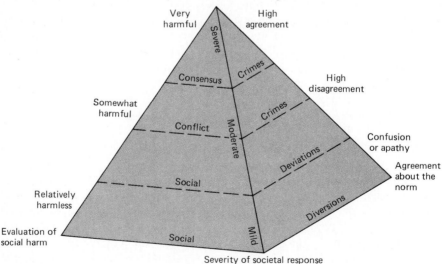

serious acts of crime and deviance in a society tend also to be less frequent, while less serious acts may be considerably more common. Acts included in the pyramid include two general categories (criminal and noncriminal forms of deviance) and four subdivisions (consensual crimes and conflict crimes; social deviations and social diversions). The divisions between these categories are represented with broken lines in Figure 2-2. Our purpose is to indicate that across time and place, the particular location of behaviors on the pyramid will vary. In other words, the divisions between the categories are intentionally imprecise. Nonetheless, each of the categories can be discussed individually.

KINDS OF CRIME AND DEVIANCE

Our discussion proceeds generally from the most to the least serious forms of crime and deviance. It needs to be emphasized, however, that the designation of seriousness is empirically, rather than ethically, determined. Some students of crime and deviance point out that unethical but noncriminal business practices are often morally more serious than rapes, robberies, or even murders of individuals. They argue, for example, that unethical multinational business arrangements can create conditions of poverty, inhumanity, degradation, and famine (see our earlier discussion of the human rights approach). The role of the Nestlé Corporation in exporting milk formulas for babies to third world countries where they increased the nutritional problems of already endangered children is a graphic illustration. From an ethical viewpoint, these arguments are extremely important. However, our purpose here is not to create a universal scale of immorality. Our goal is to describe and explain the institutionalization and the violations of the norms of an existing social order. The results of this approach will likely be relevant to, although not sufficient for, the formation of moral judgments.

CRIMINAL FORMS OF DEVIANCE

The forms of deviance regarded as most serious are defined by law as criminal. However, this should not be taken to mean that there is permanence to such designations. We have made the point repeatedly in this chapter and the preceding one that conceptions of crime change. Berk et al. (1977) have made this point in a unique way by actually classifying and counting changes made in the California penal code between 1955 and 1971. In doing this, all laws affecting the kinds of behavior labeled "illegal" were taken into account, with particular attention given to whether the net effect was to bring more or less behavior under control. Among the results is a graphing of the cumulative changes for all behaviors included or excluded from the California code over this period (see Fig. 2-3). Perhaps

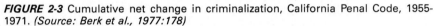

FIGURE 2-3 Cumulative net change in criminalization, California Penal Code, 1955-1971. *(Source: Berk et al., 1977:178)*

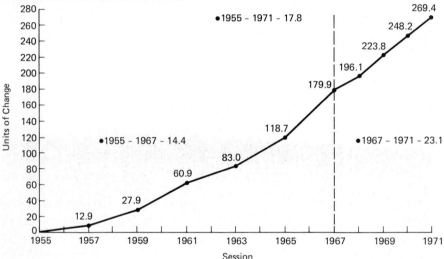

the most important finding apparent from this exercise is that for no part of this period was the overall net effect of the state legislature's actions to *de*criminalize behavior. That is, while specific kinds of behavior were taken out of the code during this period, the overall effect was to *in*crease the range of behavior included. As we will see, a variety of different kinds of behaviors are liable to this fate.

The Consensus Crimes

Our attention is directed first to the crimes that concern most of us, the more visible, predatory crimes. Legal philosophers at one time characterized such acts of deviance as *mala en se*—"wrong in themselves." However, modern sociologists emphasize that few, if any, human behaviors are universal or timeless in their criminal character. Nonetheless, for several centuries most western societies have shown considerable consensus in designating as criminal a select group of behaviors. Among the most easily listed of these offenses are premeditated murder, forcible rape, and kidnapping for ransom. A number of researchers have attempted to extend this list and to see just how widespread agreement is currently in our society and others about the seriousness of a number of different acts that are usually designated as crimes.

The pioneering work of this kind was done by Sellin and Wolfgang (1964). Using samples of judges, police, and college students in Philadelphia, they obtained ratings of the seriousness of 141 offenses. A subgroup of fifteen offenses was then selected from the larger list and supplemented with descriptions of the consequences to victims of the criminal acts (e.g., amounts of property stolen or personal injury). A set of fifteen descriptions of these criminal acts and scale scores for each resulted, along with two major conclusions. The first conclusion was that respondents were able to complete the rating tasks rather easily, suggesting that people make judgments of this kind in their everyday lives. The second conclusion was that there was considerable agreement among subgroups about both the relative ordering of criminal acts and the scale scores given. Several replications of this work suggest that American, English-Canadian, French-Canadian (Normandeau, 1966; Akman, Normandeau, and Turner, 1967), and Puerto Rican respondents rank the relative seriousness of these offenses similarly (Velez-Diaz and Megargee, 1970). Further support is found in related work in a number of other cultural settings (Newman, 1976).

Another major piece of research of this kind is reported by Rossi et al. (1974) from a survey of an adult population drawn from Baltimore, Maryland. This survey finds that in a sample of 200 adults there is very substantial agreement on the relative seriousness of 140 offenses, including various kinds of white-collar as well as more conventional crimes. The seriousness rankings are reproduced in Table 2-1 (see also Thomas et al., 1976; Blumstein and Cohen, 1980). However, despite the very high levels of agreement reported in this work, there also are two additional findings worthy of note. The first is that education and youth are correlated with the overall sample means. That is, the more highly educated and the younger the respondents, the more likely they are to agree with average ratings computed over the entire sample. The second finding of note is that less-educated blacks are the subgroup most deviant from the overall consensus—especially in regard to their lower seriousness rankings of interpersonal violence between people who know one another. These findings begin to suggest the bases for a key distinction we will draw between what we will call "consensus crimes" and "conflict crimes."

Social scientists have two different empirical conditions in mind when they speak of consensus and conflict. They refer first to sentiments of the general population on a particular issue, as measured, for example, by a frequency distribution of attitudinal expressions indicating what proportion of a group as a whole approves or disapproves of a particular behavior. They refer second to the attitudes of specific status groups, as related to a particular issue, and indicated by some measure of association; for example, the difference in the percentage of black as contrasted with white Americans who approve of assault. Using both of these criteria, consensus can be said to exist where a population generally is agreed in its attitudes and where these attitudes are related weakly, if at all, to few, if any, status-group memberships. In contrast, conflict can be said to exist where attitudes are related more widely and more strongly to status-group memberships (regardless of whether members of the society at large are generally agreed or disagreed). Using these criteria, criminal behaviors can be located relative to one another and with reference to an overall continuum of attitudes toward criminal behaviors. Our position is that "consensus crimes" are located toward one end of this continuum, while "conflict crimes" are located toward the other (see Hagan et al., 1977). We talk further about the conflict crimes below.

Meanwhile, it is essential to note that the group of behaviors we have called "consensus crimes" is neither immutably nor permanently criminal. Nonetheless, the fact that some behaviors have been consensually defined as crimes for successive generations makes them of primary interest to some criminologists. These criminologists ask the same question posed by an outraged and scared public: Why do some people dare to defy social norms that so many of us feel so strongly about? In following chapters, we will note that the theories of undercontrol are well-suited to address this question. Meanwhile, we turn our attention next to a second variety of criminal deviance.

TABLE 2-1
AVERAGE SERIOUSNESS RATINGS GIVEN TO 140 OFFENSES IN BALTIMORE SURVEY (N IS AT LEAST 100)

Rank	Crime	Mean	Variance
1	Planned killing of a police officer	8.474	2.002
2	Planned killing of a person for a fee	8.406	2.749
3	Selling heroin	8.293	2.658
4	Forcible rape after breaking into a home	8.241*	2.266
5	Impulsive killing of a police officer	8.214	3.077
6	Planned killing of a spouse	8.113*	3.276
7	Planned killing of an acquaintance	8.093	3.273
8	Hijacking an airplane	8.072	2.776
9	Armed robbery of a bank	8.021	8.020
10	Selling LSD	7.949	3.048
11	Assault with a gun on a police officer	7.938	3.225
12	Kidnapping for ransom	7.930	3.844
13	Forcible rape of a stranger in a park	7.909	3.737

Rank	Crime	Mean	Variance
14	Killing someone after an argument over a business transaction	7.898	3.536
15	Assassination of a public official	7.888	5.400
16	Killing someone during a serious argument	7.867	3.663
17	Making sexual advances to young children	7.861	3.741
18	Assault with a gun on a stranger	7.847*	2.172
19	Impulsive killing of a spouse	7.835	3.952
20	Impulsive killing of a stranger	7.821*	3.429
21	Forcible rape of a neighbor	7.778	3.726
22	Impulsive killing of an acquaintance	7.717	4.205
23	Deliberately starting a fire which results in a death	7.707	4.189
24	Assault with a gun on a stranger	7.662†	2.976*
25	Manufacturing and selling drugs known to be harmful to users	7.653	3.280
26	Knowingly selling contaminated food which results in a death	7.596	5.202
27	Armed robbery of a company payroll	7.577	3.080
28	Using heroin	7.520	4.871
29	Assault with a gun on an acquaintance	7.505	3.482
30	Armed holdup of a taxi driver	7.505	3.336
31	Beating up a child	7.490	3.840
32	Armed robbery of a neighborhood druggist	7.487*	3.221
33	Causing auto accident death while driving when drunk	7.455	3.904
34	Selling secret documents to a foreign government	7.423*	5.722
35	Armed street holdup stealing $200 cash	7.414	3.633
36	Killing someone in a bar room free-for-all	7.392	4.637
37	Deliberately starting a fire in an occupied building	7.347	5.177
38	Assault with a gun on a spouse	7.323	4.650
39	Armed robbery of a supermarket	7.313	3.911
40	Assault with a gun in the course of a riot	7.245	3.218
41	Armed hijacking of a truck	7.198	3.866
42	Deserting to the enemy in time of war	7.194	4.673
43	Armed street holdup stealing $25 in cash	7.165	4.431
44	Armed robbery of an armored truck	7.163	5.210
45	Spying for a foreign government	7.135	7.024
46	Killing a pedestrian while exceeding the speed limit	7.122	3.964
47	Seduction of a minor	7.021	5.729
48	Beating up a police officer	7.020	5.734
49	Selling marijuana	6.969*	7.216
50	Father-daughter incest	6.959	7.112
51	Causing the death of an employee by neglecting to repair machinery	6.918	4.556
52	Breaking and entering a bank	6.908	4.641
53	Mugging and stealing $25 in cash	6.873*	5.305
54	Selling pep pills	6.867	5.683
55	Cashing stolen payroll checks	6.827	4.784
56	Mugging and stealing $200 cash	6.796	5.051
57	Causing the death of a tenant by neglecting to repair heating plant	6.704	6.314

Rank	Crime	Mean	Variance
58	Killing spouse's lover after catching them together	6.691	7.695
59	Blackmail	6.667	5.122
60	Advocating overthrow of the government	6.663	7.715
61	Neglecting to care for own children	6.660	6.977
62	Forcible rape of a former spouse	6.653	6.394
63	Manufacturing and selling autos known to be dangerously defective	6.604	5.968
64	Beating up a stranger	6.604	5.379
65	Using LSD	6.557	7.479
66	Driving while drunk	6.545	6.006
67	Practicing medicine without a license	6.500*	6.908
68	Burglary of a home stealing a color TV set	6.440*	5.048
69	Knowingly passing counterfeit money	6.302	5.220
70	Beating up someone in a riot	6.368	5.788
71	Performing illegal abortions	6.330	5.723
72	Passing worthless checks for more than $500	6.309	5.119
73	A public official accepting bribes in return for favors	6.246	6.467
74	Employee embezzling company funds	6.207*	6.030
75	Knowingly selling stolen stocks and bonds	6.138*	4.960
76	Refusing to obey lawful order of a police officer	6.118*	5.806
77	Burglary of a home stealing a portable transistor radio	6.115*	5.871
78	Theft of a car for the purpose of resale	6.093*	5.085
79	Knowingly selling defective used cars as completely safe	6.093	5.023
80	Burglary of an appliance store stealing several TV sets	6.062	5.371
81	Looting goods in a riot	6.043	5.052
82	Knowingly selling stolen goods	6.021	4.463
83	Leaving the scene of an accident	5.949	6.620
84	Printing counterfeit $10 bills	5.948	6.820
85	Shoplifting a diamond ring from a jewelry store	5.939	5.466
86	Mother-son incest	5.907	9.189
87	Theft of a car for joy-riding	5.876	6.047
88	Intimidating a witness in a court case	5.853	4.850
89	Brother-sister incest	5.825	8.709
90	Knowingly selling worthless stocks as valuable investments	5.821	5.021
91	Beating up a spouse	5.796	7.051
92	Selling liquor to minors	5.789	7.572
93	Burglary of a factory stealing machine tools	5.789	5.317
94	Using stolen credit cards	5.750	5.832
95	Using pep pills	5.656	9.512
96	Joining a riot	5.656	6.750
97	Lending money at illegal interest rates	5.653	5.775
98	Knowingly buying stolen goods	5.596	5.794
99	Refusal to serve when drafted in peace time	5.535	8.863
100	Resisting arrest	5.449	6.271
101	Impersonating a police officer	5.449	7.405

Rank	Crime	Mean	Variance
102	Using false identification to obtain goods from a store	5.438	6.628
103	Bribing a public official to obtain favors	5.394	6.198
104	Passing worthless checks involving less than $100	5.339*	5.921
105	Desertion from military service in peace time	5.323	7.526
106	Under-reporting income on income tax return	5.305	6.321
107	Willfully neglecting to file income tax returns	5.157*	6.470
108	Soliciting for prostitution	5.144	7.687
109	Proposing homosexual practices to an adult	5.140	9.361
110	Overcharging on repairs to automobiles	5.135	6.455
111	Shoplifting a dress from a department store	5.070	6.308
112	Beating up an acquaintance	5.032	5.644
113	Driving while license is suspended	5.031	7.988
114	Pouring paint over someone's car	4.938	7.449
115	Shoplifting a pair of shoes from a shoe store	4.990	6.781
116	Overcharging for credit in selling goods	4.970	6.213
117	Shoplifting a carton of cigarettes from a supermarket	4.969	6.793
118	Smuggling goods to avoid paying import duties	4.918	5.618
119	Killing a suspected burglar in home	4.868*	8.930
120	False claims of dependents on income tax return	4.832	6.801
121	Knowingly using inaccurate scales in weighing meat for sale	4.786	5.902
122	Refusal to make essential repairs to rental property	4.781	6.678
123	Engaging in male homosexual acts with consenting adults	4.736	9.393
124	Engaging in female homosexual acts with consenting adults	4.720	9.042
125	Breaking a plate glass window in a shop	4.653	6.697
126	Fixing prices of a consumer product like gasoline	4.629	6.069
127	Fixing prices of machines sold to businesses	4.619	6.218
128	Selling pornographic magazines	4.526	7.826
129	Shoplifting a book in a bookstore	4.424*	6.551
130	Repeated refusal to obey parents	4.411	9.074
131	Joining a prohibited demonstration	4.323	6.486
132	False advertising of headache remedy	4.083	7.972
133	Refusal to pay alimony	4.063	6.670
134	Refusal to pay parking fines	3.583*	6.475
135	Disturbing the peace	3.779	7.174
136	Repeated truancy	3.573	7.658
137	Repeated running away from home	3.571*	6.342
138	Loitering in public places	3.375	8.111
139	Refusal to answer census taker	3.105	7.329
140	Being drunk in public places	2.849	6.021

Note: Scores have a range of 9 (most serious) to 1 (least serious).
*Crimes rated by all members (200) of the Baltimore sample.
†This offense was inadvertently repeated (see crime rank no. 18), indicating that differences in scores as much as .185 can be obtained through response unreliability.

The Conflict Crimes

Continuing controversy surrounds the presence of many offenses in our criminal codes. These crimes are sometimes referred to as *mala prohibita,* or "wrong by prohibition," for example, as proscribed and punished by statute. As one moves away from the statutes, however, it becomes clear that public opinion is divided about the appropriate status of such offenses. Most importantly, social class and interest groups are the frequently cited roots of such conflict. The sociological concern is that the criminal law may be used by one class or interest group to the disadvantage of another.

Included in a nonexhaustive list of the conflict crimes are the public-disorder offenses (malicious mischief, vagrancy, and creating a public disturbance), chemical offenses (alcohol and narcotics offenses), political crimes (treason, sedition, sabotage, espionage, subversion,and conspiracy), minor property offenses (petty theft, shoplifting, and vandalism), and the "right-to-life" offenses (abortion and euthanasia). The feature that unites these offenses is the public debate that surrounds them. This is a different way of saying that we lack societal consensus on the dimensions of public disorder, the use of comforting chemicals, permissible politics, the protection of private property, and the limits of life. Lacking a consensus, many of us, given the opportunity or need, may feel free to deviate.

It is not surprising, then, that criminologists usually are less interested in asking why individuals are involved in conflict crimes, and are more concerned with the reasons why such persons are considered criminals by law. We will argue in following chapters that the theories of overcontrol are well-suited to address this question. These theories can be helpful in explaining the status of the noncriminal forms of deviance we consider briefly next.

NONCRIMINAL FORMS OF DEVIANCE

Not all forms of deviance are designated as criminal, yet many noncriminal forms of deviance are treated in ways analogous to those required by criminal law, while other forms of noncriminal deviance are not. In general, the more serious a noncriminal form of deviance is considered, the more likely it is to be treated in a criminal fashion. Because our scientific interest is as much in behavior and its treatment as in its stated definition, and because these forms of noncriminal deviance constitute a pool of behaviors that in the past may have been, or in the future may become, criminal, the noncriminal forms of deviance also are an important source of concern for criminologists. Two types of noncriminal deviance concern us: what we call the "social deviations" and the "social diversions."

The Social Deviations

Although social deviations are sometimes treated as if they were criminal, there are clearly some very important differences. The most frequent of these deviations are of three types: adolescent (juvenile delinquency), vocational (noncriminal violations of public and financial trust), and interpersonal (psychosocial disturbances). The feature that unites these experiences is that although they are not considered criminal, they are nonetheless considered disreputable. Of particular interest is the stigma that may follow contact with noncriminal agencies of social control, and how this stigma may compare to that consequent to processing by agencies of crime control. Noncriminal agencies typically attempt to minimize their stigmatizing effects. Juvenile courts "treat" rather than convict "delinquents"; professional bodies "suspend" and "expel" occupational "violators"; civil courts "process technical violators"; and psychiatric agencies protect the identities of their "patients." These efforts vary in their effectiveness, and sociologists and criminologists have been particularly interested in determining how access to personal resources and professional protection affect the outcomes. For example, in an innovative piece of research, Schwartz and Skolnick (1964) have demonstrated that while doctors can be found in malpractice without experiencing a loss of income, "common criminals" encounter a stigma that makes earning their future livelihoods difficult. This study illustrates how significant the distinction between criminal and noncriminal forms of deviance can be, and the relevance to criminology of their comparative study.

The Social Diversions

The social diversions are regarded as less serious forms of deviance, and consequently are less likely to be criminalized. Included among the social diversions are varied expressions of preferences with regard to sex, clothing, language, and leisure. We include them in our discussion partly for the sake of completeness, but also because they too are occasionally liable to criminalization, and because they display some significant parallels to things called "criminal." The latter point has been made in a number of interesting ways. Sykes and Matza (1961), for example, note that in our society there is a set of "subterranean values," including the search for adventure, excitement, and thrills, that exists alongside such conformity-producing values as security, routinization, and stability (see also Davis, 1944; Veblin, 1967). A result is that the lines drawn between crime, deviance, and diversion in our society are uncertain and subject to change. It is to the prospect of change that we turn last.

THE COMINGS AND GOINGS OF CRIME

In this chapter we have considered a wide range of criminal and deviant acts, from the less frequent consensual crimes to the much more common social diversions. We have argued that among the varieties of deviance, the criminal forms are the more serious, and the noncriminal forms less so. This conclusion is not based on our own moral evaluation of the acts involved, but rather it is based on an index measuring the perception of harm, agreement about the norm, and the severity of societal response to infractions. Most significantly, however, we have emphasized that the location of persons and acts within subcategories of this scale necessarily will vary by time, place, and circumstance. In other words, behaviors will be variably located on this scale according to the context considered. Further discussion of an example introduced at the beginning of the chapter may help to confirm this point.

During the early 1960s, as the Vietnamese war gradually became an American war, enforcement of the Selective Service Act became an increasingly important responsibility of the federal district courts. During this early period, there was widespread acceptance of the Selective Service Act as a necessary part of American life, providing enforcement of the statute with the type of support we have associated with *consensus crimes* (Cook, 1977). It was generally agreed that violation of the act was wrong, that such violations were harmful to the nation and its defense, and that severe penalties, such as imprisonment, were required for effective enforcement. However, by 1969, the mood of the nation had changed, and support of the act had so diminished that violation of the statute now took on the character of a *conflict crime*. There was no longer public agreement that such violations were wrong; instead they were increasingly thought to be consistent with, rather than harmful to, the national interest, and imprisonment was increasingly thought to be an *in*appropriate sentence for violators. Nonetheless, the Selective Service Act was never repealed. Instead, federal court judges whose responsibility it was to enforce this now unpopular law turned to the use of probation. Thus in a prominent American city where much of the draft-resistance effort was focused, Hagan and Bernstein (1979) report that from 1963 through 1968 the use of imprisonment to punish convicted violators was pervasive, with an overall imprisonment rate of 76.8 percent. However, between 1968 and 1969, the imprisonment rate decreased from 72.7 percent to 42.9 percent, and from 1969 through 1976, the overall imprisonment rate was 33.7 percent. During the latter period, the most common disposition was probation. By the end of the Vietnamese war, almost all draft offenders were receiving probation.

The point of the above discussion is not that draft resistance is a good or bad thing, moral or immoral. The point is that over time the public evaluation of the seriousness of Selective Service violations changed in a measurable way, and doubtless it will change again as time and circumstances demand. The approach to the definition of crime and deviance presented in this chapter allows us to take changes of this kind into account. Recognition and study of such changes are an important part of modern criminology, and therefore of our approach to the definition of its subject matter.

We have considered in some detail, then, the various kinds of crime and deviance and the more general link between law and morality. In doing so we noted briefly a fundamental division of views as to whether law is the product of consensual morality or of a conflict between moralities. Our approach to the definition of crime and deviance, with its enumeration of consensus crimes and conflict crimes, implies that both processes are at work. In the following chapter we examine this issue in greater detail by focusing on the way in which specific kinds of criminal laws have come into being.

LEGISLATING CRIME AND DELINQUENCY: THE MAKING OF STATE MORALITY

3

THE ISSUE: WHO MAKES THE LAW?

We have addressed in a general way the issue of what should be called a "crime." In this chapter we address the more concrete issue of how, and more importantly by whom, such laws are made. The issue of who makes the law has two kinds of answers, both of which we have considered briefly in earlier chapters: the first derives from the older consensual perspective, the second from the newer conflict perspective. However, we argue in this chapter that neither answer is adequate. The making of law is a more complicated process than either perspective separately suggests. We will make this point by considering several kinds of crime and delinquency legislation. First, we restate the consensus and conflict positions as they relate to the issue of lawmaking.

LAW FOR THE MASSES OR LAW FOR THE CLASSES?

The Consensus View of Lawmaking

Consensus theorists, including Durkheim (1949), Pound (1943), Parsons (1951, 1966), Hall (1960, 1963), Bohannan (1965), and Friedman (1959), contend that Anglo-American laws are an expression of the state of values and customs that are shared widely in society and reflect common interests. For example, Paul Bohannan (1965, p. 36) refers to the law as a form of "double institutionalization" in which "some of the customs of some of the institutions of society are restated in such a way that they can be 'applied' by institutions designed . . . specifically for that purpose." From this perspective, the law is seen as a means of resolving disputes, as a set of mechanisms "by which rights and wrongs can be decided without recourse to violence, and by which parties deemed in the wrong can be constrained from acting upon interpretations, interests or sentiments at the expense of others" (Parsons, 1966, p. 14). In other words, the consensus perspective sees the law as serving a protective function. Furthermore, this service is seen as the consequence of a mediation among competing interests: "looked at functionally, the law is an attempt to satisfy, to reconcile, to harmonize, to adjust . . . overlapping and often conflicting demands . . . to give effect to the greatest totality of interests that weigh most in our civilization, with the least sacrifice of the . . . whole" (Pound, 1943, p. 39). The latter position has been called a "consensus theory of interests" (Quinney, 1970). In any event, what unifies this school of thought is the assumption that law functions to reconcile differing individual or group interests in favor of "the common good." As we will see, the common good can be difficult to evaluate or measure.

The Conflict View of Lawmaking

While the perspective we considered above emphasizes the virtues of our legal system in protecting the common good, the conflict perspective on lawmaking, particularly the more radical versions of this perspective, offers a less sanguine view. There are some striking examples. Some Marxian conflict theorists, including Quinney (1975*a*, 1975*b*), Platt (1975), Chambliss (1973, 1974), and Taylor, Walton, and Young (1973, 1975), contend that our laws are an expression of a *fusion of economic and political interests* to the *exclusion* of other concerns (e.g., the common good). For these conflict theorists, there is only *one* prevailing interest: a "ruling-class" or "governing-class" interest formed in an "alliance of capital and the state" (Taylor et al., 1973, p. 264). Quinney (1975*b*, p. 291) summarizes this viewpoint as it relates to criminal law:

• The state is organized to serve the interests of the dominant economic class, the capitalist ruling class.
• Criminal law is an instrument the state and dominant ruling class use to maintain and perpetuate the social and economic order.
• The contradictions of advanced capitalism . . . require that the subordinate classes remain oppressed by whatever means necessary, especially by the legal system's coercion and violence.
• Only with the collapse of capitalist society, based on socialist principles, will there be a solution to the crime problem.

With specific reference to the origins of laws, then, many Marxian conflict theorists see the legal system as "an apparatus that is created to secure the interests of the dominant class" (Quinney, 1975*b*, p. 192), or, said differently, "The criminal law is . . . first and foremost a reflection of the interests and ideologies of the governing class" (Chambliss, 1974, p. 37).

Clearly, the consensus and conflict theorists discussed above have arrived at quite different judgments about the origins of our criminal and penal laws. We should not leave the impression that these are the only perspectives on law; for example, an emerging division between "instrumental" and "structural" Marxian theory is noted in Chapter 7. The version of Marxian conflict theory we have discussed here is instrumental in its emphasis on the direct control the "ruling class" is presumed to exercise over lawmaking. We have selected the versions of consensus and conflict theory outlined above because they highlight very different factors involved in lawmaking. As we will see, some of the claims of each of these perspectives can be tested; others cannot. Many of the claims that cannot be tested suggest a tendency on the part of both perspectives to strive to support moral prejudgments; that is, advocates of each perspective tend to see any particular legal development as a "good" or "bad" solution to a set of social and/or economic problems regarded as endemic to the system itself. This point can be illustrated through a discussion of work on the origins of theft and vagrancy laws, and through a consideration of the different inferences that have been drawn from this work.

THE ORIGINS OF THEFT AND VAGRANCY LAWS

Jerome Hall (1952) examined the origins of contemporary theft law in England in the Carrier's Case of 1473, the facts of which were as follows. A defendant hired to transport several bales broke them open and took the contents instead of delivering them. At this time, such an act was not clearly criminal, since the defendant was lawfully in possession of property that had been assigned to him for the purpose of transportation. This contradiction was resolved by treating the rupture of the bales as the termination of the defendant's legal possession. Although there was no precedent for this interpretation, "the door was opened to admit into the law of larceny a whole series of acts which had up to that time been purely civil wrongs" (ibid., p. 10).

Hall goes on to identify the political and economic conditions that influenced this reinterpretation. The Carrier's Case arose during a period when feudal relationships were giving way to a new and rising middle class associated with rapidly expanding trade. The accompanying changes in the social organization of everyday life were dramatic: the use of large amounts of capital and of credit facilities, the appearance of numerous intermediate agents and dealers, a division of labor, and the employment of hundreds of persons by single firms.

Previously it had been possible for those who wished to transport property to protect themselves by selecting trustworthy persons. With the expansion of trade this became more difficult, and merchants therefore sought the protection and control of the state. Indeed, Hall observes that the king of England was himself a merchant, "carrying on many private ventures" (ibid., p. 28); the fact that the Carrier's Case was heard first in the Star Chamber "made the likelihood of royal control extremely probable" (ibid., p. 18). "The conclusion that the merchandise taken in the Carrier's Case was very probably wool or cloth means no less than that the *interests of the most important industry in England were involved in the case*" (ibid., p. 31, emphasis in the original). In short, the most powerful political and economic groups in England seemed able to determine the content of a significant legal decision.

Although the historical facts of this case study are clear, the theoretical inferences drawn from them differ dramatically. Hall himself interprets the facts from what we have called the "consensual" view of lawmaking. He suggests (1963, pp. 108–09) that "it makes sense to say that there are better and worse ways of solving problems and to speak of the 'function' of laws in relation to the values they reflect and serve." Thus, Hall looks for the "needs served" or "problems solved" by laws and evaluates the resolutions as "good" or "bad," though he concedes that "it is not easy to determine the criteria of 'best solution' " (ibid.). His response (1952, p. 28) to the emergence of theft laws was one of resignation and acceptance verging on admiration.

It was to be expected that a King who was so definitely and so greatly indebted to mercantile interests, both native and foreign, would be sympathetic to these interests; but that he should bring considerable ability to his participation in the economic life of the country and that he should persistently foster its development were rare qualities in an English monarch.

Furthermore, Hall (1963, p. 613) regarded laws of theft as part of the "natural" core of penal law: "The laws on homicide, theft, treason and incest, e.g., have not been arbitrarily imposed. . . . Not only are they among the norms which appear to be practically universal, they also have rational, normal interrelations with economic and political institutions and changes." In other words, Hall saw theft as one among a group of behaviors that in the preceding chapter we called the "consensus crimes."

Although Hall's findings have gone unchallenged, they are now regularly given a different theoretical interpretation by conflict theorists. In doing this, some of the same functional language used by consensus theory is incorporated into the conflict account. However, the difference is that the "functions fulfilled," the "problems solved," or the "needs served" are now for a specific *class* rather than for the *common good*. For example, Chambliss (1974, p. 25) reinterprets Hall's findings as follows:

There was no possibility that the new law could be justified logically but it was possible for the judges to create legal fictions that justified the decision. In this way the interests of the new upper class were protected . . . through the "perceived need" of the judges sitting on the highest courts of the time. The "perceived need," of course, represented the mobilization of a bias which favored the interests of the dominant economic class.

The new conflict interpretation offered by Chambliss again sees theft laws as serving a function, but now for one class in conflict with another, and he therefore evaluates them as a "bad" solution to the emerging problems of a capitalist society. Others have gone further in developing these conclusions (Quinney, 1975*b*, p. 49). What is significant from a theoretical and methodological viewpoint, however, is that neither value judgment is grounded in the facts of the case study. No evidence is offered to show that different classes experience economic advantage or disadvantage because this *particular* solution was chosen in contrast to another. Nor is there any evidence for the contention that classes differed in their support of theft laws. Rather, each school of thought seems to base its theoretical inferences on implicit comparisons with alternative economic arrangements, one of which, feudalism, was vanishing, and the other of which, modern socialism, had not yet arrived. In any case, no comparative exercises are conducted before the moral judgments are rendered.

A similar problem is apparent in an analysis of the origins of vagrancy laws by Chambliss (1974). The original vagrancy statute was passed in England in 1349. Prior to this, religious houses provided assistance to the poor, sick, and feeble. Passage of the statute made offering and receiving such aid illegal. The temper and purpose of the statute is suggested in its original wording: "Because . . . many beggars . . . refuse to labor, giving themselves to idleness and vice, . . . it is ordained, that none . . . shall . . . give anything to such which may labor . . . so that thereby they may be compelled to labor for their necessary living" (cited in Chambliss, 1964, p. 68).

Several factors contributed to this legislative turn of events. First, the church was no longer anxious to assume the financial costs of supporting the growing number of poor people. Second, a desperate labor situation was facing the feudal landowners. The Black Plague had ravaged England, taking in its death toll nearly 50 percent of the labor force. The problem was aggravated by the landowners selling many of their serfs into freedom to raise money in support of the crusades. Thus, religious and feudal interests were combined in support of vagrancy legislation that forced laborers to accept employment at low wages.

In time, feudalism died and the vagrancy statutes lapsed into a period of dormancy. However, in 1530, the laws were reactivated to serve a new purpose. England was now experiencing rapid growth in trade and commerce. As patterns of trade developed, business interests perceived a need, beyond that satisfied by the use of the theft laws, to protect their goods during the period of their transportation between sellers and buyers. In this context, the vagrancy statutes found new purpose as a flexible means of controlling persons in the countryside who seemed to threaten the safe transportation of goods and materials. Thus, the vagrancy laws were revived and refocused to include "any ruffians . . . [who] shall wander, loiter, or idle use themselves and play the vagabonds" (cited in Chambliss, 1964, p. 72).

There is little doubt that the vagrancy laws were used in the manner that Chambliss describes, particularly in the period following the Black Plague. It is also clear that the vague character of vagrancy laws, with their tendency to refer to a condition or subjective state rather than an objective set of behaviors, makes them liable to indiscriminate use. What remains uncertain, however, is whether the original use of these laws was *only* in the service of a dominant or ruling class, and therefore a bad solution to the social and economic problems involved. Again, there are no comparative data on alternative means used to remedy similar problems in like or unlike circumstances. How good or bad a solution the vagrancy laws represented to the problems caused by the Black Plague is difficult, if not impossible, to judge. In any case, such problems are not unique to capitalist societies. Greenberg (1976:619) makes this point when he notes that "in view of the persistence of crime in state and market socialist economies, it is plausible to assume that *all* societies contain contradictions that will generate disputes involving behavior that will be perceived as sufficiently reprehensible to warrant punitive intervention, and that in *modern* societies this intervention will at least some of the time take the form of criminalization." Therefore instead of attempting to judge in moral terms whether various forms of crime and delinquency legislation are "good" or "bad" solutions to the problems they attempt to solve, it may be more productive for our purposes to examine the following more specific set of issues that the consensus and conflict perspectives raise without resolving.

First, the Marxian conflict perspective we have considered is premised on the assumption that particular interests—specifically business interests —regularly prevail in the legislation of crime and delinquency. This perspective assumes that there is an implicit or explicit *alliance* between *business interests* that want particular kinds of criminal laws passed and the *state* that imposes them. In the remainder of this chapter, we will be attentive to any identifiable part business interests may play in forming alliances that influence the state's role in the legislative process. Second, the contrasting assumptions of the two perspectives about the role the public plays in the legislative process encourage consideration of whether the interest groups involved exercise their influence with or without *opposition* from other groups and/or the community at large. The absence of a visible opposition makes a conflict view of lawmaking more complicated to sustain. Third, it is important to know whether those seeking to change the law appeal to *dominant social values* and whether their ability to do so affects their chances of success. Interest groups may regularly and effectively use dominant social values to accomplish their lawmaking goals. If they are able to do so, they may be particularly effective in avoiding the overt kinds of opposition noted above (Hopkins, 1975).

The following discussion of three kinds of crime and delinquency legislation speaks to the above issues, while offering some illustrative descriptions of the law-creation process. Because the following laws are more recent in origin than the theft and vagrancy statutes already discussed, our review of them can address the issues in a more direct and concrete fashion than has been possible thus far.

ALCOHOL AND DRUG LAWS

America has experimented with prohibiting two kinds of "chemical crimes": the use of alcohol and the use of narcotic drugs. Fifteen case studies of alcohol and drug legislation are listed in Table 3-1. These studies collectively make the point that some of the most important North American alcohol and drug statutes developed alongside one another during the progressive era as part of a cross-national effort to protect middle-class values against the alleged threat posed by users of habit-forming chemicals. These studies raise some fascinating questions: Why did the prohibition of narcotics outlast the prohibition of alcohol? What roles did interest groups, elites, moral entrepreneurs, and the media play in the generation of these laws?

Bonnie and Whitebread (1974) offer a convincing explanation of why narcotics laws outlasted alcohol prohibition. Narcotics legislation had its roots in a wave of ethnic and racial prejudices directed against isolated minority groups, particularly Chinese, black, and Mexican Americans. These prejudices led to what Bonnie and Whitebread call a "moral consensus" focused on a presumed link between these groups and the use of narcotic drugs. We talk more about the formation of this consensus

TABLE 3-1
ALCOHOL AND DRUG LAWS

Author(s)	Legislation	Place	Period	Causal agent(s) cited
Sinclair (1962)	Alcohol prohibition	United States	1784–1933	Progressive politicians, medical researchers, WCTU, Anti-Saloon League, "Old Order of the Country"
Gusfield (1963)	Alcohol prohibition	United States	1826–1933	Rural, populist, Protestant native Americans; WCTU; Anti-Saloon League
Musto (1973)	Opiates and marijuana	United States	1832	Southerners' and westerners' hostility toward blacks and Chinese, State Department
Duster (1970)	Opiates	United States	1856–	Medical practitioners
Reasons (1974)	Opiates	United States (state and federal)	1870–	Charles Brent, Hamilton Wright, hostility toward Chinese and blacks, Treasury Department
Odegard (1928)	Alcohol prohibition	United States	1874–1928	Anti-Saloon League
Timberlake (1963)	Alcohol prohibition	United States	1900–20	Old stock, middle-class Protestants; WCTU; Anti-Saloon League
Cook (1969, 1970)	Opiates	Canada	1908–23	Hostility toward Chinese
Bonnie & Whitebread (1974)	Marijuana	United States	1911–	Prejudice against Mexican-Americans, Federal Bureau of Narcotics

TABLE 3-1 *cont'd*
ALCOHOL AND DRUG LAWS

Author(s)	Legislation	Place	Period	Causal agent(s) cited
Dickson (1968)	Marijuana	United States	1913–44	Bureau of Narcotics
Lindesmith (1959)	Opiate legislation as interpreted by the courts	United States	1914–59	Treasury Department, Federal Bureau of Narcotics
Lindesmith (1967)	Opiate legislation	United States	1914–	Treasury Department, Federal Bureau of Narcotics
Becker (1963)	Marijuana	United States	1925–51	Values regarding self-control, ecstasy, and humanitarianism; Federal Bureau of Narcotics
Galliher & Walker (1977)	Marijuana	United States	1930s	Symbolic reassurance
Galliher, McCartney, & Baum (1974)	Marijuana revision	Nebraska	1968–	Spread of marijuana use to middle class

below. In contrast, the prohibition of alcohol never fully achieved this level of consensual support, largely because it was aimed at urban immigrants who, although poor, had the potential for forming an active and organized opposition to prohibition through urban machine and union politics. In the terms of the previous chapter, alcohol prohibition remained a conflict crime. Before elaborating the latter point, we will review the development of narcotic drug policy in America.

There is little doubt that narcotics legislation was partly an expression of hostile attitudes toward minority groups associated with drug use. Musto (1973, p. 5) observes that "in the nineteenth century addicts were identified with foreign groups and internal minorities who were already actively feared and the objects of elaborate and massive social and legal constraints." For example, the Chinese were associated with opium (Musto, 1973; Cook, 1969, 1970; Reasons, 1974), southern blacks with cocaine (Musto, 1973), and Mexicans with marijuana (Bonnie and White-

Reaching Over

(Source: Atlanta Georgian, 17 March 1934. Media image of the drug problem, circa 1934.)

bread, 1974). Mackenzie King, later prime minister of Canada, acquired much of his early reputation by lobbying for passage of Canada's first narcotics legislation in terms of the "threat" posed by Asian immigration (Cook, 1969).

It made little difference in Canada or the United States that the "evidence clearly indicates that the upper and middle classes predominated among narcotic addicts in the period up to 1914" (Duster, 1970, p. 9). As we noted in the previous chapter, until the turn of the century in America many patent medicines that could be bought in stores or by mail order contained morphine, cocaine, and heroin. There was no requirement that patent medicines containing opiates be labeled as such in interstate commerce until the Pure Food and Drug Act was passed in 1906. Among other things, hay fever remedies commonly contained cocaine as their active ingredient, Coca-Cola contained cocaine until 1903, and even advertised "cures" for the opium habit frequently contained large amounts of opiates. Manufacturers of such products were remarkably effective during the nineteenth century in preventing any legislative action to require even the disclosure of dangerous drugs in these commercial preparations. The middle classes consumed these products with considerable frequency.

Only after the passage of the Harrison Act in the United States in 1914 did the picture seem to change, so that "by 1920, medical journals could speak of the 'overwhelming majority [of drug addicts]' from the 'unrespectable parts' of society" (Duster, 1970, p. 11). Originally the Harrison Act was simply a tax measure that made no direct mention of addicts or addiction (Lindesmith, 1959). However, by gradually persuading the public to associate narcotics use with disenfranchised minorities, lobbyists laid a foundation for a broader legislative prohibition. This campaign also was advanced by the facts that regardless of the class distribution of users, use was still a minority phenomenon (Musto cites estimates that 2 to 4 percent of the population was addicted in 1895), and that opiate use was known to produce pronounced physiological consequences within a fairly short period of time (i.e., the withdrawal effects were pronounced). We do not know what the relative significance of these different factors was in getting the legislative prohibition on narcotics passed.

We do know, however, that every legislative movement has a leadership. The leaders of campaigns striving for official control of crime and deviance are called "moral entrepreneurs," a term coined by Becker (1963). They are the people whose initiative and enterprise are essential in getting the legal rules passed that are necessary to "do something" about a particular type of deviant behavior. Often such individuals seem to be undertaking a "moral crusade" in that they perceive some activity as an evil in need of legal reform, and they pursue this task with missionary zeal (Gusfield, 1963). Moral entrepreneurs and crusaders assume that enforcement of desired legal rules will improve the lives of those who are ruled. That this is often a very dubious assumption will become clear as we consider the moral crusades that brought legal control to marijuana and alcohol use in America. As we will see, there are interesting parallels between the two areas of legal development.

In 1930 an important event occurred: the federal government established a Bureau of Narcotics to be housed in the Treasury Department, separate from the Bureau of Prohibition, where federal narcotics work previously had been done. Selected out of the Bureau of Prohibition to be director of the new agency was a moral entrepreneur by the name of Harry Anslinger. Although Anslinger was convinced early on that legal control of marijuana was necessary, in the beginning he was doubtful of the role the federal government should take. His concern was that expansion of the federal role in the control of marijuana might lead to a questioning of what the federal authority to deal with narcotics was in the first place. The federal government had entered the field under the pretense of generating tax revenues. To avoid attracting attention to this issue, Anslinger limited his early efforts to the active support of new and extended state marijuana laws.

Anslinger's early activities took the form of attracting public attention to what he called the "marijuana menace." Representative of these activities was the article "Marijuana: Assassin of Youth," which appeared in the widely circulated *American Magazine*. By 1932, Anslinger was joined in these efforts by the Hearst newspaper chain. This chain of newspapers editorialized in favor of the enactment of state marijuana laws. It is plausible that the use of marijuana actually increased as a result of this publicity. However, Anslinger expressed the issue quite the other way round when he argued, for example, that "fifty percent of the violent crimes committed in districts occupied by Mexicans, Greeks, Turks, Filipinos, Spaniards, Latin Americans, and Negroes may be traced to the abuse of Marijuana" (cited by Bonnie and Whitebread, 1974, p. 146).

Anslinger ultimately was convinced that there was sufficient public support to try a federal bill: another tax measure, separate from the Harrison Act. Testifying before a congressional committee, Anslinger used three unsubstantiated arguments to get a federal marijuana law passed.

1 Acknowledging first that *medical properties* of the drug were in doubt, Anslinger argued that it nonetheless presumably was known that *violent crime* was linked to its use: "Despite the fact that medical men and scientists have disagreed upon the properties of marijuana, and some are inclined to minimize the harmfulness of this drug, the records offer ample evidence that it has a disastrous effect upon many of its users. Recently we have received many reports showing crimes of violence committed by persons while under the influence of marijuana" (cited in Bonnie and Whitebread, 1974, p. 155).

2 Anslinger also argued that marijuana use had spread alarmingly in recent years, provoking a public demand for action. The newspaper campaigns noted above were cited to document the alleged public hysteria, despite the fact that there is no convincing evidence of public hysteria independent of Anslinger's efforts to create it, and that more media attention followed than preceded the passage of marijuana legislation (Galliher and Walker, 1977).

3 Finally, Anslinger argued that even though every state now had marijuana legislation, local authorities could not cope with the growing of "marijuana menace." Anslinger testified that states were requesting federal help, although it was not entirely clear why, in constitutionally acceptable terms, this help was needed.

Such arguments were persuasive, albeit dubious, and a federal marijuana statute was soon passed.

One of the most interesting consequences of the passage of this act was a sudden change in bureau policy. Before the act, Anslinger had urged in the press the idea that marijuana use was spreading among the young and that this was leading to violent crime. After passage of the act, Anslinger argued that "our present policy is to discourage undue emphasis on marijuana for the reason that in some sections of the country recently press reports have been so exaggerated that interest in the subject has become almost hysterical and we are therefore trying to mold public opinion along more conservative and saner lines" (cited in Bonnie and Whitebread, 1974, p. 178). Anslinger had encountered the paradoxical problem that many successful moral entrepreneurs eventually face: how to stop the hysterical belief that a problem is growing, once given the presumed means to control it.

Alcohol prohibition involved a somewhat different combination of factors. Most conspicuously, prohibition followed from the well-organized lobbying activities of the Women's Christian Temperance Union and the Anti-Saloon League. However, this lobby did not work in a vacuum. For a century, as Gusfield (1963) notes, the American temperance movement drew its support from a number of groups in American society that were declining in social and economic status. These groups ranged from the New England Federalists down through the lower middle strata. Then, in 1896, the temperance movement took a new turn and began a symbolic struggle against the forces of industrialization. This "symbolic crusade" was waged in defense of traditional Protestant and rural values, which were regarded as declining and thought to be under attack by the forces of American industrialization: particularly non-Protestant immigrants, and more generally the rise of the city itself. The face of America was changing, and rural, American-born Protestants saw the changes as a symbolic threat to an established, but apparently declining, way of life. Note that this picture of symbolic status-group conflict contrasts sharply with the finding of Bonnie and Whitebread (1974, p. 13) that "narcotics policy . . . was supported by a latent popular consensus." Undoubtedly, a major portion of the difference derives from the widespread use of alcohol in America, which had developed over a considerable period of time. Therefore, although a concerted attempt was made to link alcohol with poverty, crime, and insanity, it was possible for an organized opposition to these efforts to form.

Thus Timberlake (1963, p. 99) observes that although wage earners were unable to thwart the enactment of temperance legislation, they were strong enough to ensure its ultimate failure. "Many working men . . .

The Devil's Roost

(Source: Washington Herald, 26 February 1937, Copyright, 1937, by American
Newspapers, Inc. Media image of the drug problem, circa 1937.)

opposed prohibition because it smacked of paternalism and class exploitation. To them it was a hypocritical and insulting attempt to control their
personal habits in order to exact greater profits for their employers, who
themselves had no intention of giving up liquor" (ibid., p. 93). As much as
81 percent of the membership of the American Federation of Labor was

"wet" (ibid., p. 95), i.e., opposed to restrictions on alcohol use, which is consistent with the claim of Samuel Gompers that the great majority of the members opposed prohibition.

Economic considerations may also have affected the rise and fall of prohibition, but these considerations were often in conflict. Some business executives believed that temperance would increase industrial efficiency, redistribute money spent on liquor, decrease welfare expenditures on crime and poverty, and reduce threats of disorder during strikes. Others argued that prohibition would diminish public revenues, increase unemployment in liquor and related industries, shift political power balances, and increase government regulation of business. World War I seemed to strengthen the former set of arguments, but the balance was to shift again during the depths of the depression (Timberlake, 1963). The contradictory nature of these arguments seems to support Gusfield's contention that the prohibition of alcohol was more a result of symbolic than economic conflict. The passage of prohibition appears to be explained by the perception that urban, immigrant alcohol use threatened the status of rural American-born Protestants rather than the economic foundations of capitalism.

Finally, something should be said about the role of the media in molding public and political opinion about alcohol prohibition. Two progressive era journals, the *Outlook* and the *Independent,* and two popular muckraking periodicals, *Collier's Weekly* and *McClure's Magazine,* cultivated popular support for alcohol prohibition. Timberlake (1963, p. 156) writes,

> . . . because they enjoyed a nation-wide circulation, these large middle-class journals were more powerful molders of public opinion than the newspapers. But the latter also continued to exert an important influence and, like the periodicals, soon began to devote increasing attention to the liquor question. Superintendent Baker remarked upon this at the Anti-Saloon League's national convention in 1907 and noted with approval that more than one-half of the nation's press was friendly.

Thus there is little doubt that the media contributed significantly to the passage of temperance legislation.

A number of points emerge from the research on alcohol and drug legislation that we have reviewed. First, the concern of the middle class for the supremacy of its values is seen by most researchers as the primary explanation for the passage of alcohol and narcotics legislation. This class base of support was mobilized by powerful organizations, the WCTU and the Anti-Saloon League in the case of alcohol prohibition, and the Treasury Department and its Bureau of Narcotics in the case of narcotics.

Although the latter organization clearly had its own bureaucratic interests, the former, private organizations might appear to have been dominated by elite philanthropists. But Timberlake (1963, p. 136) reports that "the [Anti-Saloon] league always received the bulk of its funds from people of modest means who customarily pledged from 25 cents to $2.00 a month." Yet if the proponents of this legislation were not all upper class, its objects were uniformly poor. However, differences emerge even here: when alcohol prohibition attempted to criminalize the mass of the poor, it ran into the opposition of unions and urban political machines. In contrast, narcotics legislation focused more narrowly, and more successfully, on minorities of the poor who could be defined as disreputable. "Increasingly associated with the slothful and immoral 'criminal classes' who degraded the nation's cities, narcotics use threatened to retard national growth with pauperism, moral degeneracy, and crime. A consensus had emerged: the nonmedical use of 'narcotics' was a cancer which had to be removed entirely from the social organism" (Bonnie and Whitebread, 1974, p. 17). We have seen evidence that the media played a significant role in the creation of this consensus.

DELINQUENCY AND PROBATION LAWS

The origins of juvenile delinquency and adult probation laws have been analyzed frequently. Fifteen such studies are summarized in Table 3-2. Studies of delinquency and probation laws are grouped together in this section for three reasons: (1) most juvenile court laws contained provisions for probation, (2) many of the same reformers fought for both juvenile court and adult probation statutes, and (3) themes of the progressive era in American politics were prominent in the successful passage and implementation of both types of laws.

Conventional wisdom has it that juvenile delinquency legislation emerged as a means of getting adolescents out of adult jails and the slum neighborhoods from which they came. However, few analysts of juvenile delinquency laws have accepted this simple assessment. Parker (1976a, p. 168) offers the following antidote to the conventional view.

> To a great extent, the history of child-saving in the twentieth century is not the history of improving the general conditions of child-life (because most of the battles had been won), or the history of juvenile institutions (which changed very little after the initial efforts of the Founders of the House of Refuge and their imitators). It is not even the history of the juvenile court itself because it provided, as legal institutions tend to do, a purely

TABLE 3-2
JUVENILE COURT AND ADULT PROBATION LAWS

Author(s)	Legislation	Place	Period	Causal agent(s) cited
Schlossman (1977)	Juvenile court	Milwaukee	1825–1920	Benjamin Lindsey, progressive reformers, and advocates of probation
Lemert (1970)	Juvenile court	California	1850–	Humanitarian concern; Puritan, Calvinist values; women and women's organizations
McFarlane (1966)	Adult probation	Ontario	1857–	J. J. Kelso, W. L. Scott, and other urban reformers
Boyd (1978)	Probation	Canada	1857–1921	Middle-class reformers
Hagan & Leon (1977)	Juvenile court	Toronto	1857–1952	J. J. Kelso, W. L. Scott, and advocates of probation
Young (1976)	Probation	England	1860–	Middle-class reformers responsible for social work innovation generally
Lou (1927)	Juvenile court	United States	1869–1927	Industrial revolution and religious and moral revival; factory legislation and women's movement
Platt (1969)	Juvenile court	Chicago		Native, feminist, middle-class reformers
Platt (1974)	Juvenile court	United States	1870–	Upper-class interests operating through and with middle-class reformers
Parker (1976b)	Juvenile court	Illinois	1880s–	Moral reformers, women's groups
Fox (1970)	Juvenile court	Illinois	1899–	Urban reformers; private sectarian interests running institutions
Schultz (1973)	Juvenile court	Illinois	1899–	Advocates of probation

TABLE 3-2 cont'd
JUVENILE COURT AND ADULT PROBATION LAWS

Author(s)	Legislation	Place	Period	Causal agent(s) cited
Mennel (1973)	Juvenile court	United States	1899–1940	Progressive reformers, Protestant children's aid societies, urban women's clubs
Bryant (1968)	Juvenile court	Oklahoma	1904–15	National reform figures (Benjamin Lindsey, Kate Barnard); social workers, particularly women
Hagan (1979)	Federal probation	United States	1915–	Urban status groups, Charles Chute, and National Probation Association

symbolic quality to child work. The real history of the period is a history of probation.

Not all students of juvenile court legislation agree with Parker's conclusion, and as we will see, it is a quarrel over the role of probation in the juvenile court movement that focuses much of the debate in this area. Anthony Platt, (1974, p. 369) for example, adopts a conflict perspective in arguing that the impetus for delinquency legislation flowed from close and compromising links between members of the middle and upper classes, and (ibid., p. 377) that "the juvenile court system was part of a general movement directed towards developing a specialized labor market and industrial discipline under corporate capitalism by creating new programs of adjudication and control." Essential to this argument is Platt's emphasis (1969, chap. 3) on the emergence of a "new penology" and his disregard for the expansion of probation.

Platt (1969) argues that the "child-saving movement," like the temperance movement, was a symbolic crusade mobilized by feminist reformers. The affluent women who worked in this movement at the turn of the century were living in a changing world: organized religion was in decline, public education was taking children out of the home, leisure time and boredom were increasing, and the nuclear family seemed to be breaking down in the impersonal, crowded city. Against this background, the child-saving movement offered an opportunity for women to fulfill new roles that included elements of the old, both in terms of the movement's concern with children and in the new occupational roles (e.g., juvenile court workers, house parents, etc.) it encouraged. However, in all of this, Platt (ibid., 1969, p. 99) suggests, "the child-savers were more concerned with restriction than liberation. . . . The austerity of the criminal law and criminal institutions were not their major target of concern." Instead, Platt argues that the child-savers merely wanted to replace one set of institutions (penitentiaries) with another (reformatories).

Another student of juvenile court legislation, Sanford Fox, also focuses on the connection between this legislation and institutionalization, but in ways different from Platt. Fox (1970, p. 1224) argues that the effort to enact a delinquency law in Illinois was mainly an attempt to change existing institutional conditions and the role of private interests in operating these institutions. He regards the failure of this effort as a "triumph of private enterprise and sectarianism." Significantly, though, he attributes the outcome not to the influence of *elite* economic interests but to private *sectarian* interests that ran institutions in the state, and he acknowledges (ibid., p. 1229) that the "Illinois law spoke of probation for the first time."

Still, it is the lack of attention to probation that distinguishes Platt and Fox from other students of delinquency legislation. Schultz (1973, pp. 463–465) notes that the Illinois legislation discussed above had dramatic national implications for adults as well as adolescents.

> Although probation was never limited to juveniles before or after 1899, that date is almost as important to the growth of probation nationally as it is to the growth of juvenile courts. The use of probation had been sporadic and desultory until it became tied with the juvenile reform movement. It then spread to every state that enacted juvenile court legislation. By 1927, all but two states— Maine and Wyoming—had juvenile court laws, and every state except Wyoming had a juvenile probation system.

A more recent investigation of the origin of delinquency legislation in Canada corroborates the findings of Schultz and Parker (Hagan and Leon, 1977). Drawing on the lengthy correspondence between two key participants in the passage of the Canadian Juvenile Delinquents Act of 1908, this study reports an ongoing struggle between two professional groups, the police and the advocates of probation. The police argued for the continuation of an explicitly punitive approach based on institutionalizing juveniles, whereas supporters of probation advocated a less formal set of arrangements directed toward the "treatment" rather than the "punishment" of juveniles. No evidence is found that the use of institutions increased as a result of this legislation (although probation work clearly *was* growing) or that elite economic groups took any active interest in the legislation. Rather, the professional groups seemed to be the significant contestants in the struggle.

A study of the emergence of the juvenile courts in Milwaukee by Schlossman (1977, p. 60) suggests that the emphasis on probation within the juvenile court movement reflected a concern for the family that pervaded the progressive era: "Rehabilitation of delinquents in their own homes, as contrasted with the nineteenth-century preference for quick removal of problem youth to reformatories, was the primary goal of Progressive juvenile justice." The result was the emergence of a system of social control that was less formal and less coercive, but nonetheless more extensive, exerted over the families of urban poor, often outside of court. Thus in Milwaukee (Schlossman, 1977), as in Toronto (Hagan and Leon, 1977), probation officers soon expanded their influence not only within the structure of the court but also outside it by handling cases that they themselves had generated. However, Schlossman (1977, p. 53) also notes that the officers did little beyond making an initial inquiry and concludes that this new framework of social control was probably "more threatening in its potential than [in] its actual use." Finally, Schlossman (ibid., p. 156) acknowledges that though few adolescents were institutionalized for lengthy periods during the early years of the Milwaukee court (indeed, the number of such dispositions actually declined), and though the court relied heavily on probation during this era, it did impose an increasing number of short-term sentences in a newly built detention center: "short-term detention served as a mechanism of deterrence in a way that long-term reformatory commitals could not, and it also served as an alternative— symbolically, perhaps, even as a rebuke—to the institutional approaches that had been so ineffective in curtailing delinquency during the previous century."

A diminished reliance on institutions combined with increased control, particularly through the use of probation personnel, is apparent in other fragmentary data. The prominent reformer Frederick Almy (1902, p. 281) wrote from Buffalo that "the . . . Juvenile Court has not quite completed its first year, and no definite records have been compiled, but two results already are notable—the decrease in the number of commitments to the truant school and to reformatories, and the increase in the number of children arrested." Haller (1970, p. 629) observes that in Chicago "between 1913 and 1914 the number of delinquents referred to court rose from 1,956 to 2,916, an increase of nearly 50 percent in the delinquency rate for Cook County. The reason for the increase was that twenty-three additional probation officers were hired in 1914." Finally, Parker (1976a, p. 169) argues that "Massachusetts had the most advanced system of probation.

The number of children under the direct care of the State Board of Lunacy and Charity as 'minor wards of the state' had increased from 2065 in 1866 to 3004 in 1897. . . . The numbers in institutions had been reduced from fourteen hundred in 1866 to about four hundred in 1897."

A general picture begins to emerge out of these studies of juvenile court and adult probation legislation. The progressive era was characterized by a widely shared view that rehabilitation should be family-centered. Advocates of such legislation therefore focused on the offender's home as the locus of treatment and on the probation officer as the key remedial agent. Among the most vigorous proponents were members of women's groups and persons who eventually became the "professionals" charged with responsibility for probation (see Table 3-2). Juvenile courts and probation officers exerted new forms of social control that were disproportionately targeted at the urban poor. What remains unclear, however, is what inferences we can fairly draw from the increased attention to this group.

Although there is evidence that wealthy individuals contributed money and volunteered their time to the early juvenile courts, there is little concrete information about the motives for this "philanthropy" or the unique benefits they thereby obtained. Furthermore, there is much to suggest that the families who received judicial attention were not reluctant to obtain it. Schlossman (1977, p. 188) comments on "the willingness of many poor parents to use the courts to unburden themselves of child-rearing responsibilities," and Schultz (1973, p. 472) similarly suggests that "the greatest obstacle to interpreting juvenile court acts as instruments of class oppression is the evidence that *parents* liberally availed themselves of the court's broad jurisdiction and easy access by turning in their own children" (emphasis in original). An alternative hypothesis that accommodates these several studies is that families of the urban poor, particularly those who were most desperate, presented an inviting object for the "help and treatment" that middle-class women's and professional groups were anxious to extend. This does not deny the ominous *potential* of such laws for class control, but it may explain why these efforts were so successful in building juvenile court bureaucracies and so superficial in responding to problems of the poor.

SEXUAL PSYCHOPATH AND PROSTITUTION LAWS

Laws governing sexuality are subject to radical change, providing a good example of the frequently thin line between crime and deviance, discussed in the preceding chapter. Thus only a small part of the sexual behavior punished by criminal law in North America today was similarly punished in

Tudor England. For example, Ploscowe (1960, p. 218) notes that although forcible rape, sexual intercourse with a female under 10, the sexual corruption of children, lewd and indecent acts in public, bestiality, and buggery were punishable under old English criminal law, large areas of sexual behavior, such as fornication, adultery, incest, fellatio, cunnilingus, and mutual masturbation, were treated as sins or ecclesiastical offenses by the Church of England. That much of the latter behavior has since come under the criminal law is a reminder of the important point that the law is an expandable entity. Two types of sex laws, those concerning sexual psychopaths and those concerning prostitution, have received sustained and detailed historical consideration (see Table 3-3).

Sutherland (1950, p. 553) observes that "although . . . sexual psychopath laws are dangerous in principle, they are of little importance in practice" because they have seldom been used. Why, then, were these laws passed in the first place? Three of the four studies summarized in Table 3-3 (Swanson, 1960; Sutherland, 1950, 1951) emphasize the activities of the news media and community groups. And Tappan's conclusions (1950, p. 34) are at least consistent: "it is the public anxiety about serious sex crimes that has motivated new legislation on the sex problem."

Michigan enacted the first sexual psychopath law in 1937, and other states quickly followed suit. Sutherland (1951) saw in the diffusion of these laws a recurring pattern: a community is thrown into panic by a few serious sex crimes that are given widespread publicity; the community responds in an agitated fashion, and a variety of proposals are made; a committee is appointed to study the situation and make recommendations; finally, the committee recommends a sexual psychopath law as a "scientific" crime-control procedure that is presumably consistent with a preference for treatment over punishment. Sutherland did not deny that serious sex crimes occur, but he questioned the ideology (promulgated by people like the then director of the FBI, J. Edgar Hoover) that surrounded these crimes. This ideology maintained that (1) serious sex crimes are prevalent and increasing; (2) nearly all are committed by "sexual psychopaths"; (3) the latter continue to commit serious crimes throughout their lives; (4) sexual psychopaths can be identified accurately before the crimes occur; (5) society fails in its responsibilities when it allows the early release of such persons; (6) long confinement is the solution to the problem; and (7) psychiatrists should be the source of professional advice on the diagnosis, treatment, and release of these "patients." Sutherland criticized this ideology as inconsistent with known facts about serious sex offenders. Yet neither he nor others who have studied the passage and administration of these laws conclude they reflect political, economic, or even professional interests. Rather, they are seen mainly as a response to panic, albeit a

TABLE 3-3
SEX LAWS

Author	Legislation	Place	Period	Causal agent(s) cited
Davis (1966)	Sex laws generally	Cross-cultural	Broadly historical	Maintenance of the family
Pivar (1973)	Prostitution	United States	1868–1900	Purity reformers, the women's movement, urban progressivism
Holmes (1972)	Prostitution	United States	1892–	Society of Sanitary & Moral Prophylaxis, Bureau of Social Hygiene, American Social Hygiene Association, Illinois Vigilance Association, New York Society for the Prevention of Crime, women's groups
Lubove (1962)	Prostitution	United States	1894–1921	Vice commissions, progressive reformers
Anderson (1974)	Prostitution	Chicago	1910–15	Chicago vice commission, the muckrakers, the social hygiene movement, prominent Chicago philanthropists, concern about the family
Feldman (1967)	Prostitution	United States	1910–15	Nativists and antinativists, feminists
Waterman (1932)	Prostitution	New York City	1910–31	Health interests of the community
Sutherland (1951)	Sexual psychopath	United States	1937–50	Community panic following serious sex crime(s) given media publicity and followed by community activity
Tappan (1950)	Sexual psychopath	United States	1939–50	Public anxiety about serious sex crimes
Sutherland (1950)	Sexual psychopath	United States	to 1950	Ideological myths about "sexual psychopaths" spread through the media

TABLE 3-3 cont'd
SEX LAWS

Author	Legislation	Place	Period	Causal agent(s) cited
Swanson (1960)	Sexual psychopath	United States	to 1957	News media, desire to protect society and rehabilitate offenders
Roby (1969)	Prostitution	New York State	1962–65	A variety of interest groups including Judge Murtagh and his supporters, lawyers, American Social Health Association, hotels and business interests, civil liberties groups, police
Roby (1972)	Prostitution	New York State	1961–69	As above, with particular emphasis on lawyers with expertise seeking clarification of the law

panic aggravated and focused by the news media. An unresolved question concerns the media's motivation in giving so much attention to sexual crimes. One obvious motive, however, is the desire to increase circulation.

The media also were involved prominently in the development of prostitution laws. Prostitution became an issue of public debate during the first decade of this century, assisted in large part by the revelations of the muckrakers. In a famous *McClure's Magazine* article (1907), George Kobbe Turner captured a ready audience with provocative descriptions of prostitution in Chicago. Louis Filler (1950, p. 288) wrote in his history of the muckrakers that "the effect of this single article was indescribable." This and later articles stressed the prevalence of prostitution and the accompanying dangers of disease. But the call for action met with an ambivalent response, which we cannot understand without first considering the circumstances surrounding prostitution at the turn of the century.

Prostitution is first talked about in the United States during the colonial period, where it seems to have been most common in the major seaports. However, "commercialized vice" did not become a prominent feature of

American life until the onset of industrialization and urbanization. Meanwhile, Waterman (1932) points out that prostitution was not an offense in either English or American common law. It was only when activities associated with prostitution annoyed others that legal action was justified. For example, an early New York statute defined as a disorderly person "every common prostitute or night-walker loitering or being in any thoroughfare or public place for the purpose of prostitution or solicitation to the annoyance of inhabitants or passersby" (quoted in Waterman, 1932, p. 12). Such provisions reflected the American (and European) preference at the turn of the century for regulating rather than repressing prostitution. A result was well-known areas of prostitution ("deviance service centers," as we called them in the preceding chapter) in most large American cities: New Orleans's Basin Street, San Francisco's Barbary Coast, Denver's Market Street Line, and New York's Bowery and Five Points (Holmes, 1972, p. 85). The muckrakers, purity reformers, and urban progressives were determined to change all this.

They eventually achieved considerable success. The regulationists and the reformers clashed repeatedly in the 1860s and 1870s. During this period many states and cities considered legalizing prostitution as a means of regulating it, but they increasingly were defeated by the reformers. For example, St. Louis initiated a registration system to regulate prostitution, but this policy lasted only four years before it was repealed. During the debate on this law, a petition "praying" for the repeal of the law and signed by more than 100,000 citizens was wheeled into the legislature accompanied by a group of young women attired in spotless white gowns. This was a kind of symbolism that was difficult to fight.

With this kind of symbolism and attendant publicity the reformers formed a "social hygiene movement" that fought militantly for the "abolition" of prostitution. The publicity that accompanied this movement spoke provocatively of such practices as the frequent kidnapping of young and innocent girls by "slave traders" who forced them into lives of sin and disease. By 1910, few Americans doubted that a commercialized network of "white slavery" existed in the United States. The result was the establishment over a five-year period of "vice commissions" in forty major cities and states. It is said that while in 1910 nearly every large city in the United States had a red-light district, only eight years later these districts had been closed in 200 of America's largest cities (Holmes, 1972).

The sizable number of interest groups enumerated in the last column of Table 3-3 and cited by analysts of prostitution law suggests diversified support for the movement to criminalize prostitution. It included groups as far apart as those who had advocated the abolition of slavery (Pivar, 1973) and those who fought against immigration and for the integration of the foreign-born into American society (Feldman, 1967). It is not surprising, then, that a basic ambivalence characterized this social movement.

This is clearly recognized in the work of Feldman (1967), Anderson (1974), and Pivar (1973). Holmes (1972, p. 84) distinguishes two forces: the "humanitarians" and the "control group." "The purpose of the one was the rescue of misguided girls; the purpose of the latter was the preservation and protection of the 'moral upper classes' from a potentially expandable and 'dangerous class.' " The latter, the control group, was the more heavy-handed in its views, arguing that prostitutes were an ethnic, economic, and intellectual group of the lowest level. The vehemence of these views is reflected in the following excerpt from a speech given at a meeting of the American Society of Sanitary and Moral Prophylaxis: "We must sterilize all [these] lilly livered loons who would prey on an individual to perpetuate defectiveness and spread horrible diseases which bring pain, sorrow, agony and torture to the tender and innocent and which may destroy the race!" (cited in Holmes, 1972, p. 91). In contrast, the humanitarians offered the more liberal view that prostitutes were forced into the profession either by white-slave traders or by bad economic conditions.

Both of the above groups agreed, however, that prostitution threatened the physical health of individuals and, even more significantly, the social health of the family. "A deep concern for the family, in some cases a conviction that family discipline could not 'cope with existing social conditions,' inspired much of the agitation against prostitution" (Anderson, 1974, p. 223; cf. Davis, 1966). In this sense, antiprostitution efforts were built on consensually shared values. Antiprostitution efforts manifested themselves in the formation of vice commissions in many American cities and in the generation of considerable publicity.

Laws were also passed: the Injunction and Abatement Act (often called the "Red Light Abatement Act") was first enacted in Iowa in 1909. It provided that any private citizen could maintain an equitable action to close a house of prostitution without having to show any particular damage or injury. Between 1911 and 1915, twenty-one states and the District of Columbia passed similar laws, and in 1910 the federal Mann Act made it illegal to import aliens for immoral purposes and permitted the deportation of aliens engaged in prostitution. In the end, repression replaced regulation in North America, and its weight fell most heavily on prostitutes who practiced openly: those who could not afford, or did not wish, to be less visible or more discrete in their activities.

Nineteen states promulgated antipandering statutes during the same period (Anderson, 1974). Many new laws controlled the prostitute and dealt with her health, but during this period more laws were directed, in theory at least, against the procurer and brothel-keeper than against the prostitute (Holmes, 1972). This may reflect the activity and influence of humanitarian reformers like Jane Addams (1912). However, laws against "panderers and procurers"—not to mention their clients—have rarely been enforced (Roby, 1969, 1972). An interesting example of how this occurs involves a revision of the New York State Penal Code in 1965. Under this revision prostitution was reclassified as a "violation" rather than an offense, and the penalty was reduced from one year to fifteen days in jail. The revision also included a "patron clause" that stipulated the same penalty for the prostitute's customer. However, between September 1967 and August 1969, less than 1 percent of the prostitution and patronizing convictions in New York State were for patronizing. Ultimately, business interests and state legislators also complained about the lenient sentences and were able to get more rigid measures passed.

Beyond this, patron clauses have sometimes been employed as weapons against prostitutes instead of the patrons. For example, in 1961 Illinois passed a law making the customer subject to a fine of up to $200 and six months in jail. A number of patrons were arrested, but none were convicted. Apparently the clause was used to turn the accused persons into informers who later were released.

Finally, we should note that there is considerable evidence about the characteristics of this century's purity reformers. They were, in large part, the same kind of people, and in some cases the very same individuals, who were involved in temperance work. Most were drawn from the middle and upper classes, including a substantial number of doctors, lawyers, social workers, probation workers, and wives of professional men (see Holmes, 1972; Pivar, 1973; Anderson, 1974). Women predominated among the humanitarian group, whereas the control group contained more administrators of training schools, mental hospitals, and clinics (Holmes, 1972); the participation of the latter suggests that professional interests may also have played an important role in the development of prostitution laws.

CONCLUSIONS

This chapter has offered a selective review of research on the legislation of crime and delinquency. We have focused on the laws that have been most frequently examined by social and legal researchers and on the studies that are most widely cited. Still, there are a variety of crimes that have not been considered (e.g., homicide, kidnapping, and rape), and the subjects and time periods of the studies that have been considered are themselves of interest: they focus disproportionately on laws against victimless crimes enacted during the progressive era and were published since the mid-1960s. One reason research may have focused heavily on these laws is that our attitudes toward victimless crimes have changed considerably since the progressive era, adding interest to the question of how and why these laws were passed in the first place. In any case, the resulting body of research provides a unique and important opportunity to expand our theoretical understanding of how laws that define and penalize crime and delinquency are made.

In the beginning of this chapter, we noted that consensus and conflict perspectives on lawmaking tend to characterize crime and delinquency laws as good or bad solutions to social problems. However, we also noted that a difficulty these approaches confront is that of finding objective measures of "good" or "bad" solutions; a consequent tendency of these approaches is to engage in subjective moral judgments. Nonetheless, the interface of the competing perspectives is useful in leading us to consider the influence that business or capitalist interests may have on the passage of these laws, the opposition or support these laws receive, and the role of dominant societal values in the passage of these laws. Some conclusions related to these points now can be offered.

First, although there is evidence that business or capital took an active interest in the passage of some of this legislation, we cannot conclude that this influence predominated. In fact, the clearest finding to emerge from the summary tables we have presented in this chapter is the large number of interest groups that took part in these legislative activities. The picture is complicated further by the fact that these groups and their members often differed on the issues that confronted them. Gusfield (1963) observes a fundamental ambivalence among temperance forces; Hagan and Leon (1977; see also Hagan, 1980) identify a basic division of views on the character of delinquency legislation; and Holmes (1972) outlines an important disparity in legislative approaches to prostitution.

Furthermore, we lack a clear understanding of the connections among such groups, particularly during the progressive era. Knowledge of the connections would help us to understand similarities and differences among the groups and the degree of influence or indifference that characterized their relationships.

However, the problems of identifying relationships between active interest groups pale in comparison with the difficulties of discovering the opposition or support these legislative efforts elicited in the general population. There is simply very little evidence on this issue. Of the laws we considered, only prohibition is known to have encountered concerted opposition, and of course it ultimately was repealed. This renders ambiguous the theoretical meaning of the otherwise significant fact that almost all the legislation we have examined appears to have been directed against portions of the urban poor. The problem is that it may be just as plausible to assume that legislation (other than prohibition) received passive acceptance, or even support, from the urban poor as it is to assume that a substantial number of citizens offered active resistance to passage of these laws. This raises the interesting question of why so few resisted the intrusion of criminal law into what were previously noncriminal domains.

A part of the answer to this question may involve the role in the legislative process of dominant societal values. Delinquency, probation, and prostitution laws all were justified as essential to the preservation of the family, and alcohol and drug laws also were associated with general middle-class values. The progressive era was a period in which these values were perceived to be challenged by urbanization and rapid social change. The real issue, then, is how these values were connected to various legislative reform efforts in the public mind.

The key to this issue may be the media. Delinquency, alcohol, drug, sexual psychopath, and prostitution laws all received considerable media attention. Our review has noted this publicity repeatedly; indeed, much of the research itself is based on contemporary publicity in newspapers and magazines. The recent study by Berk, Brackman, and Lesser (1977) of changes in the California Penal Code from 1955 to 1971 adds to this picture. Berk et al. find that editorials published in the *Los Angeles Times* had a persistent, nonspurious, and substantial correlation with legislative outcomes. Specifically, the number of column inches in *Times* editorials devoted to crime-related issues anticipated by one year each of the following: greater increases in criminalization, greater increases in the severity of penalties, greater increases in the rights and resources provided for prosecutors, and smaller increases in the rights and resources provided for defendants. These researchers then note that the *Times* is an influential paper published by a prominent family closely linked to elite circles of policy discussion, if not policy decision. Yet Berk and his colleagues (ibid., p. 294) acknowledge that problems remain in spelling out the causal implications of this situation: "it was often not at all clear to us which *specific* criminal justice proposals automatically favored business interests, and we suspect that economic elites frequently confront similar complexities" (emphasis in original). Thus elites clearly have a role to play in the legislation of crime and delinquency, but so also do interest groups more generally, dominant social values, and the media. In the end, the most important point to be made in this chapter is that the social and economic origins of our criminal laws cannot be taken for granted; the origins of the laws often are as worthy of study as the behaviors they seek to control.

The last point is particularly important to keep in mind as we move to the topic of the next chapter, the measurement of crime. Measurements can do no better than the definitions on which they are based. As we will see, shifting definitions of crime often have produced dubious understandings of the distribution and correlates of crime.

COUNTING CRIME: THE MANY MEASURES OF CRIMINALITY

4

THE ISSUE: WHO, WHAT, WHEN . . .

Who does what? When? How often? To whom? These are the perennial questions about crime. There is no scarcity of answers. Indeed there is a surplus. The problem is that the answers seldom satisfy. Dissatisfaction follows from the fact that our measures of crime are of doubtful accuracy. This is, of course, true of all social and economic indicators (e.g., rates of inflation and unemployment). All known measures are assumed liable to error. And therefore the counts continue. These efforts are encouraged by the assumptions that some inadequacies of our measures can be corrected, and that even inadequate measures can tell us things that we otherwise would not know. In this chapter we adopt these assumptions and try to answer questions like the following: Are rates of crime increasing? Are men more criminal than women? Are there class differences in criminal behavior? How criminal are the corporations? But before we offer answers to such questions, it is necessary that we ask several questions about the counting of crime itself.

ACCOUNTABLE COUNTS

Who is counting what, whom, and why? The purpose of posing the preceding questions is to encourage some healthy skepticism. The counting of crime is a socially organized activity, with its own intrinsic causes and consequences. Numerous governmental agencies, for example, the police, courts, and correctional institutions, are involved in the official counting of crime—and all of these agencies have budgets and are managed by individuals whose careers may be influenced by the counts of crime they produce. Apart from the criminal behavior to be counted, then, there are factors at work that can influence the tallies rendered. For example, Seidman and Couzens (1974) report on the period in 1969 when Jerry V. Wilson was appointed chief of police in Washington, D.C. Wilson announced that police officers who could not reduce crime in their jurisdictions would be replaced. It will perhaps come as little surprise that the *official* figures "improved." Seidman and Couzens surmise that "the political importance of crime apparently caused pressures, subtle or otherwise, to be felt by those who record crime." Similarly, New York City was once excluded briefly from the FBI's *Uniform Crime Reports* for suspect reporting, and Graham and Gurr (1969, p. 380) reports that Philadelphia was once found to have 5,000 more crime reports on file than recorded officially. Another city was found to have a secret "file 13" containing a catalog of complaints that were not officially reported. Counts of crime from such cities, then, may say as much or more about the sources and circumstances of their collection as about the persons and events counted (Kitsuse and Cicourel, 1963; McCleary et al., 1982). A reasonable question is whether some sense can be made of such statistics.

The response we propose to this question begins with the assumption that all such statistics consist of several components. The first component derives from the persons and their behaviors that we presumably wish to count. We will call this the "behavioral component." A second component derives from the errors that lead to persons and their behaviors being overreported or underreported in the counts we consider. We will call this the "error component." All counts of crime of any magnitude will at least contain some random errors of measurement. Most, for reasons like those indicated above, also contain systematic sources of error. To the extent that we can identify systematic errors, we will be able to isolate a third component of crime statistics. We will call this the "response component," since it consists of errors that derive from the individuals and organizations that respond to crime. Criminologists are increasingly interested in the response component of crime counts (Black, 1970). This interest derives from the knowledge that systematic sources of error can serve significant social purposes, including the political motivations we have noted, and other kinds of interests discussed below.

Fortunately, the several components of crime statistics we have discussed can be explored and even estimated through the use of alternative (or multiple) measures (cf. Campbell and Fiske, 1959). For example, imagine that we are interested in knowing the extent of heroin addiction in a jurisdiction. Arrests for possession or sale of heroin represent one source of information. However, because drug use is often a private pursuit without persons to complain about it, most heroin use will escape official detection. The heroin addiction that comes to official attention will be the product of various kinds of systematic as well as random sources of error. An alternative measure of heroin addiction can be derived from hospital records of deaths due to heroin overdoses. These records will also contain errors. However, to the extent that the different measures agree, we will be encouraged as to the accuracy of the results; to the extent that the various measures disagree, we may be directed to possible sources of error. It is to this kind of comparative assessment that this chapter is devoted.

Data useful in the kind of comparative assessment we are encouraging come from five sources: (1) official agencies of crime control; (2) nonofficial agencies of crime control; (3) first-person accounts; (4) victimization surveys; and (5) observational reports. We will use such sources to answer the kinds of questions posed at the outset of this chapter. Before doing so, however, we first will introduce in some additional detail the different sources of our data and the ways that we will comparatively use them.

OFFICIAL CRIME DATA

Official crime counts are readily available from the various government agencies assigned responsibility for controlling crime. The best-known of the counts in the United States is the *Uniform Crime Reports (UCR).* These reports are organized and reported by the Federal Bureau of Investigation on the basis of data it receives from most, but not all, U.S. police departments. The reports deal primarily with "crimes known to the police" (CKP). These are crimes that in one way or another come to police attention and are "found"—or in other words confirmed, at least to the extent that the police believe the behavior occurred and was a crime. Most discussions of *UCR* statistics focus on what are called "index crimes," eight crimes that the FBI argues are most likely to be reported to the police and that occur with enough frequency to allow comparisons across times and places. The index crimes include murder and nonnegligent manslaughter, forcible rape, robbery, aggravated assault, burglary, larceny-theft, motor vehicle theft, and arson.

Index crime rates are presented at length in the *Uniform Crime Reports,* along with percentage changes in the rates. The statistics frequently are subject to discussion in the media. It therefore is important to note briefly how they are calculated. To calculate a rate we need to know the number of events (e.g., crimes) that have occurred during a specified period of time (e.g., a year) and the population (e.g., persons, cars) at risk. The point is to draw a comparison between events and the risk of them. Note that the population at risk may appropriately be cars, men, women, children or any other relevant base we wish to choose, depending on whether the event considered is car theft, rape, child molesting, or some other crime (see also Gibbs and Erickson, 1976). The idea is to make the comparison of the event and the population at risk meaningful. Unfortunately, the event and population measures seldom come from the same source—crime statistics usually come from the police, population statistics from the census—and this may lead to further problems of comparison. With all of this in mind, a crime rate will take the form of $(A/B)C$, where A is the event counted, B is the population, and C is a constant, usually the number of 100,000 persons in the population.

Official crime statistics like those provided by the UCR serve one very important purpose: they indicate the extent to which, and the methods whereby, government agencies of crime control are dealing with the behavior they officially define as criminal. Notwithstanding this important purpose, some common deficiencies of official crime data should be noted:

1 An indeterminable amount of criminal behavior goes undetected, is handled by private means, or otherwise remains beyond public knowledge (e.g. crimes against bureaucracies [Smigel and Ross, 1970]), including much white-collar crime.

2 Some criminal behavior that is reported to the police is not recorded (see Hood and Sparks, 1970, p. 35).

3 Categories of criminal behavior are defined vaguely and variously recorded (see discussion below).

4 Bases used in computing crime rates vary, and are frequently inappropriate (e.g., using the number of females *and* males as the base for computing rape rates).

A challenge of working with official crime data is to identify the sources of the deficiencies, and to correct or compensate for them. Hindelang (1974, p. 2) makes this point well when he observes that "researchers who refuse to examine even a blurred reflection of the phenomenon may be discarding an opportunity to reduce ignorance about the phenomenon in question; further, by refusing to explore ways in which prior indicators of a phenomenon may be improved, lack of progress toward more satisfactory measurement is more likely to be ensured." The problem is that official crime statistics are both errorful and essential, leaving us little choice but to seek better understanding of, and reductions in, the errors.

A creative example of this kind of effort is found in McCleary et al.'s (1982) study of *Uniform Crime Reports* in three cities. *Uniform Crime Report* burglaries are charted in Figure 4-1 from 1975 to 1981 for one of the cities. Prior to July 1979, the trend is downward, but from then on the trend is up. While one explanation of this change is obviously that the actual incidence of burglary increased, McCleary et al. also note that the *UCR* "crime wave" coincided with the retirement of an incumbent police chief. The *UCR* coding bureau of the department was altered substantially by an ensuing administrative shake-up. As the bureau's chain of command changed, *UCR* coding clerks gradually began to make coding decisions that had been made previously by "higher-ups." McCleary et al. note that

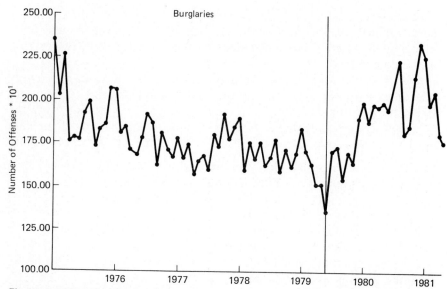

Figure 4-1 Monthly UCR burglaries from January 1975 to May 1981 *Note*: Vertical dotted line indicates the month in which an incumbent chief resigned. (*Source: McCleary et al., 1982:23*)

crimes that appear to fit the *UCR* burglary definition on the basis of field reports are often better categorized as "no crime," theft, vandalism, or trespass. They further note that the increase shown in Figure 4-1 represents a change in only two or three *UCR* burglaries per day, and this is well within the range one could expect from a slight change in the decision-making process. The implication is that while previously the authority hierarchy of the department was suppressing these crimes and, rightly or wrongly depending on your point of view, deflating the burglary rate, after the change in administration this policy dissipated. McCleary et al. observe that the resulting "crime wave" was not unlike others reported in Chicago (Campbell, 1969; Glass et al., 1975), Kansas City (Guyot, 1976), and Washington, D.C. (Seidman and Couzens, 1974). The challenge is to obtain a better understanding of organizationally induced fluctuations of this kind.

NONOFFICIAL CRIME DATA

Nonofficial sources of data offer an intriguing and increasingly important alternative source of information on crime. One nonofficial measure of variations in property crimes is provided in the premium rates charged by insurance companies offering coverage against criminal property losses, including losses by arson and theft (e.g., Price, 1966). Calculated on the basis of past losses, these rates are profit-inspired. Thus insurance companies have a financial interest in achieving accuracy. Insurance statistics have not been used to any great extent, but they have an interesting potential.

The mortality records of public and private hospitals and public health agencies are a second source of nonofficial data. These records are used most effectively in estimating the prevalence of alcohol- and drug-related crimes (e.g., Ross, 1982; Brenner, 1967), through deaths designated as resulting from alcoholism, liver cirrhosis, drug abuse and overdoses, and the incidence of homicide. Of course, a limitation of such estimates is the accuracy of the health and hospital records themselves (see Leon, 1975).

. Private policing organizations (Shallo, 1933; Becker, 1974) and the security forces of large department stores (Cameron, 1964; Hindelang, 1974a; Feuerverger and Shearing, 1982) provide some of the most interesting nonofficial crime data. Private policing is a growth industry (Spitzer and Scull, 1977; Shearing and Stenning, 1983), with most large commercial enterprises having either an internal security division or contracted coverage from an outside policing agency. Much of the criminal activity these organizations and departments monitor, particularly shoplifting and employee theft, is never reported to the police. This makes these sources of data that much more important. Business accountant and consultant firms often uncover similarly important information on patterns of internal theft (Jaspan and Black, 1960). Concerns about the confidentiality of such records have limited the use made to date of the kind of information they provide.

In more general terms, while nonofficial sources of data will seldom constitute a sufficient basis for the calculation of actual crime rates, they nonetheless constitute an important resource for confirming and expanding our knowledge of various kinds of criminality.

FIRST-PERSON ACCOUNTS

The measures we have considered to this point have in common the liability that they usually are removed several steps from the phenomenon we wish to study. In effect, they are third-person records of the criminal events to be examined. As we have noted, there are serious possibilities of bias involved in the transmission of data from source to record. The error-producing distance from the source is reduced by some relatively recently developed strategies for collecting first-person accounts. These strategies include (1) self-report surveys, and (2) field interviews.

Self-report surveys typically involve paper-and-pencil instruments that ask (usually anonymous) respondents to confess, in Kinsey-like fashion, the quality and quantity of their indiscretions. Such surveys have been used for some time now with students in the classroom (e.g., Porterfield, 1946; Nye and Short, 1957), as well as with adults (e.g., Wallerstein and Wyle, 1947). The weaknesses of the self-report approach include memory lapses and deceit among subjects, as well as vaguely stated test items and indefinite periods of coverage. Noting such weaknesses, prominent criminologists have suggested that "the methodological and technical foundations of those [self-report] studies do not invite confidence in the conclusions" (Reiss, 1975, p. 214), and that "confessional data are at least as weak as the official statistics they are supposed to improve upon" (Netter, 1974, p. 86).

Nonetheless, self-report data are suggestive of the volume and social location of various forms of crime and delinquency, and if appropriate questions and sampling procedures are used, the findings can be generalized and usefully compared with official data sources. Self-report measures have also proved useful in studying the causes of crime and delinquency, as illustrated by much of the research on what we call in Chapter 5 the theories of "undercontrol." Hindelang et al. (1981, p. 212) make the point well when they note that,

> The self-report method easily demonstrates that people will report crimes, that they will report crimes not known to officials, that they are highly likely to report those crimes known to officials, and that their reports of crimes are internally consistent. These facts are rightly taken as evidence that the procedure is potentially useful as an alternative to traditional procedures, particularly for studying the etiology of delinquency. These facts, of course, do not guarantee that the method will produce equally reliable and valid results in all demographic subgroups and under all research conditions. Once it has been determined, however, that the method works at all . . . , the next step is to deal with the traditional reliability and validity criteria in some more direct way.

The same attitude is adopted in this book.

Field interviews offer the opportunity of moving one step closer to the source by meeting the subject population in its own setting. This first-hand strategy for the collection of crime data is not commonly used by criminologists. An obvious reason such a strategy is uncommon involves the problem of getting subjects to talk to. However, Ned Polsky (1969, p. 124), a forceful advocate of this approach, asserts that "from students, faculty, and others I have had more offers of introductions to career criminals—in and out of organized crime—than I could begin to follow up." From there, Polsky suggests the task is simply one of accumulation: "get an introduction to one criminal who will vouch for you with others, who in turn will vouch for you with still others." Polsky does not propose that researchers participate in, or even witness, their subjects' acts. Instead, the emphasis is placed on in-depth interviews and group discussions. One example of this kind of field research is found in Peter Letkeman's (1973) intriguing study of bank robbers and safecrackers. Perhaps in part because he was able to study these offenders in their natural settings, Letkeman found his subjects rather conventionally *un*conventional in their careerist aspirations; and thus the title of his book, *Crime as Work*.

VICTIMIZATION SURVEYS

Criminal acts of deviance often involve a victim as well as an offender. Victims too, then, are a source of information about criminal deviance. Victimization surveys are the modern means of tapping this resource. The first of these surveys was conducted in the United States in the mid-1960s (Biderman et al., 1967; Ennis, 1967). The significance of this new approach to the measurement of crime is now well-recognized, as is reflected by the federal government's funding of a National Crime Survey, as well as several local and state-level investigations (e.g., Crime in Eight American Cities, 1974).

Victimization surveys initially were conducted on a house-to-house basis. It is significant to note that the focus of victimization surveys is somewhat different from that of official crime statistics: "Unlike the official system, whose interest is not ordinarily in the victim *qua* victim, but rather as complainant or witness, the victim is the survey's unit and focus" (Biderman, 1981, p. 810). Respondents in the early surveys were asked: (1) whether they personally had been victims of specific crimes in the past year; (2) whether any member of the household had been victimized; (3) the "very worst crime" that had ever happened to the respondents; and (4) the "very worst crime" that had ever happened to anyone currently living in the household. More recent innovations have included the use of telephone interviews based on random-digit dialing, and more intensive attention to the personal experiences of victims. Regardless of method, victimization surveys have consistently informed us that the volume of crime unreported to official agencies is large. The first national victimization survey, conducted by the National Opinion Research Center (NORC) and reported by Ennis, found that over a one-year period *twice* as many major crimes were reported to survey interviewers as were reported nationally in the *UCR*.

It should be emphasized that victimization surveys do not deal with all kinds of crime. They usually are concerned with crimes committed by individuals against other persons and/or their property. They are obviously not concerned with the "victimless crimes": gambling, prostitution, public-disorder offenses, and alcohol and drug abuse. With some noteworthy exceptions discussed below, they also ignore crimes by, and against, corporations. Inevitably, there are problems of method. For example,

- Respondents who are unwilling or unavailable to participate (e.g., commuters less frequently are available than homemakers and old people).
- Problems of memory, deception, and the reluctance to recall some types of events (e.g., family quarrels or sexual attacks).
- Varying interpretations of survey categories and the events included within them.
- "Forward and backward telescoping," or the process of remembering events as more recent or distant than they are, thus invalidating the intended time coverage of the survey (Skogan, 1975).

The existence of these deficiencies should be balanced against the unique kinds of findings victimization surveys provide, and the promise the method offers. A balanced viewpoint is urged by one of the method's pioneers, Albert Biderman (1981, p. 812), who suggests that "while it [the victim survey] undoubtedly is the single most important recent development in criminological methodology, and while it already has had profound results in reorienting the conceptual structure and problem agendas of the pertinent disciplines, the revolutionary potential of the victim survey will not be realized for a considerable period of time."

Finally, it is interesting and potentially important to note that while victimization research has tended to be "person-centered" (Reiss, 1981), organizations—particularly commercial corporate organizations, and especially large retail stores—also are victims of crime (Hagan, 1983). Some victimization data have been collected on these victims as well, and are considered later in this chapter.

OBSERVATIONAL DATA

Direct observation takes us a final step beyond first-hand accounts and victim reports. Observational studies are not frequent in criminology, but the methods involved are receiving increased attention (e.g., McCall and Simmons, 1969; Reiss, 1971*a*, 1971*b*). Work of this kind usually takes one of two forms: where the observers are overt or covert participants in the situations observed, typically called "participant observation studies"; and where the participants are less aware of the observers' presence, often called "field observation studies."

A provocative example of a participant observation study is Laud Humphreys's (1970) research on homosexual encounters in public washrooms. The initial problem to be faced in this research was predictable: how "to take a 'natural part' in the action without actual involvement of a sexual nature" (ibid., pp. 26–27). Humphreys's "solution" (ibid., p. 27) was premised on an organizational role that derives from the threat of criminalization involved in the behaviors to be explained.

> The very fear and suspicion encountered in the restrooms produces a participant role, the sexuality of which is optional. This is the role of the lookout ("watchqueen" in the argot), a man who is situated at the door or windows from which he may observe the means of access to the restroom.

The use of these and other research strategies resulted in a set of findings that are relevant to the issue of criminalization. For example, Humphreys reports that adult homosexuals seeking sex in public washrooms avoid, rather than approach, persons under the age of consent. More recently, Weinberg and Williams (1975) have offered a detailed account of the social organization of homosexual contacts in gay baths. This kind of research has not always earned the praise of professional peers. Krisberg (1972), for example, suggests that some of the more explicit passages of Humpreys's account constitute "sociological pornography" (to be more explicit, a "blow-by-blow account"!). However, it does seem appropriate that as a society we know something about the persons we harass and the behaviors we condemn. We address this point further below.

Systematic field observation with a reduced participatory role is well illustrated by Albert Reiss's research (1971*b*) on police behavior and the processing of criminal and delinquent behavior. In this study, thirty-six trained observers recorded observations in three of North America's largest cities. For seven consecutive weeks observers rode in patrol cars and walked with police officers on their beats on all shifts in each of the three cities. A major concern in this research was that the presence of the observer not alter or disturb the encounters between officers and citizens who were the subject of the study. To minimize the influence the observers might have on police behavior, officers were told that the primary purpose of the study was to observe the behaviors of suspects. The observers were also instructed to avoid any direct participation in the encounters. Of course, this was not always possible, as the following incident report (Reiss, 1971a, p. 20) makes clear:

> Both officers were very grateful to have this observer along in an on-view incident. A fight ensued in No. 3 incident where both officers lost control of the offender and this observer had to restrain him. . . . I might add that in the process of the fight either I was bitten by the offender or my hand scraped against his mouth, because I have two lovely abrasions on my hand.

There are also ethical and legal problems that accompany observational studies. Informed consent cannot usually be obtained from the persons observed in this kind of research. The situation was further complicated in Humphreys's research by the use of a disguised follow-up interview. Humphreys had noted the license numbers of his subjects' cars as they departed from the public washrooms. The license numbers were then used to track down respondents for the follow-up interviews. The interviews were conducted under the pretext of being social health surveys. This strategy later attracted considerable attention and debate (see, for example, Horowitz and Rainwater, 1970; Von Hoffman, 1970). To some, the strategy was a deceit and an intolerable invasion of privacy (Sagarin, 1973). Others argued that if you do not "exploit," reveal, or otherwise demean subjects, little or no harm is done. To assure this, some observers offer to guarantee the confidentiality of their findings. However, such guarantees ignore the fact that court subpoenas and other legal devices can be used to force disclosure. Thus Reiss (1971a, p. 16) observes that "one cannot be certain that one's observers will fulfill the guarantees given, and lacking the professional privileges of confidentiality of information, one cannot protect one's employees against legal sanction." On the other hand, Reiss (ibid.) concludes that "this is not to say that one must simply inform organizations that no such guarantees can be given." Furthermore, none of the legal and ethical questions we have considered diminishes the "quality of closeness" provided by observational methods we have described.

MAKING THE MANY MEASURES MEANINGFUL

We have introduced various ways of counting crime, but the task remains of showing how these different counts can be compared and thereby used to improve our knowledge of crime. Criminologists, like other scientists, want two things from their measures: reliability and validity. Measures usually are considered reliable to the extent that they attain consistency or stability in the measurement of a phenomenon. Measures typically are considered valid to the extent that they are judged to measure faithfully what we want them to measure, in this case criminal or delinquent behavior. Thus reliable measures count the same thing with the same results over and over again, while valid measures count what it is we think we want counted in the first place. Criminologists more easily have been convinced of the reliability than of the validity of their measures (Clark and Tift, 1966; Farington, 1973; Bachmann et al., 1978). We will give greater attention, then, to issues of validation.

Measures of crime and delinquency can be tested for their convergent and discriminant validity (Campbell and Fiske, 1959). Convergent validity is tested by the degree to which measures thought to have similar meanings are related strongly to one another. Discriminant validity is tested by the degree to which measures thought to have different meanings are related weakly. Our interest is in how the notions of convergent and discriminant validity can be used to make the many measures of crime and delinquency more meaningful.

An example of how this can be done is found in an effort by Hindelang, Hirschi, and Weis (1981) to assess the validity of self-report measures of delinquency. Incorporating most of the measures introduced above, Hindelang et al. use several validation strategies, outlined in Figure 4-2. The figure identifies links between different measures of delinquency, all of which are relevant to issues of validity. Note that in the figure delinquent

Figure 4-2 Validation strategies. (*Source: Hindeland et al., 1981:98*)

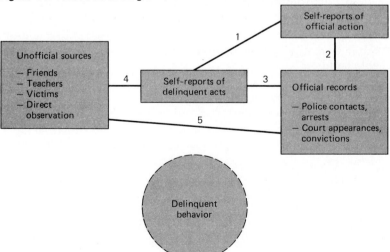

behavior is represented within a broken circle. This is meant to symbolize the fact that the actual behavior is known only indirectly, on the basis of our imperfect and incomplete measures. The idea is to use the interrelations among the measures to tell us something about each of the measures and its validity as an indicator of the *indirectly* known behavior.

Link 1 in the figure reflects the extent to which self-reports of delinquent acts correspond to self-reported contacts with the law. Since many delinquents' acts are undiscovered, unreported (both by the delinquents and by the police), and unrecorded, we should not expect the relationship between these measures to be extremely high. Nonetheless, there should be some correspondence. Furthermore, the relationship should probably be stronger than that represented by line 3, the connection between self-reported delinquent acts and official records, since official actions (e.g., warnings) do not necessarily lead to official records. Meanwhile, line 2, between self-reported official actions and official records, should be fairly strong. That is, to the extent that self-report questions ask about the kinds of official actions that lead to official records (e.g., arrests), there should be a high degree of correspondence. Link 4 represents the connection between self-reported delinquent acts and nonofficial measures, including victimization surveys, teachers' and friends' reports, and direct observations. To the extent that these different measures are directed at a common set of events, a correspondence should be found. Finally, link 5 considers the extent to which nonofficial and official measures correspond. This is the only linkage that does not involve any reliance on self-report data. However, the existence of such a link can still be important to the consideration of self-report measures. For example, if self-report measures were found uncorrelated with the official measures (link 3), then a positive correlation between unofficial and official sources of information (link 5) would suggest that the self-report measures were of questionable validity.

Fortunately, recent studies using combinations of the above measures provide enough evidence of the above links to give us some confidence in using their results to answer questions like those posed at the outset of this chapter. For example, the efforts of Hindelang et al. to estimate links in Figure 4-2 using self-report and official data regarding adolescents in Seattle yields the pattern of results, broken down by sex and race, indicated in Figure 4-3. Without belaboring the details of this study, several points should be noted. First, the link 2 relationships between self-reported official contacts and official measures of delinquency are, as expected, the strongest overall. Second, the link 1 and 3 relationships between self-reported behavior and, respectively, self-reported official contacts and official records are, again as expected, smaller but still substantial. Finally, the link 4 and 5 measures are slightly smaller still, but

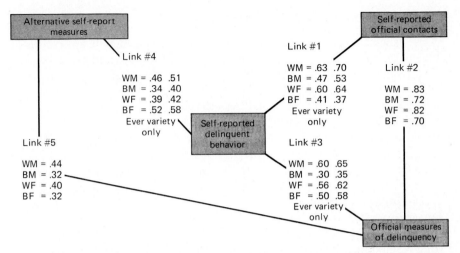

Figure 4-3 Mean gamma's for the relationships among various indicators of delinquency, by race and sex. Seattle study. Weighted data. (*Source: Hindelang et al., 1981:13*)

nonetheless clearly indicate that there is some correspondence between the unofficial sources and self-reports of delinquency, and between the former and official records. Hindelang et al. (1981, p. 114) conclude from all this that "the self-report method appears to behave reasonably well when judged by standard criteria available to social scientists."

None of this is to say that self-report and other measures are without problems. There is, for example, considerable difficulty involved in developing self-report items and samples that tap delinquent behaviors of equal seriousness to those found in official data. We address this issue further below. There are also problems of racial differences in the self-reporting of offenses apparent in Hindelang et al.'s results. Note that in Figure 4-3 smaller relationships are generally reported for black males (see link 3 in particular) than for other groups. Black delinquents appear to report less fully than white delinquents. Hindelang et al. speculate that this follows from the low saliency of such behavior for those who are more likely to be involved. However, data from this study (ibid., p. 123) also indicate that racial differences in reporting are smallest when the reports are received in nonanonymous interviews. The implication may be that a greater sensitivity in methodology—for example, involving the use of more personalized and natural settings (see discussion of Polsky's field interview techniques above)—could further improve the results.

We have now laid the groundwork for our comparative use of the various measures of crime and delinquency to answer the questions posed at the outset of this chapter.

ARE CRIME RATES INCREASING?

There is widespread agreement that crime rates, most significantly rates of violent crimes, increased in the United States, Canada, and most western European societies during the 1960s and 1970s. However, to say only this, and leave it at that, would be misleading and would miss much that is most intriguing about the rise and fall of crime rates in western societies like the United States. For one thing, we may be entering a period of decline or stabilization in crime rates. For another, it may be misguided to believe that crime is at some sort of all-time high. In any case, to think more broadly about crime rates is to entertain the possibility that things are somewhat different from what they may otherwise currently seem to be.

Criminologists have long been skeptical of ever-increasing crime rates, and with good reason. We have already encouraged a healthy skepticism with regard to official crime data, the data that must be relied on for any long-term view of variations in crime. Unfortunately, it is when we start to look at the official data on crime over time in America that the sources of this skepticism become most apparent. We begin with the fact that most available studies indicate that the crime rate in America rose rapidly after World War I and the economic boom of the twenties, and then nose-dived within a year or so after the crash of 1929 (Graham and Gurr, 1969, p. 375). However, when the FBI publishes its own crime charts in the *Uniform Crime Reports,* it cuts off the downward years. A result is to dramatize the upward swing that begins in the 1960s. (You can get a sense of what difference this makes by covering up the period to 1960 in Figure 4-4.) One consequence of this practice is that even before crime rates quickly began to move upwards in the mid-1960s, the FBI was already "crying wolf." Equally disturbing was the FBI's annual publication of "crime clocks." As Graham and Gurr (1969, p. 382) notes:

> This baffling presentation, year after, of the shrinking average interval between the commission of various offenses across the country, seems to have no purpose other than sheer terror. Because the population is growing, the interval between crimes would necessarily narrow each year, even if the crime rate was not increasing. Thus the hands of the F.B.I.'s "crime clocks" invariably show fewer minutes between crimes than for the previous year.

Still, all official data are not equally bad, and some of the data actually show encouraging signs of validity. Homicide statistics are a case in point. The national victimization survey reported by Ennis (1967) reveals only slightly *fewer* reports of murder than the official data (the disparity is

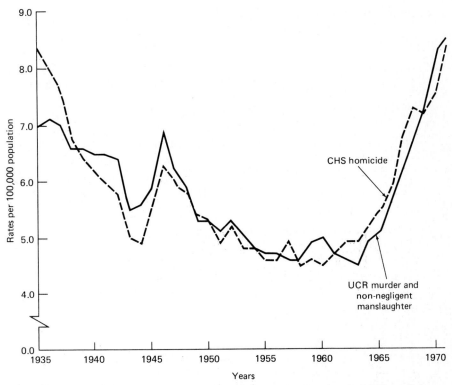

Figure 4-4 Rates of homicide in the United States as reported by the Uniform Crime Reports and The Center for Health Statistics, 1935-1971. (*Source: Hindelang, 1974:4*)

presumably a comment on "how soon we forget" and the inability of victims to provide a reminder!), while a comparison of data from the Center for Health Statistics (CHS) and the *Uniform Crime Reports* over a thirty-six-year period in the United States (see Fig. 4-4) yields nearly an identical picture of annual homicide rates (Hindelang, 1974). This at least confirms our suspicion that bodies are difficult to hide and that this official measure deserves some credibility. Meanwhile, as other kinds of official data are collected over long periods of time, across many places, and with some consistency, and as contrasting assumptions are brought into play to make sense of their results, it may be possible to discern broad and meaningful trends. The remainder of this section is devoted to identifying such trends.

One trend-setting study in its own right was Ferdinand's (1967; see also 1972) research on criminal patterns in Boston since 1849. This study examines approximately a century of annual arrest reports from Boston for the period from 1849 to 1951 for seven major crimes. What is interesting about this study is that it shows a general pattern of *decline* from the 1870s to the 1950s. As indicated in Figure 4-5, the period immediately before the Civil War saw a high rate of major crime, but during and shortly after the Civil War, crime declined, only to rise to an all-time peak in 1875–1878. From that time until the middle of the twentieth century, the crime rate declined steadily in Boston to a level about *one-third* that in 1875–1878. When Ferdinand turned his attention to specific crimes he found that most offenses, including probably the most accurately measured crime of murder, showed a pattern of decline. Only forcible rape showed a clear tendency to increase over the 100-year period.

Figure 4-5 Rate of major crimes in Boston per 100,000 population, 1849-1951. (*Source: Ferdinand, 1967-87*)

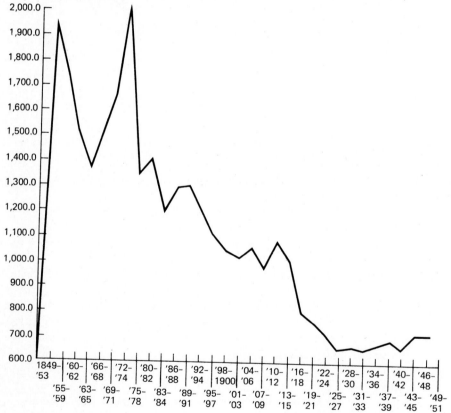

Similarly, Lane (1968) used crime statistics from nineteenth-century Massachusetts to make the point that the metropolis at the end of the nineteenth century was a less violent and disorderly place than the small commercial city of the 1840s. This study indicates that while "public-disorder" offenses, notably drunkenness, were increasing, "real" criminal activity, defined as the commission of offenses against persons and property, was decreasing. Thus Lane concludes that crime was in decline during this period despite rapid urbanization. He even argues that the increase in public-disorder offenses is consistent with the trend, noting that with less real crime to contend with, police were concentrating on enforcing higher standards of public behavior. From this viewpoint, rising arrests for drunkenness are consistent with actual decreases in its occurrence.

Lane (1974) has gone on to make the point that British as well as American scholars are agreed that the preindustrial population of the early eighteenth century was far more criminal than the largely urbanized and more fully industrialized population of the late nineteenth century. Of Britain, Lane (1980, p. 29) notes that "first in the factory towns, then in agricultural districts dominated increasingly by rational entrepreneurs, lastly in the great commercial (nonindustrial) metropolis of London, a nation once famed for its boozy rowdiness at public hangings acquired a stereo-type involving roses, tea, and understatement." More generally, Lane (1980, p. 35; see also Monkkonen, 1975, 1981) suggests that when measured over any considerable period of the nineteenth century, most studies show that serious crime, however defined, was either declining or, at worst, stable. The evidence of decline is particularly strong in England.

Monkkonen (1981) has put together data on public-disorder offenses from a large number of American cities for the years 1860 to 1980. In contrast to the findings (but not necessarily the conclusions) of the earlier study by Lane, these data indicate overall decline in per capita arrests for public misbehavior from the onset of the Civil War to the present (see Fig. 4-6). There are of course interruptions in this trend, the most spectacular of which is a burst in drunk and disorderly-conduct arrests which occurred between 1945 and 1946. Monkkonen speculates that three factors linked to the demobilization following World War II produced this burst: the increased numbers in arrest-prone age groups (young men), the return to work of younger police officers, and the increased postprohibition consumption of alcohol. While Monkkonen (1981, p. 545) acknowledges the difficulty in knowing whether these rates reflect actual changes in public behavior and an overall decline in public order, and also that not all cities followed this pattern, he nonetheless concludes that "if anything, the

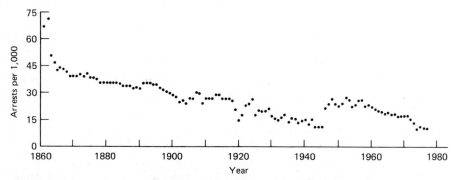

Figure 4-6 Arrests for drunkenness and disorderly conduct per 1,000 population, urban data, 1860-1977. (*Source: Monkkonen, 1981:543*)

biases in the data should have distorted the trend in an upward direction, making the actual downward direction seem all the more reliable."

However, easily the most interesting finding in the literature on variations in crime rates over time is the suggestion of a U-shaped curve in the occurrence of serious crimes. This curve has been discussed most extensively by Gurr (1979, 1981, see also Gurr et al., 1977), but it can be discerned in the work of Monkkonen (1981), and has been observed by Lane (1980, p. 36; see also 1979) as well. While Gurr (1981, p. 296) is cautious in his assessment of evidence for the curve, noting that "the evidence for it is substantial in some societies, especially the English-speaking and Scandinavian countries, but either lacking or contradictory in others," Lane (1980, p. 36) is somewhat less guarded in pointing to the "exciting possibility that there is a single comprehensive explanation for long-term trends in the Western world as a whole over the past two centuries." Here we can note only a small part of the evidence for the curve.

One part of the evidence involves a long-term trend from about 1200 to the present in English homicide. This trend is traced in Figure 4-7 and is predominantly and dramatically downward, with the beginning of an upward turn in the mid-twentieth century. What is most dramatic in the figure, and perhaps most important in adding perspective to our current circumstances, is that rates of violent crime were far higher in medieval and early modern England than in the twentieth century—probably ten and possibly twenty or more times higher. This is the case in spite of the increases that seem to have begun since the 1950s, and in spite of many ups and downs along the way (Beattie, 1974).

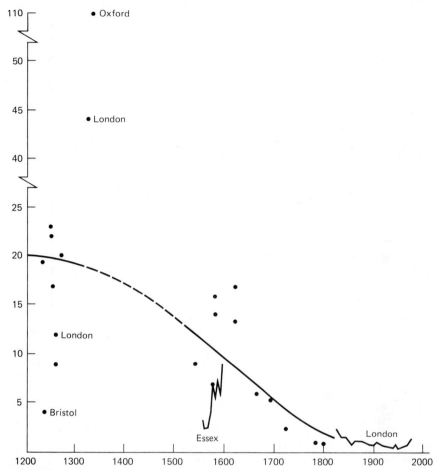

Figure 4-7 Indicators of homicides per 100,000 population in England, thirteenth to twentieth centuries. Each dot represents the estimated homicide rate for a city or county for periods ranging from several years to several decades. (*Source: Gurr, 1981:313*)

More complicated is the evidence from the United States, graphed in Figure 4-8. This figure broadly documents three surges of interpersonal violence at approximately fifty-year intervals: 1860, 1900, and 1960. Gurr (1981, p. 326) notes that these waves or cycles are of such amplitude that it is impossible to say conclusively whether they are superimposed on a longer-run decline. However, he then provocatively suggests the following:

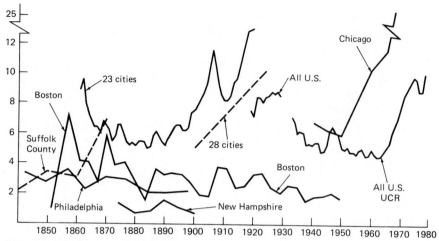

Figure 4-8 Indicators of homicides per 100,000 population in the United States, 1840-1980. (*Source: Gurr, 1981:325*)

To the extent that North America from settlement to industrialization was an extension of British culture and society, I suspect that
the underlying trend was downward. But as Lane points out
(personal communication), non-English immigrants have unques-
tionably added to the violence of American cities: the Irish,
especially from the 1840s through the 1860s; possibly the Italians,
in the early twentieth century; and in-migrating blacks throughout.

In the end Gurr and also Lane seem convinced of the long-term downward
trends they have observed, even more than the U-shaped curve. Indeed,
Gurr ultimately (1981, p. 342) describes the upturn of recent years in
violent crime as "simply the latest, and best-documented, deviation from
the underlying trend."

Are, then, crime rates increasing? Almost nobody seems to doubt a real
increase in violent crime in most western societies in the 1960s and 1970s.
But the most sophisticated forecasts, taking into account the movement of
baby-boom children out of the violence-prone years and other significant
factors, today suggest a new stability or even a decline in crime rates. One
such forecast, predicting declines for two of three crimes in the 1980s, is
summarized in Table 4-1 (Cohen et al., 1980). The increasing crime rates of
the 1960s and 1970s are of real and immediate importance, but over the
longer term, they may come to seem much less so.

TABLE 4-1
EQUILIBRIA FORECAST COMPARISONS FOR ROBBERY,
BURGLARY, AND AUTOMOBILE THEFT RATES, UNITED
STATES, 1977 AND 1985

Equation used to forecast	Equilibria	
	1977 (ex post)	1985 (ex ante)
Robbery rate, (3)	318.3	236.3*, 217.4†
Burglary rate, (5)	1,509.6	1,798.2*, 1,821.4†
Automobile theft rate, (8)..	536.0	492.3*, 454.1†

*Assumes a 5% unemployment rate.
†Assumes a 6% unemployment rate.
Source: Cohen et al., 1980 p. 113.

ARE THERE CLASS DIFFERENCES IN CRIMINAL BEHAVIOR?

Few issues in criminology cause more controversy than the question of
whether criminal behavior is differentially distributed by class. Much of the
controversy derives from two assumptions about the occurrence of criminal
behavior in the "underclass." The first assumption is that poverty induces
many socially injurious experiences and an unequal distribution of opportunities, both of which are conducive to increased criminal behavior. The
second assumption is that the poor are victims of discrimination by
authorities, leading to their more frequent apprehension, prosecution,
conviction, and punishment for criminal behavior. The first assumption
suggests that members of the underclass are more criminal in their
behavior. The second assumption suggests that apart from any behavioral
differences, members of the underclass are more likely to be processed as
criminals. However, note that while these assumptions are quite different
from one another, both may still be true. Indeed, we will argue that both of
these assumptions *are* true. The interesting question is, How true is each?
The first of the above assumptions, that criminal behavior is class-linked, is
examined in this section. The second assumption, that class differences
derive from discriminatory enforcement, is considered in Chapter 8.

Official records of crime and delinquency suggest an uneven distribution
of offenses by class. As early as 1889 in Italy, Bonger (1916) noted that
indigents constituted from 74.7 to 88.1 percent of convictions for all
crimes, excluding forgery. It comes as little surprise that in nineteenth-
century Italy the "well-to-do" were less likely to commit crimes and less

likely to be convicted for doing so. However, early American research conducted at the census tract and neighborhood level of analysis produced a similar picture. For example, Shaw and McKay (1942) reported a correlation of .89 between rates of delinquency and rates of families on relief across 140 ecological units in Chicago, and subsequent studies in other large U.S. cities produced similar results (Lander, 1954; Bordua, 1958; Chilton, 1964; Schmid, 1960*a*, 1960*b*).

However, the meaning of the above findings is not as straightforward as may at first seem apparent. First, it is well-known that ecological correlations (relationships based on data collected from areal units like census tracts) tend to be substantially larger than correlations based on data collected from individuals (Hannan, 1971). Second, we have noted that official data may often reflect a "response" as well as a "behavioral" component. To begin to sort out these components, we must first get some sense of what is going on in the official data at the individual level.

Two recent literature reviews (Tittle, Villemez, and Smith, 1978; Braithwaite, 1981) have considered individual-level studies using official data. Both conclude that there is some relationship between the class position and official delinquency of individuals, although Tittle et al. find this relationship to be declining. We consider these studies further below. Meanwhile, an unfortunate problem with the individual-level studies of official delinquency these reviews consider is that they usually are based on nonrepresentative samples. Hindelang et al. (1981) make this point and demonstrate with one such study that the class-official delinquency relationship reduces from .45 to .11 when more appropriate estimation procedures are used. All of this is to suggest that at the level of individuals, and considering official data, there well may be some relationship between class position and delinquent behavior, but that the relationship is not large. We turn now to the self-report studies.

As we have noted, the self-report method was first applied in the 1940s. Porterfield (1943) compared the delinquency of Texas college students with that of children who had been brought before a juvenile court. The findings revealed that while every college student surveyed reported at least one offense, there were no class differences in self-reported delinquency. Many studies later, the existence of a class–self-reported delinquency relationship remains at issue. Tittle et al. (1978) have concluded that such a relationship is a "myth." Using summary measures to bring together the results of thirty-five studies, Tittle et al. find a small overall relationship (official and self-report) between class and delinquency (gamma = −.09), but a very weak relationship when only self-report measures are used (gamma = −.06). A subsequent review by Braithwaite

(1981) finds more substantial evidence of a relationship between official delinquency and class, but the situation with regard to self-report measures remains unclear. Thus forty-seven of the studies reviewed by Braithwaite are summarized in Table 4-2, with twenty-five of them finding some evidence of the expected relationship, and twenty-two reporting no relationship at all. In sum, the official data are more supportive of a class-delinquency relationship than are the self-report data. The issue is why?

One answer we have already suggested and will consider further in Chapter 8 is that the official data are class-biased, reflecting class prejudice and discrimination. However, it is equally important to consider the possibility that self-report and official data are measuring different things. Self-report instruments vary widely in content (Gold, 1970). Some contain many items of only minor seriousness, while others tap more serious infractions. As well, many self-report studies only crudely measure the frequency with which various infractions occur. Finally, as suggested by the work of Hindelang et al., some offenders may recall more infractions than others.

Self-report studies have sometimes candidly acknowledged these points. For example, in a pioneer study of middle-class delinquency, Edmund Vaz (1966) finds no higher incidence of delinquency among lower-class respondents than among respondents from the middle and upper classes. This study usefully emphasizes that much middle- and upper-class delinquency remains "hidden." However, Vaz (ibid., p. 25) nonetheless concludes his study with the observation that "the largest amount and toughest kind of delinquency is found usually in the slum or 'disorganized' areas of large cities." Vaz (ibid.) bases his conclusion on the assumption that his own research "does not include the hard-core nor variety of delinquency found in metropolitan centers." Meanwhile, another indication that different types of behaviors probably *are* class-linked is found in the derivation by Vaz (1965, 1967) of two unidimensional scales for the measurement of middle-class delinquency (see also Casparis and Vaz, 1973; Clark and Wenninger, 1962). These scales (1967, p. 141) include the following kinds of items: "taken little things that did not belong to you; gambled for money at cards, dice, or other games; driven a car beyond the speed limit; skipped school without a legitimate excuse; been feeling *high* from drinking beer, wine, liquor; bought or tried to buy beer, wine, or liquor from a store or adult; taken a glass of beer, wine, or liquor at a party or elsewhere with your friends; tried to be intimate (go the limit) with a member of the opposite sex." Most of these behaviors neither require nor inspire an official response!

TABLE 4-2
A COMPARISON OF STUDIES ON THE RELATIONSHIP BETWEEN SOCIAL CLASS AND SELF-REPORTED
JUVENILE CRIME

Author(s)	Location of study	Sample size	Interview or questionnaire	Number of items	Lower-class juveniles more criminal?
Akers (1964)	Washington	836	Q	7	No
Allen and Sandhu (1968)	Tampa, Florida	198	Q	6	Yes[a]
Arnold (1965)	Unnamed U.S. city	180	Q	32	No
Belson (1969)	London	1,425	I	44	Yes
Belson (1978)	London	1,565	I	53	Yes
Berger and Simon (1974)	Illinois	3,100	Q	11	No
Braithwaite (1979)	Brisbane	344	I	15	No
Braithwaite and Braithwaite (1978)	Brisbane, Melbourne, Ipswich, Australia	422	Q	32	No
Casparis and Vaz (1973)	Rural Switzerland	489	Q	23	No
Cernkovich (1978)	Midwestern U.S. city	412	Q	30	Yes
Christie et al. (1965)	Oslo, Bergen, and rural areas of Norway	3,372	Q	25	No
Clark and Wenninger (1962)	4 U.S. communities	1,154	Q	38	Yes and No[b]
Dentler and Monroe (1961)	3 U.S. communities	912	Q	5	No
Elliott and Ageton (1980)	National sample, U.S.	1,726	I	47	Yes

Study	Location	Sample size		Number	Result
Elliott and Voss (1974)	California	2,617	Q	12	Yes and No[c]
Elmhorn (1965)	Stockholm	950	Q	21	Yes
Empey and Erickson (1966)	Utah	180	I	22	Yes and No[d]
Engstad and Hackler (1971)	Seattle	200	Q	Unknown (Nye-Short scale)	Yes
Epps (1959)	Seattle	356	Q	11	Yes and No[e]
Erickson (1973)	Rural Utah	336	—	14	No[f]
Gold (1970)	Flint, Michigan	522	—	51	Yes and No[g]
Hassall (1974)	Christchurch, New Zealand	872	Q	Unknown (Hirschi and Nye-Short scales)	No
Himelhoch (1965)	Rural Vermont	Unknown	Q	Unknown (Nye-Short scale)	No
Hirschi (1969)	Richmond, Virginia	1,121	Q	6	Yes and No[h]
Johnson (1969)	Baton Rouge	Unknown	Q	Unknown	No
Johnstone (1978)	Chicago	1,124	Q	30	Yes
Kelly (1974)	2 small towns in New York	173	Q	25	No
Kelly and Pink (1975)	Unnamed U.S. county	284	I	2	Yes
Kratcoski and Kratcoski (1975)	Unnamed U.S. city	Unknown	Q	25	No
Lanphier and Faulkner (1970)	Small U.S. town	739	Q	6	Yes
McDonald (1968)	London and S.E. England	851	Q	44	Yes
Marsden (1979)	Illinois	2,467	I	28	Yes
Natalino (1979)	Northcentral U.S.	1,174	Q	36	No
Nye, Short and Olson (1958)	6 small Ohio communities	2,350	Q	18	No

TABLE 4-2 cont'd
A COMPARISON OF STUDIES ON THE RELATIONSHIP BETWEEN SOCIAL CLASS AND SELF-REPORTED JUVENILE CRIME

Author(s)	Location of study	Sample size	Interview or questionnaire	Number of items	Lower-class juveniles more criminal?
Phillips (1974)	Unnamed U.S. city	469	Q	Unknown	Yes
Quensel (1971)	Cologne, Germany	599	Q	16	Yes
Reiss and Rhodes (1961)	Nashville	158	I	Unknown	Yes
Sherwin (1968)	Middletown, Ohio	280	Q	20	Yes and No[i]
Slocum and Stone (1963)	Washington State	3,242	Q	5	Yes
Vaz (1966)	Canada	1,639	Q	21	No
Voss (1966)	Honolulu	620	Q	16	No
Wallberg et al. (1974)	Chicago	430	Q	13	Yes[j]
West (1973)	London	411	I	38	Yes
Wilcox (1969)	Rocky Mountain area	403	Q	Unknown	No
Williams and Gold (1972)	National sample, U.S.	847	I	16	No
Wilson et al. (1975)	Brisbane	129	I	8	No
Winslow (1967)	Los Angeles	259	Q	9	No

[a]Allen and Sandhu seem to misinterpret their data at one point in their paper as showing that adolescents from high income families are more delinquent than those from low income families. Why they do this is puzzling....It is quite clear that while 46% of those in the low family income category are high on self-reported delinquency, only 37% of those in the higher income category are high on self-reported delinquency.
Calculated from Allen and Sandhu

	Delinquency		
Family income	Low	High	Total
Low	54%(57)	40%(48)	100%(105)
High	63%(59)	37%(34)	100%(93)

[b]"Yes" for the "Industrial city" sample, "No" for other areas. There is an association between social class and the more serious self-report delinquency items, even in the latter areas.

[c]This is a longitudinal study in which the relationship between class and crime is examined at two time periods, junior and senior high school. For neither time period were the Nye-Short items classified as nonserious significantly related to social class. Serious delinquency was significantly associated with social class at the junior high school level, but not at the senior high school level.

[d]This study is based on an unusual nonrandom sample of 50 high school boys, 30 boys with one court appearance, 50 boys on probation and 50 incarcerated offenders. Three subscales, "general theft," "serious theft," and "common delinquency" showed correlations of .20, .17, and .17 respectively with social class. But when these results were broken down into more detail, the correlations were due to middle- and lower-status respondents reporting more delinquency than those in the upper-class category, while there were no differences between middle- and lower-status boys.

[e]"Yes" for females, "No" for males. A number of items in this study represent crimes without victims.

[f]This study is based on an unusual nonrandom sample. The sample consisted of 100 incarcerated offenders, 136 "Provo Experiment" offenders, and 100 youths who were officially nondelinquent.

[g]"Yes" for males, "No" for females.

[h]See the discussion of this study in the text.

[i]Lower-class youth did not admit to committing a greater number of different offenses. However, they admitted to committing most offenses with greater frequency than middle-class youth.

[j]The independent variable here is "family background" rather than social class as such. "Family background" is indexed by the number of middle-class, school-relevant objects in the home (telephone, dictionary, encyclopedia, etc.) and the nature of the psychological relationship between parent and child, particularly with regard to school expectations. That is, the independent variable purports to be an index of the existence of a middle class ethos in the family situation.

Source: Braithwaite, 1981, pp. 43–44.

What is done with the answers provided by self-report surveys can also be significant. Answers to such surveys frequently are summed to provide a cumulative score on a delinquency scale for each individual. In turn, a "cut point" is often designated for the purpose of distinguishing "delinquents" from "nondelinquents." Often the mean or median score on the scale is chosen to draw this distinction. The scale scores then are correlated with the social class backgrounds of the respondents to determine the existence and/or extent of a relationship (see, for example, Chambliss and Naga-sawa, 1969). The problem, Nettler notes (1974, p. 95), is that "since it is not known what score on the questionnaire represents activities equivalent to those for which the same people . . . [would be] *arrested,* the cutting points are arbitrary" (emphasis added). The concern is that a small change in the cut point may make a substantial difference in the findings that result. For example, it is unlikely that a median cut point on a scale of trivial items would produce any other finding than that behaviors are rather evenly distributed across class positions.

Several recent studies address the above issues by emphasizing behaviors that are legally sanctionable, and report some relationship between class and delinquency. For example,

• Elliot and Ageton (1980) find a weak but significant relationship for predatory crimes against persons and a total offense index.
• Thornberry and Farnworth (1982) find that white males with fathers of lower class position are more likely to have committed violent offenses.
• Johnson (1980) finds a weak but significant relationship between seriousness of offense and class.

The implication of these studies is that if offenses considered in self-report surveys are made commensurate with those found in official data, a class-offense relationship will be observed; albeit a relationship that is small, and in this respect similar to that found in official data collected for individuals.

Two further factors complicate the search for a class-offense relationship. First, there is little consistency in, or consensus about, the measurement of class in criminology (Thornberry and Farnworth, 1982). For the most part, American research has measured class in terms of graded levels of occupational status. However, it recently has been argued that class should be measured in terms of the positions persons occupy in relation to one another in and out of the workforce (e.g., Clelland and Carter,1980; Greenberg, 1981). Unfortunately, there are too few efforts of the latter type to assess what differences new measures of class might make. The differences may be important. Meanwhile, it also has been argued that for adolescents it is status in school, rather than parents' status, that should make the difference (Stark, 1979). There are studies that make a convincing case that stream or track and other indicators of school status do correlate with delinquent behavior (Kelly, 1975; See Polk, 1957/1958, 1983).

The second factor that complicates the search for a class-offense relationship is the high correlation between class, however measured, and race. One attempted solution to this problem, adopted by Hindelang et al. (1981), is to consider only whites in assessing the relationship between class and delinquency. Using this approach, they find little relationship. Alternatively, Hindelang et al. do find a significant relationship between race and self-reported delinquency, a relationship that is most noteworthy when serious offenses are considered. More specifically, these findings indicate (ibid., p. 170) that "black males disproportionately and consistently . . . report being involved in what could be characterized as face-to-face *violent* offenses often involving theft: used club, knife or gun to get something; threatened to beat someone up if he didn't give you money; used physical force to get money; carried a razor, switchblade, or gun; pulled a knife; hit a teacher; beat up someone so badly they probably needed a doctor; and jumped or helped jump somebody." Note the difference in these items and those linked to middle-class delinquency above. The focus on these kinds of items is consistent with the finding of Hindelang (1978) that there are substantial differences by race of offender in the reporting of victims of common-law personal crimes.

Such findings lead us to the conclusion that when various kinds of data sources are used to collect information on the kinds of serious offenses that are most likely to result in official sanctions, some relationship between class and criminality is apparent. It should be emphasized that the relationship is not large, but that it also may be found to increase in size as attention is given to samples that include black respondents and offenses of a serious or violent nature as they occur in large American cities. Past self-report research has often glossed over the potential importance of the latter factors, providing data on whites, for minor offenses, committed in small and middle-sized cities where research is often more easily conducted. One consequence is that today the data, as well as available data analytic techniques, do not allow us to be very certain of the separate and interacting effects of race and class on criminal and delinquent behavior. This in particular remains an important and difficult issue for further research.

Finally, it requires mention that our conception of what constitutes a serious criminal or delinquent act is subject to change. Perhaps even more to the point, there is evidence that as some activities become more common in the upper classes, they come to be considered less serious in nature. For example, in the period of one generation, marijuana use shifted in status from a presumed source of "reefer madness" to a "radical chic" social lubricant readily available to those who could afford it. Self-report studies reflect this change in status: Barter et al. (1970) and Suchman (1968) report a higher incidence of marijuana use among persons from high-income families, and a California study (Blum, 1969) comparing patterns of usage in working and middle-class high schools, reveals higher figures in the latter. Acknowledging such changes, however, should not obscure the importance of our more general conclusion that the disadvantages of social class are correlated with the increased likelihood of those forms of crime and delinquency now considered more serious, and dealt with as such.

ARE MEN MORE CRIMINAL THAN WOMEN?

Although criminologists only recently have begun to study seriously the crimes of women, a large volume of research already has accumulated. This research focuses primarily on three issues: (1) the *extent* to which men are more criminal in their behavior than women; (2) whether this gap is *narrowing,* and (3) the *comparability* of the criminal behavior patterns of men and women. Various sources of data have been used to explore these issues.

Official agency data tell us only part of the story of crime and gender, but they are an important part and remarkably consistent. With the exception of peculiarly female crimes, such as prostitution and infanticide, and various "victimless crimes" on which credible statistical data are seldom available, men are nearly always shown to be much more involved in criminal activity than women. Table 4-3 shows *UCR* arrest rates and ratios per 100,000 population by sex for selected property offenses for the period 1969–1975. From the pioneering explorations of official crime statistics by Quételet (1842) to the modern tabulations by Radzinowicz (1937), Pollak (1961), Adler (1975), Simon (1975), and Smart (1976), such statistics have consistently shown that men are more criminal than women. However, although this pattern is apparent in Table 4-3 as well, it is also the case that the *ratio* of male to female arrest rates has declined in recent years. For example, we see in Table 4-3 that between 1960 and 1975 the ratio of male to female rates of index property crimes (combining the offenses of burglary, larceny, and auto theft) decreased from 9:43 to only 3:93. Similar declines in the ratio of male to female rates are also apparent in Table 4-3 for the individual crimes of burglary, larceny theft, auto theft, fraud/embezzlement, and stolen property. The question commonly asked

TABLE 4-3
PROPERTY CRIME RATES AND RATIOS PER 100,000 FOR FEMALES AND MALES, 1960–75

Year	Three property crime index			Burglary			Larceny theft		
	Female	Male	Male/female	Female	Male	Male/female	Female	Male	Male/female
1975	421.2	1657.1	3.93	31.0	588.4	18.98	379.6	913.8	2.41
1974	428.1	1708.0	3.99	31.7	592.9	18.70	384.5	930.5	2.42
1973	339.6	1364.7	4.02	25.4	479.6	18.88	303.6	706.8	2.32
1972	327.0	1387.4	4.24	23.6	464.8	19.70	293.3	743.6	2.54
1971	321.8	1470.1	4.57	23.4	468.1	20.00	286.7	786.3	2.74
1970	298.7	1400.5	4.69	20.8	455.3	21.88	267.8	742.9	2.77
1969	252.1	1313.3	5.21	18.4	434.8	23.63	222.8	667.0	2.99
1968	213.7	1265.0	5.92	17.6	434.1	24.66	186.0	620.3	3.33
1967	200.9	1210.0	6.02	16.0	406.8	25.42	176.6	602.7	3.41
1966	183.2	1128.5	6.16	13.6	361.1	26.55	162.0	576.6	3.56
1965	176.6	1138.1	6.45	13.4	369.2	27.55	155.4	579.6	3.73
1964	156.0	1102.0	7.06	12.7	355.1	27.96	135.6	563.2	4.15
1963	134.9	1044.3	7.74	10.9	342.5	31.42	117.6	529.8	4.51
1962	134.0	1040.5	7.76	11.9	342.7	28.80	115.5	530.8	4.60
1961	112.3	1002.9	8.93	10.9	349.3	32.04	96.0	502.3	5.23
1960	101.9	961.3	9.43	9.8	324.7	33.13	87.3	487.4	5.58

TABLE 4-3 *cont'd*
PROPERTY CRIME RATES AND RATIOS PER 100,000 FOR FEMALES AND MALES, 1960–75

Year	Auto theft			Fraud/ embezzlement			Stolen property		
	Female	Male	Male/ female	Female	Male	Male/ female	Female	Male	Male/ female
1975	10.6	155.0	14.62	67.1	142.2	2.12	13.7	124.9	9.12
1974	11.9	184.5	15.50	53.7	121.0	2.25	13.4	127.3	9.50
1973	10.5	178.4	16.99	41.9	101.0	2.41	10.5	101.2	9.64
1972	10.1	179.1	17.73	44.2	113.9	2.58	10.1	101.0	10.00
1971	11.8	199.6	16.92	44.0	119.3	2.71	10.6	111.0	10.47
1970	10.1	202.3	20.03	35.5	104.1	2.93	8.9	93.3	10.48
1969	10.9	211.5	19.40	29.6	92.0	3.11	6.5	75.0	11.54
1968	10.2	210.6	20.65	24.3	84.6	3.48	4.8	61.6	12.83
1967	8.3	200.5	24.16	24.2	87.8	3.62	3.6	46.9	13.03
1966	7.7	190.7	24.77	22.0	86.4	3.92	2.9	36.6	12.62
1965	7.7	189.2	24.50	21.7	92.5	4.27	2.9	33.9	11.69
1964	7.7	183.8	23.66	19.1	87.4	4.58	3.3	32.3	9.79
1963	6.3	171.9	27.29	18.7	90.9	4.86	2.4	28.7	11.96
1962	6.6	167.0	25.30	16.7	87.4	5.23	2.5	28.8	11.52
1961	5.5	151.3	27.50	16.1	89.7	5.57	2.4	27.3	11.38
1960	5.4	149.2	27.62	14.7	87.9	5.98	2.3	26.3	11.43

Source: Steffensmeier, 1978, table 1, reformulated.

of these kinds of data is whether the gap between males and females in rates of property crime has therefore declined.

Different answers have been given to this question, and there is reason to think that the differences derive from the kinds of measures applied. Steffensmeier (1978, 1980) notes that disparities between the sexes can be measured in absolute and relative terms. He advocates the former. Some ratio and percentage measures of relative differences, he argues, can be misleading because, if the starting point is low, small absolute changes will look *relatively* large. This may often be the case with female crime rates. Furthermore, he notes that percentage or ratio measures of relative change may be unstable when the measure is premised on part-to-part rather than part-to-whole comparisons. In place of the part-to-part ratio measures, Steffensmeier calculates the percentage that the female rate contributes (% FC) to the male rate *plus* female rate for each offense. He also calculates absolute differences between male and female rates. These various kinds of measures are presented in Table 4-4 to illustrate the point that a *relative* gap in crime rates between the sexes can narrow while the *absolute* gap actually widens.

Indeed, for all crimes except forgery and embezzlement in Table 4-4, the relative gap does decline, while the absolute difference increases. Using larceny as an illustration, the arrest rate for females was 87.3 in 1960 and 376.2 in 1978. For males it was 487.4 in 1960 and 870.4 in 1978. The two relative measures of change presented in this table both indicate a narrowing of the male/female gap: the ratio of rates declined from 5:58 to 2:31, and the % FC increased from 15:2 to 30:2. However, Steffensmeier's point is that only limited significance can be attached to these changes because, during the same period, the absolute difference between male and female rates widened to 494.2 (870.4 − 376.2) from 400.1 (487.4 − 87.3). Based on the kinds of calculations presented in Table 4-4, Steffensmeier concludes that the relative gains made by women in their rates of crime are often more apparent than real. However, there are important differences of opinion on this point.

Rita Simon, whose work (e.g., 1975) may have had the greatest influence in this area, offers a convergence theory in which patterns of criminality for women increasingly resemble those for men. For example, she has analyzed arrest statistics for a forty-year period (1932 to 1972) and concluded that: (1) the proportion of all persons arrested in 1972 who were women was greater than was the case one, two, or three decades earlier; (2) the increase was greater for serious offenses than for other kinds of offenses; and (3) the increase in female arrest rates among the serious offenses was caused almost entirely by women's greater participation in property offenses, especially larceny. Simon (1976*b*) extrapolates from the

TABLE 4-4

ARREST RATES AND RATIOS PER 100,000 MALES AND FEMALES FOR PETTY PROPERTY CRIMES AND FOR MASCULINE PROPERTY CRIMES, 1960 (64) AND 1977[a]

Type of crime	Female rate	Male rate	Male/female	% FC	AD[b]	% of all female arrests	% of all male arrests
Petty							
Larceny							
1960	87.3	487.4	5.58	15.2	400.1	8.5	5.4
1978	376.2	870.4	2.31	30.2	494.2	9.0	22.2
Fraud							
1964	16.3	73.4	4.50	18.2	57.1	1.6	0.9
1978	100.3	185.3	1.85	35.1	85.0	5.9	1.9
Forgery							
1960	9.2	52.0	5.65	15.0	42.8	0.9	0.6
1978	23.8	60.6	2.55	28.2	36.8	1.4	0.6
Embezzlement							
1964	2.8	14.1	5.03	16.5	11.3	0.3	0.2
1978	2.1	6.8	3.23	23.6	4.7	0.1	0.1
Masculine							
Robbery							
1960	3.5	76.5	21.86	4.4	73.0	0.3	0.9
1978	10.9	154.7	14.19	6.6	143.8	0.6	1.6
Burglary							
1960	9.3	324.7	34.91	2.8	315.4	0.9	3.6
1978	32.7	536.1	16.39	5.7	503.4	1.9	5.5
Auto theft							
1960	5.4	149.2	27.6	3.5	143.8	0.5	1.7
1978	14.0	165.2	11.8	7.8	151.2	0.8	1.7

Arson							
1964	0.9	9.4	10.44	8.7	8.5	0.1	0.1
1978	2.4	18.7	7.79	11.4	16.3	0.1	0.2
Vandalism							
1964	8.6	142.3	16.55	5.7	133.7	0.8	1.7
1978	20.5	240.6	11.74	7.9	220.1	1.2	2.5
Stolen property							
1960	2.3	26.3	11.43	8.2	24.0	0.2	0.3
1978	13.5	177.5	13.15	10.3	104.0	0.8	1.2

Note: In some cases 1964 data were used because this was the earliest year for which data were reported separately for these categories.

[a]Percentage of female contribution.

[b]Absolute difference.

Source: Steffensmeier, 1981, table 1, reformulated.

latter findings and predicts that "if present rates in these crimes persist, approximately equal numbers of men and women will be arrested for fraud and embezzlement by the 1980's, and for forgery and counterfeiting the proportions should be equal by the 2010's. The prediction made for embezzlement and fraud can be extended to larceny as well."

Steffensmeier is most at odds with Simon on these last points. He finds that arrest-rate projections for larceny show a *widening of the absolute gap* with each passing decade to the year 2000, with similar results for fraud and forgery. He concludes (1980, p. 1098) that "female gains have been leveling off in recent years and it is likely that crime will be as much a male-dominated phenomenon in the year 2000 as it is in 1977." Still this does not deny Simon's more fundamental point that, in *relative* terms, women are now significantly more involved in crime than they were in the past.

In terms of crime patterns, Simon emphasizes that the relative increases in adult women's crime rates are concentrated in the area of property crime. This point is important to Simon's theoretical argument that as women increase their participation in the labor force, their opportunity to commit certain types of crime also increases. Steffensmeier does not reject this argument; rather, he seeks to diminish its significance. His point is that, while the female contribution to property crime generally, and again in a relative sense, has increased, the amount of the increase that is occupationally related (e.g., embezzlement) is small. A problem here involves the vagueness of general offense categories like larceny. When categories are broken down, Steffensmeier argues that the greater contributions of women are in the areas of petty theft and fraud.

Some support for Steffensmeier's suggestions is provided in Table 4-4. This table includes a division between "masculine" and "petty property" crimes. As both Steffensmeier and Simon suggest, "masculine" crimes like robbery, burglary, and auto theft remain predominantly male phenomena, in spite of some recent relative increases in female participation. In contrast, the petty property crime rates of women have increased notably, and the absolute differences between the male and female rates for petty crimes like forgery and embezzlement have actually declined: between 1960 and 1978 the sex difference in forgery rates declined from 42.8 to 36.8, and for embezzlement from 11.3 to 4.7. Still, the absolute differences between male and female rates of other petty property crimes like larceny and fraud have increased over this period, and it may be important to note that embezzlement represents only a very small part of female arrests: 0.1 percent in 1978, down from a similarly small 0.3 percent in 1964. Steffensmeier's point is that women are being arrested for traditionally female kinds of larceny like fraud rather than for nontraditional kinds of female crime such as embezzlement. However, this does not make the nontraditional gains any less important; indeed, in terms of dollars and the threat posed to the economic order, the nontraditional female crimes may be very important. Simon and Steffensmeier here offer different interpretations of similar empirical findings.

Last, there is the issue of female involvement in violent crime. Simon's findings seem to contradict Adler's prediction of growing female violence. Other sources of data seem to be consistent with Simon's position as well, at least for adult women (see Noblet and Burcart, 1976; Hill and Harris, 1981; Steffensmeier, 1980). Thus the violence of adult women is clearly patterned differently from the violence of men (Ward, Jackson, and Ward, 1969; Wolfgang, 1958), and the patterning has not shown much sign of change. However, this point is less clear for adolescent women. Noblet and Burcart (p. 655) find that arrests for violent crimes and property crimes increased equally among adolescent women between 1960 and 1970, and Hill and Harris (1981) report sex-ratio drops between 1963 and 1974 in the population under 18 for a variety of violent crimes. We will return below to the issue of changing patterns of violence among adolescent women.

Hindelang (1979) has analyzed data on the sex of offenders reported by victims derived from the 1973 through 1976 surveys of American crime victims, called the National Crime Surveys (NCS). The findings of these surveys are summarized in Table 4-5 along with 1976 *Uniform Crime Reports* data. A comparison of the NCS and *UCR* data (see Table 4-5) reveals a very similar picture, leading Hindelang (1979, p. 152) to surmise that "in general, it appears that even at the earliest stage in the offending process for which data are available, the conclusions we can draw about sex and involvement in crime from victimization survey data are essentially the same as those derived from arrest data for the same types of crimes." Thus these data indicate that (1) women offenders are a small portion of all offenders reported by victims (e.g., in 1976 they accounted for 4 percent of all robberies, 8 percent of all aggravated assaults, 14 percent of all simple assaults, 5 percent of all burglaries, and 5 percent of all motor vehicle thefts reported by victims), and (2) what increase in female involvement in crime has occurred during the short period of these surveys is most conspicuously in the area of larceny offenses (women accounted for 14 percent of all larcenies reported by victims in 1972, and 17 percent of such larcenies in 1976). Again, these data indicate that petty property crimes are the "traditional female crimes," and that they are the crimes in which increases in female involvement are most clearly occurring. Finally, Hindelang reports that, when the sex of the victim was held constant in his analyses, there was no evidence that male chivalry (males' reluctance to report crimes against them by women) had the effect of reducing the

TABLE 4-5
ESTIMATED PERCENTAGES OF OFFENDERS REPORTED BY VICTIMS TO HAVE BEEN FEMALES, BY TYPE OF CRIME IN NATIONAL CRIME SURVEY, 1972–76, AND FEMALE ARRESTS IN *UNIFORM CRIME REPORTS*, 1976 ONLY

Type of crime	NCS 1972[a]	NCS 1973[a]	NCS 1974	NCS 1975	NCS 1976	UCR 1976
Rape	0% (232,845)[c]	1% (203,733)	0% (223,721)	3% (222,050)	1% (161,000)	1%
Robbery	6%[a] (2,365,176)	4%[a] (2,070,110)	7% (2,122,945)	4% (2,248,777)	4% (2,126,622)	7%
Aggravated assault	8% (1,895,089)	8% (2,191,050)	7% (2,086,011)	6% (1,982,910)	8% (1,986,360)	13%
Simple assault	15% (3,047,491)	15% (3,364,001)	15% (3,228,297)	15% (3,283,535)	14% (3,374,864)	14%
Burglary	5% (563,470)	5% (493,526)	4% (604,949)	7% (458,304)	5% (502,293)	5%
Motor vehicle theft	3% (127,933)	3% (161,621)	4% (87,213)	2% (69,030)	5% (110,205)	7%
Larceny[b]	14% (2,039,625)	14% (1,636,759)	14% (1,709,704)	15% (1,818,003)	17% (1,670,439)	—
Personal larceny	11% (409,217)	11% (351,611)	11% (380,437)	11% (507,332)	14% (383,957)	—
Larceny from household	15% (695,064)	16% (568,833)	16% (535,966)	14% (507,332)...		

| Larceny from household | 15% (695,064) | 16% (568,833) | 16% (535,966) | 14% (515,022) | 17% (507,345) | — |
| Larceny of unattended property | 14% (935,344) | 15% (716,315) | 16% (793,301) | 19% (795,649) | 19% (779,137) | — |

[a]Commercial robberies for 1972 and 1973 (or about one-fifth of all robberies) have been excluded because the raw data were not available for analysis. Female offenders generally constitute fewer than 2 percent of the commercial robbery offenders; hence, if they were included in the 1972 and 1973 robbery data, the robbery percentages for females might decline by half a point.

[b]The *UCR* and NCS larceny categories are not comparable (see Hindelang, 1979, p. 148).

[c]Number of cases in parentheses.

number of female-offender victimizations reported to the police. In sum, victimization data seem to confirm the picture of women and crime portrayed in public agency data.

The gender-crime patterns we have seen in public agency and victimization data reappear in the self-report studies, but with significant variations in degree. For example, official arrest ratios by sex are substantially higher than the sex ratios by offense found in self-report surveys. Nye and Short (1957) find a sex ratio among adolescents of 2.42 in a midwestern setting and 2.82 in a western setting. Wise's (1967) New England study yields an adolescent differential of 2.30; Hindelang's (1971) California data yield a sex ratio of 2.56; Kratcoski and Kratcoski (1975) report a 2.00 sex ratio; and Cernkovich and Giordano (1979) find a ratio of 2.18 (see also Hagan, Simpson, and Gillis [1979]; Jensen and Eve [1976]; Hindelang et al. [1981]). In each of these instances, males exceed females in self-reported delinquencies by more than two to one. However, this figure is still considerably less than that indicated by public agency data. The 1975 FBI *Uniform Crime Reports* indicate that the male/female arrest ratio for those under 18 years of age is 3.72. One explanation for this disparity is that police are more sensitive and responsive to male delinquencies.

In an attempt to estimate how police selection practices might influence delinquency sex ratios, Feyerherm (1981) has calculated a series of "transition probabilities" that reflect the likelihood that male and female adolescents will be processed through a series of steps beginning with police contact and leading to arrest. The results of these calculations reveal that, while the ratio of male to female delinquency at the stage of self-report was on the order of 1.70, at the point of arrest the ratio had increased to 3.88, more than doubling the apparent difference between males and females and approximately the figures found in public agency data.

Two explanations are offered: (1) that police are biased in their arrest practices, and (2) that male adolescents are involved in more serious kinds of delinquency. This brings us to the *kinds* of self-reported activities in which male and female adolescents are involved.

The important point to be made here is that, while female adolescents may be more "versatile" in their delinquencies than female adults are in their criminal behavior, nonetheless, as the seriousness of the events increases, so also do the differences between levels of male and female participation, among both adolescents and adults. A first indication that female adolescents may be unexpectedly versatile in their delinquencies is found in the work of Hindelang (1971). Hindelang reports that, while males may be much more delinquent than females, female delinquencies, much like those of males, stlll are spread across a broad range of activities.

However, more recently Feyerherm (1981) has pointed out that the seriousness of such activities may differ substantially by sex. Thus, in Feyerherm's data, three levels of theft are examined, with the following results: in the lowest level, under $10, the ratio of male to female participation is 1.80; between $10 and $50 the ratio increases to 4.56; over $50, it increases to 22.00. The conclusion (ibid., p. 88) is that "since the sets of arrest statistics most often examined are designed to deal primarily with serious offenses, this tendency may explain why arrest information is more likely to show strong male-female differences."

A key difference between the self-report studies and those based on public agency data is that the former are generally time-bound in their coverage. This makes it more difficult to answer questions about change over time when using self-report data. Fortunately, however, Smith and Visher (1980) have brought together many of these studies, along with those focusing on public agency data, and have offered a "meta-analysis" of the data they review. Their analysis indicates that the relative involvement of males and females in crime is trending toward similarity for *both* self-report and official measures, but that the rate of the trend is significantly greater for the self-reported measures. Beyond this, Smith and Visher report that, although women are closing the gap in terms of *minor* forms of crime and delinquency, there is no indication that equal gender representation in the area of serious criminal behavior has yet occurred. Finally, and perhaps most significantly, they note that, while the gender-deviance relation is diminishing for both youths and adults, their data indicate that this trend is stronger for youths.

The last point is significant because, as Smith and Visher (1980) note, "It is at least plausible that shifting sex-role ideologies may be more salient for younger females and, thus, may have a greater impact upon the behavior of this group." This hypothesis and an analysis of public agency data in support of it are found in the work of Hill and Harris (1981).

There remain three other sources of data on women and crime. First, the records of the internal security departments of corporate entities have been used to study shoplifting and the crimes of employees against these bureaucracies. The studies of shoplifting indicate that this is a traditionally female crime in that it has involved large numbers of women for some time (Cameron, 1964).

Employee theft is another area in which private agency data have been put to interesting use. Franklin (1979) finds, in a study based on the reports of a large retail organization, that although a majority of the employees were women, the majority of employee thieves were men. Similarly, it is also found that the greater the value of the theft, the greater the likelihood that it was committed by a male employee. Indeed, the female thefts were relatively petty, with 80 percent of the thefts valued between $1 and $150 committed by females. These private agency data, then, seem to further confirm the impression that women continue to be involved in the "traditional" types of female crime.

The latter point is made in a somewhat different way by observational case studies of different types of criminal behavior. Miller (1973) reports on the basis of his work with street-corner gangs that females continue to play largely ancillary roles. As Steffensmeier (1980, p. 1102) notes, this does not mean there have been no serious and significant female criminals: there are now and always have been cases of female professional thieves, robbers, and so on (Block, 1977; Byrnes, 1969; Inanni, 1974; Jackson, 1969; Lucas, 1926; Reitman, 1937). However, the female role, then and now, has typically been as an accomplice to a male who both organized the crime and was the central figure in its execution (although see Giordano, 1978).

A study based on archival records puts much of the preceding discussion into a broader historical perspective. This study, by Cernkovich and Giordano (1979), is based on police blotters from the city of Toledo, Ohio, for the years 1890–1973. The length of the time period covered is unique to this study, and these conclusions are drawn: (1) women are now being arrested for offenses that are increasingly similar to those for which males are arrested; (2) female rates of arrest are increasing more rapidly than male rates; and (3) male-to-female ratios are declining for many offenses. The changing character of female crime is noted in qualitative as well as quantitative terms. Thus, notes made by police officers in the margins of the blotters indicate that, whereas in the earliest periods a higher percentage of the total number of women arrested were somehow tied to "houses of ill fame" (see also Heyl 1979), by the 1930s there began to be a more active, independent-from-hearth-and-home (as well as from house-of-prostitution) quality to the offenses. Indeed, the 1930s show significant increases in such property offenses as robbery, burglary, theft, and embezzlement. The significance of the timing of this shift is that it also marks the onset of the great depression, a time that was particularly precarious for women. Thus Giordano, Kerbel, and Dudley (1981) conclude that "this analysis of offense types as well as the characteristics of women arrested suggests that the increases may reflect the fact that certain categories of women (e.g., young, single, minority) [were] now in an even more unfavorable position in the labor market at the same time they [were] . . . increasingly expected to function independently."

We are now in a position to draw some conclusions about the relation between gender and crime. We have noted that this relationship is strong and that it is likely to remain so into the near future, at least in an absolute sense. On the other hand, in a relative sense, there is evidence that women are becoming more like men in their levels of involvement in crime, with this being particularly true of younger women and in the area of property crime. The areas of female criminality that are changing fastest are those that have been traditionally female, including petty forms of theft and fraud. In the more traditionally male areas of crime, the differences appear more durable.

HOW CRIMINAL ARE THE CORPORATIONS?

In the preceding sections we have placed great emphasis on the seriousness of crime and its relationship to class and gender. We have noted that when consideration is limited to the crimes widely considered serious by the public, criminal behavior is found to be disproportionately male and underclass in incidence and prevalence. However, we have also emphasized that conceptions of seriousness are variable. This point becomes particularly important when we turn to white-collar and corporate crimes, for these crimes traditionally are not taken as seriously as more conventional "street" crime by the public and its governments. Edwin Sutherland (1949, p. 9) in his classic study of *White Collar Crime,* noted the practical and theoretical inadequacy of such conceptions, in terms of their neglect of much upperworld crime and policies toward such crimes.

> The thesis of this book, stated positively, is that persons of the upper socio-economic class engage in much criminal behavior; that this criminal behavior differs from the criminal behavior of the lower socio-economic class principally in the administrative procedures which are used in dealing with the offenders; and that variations in administrative procedures are not significant from the point of view of causation of crime. Today tuberculosis is treated by streptomycin; but the causes of tuberculosis were no different when it was treated by poultices and blood-letting.

Although Sutherland focused conceptually on what he called "white-collar crime"—i.e., "a crime committed by a person of respectability and high social status in the course of his occupation"—decisions against *corporations* were the units of his statistical analysis. In Chapter 9 we will further discuss the confusion in conceptualizations of white-collar and corporate crime; here it is enough to note that our interest in this section is in crimes committed by and through corporations. Sutherland's study covered the "life careers," through 1944, of seventy large corporations. The analysis considered the following types of law violations: restraint of trade; misrepresentation in advertising; infringement of patents, trademarks, and copyrights; "unfair labor practices" as defined by the National Labor Relations Law and a few decisions under other labor laws; rebates; financial fraud and violation of trust; violations of war regulations; and some miscellaneous offenses. "All of the cases included in the tabulation are violations of law, most of them may properly be defined as crimes, and the others are closely allied to criminal behavior" (Sutherland, 1949, p. 18). The issue of definition is important because, as we noted in Chapter 2, Sutherland favored a liberal definition of crime based on two criteria: the legal definition of a social harm and the provision of a penalty.

Sutherland found in his research that each of the seventy large corporations had one or more decisions against it, and that altogether 980 decisions had been imposed against the corporations, with an average of 14 decisions against each. Approximately 16 percent of the decisions were made by criminal courts, but even when this strict criterion of criminality was used, Sutherland found that 60 percent of the seventy corporations had been convicted of crimes and had an average of approximately four convictions each. An irony of the latter finding was that in many states a person with four convictions was defined as a "habitual criminal." When Sutherland used his own criteria to categorize the decisions, he concluded that 779 of the 980 decisions constituted criminal convictions.

The distribution of the decisions across time is presented by types of offenses in Table 4-6. Date of the first adverse decision was used. The results reveal that approximately 60 percent of the adverse decisions were rendered in the ten-year period of 1935 to 1944, while only 40 percent were rendered in the thirty-five-year period leading up to 1935. Sutherland concluded that increased violations *and* prosecutions were responsible for rising levels of official corporation criminality.

The first large-scale comprehensive investigation of the law violations of major firms since Sutherland's pioneering work is provided by Clinard and Yeager (1980). This study involves a systematic analysis of federal administrative, civil, and criminal actions either initiated or completed by twenty-five federal agencies against the 477 largest publicly owned manufacturing (*Fortune* 500) corporations in the United States during 1975 and 1976. To this is added a more limited study of the 105 largest wholesale, retail, and service corporations. The study is restricted to *actions initiated* against corporations for violations, which Clinard and Yeager regard as roughly equivalent to arrests or prosecutions, and *actions completed*, which they regard as equivalent to convictions. While it is acknowledged that official actions taken against corporations are probably only the tip of the iceberg, Clinard and Yeager argue that these actions nonetheless constitute an index of illegal behavior by large corporations. Six main forms of corporate

TABLE 4-6
DECISIONS AGAINST SEVENTY CORPORATIONS, BY FIVE-YEAR PERIODS AND BY TYPES OF LAWS VIOLATED

Dates	Restraint of trade	Misrepresentation in ads	Infringement	Unfair labor	Rebates	Other	Total	Percentages
1940–date.....	102	34	52	102	7	43	340	34.7
1935–39.......	59	42	59	50	15	20	245	25.0
1930–34.......	27	8	36	4	7	10	92	9.4
1925–29.......	28	1	26	—	—	23	78	8.0
1920–24.......	18	3	12	—	—	9	42	4.3
1915–19.......	20	7	5	—	6	7	45	4.6
1910–14.......	29	1	13	—	14	7	64	6.5
1905–09.......	17	—	9	1	14	5	46	4.7
1900–04.......	5	1	6	1	3	1	17	1.7
1890–99.......	2	—	1	—	—	3	6	0.6
Prior to 1890 ...	—	—	3	—	—	2	5	0.5
Total......	307	97	222	158	66	130	980	100.0

Source: Sutherland, 1949, p. 26.

illegal behavior were recorded: administrative, environmental, financial, labor, manufacturing, and unfair trade practices. Two notable differences between this study and Sutherland's are the consideration given here to official actions initiated as well as completed against corporations, and the attention given to the seriousness of the violations and characteristics of the corporations.

The results of this analysis (see Table 4-7) reveal that approximately 60 percent of the 475 manufacturing corporations had at least one action initiated against them, while more than 200 of the corporations, or 42 percent of the total, had multiple cases charged against them from 1975 to 1976. Thirty-eight of the 300 manufacturing corporations cited for violations accounted for 52 percent of all violations charged in 1975–1976, with an average of 23.5 violations per firm. One firm had fifty-four environmental cases brought against it. Clinard and Yeager also developed a measure of seriousness to rank these violations, using such criteria as the knowledge, extent, and size of the violation. Corporations in the oil-refining industry had nearly 60 percent of the total environmental violations, and more than a third of the serious and moderately serious environmental violations. More generally, Clinard and Yeager report that large corporations were more numerous and more serious in their violations.

In spite of the impressive statistical evidence that Sutherland and Clinard and Yeager have amassed to demonstrate that corporate criminality is extensive, their larger point is that the criminal law has been ineffectual in detecting and punishing these crimes. The significance of this important and growing body of work is therefore to demonstrate that corporate actors are ineffectively pursued as criminals (Ermann and Lundman, 1980; Schrager and Short, 1978). There is, however, another important aspect of this situation. That is, that corporations are nonetheless very active participants in the criminal-justice process, pursuing through the police and courts many individuals who commit crimes against them (Hagan, 1982, 1983). In other words, corporate actors not only have often successfully avoided large-scale criminal prosecutions, they also have proven themselves effective in mobilizing the criminal law to penalize individuals who offend against them. This is partly because corporate enterprises, especially retail stores, are attractive targets for crime, and partly because corporate actors are more and better prepared to pursue criminal prosecutions. Victimization data collected on burglary and robbery from both commercial and residential samples in thirteen American cities (U.S. Department of Justice, 1975) help to make these points (see Tables 4-8 and 4-9).

For example, in every city, and for both burglary and robbery, the per capita rates of victimization of commercial establishments are higher than

TABLE 4-7
INDUSTRY TYPE OF 445 MANUFACTURING CORPORATIONS BY PRIMARY
VIOLATION TYPE AND PERCENTAGE, TOTAL AND SERIOUS/MODERATE
VIOLATIONS*

Industry type		Primary Vibration Type					
		Total		Administrative		Environmental	
		Violations	%	Violations	%	Violations	%
Mining and oil production	T	17	1.2	1	0.8	10	2.0
	S/M	8	1.2	1	2.9	1	1.9
Food	T	96	6.7	4	3.3	11	2.2
	S/M	49	7.4	2	5.9	3	5.7
Apparel	T	4	0.3				
	S/M	3	0.5				
Paper, fiber, wood	T	81	5.7	3	2.4	50	10.1
	S/M	28	4.2	2	5.9	3	5.7
Chemical	T	115	8.1	13	10.6	55	11.1
	S/M	49	7.4	3	8.8	12	22.6
Oil refining	T	289	20.1	6	4.9	229	46.2
	S/M	70	10.4	5	14.7	19	35.8
Metal manufacturing	T	88	6.2	8	6.5	71	14.3
	S/M	13	2.0	3	8.8	3	5.7
Metal products	T	28	2.0	8	6.5	5	1.0
	S/M	13	2.0				
Electronic and appliances	T	65	4.6	12	9.8	5	1.0
	S/M	49	7.4	1	2.9	2	3.8
Motor vehicles	T	238	16.7	20	16.3	19	3.8
	S/M	142	21.2	3	8.8	7	13.1
Aerospace	T	18	1.3	1	0.8	1	0.2
	S/M	16	2.4	1	2.9		

TABLE 4-7 cont'd

Primary Vibration Type							
Financial		Labor		Manufacturing		Trade	
Violations	%	Violations	%	Violations	%	Violations	%
		1	0.6	2	0.4	3	4.8
		1	0.6	2	0.6	3	4.9
5	12.3	12	6.7	54	10.5	7	11.0
5	13.2	12	7.5	20	6.3	7	11.5
1	2.4	2	1.1			1	1.6
		2	1.2			1	1.6
		15	8.3	1	0.2	10	15.9
		12	7.5	1	0.3	10	16.4
1	2.4	15	8.3	21	4.1	7	11.0
1	2.6	10	6.2	16	5.0	7	11.5
25	61.1	9	5.1	8	1.6	10	15.9
23	60.5	9	5.6	4	1.3	8	13.1
		4	2.3	3	0.6	2	3.2
		2	1.2	3	0.9	2	3.3
		9	5.1	4	0.8	2	3.3
		7	4.4	4	1.3	2	3.3
1	2.4	30	16.9	12	2.3	5	7.9
1	2.6	28	17.4	12	3.8	5	8.2
		20	11.2	171	33.3	8	12.7
		19	11.8	105	33.0	8	13.1
1	2.4	6	3.4	7	1.4	2	3.2
1	2.6	6	3.7	6	1.9	2	3.3

TABLE 4-7 cont'd
INDUSTRY TYPE OF 445 MANUFACTURING CORPORATIONS BY PRIMARY
VIOLATION TYPE AND PERCENTAGE, TOTAL AND SERIOUS MODERATE
VIOLATIONS*

Industry type		Primary Vibration Type					
		Total		Administrative		Environmental	
		Violations	%	Violations	%	Violations	%
Drugs	T	134	9.4	18	14.6		
	S/M	81	12.0	5	14.6		
Industry and farm equipment	T	70	4.9	11	8.9	8	1.6
	S/M	42	6.3			3	5.7
Beverages	T	11	0.8			1	0.2
	S/M	7	1.1				
Other	T	174	12.2	18	14.6	31	6.3
	S/M	97	14.5	8	23.4		
Total	T	1428	100.0	123	100.0	496	100.0
	S/M	667	100.0	34	100.0	53	100.0

*Industry classification from *Fortune,* 1976: T=total.
S/M=serious and moderately serious violations.
  Source: Clinard, 1980, pp. 390–391.

for individuals and households. Across the thirteen cities, on a per capita basis, commercial establishments experience more than three times the burglaries and five times the robberies as households and individuals. Again, in every city, and for both burglary and robbery, commercial establishments are more likely than individuals and households to report the victimization they experience to the police. Across the thirteen cities, approximately three-quarters (76.1 percent) of the commercial burglary victims report their experiences to the police, while about half (51.6 percent) of the household burglary victims report their experiences to the police. Similarly, 82 percent of the commercial robberies and 57 percent of the individual robberies are reported to the police. In sum, and on a per capita basis, commercial victims are much more likely than individual victims to require and make use of the criminal-justice system. Of course,

TABLE 4-7 cont'd

Primary Vibration Type							
Financial		Labor		Manufacturing		Trade	
Violations	%	Violations	%	Violations	%	Violations	%
		6	3.4	109	21.1		
		6	3.7	70	22.0		
		11	6.2	37	7.2	3	4.8
		10	6.2	26	8.2	3	4.9
1	2.4	4	2.3	4	0.8	1	1.6
1	2.6	4	2.5	1	0.3	1	1.6
6	14.6	34	19.1	81	15.7	2	3.2
6	15.9	33	20.5	48	15.1	2	3.3
41	100.0	178	100.0	514	100.0	63	100.0
38	100.0	161	100.0	318	100.0	61	100.0

individuals and households outnumber commercial organizations, so that when the above findings are weighted back to the population, commercial establishments are reduced in their apparent significance. Even then, however, commercial establishments are responsible for more than a third, and in some cities (e.g., Cincinnati in the case of burglary and Miami in the case of robbery) more than half, of both the burglaries and robberies reported to the police. In other words, the representation of commercial victims in the criminal-justice process is large and disproportionate. Unfortunately, the Panel for the Evaluation of Crime Surveys of the National Research Council (1976) recommended discontinuation of "commercial surveys," and they consequently have not been done in recent years. We nonetheless speculate further about the influence of "corporate victims" in the criminal-justice system, as well as about corporate criminality, in Chapter 9.

TABLE 4-8
VICTIMIZATION DATA ON ROBBERY IN THIRTEEN AMERICAN CITIES

	Boston	Buffalo	Cincinnati	Houston	Miami	Milwaukee
Robbery incidents per 1000 population	31	16	15	17	10	18
Percent reported to police	53%	51%	51%	47%	65%	51%
Incidents reported to police weighted to population	5,989 (64.9%)	2,295 (73.0%)	2,091 (54.6%)	6,157 (60.8%)	1,430 (43.4%)	4,182 (80.0%)
Robbery incidents per 1000 establishments	132	56	72	140	104	49
Percent reported to police	83%	77%	87%	78%	69%	95%
Incidents reported to police weighted to population	3,237 (35.1%)	847 (27.0%)	1,740 (45.4%)	3,978 (39.2%)	1,863 (56.6%)	1,045 (20.0%)
Per capita ratio of commercial to personal robberies	4.3	3.5	4.8	8.2	10.4	2.7
Total no. of incidents reported to police weighted to population	9,226	3,142	3,831	10,135	3,293	5,227

TABLE 4-8 cont'd

Minneapolis	New Orleans	Oakland	Pittsburgh	San Diego	San Francisco	Washington	13 cities
21	18	22	15	11	29	17	18.5
49%	53%	53%	56%	46%	44%	63%	57%
2,793 (67.9%)	3,392 (54.6%)	2,650 (52.4%)	2,744 (65.3%)	2,438 (74.0%)	6,160 (66.1%)	4,914 (70.4%)	47,235 (63.8%)
91	173	137	77	49	80	88	96.0
88%	83%	83%	97%	85%	77%	90%	82%
1,320 (32.1%)	2,822 (45.4%)	2,407 (47.6%)	1,455 (34.7%)	855 (26.0%)	3,157 (33.9%)	2,070 (29.6%)	26,796 (36.2%)
4.3	9.6	6.2	5.1	4.5	2.8	5.2	5.2
4,113	6,214	5,057	4,199	3,293	9,317	6,984	74,031

TABLE 4-9

VICTIMIZATION DATA ON BURGLARY IN THIRTEEN AMERICAN CITIES

	Boston	Buffalo	Cincinnati	Houston	Miami	Milwaukee
Burglary incidents per 1000 population	149	97	143	164	85	152
Percent reported to police	56%	50%	55%	46%	58%	54%
Incidents reported to police weighted to population	17,360 (56.7%)	7,200 (60.4%)	12,375 (48.9%)	32,016 (70.4%)	6,090 (50.4%)	19,926 (76.9%)
Burglary incidents per 1000 establishments	576	319	566	518	292	321
Percent reported to police	78%	75%	84%	71%	79%	82%
Police weighted to incidents reported to population	13,260 (43.3%)	4,725 (39.6%)	13,490 (29.6%)	6,004 (49.6%)	5,986 (23.1%)	5,986 (25.7%)
Per capita ratio of commercial to household burglaries	3.9	3.3	4.0	3.2	3.4	2.1
Total no. of incidents reported to police weighted to population	30,620	11,925	25,311	45,506	12,094	25,912

TABLE 4-9 cont'd

Minneapolis	New Orleans	Oakland	Pittsburgh	San Diego	San Francisco	Washington	13 cities
177	112	174	93	138	115	75	128.7
52%	47%	57%	50%	50%	51%	57%	57.6%
14,768 (74.3%)	10,199 (62.8%)	13,224 (56.2%)	8,100 (66.5%)	17,650 (74.4%)	16,932 (64.6%)	11,229 (62.3%)	187,069 (64.2%)
436	448	637	293	358	253	330	411.3
71%	68%	77%	73%	80%	72%	79%	76.1%
5,112 (25.7%)	6,052 (37.2%)	10,318 (43.8%)	4,088 (33.5%)	6,080 (25.6%)	9,288 (35.4%)	6,794 (37.7%)	104,033 (35.8%)
2.5	4.0	3.7	3.2	2.6	2.2	4.4	3.2
19,880	16,251	23,542	12,188	23,730	26,220	18,023	291,202

CONCLUSIONS

Crime statistics seldom, if ever, speak for themselves. They require interpretation. Helpful in this interpretation is an awareness that the components of such statistics include not only the persons and behaviors they presume to count, but also errors that lead to over- and under-reporting, some of which are random, and some of which are systematic, with origins in the individuals and organizations that respond to crime. We have called the first of the above the "behavioral component" of crime statistics, the second the "error component," and the third the "response component." In sorting out these components, modern criminologists have been informed by comparisons of alternative measures, drawn from a variety of sources, including: (1) official agencies of crime control, (2) nonofficial agencies, (3) first-person accounts, (4) victimization surveys, and (5) observational studies. We can be encouraged as to the validity of our measures when estimates based on several of these methods agree; and we can be directed to possible sources of error when the different methods disagree.

Proceeding on the basis of the above principles, we have suggested answers to four questions:

1. Are crime rates increasing? In intervals of about fifty years, the United States has experienced three important surges of violent crime: in 1860, 1900, and 1960. However, there is some possibility that these periodic surges are actually deviations from a much longer downward trend that has been traced to medieval and early modern England, when rates of violent crime were extremely high. In any case, the most sophisticated forecasts, taking into account the movement of baby-boom children out of the violence-prone years, suggest a new stability or even decline in some crime rates in the 1980s.

2. Are there class differences in criminal behavior? Analyses of official data aggregated into areal units may often exaggerate the link between social class and criminal and delinquent behavior. Nonetheless, evidence suggests that the forms of crime and delinquency currently considered most serious by the public, and treated as such, are unequally distributed across the class structure, with the underclasses experiencing more than their fair share of crime and delinquency.

3. Are men more criminal than women? When it comes to criminal forms of behavior, men clearly exceed women. This does not mean that the relationship between crime and gender is a simple one: the disparity between the sexes varies with the class of crime and the time considered. The biggest changes are occurring for younger women and in the area of property crime. Although the criminality of women will not soon equal or surpass that of men, changes are occurring.

4. How criminal are the corporations? Many corporations are not only criminal but also criminal recidivists, in the sense of being convicted repeatedly for criminal offenses. It is assumed further that far more corporations commit crimes than are caught and convicted. Corporations not only have often successfully avoided large-scale criminal prosecutions, they also have proven themselves effective in mobilizing the criminal law to penalize those (e.g., shoplifters) who offend against them. In this sense, corporations may benefit more than individuals, both as criminal offenders and as victims of crime.

Modern theories of crime have not given much attention to the crimes of women or of corporations. This issue is addressed in some detail in Chapter 9. On the other hand, much theoretical effort has been devoted to the explanation of class differences in criminal and delinquent behavior. The three following chapters consider these theories in the following groups: the theories of undercontrol; the theories of culture, status, and opportunity; and the theories of overcontrol. It is to the effort to understand variations in criminal behavior, then, that we turn next.

UNDERSTANDING CRIME I: THE THEORIES OF UNDERCONTROL

5

THE ISSUE: WHY DO PEOPLE VIOLATE LAWS THAT MOST OF US ACCEPT?

"Why," the theories of undercontrol try to explain, "would anyone violate rules of social conduct that nearly all of us accept?" As the subtitle of this chapter suggests, the answers given to this question point in various ways to the absence or ineffectiveness of social controls; that is, these theories talk about how and why some of us are beyond or out of control. However, before we consider this theory group in any detail, we should note that the question we have started with involves a crucial assumption. The question posed assumes that most of us *do* agree about the rules we are expected to follow. As we noted in Chapter 2, this assumption of consensus is subject to debate, and theories we consider in later chapters begin with rather different assumptions. Thus the theories we consider here can be regarded as "consensus theories," and they exist in apposition, if not opposition, to theories we consider later. For the purposes of this chapter, however, we will accept the assumption of consensus, noting only that it may be truer of some rules of social life (e.g., those regulating serious crimes of violence) than others.

There are at least three kinds of theories of undercontrol, and each explains lawbreaking in a different way.

• *Social disorganization theory* asserts that the growth of American cities brought breakdowns in processes that normally regulate lawbreaking behavior.

• *Neutralization theory* notes that although most of us still learn the norms and values of our society, some of us also learn to rationalize, or neutralize, their violation.

• *Control theory* observes that some people feel less constrained than others by the norms and values of our society, and therefore that they feel relatively free to deviate from them.

There is, of course, more to each of these theories than the summary statements just presented. These statements are helpful, however, in making the initial point that each of the theories of undercontrol is concerned with how persons evade, or are freed from, the control of norms and values they are assumed to share in common. Our task in this chapter will be to examine each of the theories of undercontrol in more detail. Before doing so, however, we will first introduce a concept that is fundamental not only to the theories of undercontrol but to the theories we consider later.

DURKHEIM'S CONCEPT OF ANOMIE

The concept of anomie emerged in the work of the French sociologist Emile Durkheim (1897). This concept anticipated the modern theories of undercontrol (see Hirschi, 1969, p. 3n) in the attention it gave to social bonds and cultural regulation, and more specifically, to the consequences of their absence or failure. Thus, in its initial usage, the concept of anomie referred to an absence of social regulation, or normlessness. Durkheim introduced his discussion of anomie by noting that physical and social needs are regulated in significantly different ways. For example, when physical hunger is satiated, the body *itself* will resist additional food. But the social needs—including wealth, prestige, and power—are regulated *externally,* through the constraining forces of society. Undisciplined by this guardian social order, Durkheim (1897, p. 247) assumed that our desires are an "insatiable and bottomless abyss." Further, Durkheim argued (ibid., p. 252) that humanity's darkest danger resided in the absence of regulation, or absolute freedom: "It is not true, then, that human activity can be released from all restraint. . . . Its nature and method of manifestation . . . depend not only on itself but on other beings, who consequently restrain and regulate it." For Durkheim, as for Kris Kristofferson and Bobby McGee, then, "freedom is just another word for nothing left to lose."

Suicide, the ultimate act of anomie, was the subject of Durkheim's best-known research. The assumption that guided this research was that suicide rates vary with two social conditions: social integration and social regulation. Durkheim argued that excessively low *or* high levels of integration and regulation can bring high rates of suicide. Thus, high levels of integration can result in states of *altruism,* exemplified in the human sacrifices of primitive peoples, and the brave but deadly acts of modern soldiers. On the other hand, low levels of integration are said to result in *egoism* and higher rates of suicide among unmarried persons and Protestants (as contrasted with Catholics and Jews). Excessive regulation produces *fatalism* that causes higher suicide rates among childless married women and very young husbands. Finally, low levels of regulation bring *anomie* and higher suicide rates among widows and divorced persons, as well as among business people during economic booms and slumps. For our purposes, anomie, with its attention to economic conditions and its implications for types of crime and deviance other than suicide, is the most important element in Durkheim's discussion.

Durkheim's proposed cure for anomie is found in his suggestion (ibid., p. 246) that "no living being can be happy or even exist unless his needs are sufficiently proportioned to his means." Rather than social or economic reform, then, Durkheim in his early work recommends an attitude of resignation as the solution to the problems of anomie. In particular, Durkheim was stubborn in his belief that economic reforms could not effectively resolve conditions of anomie. He insisted instead (ibid., p. 251) that "one sort of heredity will always exist, that of natural talent. A moral discipline will therefore still be required to make those less favored by nature accept the lesser advantages which they owe to chances of birth." Indeed, Durkheim went so far as to find virtue in poverty, suggesting (ibid., p. 254) that "it is actually the best school for teaching self-restraint."

As we will see in Chapter 6, Robert Merton assumed the task of extracting a more liberal sentiment from the Durkheimian tradition. Merton did this by reformulating the relationship postulated between goals and means in the concept of anomie. As we will see in Chapter 7, other theorists have also identified more radical themes in Durkheim's later work. However, for the moment our primary interest is in the emphasis Durkheim gave to processes of social integration and regulation. It is this emphasis that ties Durkheim's early work to the more modern theories of undercontrol.

SOCIAL DISORGANIZATION THEORY

We have already made reference in Chapter 1 to the importance of the Chicago school in American criminology. Social disorganization theory had its roots in the Chicago school and the work of several of its most important members: W. I. Thomas, Frederick Thrasher, and Clifford Shaw and his associates. Prominent in the work of all of the early Chicago criminologists was the idea of social control. Like Durkheim, these theorists believed that it was the absence or failure of controls that explained deviant behavior.

W. I. Thomas and "The Unadjusted Girl"

W. I. Thomas (1909, pp. 14–16) organized his work around the explicit assumption that "control . . . is the object of all purposive activity." Social control is necessary, according to Thomas (1923), because there is an inevitable contradiction between the wants and needs of individuals and society. In particular, individuals pursue their wishes for four things— security, new experience, response, and recognition—while "an organized society seeks . . . to regulate the conflict and competition inevitable between its members in the pursuit of their wishes" (1923, p. 43). The instruments of social control or regulation are "definitions of situations"; these comprise a moral code that for Thomas are society's defense against social disorganization.

However, Thomas also observed that modern, urban, capitalist societies are characterized by competing and socially disorganizing definitions of individual behavior, including such ideas as "women's rights." In turn-of-the-century Chicago, Thomas saw young women seeking new opportunities in schools, factories, stores, offices, and other previously unavailable settings. This movement away from the home and its primary relationships was seen as weakening traditional social controls and as subjecting young women to conflicting definitions of situations. Thomas was interested in using these ideas to explain the involvement of young women in prostitution.

In *The Unadjusted Girl,* Thomas argued that the processes of social change that were occurring in cities like Chicago were destroying older social controls and the force of definitions favoring such ideas as "virginity" and "purity." Particularly for young women whose economic resources were limited, Thomas (1923, p. 98) argued that sex now took on new meanings: "Their sex is used as a condition of the realization of other wishes. It is their capital." Thus Thomas saw sex as a medium through which impoverished young women could achieve their wishes for "security, new experience, and response." In sum, prostitution was seen as a product of the socially disorganizing forces of the city and the changing definitions of situations that it brought, particularly to young women who were economically disadvantaged. Note that this view of prostitution may help to explain the enthusiasm of the "humanitarians" for the types of prostitution legislation we discussed in Chapter 3. The theory of social disorganization saw *informal* social controls as in decline, and society as requiring *formal* social controls, that is, laws, to take their place. This view does not fit well with the notion that prostitution is the world's oldest profession, and therefore not the product of recent social change; nor does it fit well with the common assumption that during the first part of this century ideas about women's rights had greater currency among middle- and upper-class women than among underclass women. Nonetheless, the views held by Thomas were influential.

Thrasher and "The Gang"

Thomas's conception of the four wishes (the desires for new experience, security, response, and recognition) became the basis for Frederick Thrasher's (1937) study of juvenile gangs in Chicago. Thrasher more inclusively called these wishes the "lively energies." He argued that these "energies" made adolescent life naturally free and wild. The question, then, was what conditions would allow these energies free play. The answer given again involved the disorganization of the community and the loss of traditional controls. These conditions were to be found, according to Thrasher, in city slums characterized by physical deterioration, a rapid succession of inhabitants, and high mobility. Gangs were seen as a natural response to these conditions.

But why gangs specifically? Here Thrasher notes that a disorganized community and family life not only frees adolescent males from social control, but also fails to provide for the elemental human needs identified by Thomas. Gangs are social organizations that serve these needs. The functions of the gang are to establish order and fulfill human needs. The gang constitutes a form of collective behavior that is spontaneous and unplanned in origin.

Thrasher is also rather specific about the joining and leaving of gangs. Again, the key variable is social control. He argues that girls, preadolescent boys, and children of both sexes in certain ethnic groups rarely join gangs because they are effectively controlled by their families. On the other hand, boys leave gangs when obligations of marriage and work introduce new kinds of controls on their behavior.

In all of this, we should not lose sight of the fact that Thrasher saw delinquency as a fun and playful pursuit (Bordua, 1961). Thrasher's descriptions of the slums of Chicago are scenes of excitement, with their railroad yards, industrial properties, and waterways offering "a realm for adventure that is unexcelled in the playgrounds or in the more orderly portions of the city" (p. 479). Given these attractions, and the absence of controls, delinquency was seen as a normal and natural response.

Shaw, McKay, and Delinquency Areas

Clifford Shaw and Henry McKay (1931; 1942; 1969) conducted a series of studies beginning in the late 1920s in Chicago that sought to identify areas of social disorganization and the processes that characterize them. What they found was that a variety of measures of social disorganization—truancy, tuberculosis, infant mortality, mental disorder, economic dependency, adult crime, and juvenile delinquency—tended to occur in common. In general, the rates were highest in slums near the city center, and they diminished with movement from the center out (the zonal hypothesis on which this pattern was premised is discussed in Chapter 1.) Since these problems were assumed to be contrary to the shared values of area inhabitants, they were taken as indications that these areas were unable to realize the goals of their residents. In other words, they were taken as indicators of social disorganization.

Shaw and McKay also attempted to determine the sorts of community characteristics that were correlated with delinquency, so that they could infer from these characteristics what the central components of social disorganization were and how they caused delinquency. Three types of correlates were identified: the economic status of the community, the mobility of the community, and its heterogeneity. The implication was that poverty, high mobility, and heterogeneity lead to weak controls and, in turn, to high rates of delinquency. Of course, poverty, mobility, and heterogeneity have been distinctive features of the centers of American cities for some time, and their discussion therefore speaks directly to the issue of why America's central cities have experienced so much crime and delinquency. Nonetheless, Shaw and McKay's work and that of other social disorganization theorists has received a good deal of criticism. A discussion of some of the sources of this criticism follows.

Some Critical Comments on Social Disorganization Theory

One very basic critique of social disorganization theory has involved efforts to test the assertion that poverty is a primary determinant of community variations in rates of official delinquency. Five of these studies have attracted the most attention (Lander, 1954; Polk, 1957–1958; Bordua, 1958–1959; Chilton, 1964; Quinney, 1964). All save the next-to-last of these studies conclude that the economic well-being of an area is less important in its relationship to delinquency than social disorganization theory suggests. However, as Gordon (1967) and, more recently, Kornhauser (1978) have noted, these studies have suffered from statistical problems (most notable, multicollinearity) that make their conclusions doubtful. In the end, Gordon concludes that there *is* a correlation at the aggregate level between socioeconomic status and official delinquency rates, with the lower end of the socioeconomic continuum contributing most to the relationship. As we noted in the previous chapter, the use of

AN EXAMPLE: THE SOCIAL ORDER OF THE SLUM   A modern descendant of the Chicago school of sociology, Gerald Suttles, has offered a somewhat different view of slum communities than that provided by social disorganization theory. His research is based on a part of Chicago that he calls the "Addams area," where he lived from 1963 to 1966. Suttles notes that this neighborhood had achieved notoriety for its lawlessness, gangsterism, and general departure from the standards of the city. It became the stronghold of Al Capone, the "Gena Brothers," and the "40" gang in the 1920s. On the other hand, Hull House was founded in the neighborhood by Jane Addams, and Mother Cabrini, America's first and only Roman Catholic saint, devoted much of her life to the area.

Measured by the usual yardstick of success, Suttles observes, it is tempting to adopt the social disorganization perspective and to think of the local residents of the Addams area as inadequate and disadvantaged people suffering from cultural deprivation, unemployment, and a number of other "urban ills." However, Suttles (1976, p. 3) argues that when this area is viewed from the *inside* it can be seen that it is intricately organized according to its own standards, a set of standards that "require discipline and self-restraint in the same way as do the moral dictates of the wider community." The basis of these standards is a pattern Suttles calls "ordered segmentation," in which age, sex, ethnic, and territorial units are fitted together like building blocks to create a larger structure. This patterning is apparent in the activities that surround the adolescent male street-corner groups (i.e., gangs) that were of so much concern to social disorganization theorists like Thrasher, Shaw, and McKay.

In a manner not so different from Thrasher, Suttles (ibid., p. 220) suggests that "the street corner group provides a way of ordering people into a manageably small number of social aggregates. . . . The function of the named street corner group is rudimentary and primitive: it defines groups of people so that they can be seen as representatives rather than individuals." However, these groups often become problematic as rumors circulate about them in rather predictable, socially organized, ways. For example,

In the winter of 1964 a Mexican from Eighteenth Street was badly hurt by someone who tied him to a telephone pole and ran a car into him. Three Italians were arrested as drivers of the car but later released. Among the Mexicans on Eighteenth Street, the rumor was that the "outfit" had "got off" the three Italians. To this was added the general view that "someone from around here's gonna get one of those Dagos." Implicitly this meant any "dago" in the Addams area. Being Italian and living in the Addams area is equivalent to belonging to the "outfit" so far as those from Eighteenth Street are concerned.

The rumor circulated on Eighteenth Street until late spring when an open dance was held in the Addams area. A large number of boys from Eighteenth Street attended. Outside the dance, boys congregated and eyed one another. A group of Mexican boys congregated at one location only a few yards from several Italian boys. A shot rang out and Snout, an Italian boy, fell wounded. A policeman no more than a few yards away gave chase and wounded one of the assailants. The rest got away.

Immediately, there was a gathering among the Italian boys in the Addams area, and the question of "what will be done about those guys on Eighteenth Street" arose. On this occasion, however, they waited for a report on Snout's condition. No one was badly hurt. Later another rumor developed among the Italians: "Our (Italian) policemen are going to take care of it." From that point on, no one felt any need to retaliate against Eighteenth Street. The fact that there was no subsequent evidence that the Italian policemen had done anything did not lessen their faith in the outcome.

Suttles notes that the tendency is for such rumors to spread widely, but along a very selective path governed by the ordered segmentation of the area. Thus, he observes that such rumors usually spread among the younger males, crossing ethnic and sex boundaries at the same age level. A result is that a rumor may spread downward among the younger children of an area, but it will seldom reach upward to their parents before a number of street workers and police officers have heard some version of the rumor. It is therefore generally the latter who intervene to forestall serious conflict. When conflict does erupt, it too follows a pattern of ordered segmentation. The boys involved tend to attack others known to them, and to exploit persons they do not know. The girls hang back and evade the conflict, with the possible exception of black girls, whose status more nearly approximates that of the boys. The truth of unfounded rumors is assumed, and ethnic differences further antagonize their interpretation. Area adults seldom intercede effectively because they know so little about what is happening in the boys' world. Suttles (ibid., p. 220) therefore concludes that "in various ways, age, sex, residence, and ethnicity continually reappear to define participant and onlooker, victim and victimizer, the ignorant and the wise, and the troublemaker and the peacemaker." In this sense, slum communities *are* socially organized.

aggregated official police data in these studies may inflate such a relationship; nonetheless, this relationship is one which crime and delinquency theories must explain.

More serious criticisms of social disorganization theory have questioned the imprecision and possible circularity of the social disorganization concept and its use to characterize slum or ghetto life. The imprecision or circularity of social disorganization theory lies in its inclusion of delinquency rates as one of its indicators. Kornhauser (1978, pp. 118–120) notes that a problem here may have been the reluctance of social disorganization theorists to be explicit about the causal structure of their theory. Rather, they sometimes seem to be using the presence of delinquency to explain its occurrence, which certainly sounds like circular, or tautological, thinking. However, if what they really meant was that poverty, heterogeneity, and mobility cause social disorganization, and that crime and delinquency are its consequences, then they may be on safer ground (Kornhauser, 1978).

Still, are slums and ghettos really socially disorganized? Such conclusions often seem to be little more than middle-class value judgments about disadvantaged ways of living. In response to just this kind of concern, a number of observational studies (e.g., Whyte, 1955; Liebow, 1967; Rainwater, 1970; Suttles, 1978) have sought to determine how slum and ghetto communities are ordered. We turn now to a recent study of this kind.

NEUTRALIZATION THEORY

Neutralization theory brings with it a shift away from the objective conditions of underclass life, and a new emphasis on the *subjective* manner in which crime-producing situations are *interpreted*. At base, neutralization theory assumes that people's actions are guided by their thoughts. Thus, the question asked by this theory is, What is it about the thoughts of otherwise good people that sometimes turn them bad? It can be noted that the question posed assumes that most people, most of the time, are guided by "good" thoughts. In other words, neutralization theory, like social disorganization theory, assumes that there is general agreement in our society about "the good things in life" and the appropriate ways of obtaining them. Thus, Sykes and Matza (1957, p. 665n) are able to observe that the juvenile delinquent "recognizes *both* the legitimacy of the dominant social order and its moral 'rightness.' " With Morris Cohen, the neutralization theorists suggest that one of the most fascinating puzzles of human behavior is how individuals come to violate the laws in which they believe.

One of the most important contributions of this theoretical approach, then, was to alter the emphasis of sociological theory on crime and delinquency as lower-class phenomena. Applications of neutralization theory include the early work of Sutherland on white-collar crime, the research of his student Cressey on embezzlement, and the connections drawn by Sykes and Matza between the acts of delinquents and the lifestyles of the "leisure class." The strand that ties these works together, across several generations of sociological research, is an interest in how the thinking of "good" people sometimes leads them to deviate. The answer is found in the willingness to neutralize, through the use of what we often call "rationalizations," the norms and values that inhibit both crime and delinquency.

Sutherland and Differential Association

Edwin Sutherland (1924) organized much of his work around the concept of "differential association." His focus was not only on associations among people, as the phrase implies, but also on the connections of ideas to behavior. Sutherland's basic thesis was that people behave criminally only when they *define* such behavior as acceptable. Thus, "the hypothesis of differential association is that criminal behavior is learned in association with those who define such behavior favorably and in isolation from those who define it unfavorably, and that a person in an appropriate situation engages in such criminal behavior if, and only if, the weight of the favorable definitions exceeds the weight of the unfavorable definitions" (Sutherland, 1949, p. 234).

Sutherland applied this hypothesis most provocatively in his *White Collar Crime*. As noted in Chapter 4, this study was based on a sample of seventy large corporations, and their encounters with civil and criminal agencies of social control. From these data emerged several dramatic conclusions:

- That corporate criminality is both common and persistent.
- That convictions generally do not result in a loss of status for offenders among their business associates.
- That there is widespread corporate contempt for government regulatory agencies and the personnel involved in their administration.
- That most white-collar business crime is organized crime, in the sense that the violations are often either internally organized corporate affairs or are extended through several corporations.

Theoretically, Sutherland was concerned with how white-collar criminals come to define their illegal business practices as acceptable. His conclusion was that a general ideology grows out of involvement in specific practices, and that this ideology in turn serves to justify the practices involved. The ideology itself is transmitted in a collection of common commercial clichés, including:

"We're not in business for our health."
"Business is business."
"It isn't how you get your money, but what you do with it that counts."
"It's the law of the jungle."

Sutherland (1949, p. 247) suggests that this justificatory ideology is diffused in an atmosphere that is isolated from competing points of view. Thus, "the persons who define business practices as undesirable and illegal are customarily called 'communists' or 'socialists' and their definitions carry little weight."

Sutherland, then, laid the broad outlines for neutralization theory with the suggestion that variable definitions determine whether social conduct will be considered lawful or unlawful. We will pursue this point further in a discussion of corporate homicide below. It remained, however, for Sutherland's student, Cressey, and later Sykes and Matza, to give more specific content to this perspective. Cressey's contribution was to make the causal structure of the theory emphatic.

Cressey and "Other People's Money"

Donald Cressey (1953, 1971) developed his theoretical perspective in a study of embezzlement, and then later expanded his explanation to cover a variety of "respectable crimes" (1965). The original research was guided by a demanding methodology, called "analytic induction" (Znaniecki, 1934; Lindesmith, 1947), in which the investigator is bound by the provision that the discovery of a *single* negative case requires rejection of the hypothesis under investigation. Using this approach, Cressey tested and rejected several hypotheses before settling on an explanation that survived interviews with 133 imprisoned embezzlers and a rereading of some 200 cases in Sutherland's files. The result was a four-part explanation of the violation of financial trust.

Cressey's explanation requires first that the subjects be in positions of financial trust; second, that they think of themselves as having nonshareable (usually financial) problems; third, that they be aware of techniques for violating the financial trust; and fourth, that they have access to a set of verbalizations that rationalizes their crimes. The two most important features of this explanation are the presence of the nonshareable problem and the rationalization of guilt.

The presence of the nonshareable problem in Cressey's theory reflects the assumption that deviants and conformists alike share the basic values of the surrounding society, and therefore that some kind of problem is necessary to stimulate the violation of these values. Thus, Cressey's embezzlers are assumed to be moral people who accept in good faith the position of trust that they occupy. A nonshareable financial problem is required to initiate their decline. This problem is assumed to be so serious that it cannot be shared, discussed, or otherwise resolved with the help of others.

However, the nonshareable problem *alone* is not enough to bring embezzlement. Driven to *thoughts* of trust violation, the potential embezzler is subject to the *guilt* produced in the conflict between societal values and personal needs.

Verbalizations are the key to the neutralization of this guilt, and they are similar in form to those found by Sutherland (Cressey, 1971, chap. 4).

"Some of our most respectable citizens got their start in life by using other people's money temporarily."

"All people steal when they get in a tight spot."

"My intent is only to use this money temporarily, so I am 'borrowing,' not 'stealing.' "

"I have been trying to live an honest life but I have had nothing but troubles, so 'to hell with it!' "

We will argue in later sections that the nonshareable problem and verbalization components of Cressey's theory are subject to challenge, using the very methodology of "negative cases" that he suggests. However, for the moment, we will simply note that Cressey (1965, p. 15) believes the verbalization component of his theory to have a more general application: "The generalization I have developed here was made to fit only one crime—embezzling. But I suspect that the verbalization section of the generalization will fit other types of respectable crime as well." Sykes and Matza expand on this observation by suggesting that there may be a further link between the "respectable" acts of the leisure class and the more commonplace acts of delinquents.

Sykes, Matza, and the Techniques of Neutralization

Although many theories of deviance assume that the deviant, particularly the lower-class delinquent, is a markedly different type of person from "the rest of us," Sykes and Matza (1957, 1961) suggest that the similarities actually outnumber the differences. Their argument is based in part on the observations that delinquents usually exhibit guilt or shame when they violate the law, that they frequently accord approval to certain conforming figures, and that they often distinguish between appropriate and inappropriate targets for deviance. The delinquent, say Sykes and Matza (1957, p. 667), is an "apologetic failure" who drifts into a deviant lifestyle through a subtle process of justification: "We call these justifications of deviant behavior techniques of neutralization; and we believe these techniques make up a crucial component of Sutherland's 'definitions favorable to the violation of law.' "

Sykes and Matza suggest that there are five techniques of neutralization:

Denial of responsibility. Here delinquents picture themselves as the helpless agents of social forces (e.g., unloving parents, bad companions, or a slum neighborhood). Thus the lament of the delinquent to Officer Krupke in *West Side Story*, "I'm not a delinquent, I'm misunderstood, I'm psychologically disturbed."

Denial of injury. Here delinquents argue that their behavior does not really cause any great harm. Thus vandalism is seen as "mischief," auto theft as "borrowing," and gang fighting as a "private quarrel."

Denial of the victim. Here delinquents conceive of themselves as avengers, while victims are transformed into wrongdoers. For example, the delinquents might describe themselves as "Robin Hoods," stealing from the rich to give to the poor.

Condemnation of the condemners. Here delinquents allege that their captors are either hypocrites, deviants in disguise, or impelled by personal spite. The effect of this approach is to "change the subject" of concern, placing the focus instead on the alleged misdeeds of others.

Appeal to higher loyalties. Here delinquents see themselves as caught between the demands of society, its laws, and the needs of smaller groups (siblings, the gang, or the friendship clique). The appeal is to "friends and family first."

It can be noted that all of the above neutralizations have some support in society at large. Beyond this, Sykes and Matza (1961, p. 717) suggest that "the delinquent has picked up and emphasized one part of the dominant value system, namely, the subterranean values that coexist with other, publicly proclaimed values possessing a more respectable air." These subterranean, or latent, values include a search for adventure, excitement, and thrills, and are said to exist side by side with such conformity-producing values as security, routinization, and stability. Further, Sykes and Matza cite Arthur Davis (1944) and Thorsten Veblen (1967) in arguing that delinquents conform to society, rather than deviate from it, when they add the desire for "big money" to their value system. Summarizing, then, subterranean values make delinquency desirable, while the techniques of neutralization allow this desire to take direction.

Some Critical Comments on Neutralization Theory

Where Cressey postulates a nonshareable problem as the stimulating factor in embezzlement, Sykes and Matza suggest a simple attraction to the "good life" as the source of delinquency. It can be observed, however, that if the attraction is "big enough," then the need for neutralization might seem superfluous. Support for this view is available in the Schwendingers'

(1967) finding that delinquents, when offered the opportunity to rationalize projected deviant behaviors, seldom do so. Instead, delinquents observed in this study assessed their situations tactically, comparing the pains versus gains of contemplated acts (cf. Hirschi, 1969). A major criticism of neutralization theory, then, is that it may underestimate the pleasures of a deviant lifestyle and at the same time overestimate the guilt experienced by those who choose to pursue such pleasures. This last point can be clarified by considering further the crime of embezzlement.

Recall that Cressey (1971, p. 16) developed his theory of embezzlement with the proviso that "the discovery by the investigator or any other investigator of a single negative case disproves the explanation and requires a re-formulation." Operating under this proviso, Gwynn Nettler (1974) interviewed six Canadian embezzlers convicted during the past decade of stealing from a low of $60,000 to more than $300,000. Included among the six were two male attorneys, one female bookkeeper, one female bank cashier, one male social worker, and one male investment counselor. Only *one* of the six cases conformed to Cressey's requirement that a nonshareable problem be the stimulant to theft.

In contrast, Nettler (ibid., p. 75) suggests that the remaining five cases "are more clearly described as individuals who wanted things they could not afford and who were presented with (or who invented) ways of taking other people's money." In all of these cases there was *desire*—something one could do with the money, and in each of the cases there was *opportunity*—a way to take the money with little apparent risk. In fact, Nettler (ibid.) suggests that in two of the cases the opportunities were so open, for so long, that it would have required strong defenses or weak desires to resist the temptations offered.

> For example, a social worker in charge of a welfare.agency resisted for seven years stealing the inadequately guarded funds entrusted him. Only after these years of handling easy money did he succumb to the pleasures of acquiring some $25,000 annually in "welfare payments" made to non-existent clients. These benefits accrued for eight years before his arrest. The thefts were *not* engaged to meet a secret financial difficulty. They did, of course, *produce* an unshareable financial embarrassment. In this case, money was stolen because it was, like Everest, there.

Most individuals probably possess *neither* strong defenses *nor* weak desires, and in attractive circumstances neutralizations therefore may be as likely to occur *after* the fact as before the act. In other words, neutralizations, verbalizations, or rationalizations may *justify* as well as cause acts of deviance (cf. Hackler, 1971, p. 72). Still neutralizations can play a very important role, particularly in the area of white-collar crime. Neutralizations of white-collar indiscretions, if widely enough accepted, can prevent definition of the behaviors involved as criminal, not only by the actors involved, but also by *re*actors. As we will note next, this is precisely the issue involved in the definition of corporate homicide.

AN EXAMPLE: CORPORATE HOMICIDE AND THE FORD MOTOR COMPANY   An interesting illustration of how important definitions of crime and deviance can be is found in the prosecution, albeit unsuccessful, of the Ford Motor Company for reckless homicide resulting from design and marketing decisions made about its subcompact car, the Pinto. Swigert and Farrell (1980–1981) have charted the process by which notions of corporate homicide have gained legal recognition, with particular reference to the Ford Pinto case. They note that until recently, the dominant precedent, first established in the 1909 case of *People v. Rochester Railway and Light Company,* has been that corporations are incapable of forming the criminal intent that is necessary to constitute a provable crime like homicide against a person. Also, in many state and federal statutes, homicide is defined as the criminal slaying of "another human being," with "another" referring to the same class of being as the victim. These precedents and statutes together have acted to diminish the plausibility of the idea that corporations can, in a criminal sense, kill people. Instead, corporate misbehavior has been viewed as entailing a diffuse, impersonal kind of cost to society that should be understood in economic (i.e., civil) rather than moral (i.e., criminal) terms. This kind of thinking, it can be noted, allows corporate decision-makers to disassociate their actions from their harmful consequences for individuals; in other words, to *neutralize* potential feelings of guilt. In more practical terms, the difference amounts to that between civil claims of unsafe-product liability and criminal charges of homicide.

However, the indictment of the Ford Motor Company and the trial that followed constituted official recognition of a new public harm—homicide by a corporation. Columnists Jack Anderson and Les Whitten (cited in Swigert and Farrell, 1980–1981, p. 170) brought the issue into full public view when, on December 30, 1976, they charged that:

> Buried in secret files of the Ford Motor Company lies evidence that big auto makers have put profits ahead of lives. Their lack of concern has caused thousands of people to die or be horribly disfigured in fiery car crashes. Undisclosed Ford tests have demonstrated that the big auto makers could have made safer automobiles by spending a few dollars more on each car.

Swigert and Farrell argue that this kind of press attention was a part of a reconceptualization in the public mind of the harm that can result from corporate acts. As these harms were *personalized* in press accounts, they argue, charges of criminal homicide became more plausible.

In the beginning, Swigert and Farrell note, more attention was given in news stories to the Pinto's mechanical defect, its faulty fuel-tank design, than to the issue of personal harm; furthermore, the two issues were kept separate. For example, in the Anderson-Whitten column quoted above, a harm-oriented statement, "lack of concern [of the big automakers] has caused thousands of people to die or be horribly disfigured in fiery car crashes," was set apart from the defect-oriented comments that "in most American-made cars, the fuel tanks are located behind the rear axle. In this exposed position, a high-speed rear-end collision can cause the tank to explode, turning the car into a giant torch." Over time, however, more attention was given to the personalization of harm, and the mechanical defect and personal harm issues increasingly were fused. On February 8, 1978, for example, the *Washington Post* (cited in Swigert and Farrell, 1980–1981, pp. 173–174) reported that punitive damages were awarded to a "teen-ager who suffered severe burns over 95 percent of his body when the gas tank of a 1972 Pinto exploded." As the two issues were combined, mechanical defect ceased to compete with personal harm as an appropriate definition of the problem. "This public recognition of personal harm," Swigert and Farrell (ibid., p. 180) suggest, "was ultimately reflected in the grand jury decision that the Pinto-related deaths of three Indiana teenagers were like homicide."

However, while the grand jury and the state of Indiana saw grounds to indict, the trial jury, after listening to ten weeks of testimony and deliberating three days, returned a verdict of not guilty. The question that remains, then, is whether it will continue to be possible for large corporations to neutralize their guilt in the causation of individual harms, even deaths, as civil liabilities (i.e., as a cost and risk of doing business) or whether a new attitude toward corporate activities might prevail. Swigert and Farrell (ibid., p. 177) cite several court cases that suggest the latter and quote the president of the National District Attorneys' Association as predicting that "a psychological barrier has been broken, and the big corporations are now vulnerable." Time will tell.

CONTROL THEORY

The last group of theories we will consider in this chapter, the control theories of crime and delinquency, have their roots in social disorganization theory. Much about them may therefore seem familiar. However, there is at least one feature of the control theories that renders them unique. Sociological theories of crime and deviance typically assume that people are "good" unless they are driven "bad"—either by social injustice or by some other problem beyond their control. In contrast, control theory takes a more neutral view of the human condition, assuming that most people have an equal propensity for both "bad" and "good." In this view, people become "good" as society makes them so. "Good" and "bad" must be placed in quotation marks here because they have little or no intrinsic meaning outside of the society that defines them. That society defines these qualities through its norms and values; that these norms and values are widely (although not thoroughly or enthusiastically) shared; and that every society attempts to impose its norms and values on its members are the key assumptions of control theory. The interest of the control theorist, then, is in that which restrains us. Instead of asking of the deviant, "Why do you do it?," the control theorist wonders, "Why don't we all do it?" Agreeing that "vice is nice," one control theorist, Travis Hirschi (1969, p. 34), answers, "We would if we dared."

Traditionally, control theory sees constraints as operating inside and outside the individual. Thus, Walter Reckless (1961, pp. 44–45) offers a broad outline of the concerns of control theory by focusing on "inner containment" and "outer containment." On the one hand, "Inner containment consists mainly of self components, such as self-control, [and] good self-concept," while "outer containment represents the structural buffer in the person's immediate social world which is able to hold him within bounds." Inner containment is seen as resulting primarily from the success of the family at internalizing the "good values of society" in the minds of its offspring; when the family fails, control theorists are interested also in the role of the community, the police, and other formal agencies of outer containment.

In large part, control theory tends to regard deviance as the result of "bad" (said politely, "inadequate") socialization into "good" (said sociologically, "conforming") values. Parsons (1951, p. 320) says it this way: "The relevance of tendencies to deviance, and the corresponding relevance of mechanisms of social control, goes back to the . . . socialization process and continues throughout the life cycle." More simply stated, the problem is that of making people believe (whether through childhood socialization or adult resocialization) that they *want* what society defines as the "good life." This shared desire is the essence of what control theorists call the "social bond." According to control theory, when the social bond is weak or broken, deviant behavior is likely to follow.

Hirschi and the Elements of the Social Bond

If it is the social bond that keeps people from deviating, then we will need to know what it is that constitutes this bond, and how the absence of its binding character is associated with deviance. Travis Hirschi (1969) suggests that there are four elements of the social bond: (1) attachment, (2) commitment, (3) involvement, and (4) belief. In turn, we will consider briefly each of these elements.

The importance of *attachment* to others is that it arouses in us a sensitivity to their wishes and expectations. To be attached to siblings, parents, teachers, or anyone else is to be concerned about their feelings. Thus, although we "always hurt the ones we love," we usually do so unintentionally. More commonly, we seek to protect our loved ones from the type of hurt, loss, and embarrassment that deviant behavior can bring. It is this type of attachment that can make a person feel "tied down" or "locked in;" that the "swinging single" seeks to avoid by refusing to "get involved;" and that the transient antihero of the movie *Five Easy Pieces* calls the "auspicious beginning," and desperately leaves behind. But for most of us, most of the time, the wishes and expectations of others seem to add a meaning to our lives. As the fearful 40-year-old of the film *Middle-Aged Crazy* finally concludes from the perspective of midlife, "no strings, no people." An act of deviance is an act against the wishes and expectations of such people. Conversely, to be unattached is to be unaffected by constraints. In other words, *de*tachment provides the freedom to deviate.

Commitment refers to the investment of time and energy toward achieving a goal like getting an education, building a business, paying off a mortgage, or building a reputation. Society is structured so that many, but not all, of us develop such commitments. As a part of our normal social life, most of us acquire goods, reputations, and prospects; in other words, a way of living that we do not want to risk losing. Hirschi refers to these accumulations as society's "insurance policy" against the violation of its rules. To deviate is to risk losing these accumulations, and control theory assumes that it is this commitment (or "stake in conformity," as we will call it later) that keeps most of us "honest." In other words, it is not so much that most of us wish to be honest, but that we fear the costs of being dishonest. Alternatively, the problems of deviance involve those who feel they really have "nothing to lose."

To be *involved* is to be busy. Too busy, hopefully, to deviate. The thinking behind this proposition is as old as the homily that "idle hands are the devil's workshop," and as perennial as the desire to *do* something. The assumption is simply that if a person is busy doing *conventional* things, then there wlll be little time or opportunity to deviate. The catch, of course, is that the subject of involvement must be conventional, or, in other words, conforming.

Belief in society's values is the last of the elements of the social bond. Hirschi stresses that deviance is not caused by beliefs that *require* such behavior; rather deviance is made possible by the *absence* of beliefs that forbid deviance. Said differently, it is not that the deviant holds different values from the rest of us, but rather that he or she holds the dominant values in reduced amount. The assumption is that persons unconstrained by society's values feel no moral obligation to conform to its norms. The concluding hypthesis is that the less people believe they should obey the rules, the more likely they are to deviate from them.

According to control theory, the less committed, attached, involved, and believing individuals are, the less is their bond to society. The question, then, is how this bond is created. To this the control theorist has as many answers as there are people and processes that touch the individual. Two answers, however, receive particular attention: the first involves relationships within the family; the second the personal *stake* an individual develops in conforming to the rules of society. After considering these answers, we will then consider what may happen when the social bond is *not* created.

Nye and Family Relationships

To focus on the family as a causal factor in criminal behavior is to run the risk of seeming old-fashioned (cf. Hirschi, 1973). Wilkinson (1974) notes that family breakdown was first emphasized as a causal factor at the turn of the century, and was accepted as an important variable until about 1930. In Chapter 3 we saw the significance of this concern about the family in the generation of juvenile delinquency legislation. The architects of this legislation often seemed to be acting on the basis of social disorganization and control theories. However, from about 1930 to about 1950, family breakdown was rejected as a causal factor, and although some signs of renewed interest emerged in the 1950s, to date, concern with the family remains limited. In explanation, Wilkinson suggests that in the early 1900s the family was seen as important because of its near-exclusive control over the development of children, and because of a very negative attitude toward divorce. However, in the 1930s the family's protective, religious, recreational, and educational functions began to shift dramatically to other institutions. At the same time, attitudes toward divorce were softening. Of course none of this meant that the family was now of *no* importance, but Wilkinson suggests that we began to think and act more and more as if this were the case. Wilkinson (1974, p. 735) summarizes our situation this way: ". . . the decline in concern for the . . . home . . . came about not because scientific evidence provided conclusive grounds for rejecting it, but because cultural and ideological factors favoring its acceptance early in this century became less important." The research of F. Ivan Nye (1958) and the control theorists serves to correct this trend.

Nye suggests that the family contributes to the creation of the social bond in four ways: through the provision of (1) internalized controls, (2) indirect controls, (3) direct controls, and (4) need satisfaction. *Internalized controls* are assumed to operate through the medium of the child's conscience. Such controls consist primarily of internalized norms and values, whose binding power is based in feelings of anxiety and guilt, conditioned through parental rewards and punishments (this conditioning process is discussed further below). *Indirect controls* consist primarliy of the desire not to hurt or embarrass one's family by *getting caught* acting against their wishes or expectations. This sort of control, then, depends on affection for, or an attachment to, the family. *Direct controls*, on the other hand, depend more on restrictions and punishments. Examples here consist of rules about time spent away from home, choice of friends, and types of activities. Finally, the family's role in *need satisfaction* eventually involves its ability to prepare the child for "success": at school, with peers, and often in finding work. That some families are better able to do all these things is proposed as an influential factor in ensuring conformity, and avoiding crime and delinquency.

It is interesting to note that Nye and others (Gibbons and Griswold, 1957; Toby, 1957a) find the family more influential in preventing delinquency with girls than boys. This is explained in terms of the larger role assigned to parents in our society in restricting the activities of girls. Also interesting is the finding of a U-shaped relationship between the strictness of direct controls and delinquency. In other words, as Durkheim would have suggested, delinquent behavior is at a minimum where a *moderate* amount of direct control is exercised. The explanation is that when direct controls become too pervasive, it becomes impossible for adolescents to function as normal members of their peer group. Finally, Nye (1958, p. 51) reports that it is not so much whether a home is *legally* broken, but the happiness of the home, that influences the prospects of deviant behavior. Thus, "the *happiness* of the marriage was found to be much more closely related to delinquent behavior in children than whether the marriage was an original marriage or a remarriage or one in which the child was living with one parent only."

Toby and the Stake in Conformity

Although it is the family that is in large part responsible for the preparation of its offspring, it is society itself that must receive the final product. Thus, one measure of a "just" society is that it provides meaningful places for its members. For those who find a meaningful place in society, and for those who believe in the promise of such a place, there is a "stake in conformity." The problem, of course, is that individuals vary in the stake they feel in conformity. This problem begins in the family, gains significance in the school, and ends in the workplace.

In North America, education and occupation are closely associated, and in turn highly correlated with class position and ethnic background. Thus Jackson Toby (1957*b*, p. 516) notes that an upper-class white Anglo-Saxon Protestant schoolchild is heavily favored to have a high stake in conformity.

> He comes from a "good" family. He lives in a "respectable" neighborhood. His teachers like him; he gets good marks and he moves easily from grade to grade. These social victories provide a reasonable basis for anticipating future achievements. He expects to complete college and take up a business or professional career. If he applied his energies to burglary instead of to homework, he would risk not only the ego-flattering rewards currently available but his future prospects as well.

But the development of a stake in conformity is not *entirely* class-based. Some immigrant groups, most notably Jews and Asians, have assumed an immediate stake in conformity that in spite of prejudice and discrimination moved them from poverty to affluence in a single generation (Porter, 1965). Toby (1957*a*) notes that in the case of the Jews, their social assent was grounded in generations of respect for religious learning. In the new world, this faith was transferred to the educational system, yielding a commitment to conformity that paid off in occupational advancement. Alternatively, Porter (1965, p. 172) suggests that "those who are reared in a milieu indifferent to education are not likely to acquire a high evalution of it." It is these instances that challenge a society to demonstrate that the pursuit of education and other kinds of conforming behavior can be rewarding. Without this kind of faith in conformity, there can be no perceived stake in conformity, and the probability of deviation increases.

Akers's Social Learning Theory

Thus far, the control theories we have considered have offered good reasons why crime and deviance *may* occur; but why *does* it, and why does it assume specific forms? This question and an answer to it are posed by Ronald Akers (1977, p. 66) when he notes that "the person whose ties with conformity have been broken may remain just a candidate for deviance; whether he becomes deviant depends on further social or other rewards." Akers's answer (see also Burgess and Akers, 1966; Eysenck, 1964; Trasler, 1962) derives from his social learning theory of crime and deviance, which in turn is linked to Sutherland's differential association theory of crime. However, as Akers (1977, p. 65) notes, "control theory is the theory that is most compatible with social learning."

The most important principle of social learning theory is that deviant behavior results from a conditioning process in which rewards and punishments shape the behaviors they follow. The four ways in which rewards and punishments shape deviant and conforming behaviors are indicated in Table 5-1. Thus specific types of deviant behavior are strengthened through reward ("positive reinforcement") and avoidance of punishment ("negative reinforcement") or weakened (punished) by adversive stimuli ("positive punishment") and lack of reward ("negative punishment"). The concept of "differential reinforcement" is used to explain the specific process by which deviant behavior becomes dominant over conforming behavior in any particular situation. The idea is that given two alternative acts, both of which produce and are reinforced by the same or similar consequences, the one with the higher probability of being maintained will be the one that is reinforced most frequently and in the greatest amount. In addition, Akers notes that an individual learns to evaluate behaviors as good or bad, and these definitions themselves can be reinforced and themselves become reinforcers. A result is that the more a person defines his or her behavior as a positive good or at least justified, the more likely he or she is to engage in it. Akers (1977, p. 58) therefore concludes that "a person will participate in deviant activity . . . to the extent that it has been differentially reinforced over conforming behavior and defined as more desirable than, or at least as justified as, conforming alternatives."

Akers's version of social learning theory is particularly interesting in its accounts of how individuals move from conforming to criminal and noncriminal patterns of deviant behavior. These accounts represent a blending of the themes of control theory and the principles of social learning theory. For example, it is noted that in groups with prescriptive

TABLE 5-1

FOUR WAYS IN WHICH REWARDS AND PUNISHMENTS INFLUENCE BEHAVIOR ACCORDING TO SOCIAL LEARNING THEORY

Stimulus	Behavior increases—reinforcement	Behavior decreases—punishment
+	Positive reinforcement (reward received)	Positive punishment (punisher received)
−	Negative reinforcement (punisher removed or avoided)	Negative punishment (reward removed or lost)

Source: Akers, 1977, p. 46

norms (norms that allow some drinking) most people do drink moderately. In such groups, an alcoholic's excessive drinking may not confront the group's controls or norms until it is so far out of hand that he or she is no longer welcome in the group. A break at this point from the more moderate group opens the way for a move to other groups which tolerate and *reward* heavier drinking. According to the social learning perspective, then, it is not simply the absence of controls, but also the availability of alternative rewards, that explains criminal and deviant behavior.

Some Critical Comments on Control Theory

Many of the hypotheses of control theory have been well supported by research (Hirschi, 1969; Nye, 1958; Hindelang, 1973; Jensen, 1969; Linden and Hackler, 1973; Linden, 1976; Dinitz, Scarpitti, and Reckless, 1962; Reiss, 1951; Hagan and Simpson, 1977). A recent and extensive test of the theory (Wiatrowski, Griswold, and Roberts, 1981) demonstrates that the school as well as the family is extremely important in developing the bond to society, arguing (p. 539) that "the emergence of schools as primary socializing institutions reflects the division of labor in a complex society, where specialized social institutions perform functions of education, socialization, and preparation for adult social roles which previously occurred within the family." A slightly revised model of social control theory emerges from this research in which social class position and ability are included because of their relationship to elements of the social bond, which in turn affect involvement in delinquency. This revised model of a control theory of delinquency is pictured in Figure 5-1.

The body of evidence that has accumulated in support of a control theory of crime and delinquency is impressive. Rather than question these

Figure 5-1 A revised model of the Control Theory of Delinquency. (*Source: Wiatrowski et al., 1981:537*)

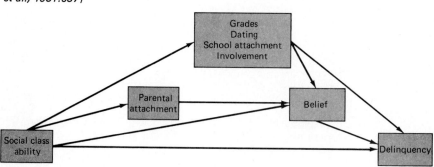

findings, or minimize their significance, our central complaint will be that the implications of control theory have not been carried through to their logical conclusions. Theoretical discussion and research in the control tradition have focused on lower- and middle-class adolescents, as in the study just discussed. Yet, it can be argued that the prevalence of social controls varies in unexplored ways with social class. In particular, we are concerned with the widespread freedom to deviate that exists among established economic and political elites (see Hagan et al., 1984). Part of the problem at this level of society is that upperworld "indiscretions" are not necessarily defined as disreputable, much less criminal, further freeing individuals to pursue their interests without moral or legal constraint. We will develop this point further by considering neutralization and control explanations of the most dramatic set of upperworld crimes of our time: "Watergate." Our argument is that expanding the attention of control theory to upperworld crime and deviance will serve to correct a limitation in its previous application.

> **AN EXAMPLE: "WATERGATE"**   The American experience called "Watergate" is a chronology of events that spanned the period from June 12, 1972, to August 8, 1974. The outline of these events will be familiar to most readers, beginning with the unsuccessful break-in at the Democratic National Committee headquarters in Washington's Watergate complex, and ending with Richard Nixon's resignation as President of the United States. The most comprehensive view of executive activity during the course of these events is provided in the *Presidential Transcripts* (1974), the abridged 1,200-page record of selected White House conversations. We will use these transcripts to consider neutralization and control explanations of the Watergate crimes. Of course, a problem in using these materials is that they are known to be incomplete. However, we will argue that in spite of the self-serving potential of the transcripts, they actually provide support for an explanation of Watergate that is far from flattering (Hagan, 1975a).
>
> At least five rationalizations, or neutralizations, of the Watergate cover-up were offered in the course of Nixon's conversations. They include: (1) the protection of national security: ". . . the whole thing was national security" (*Presidential Transcripts,* p. 125); (2) the protection of the Presidency: ". . . it isn't the man, it's the office" (ibid., p. 267); (3) support of the defendants: ". . . this was not an obstruction of justice, we were simply trying to help these defendants" (ibid., p. 339); (4) loyalty: "Well, the point is, whatever we say about Harry Truman, etc., while it hurt him, a lot of people admired the old bastard for standing by people" (ibid., p. 359); and (5) the country's future: "If there's one thing you have got to do, you have

got to maintain the Presidency out of this. I have got things to do for this country" (ibid., p. 673).

The most important of these rationalizations, judging from the attention it received from the participants, was the assertion that administration agents were simply trying to "help" defendants by offering them cash payments. However, discussions relating to the support rationalization reveal that its importance was as an excuse, or justification, rather than as a cause for the payments being made. For example, in the March 21, 1973, conversation in which the decision was made to pay Howard Hunt "hush money" (ibid., p. 133), the discussion was entirely tactical.

PRESIDENT: That's why for your immediate things you have no choice but to come up with the $120,000, or whatever it is. Right?

DEAN: That's right.

PRESIDENT: Would you agree that that's the prime thing, that you damn well better get that done?

DEAN: Obviously he ought to be given some signal anyway.

PRESIDENT: (Expletive deleted), get it.

Several weeks later, on April 14, the support rationalization appears for the first time, with little effort to deny its justificatory character. Here the former President reports: "Support, well, I heard something about that at a much later time" (ibid., p. 242). Later in the same conversation, (ibid., p. 272) the ad hoc character of the rationalization becomes even more obvious.

HALDEMAN: What Dean did, he did with all conscience in terms . . . [of] the higher good.

PRESIDENT: Dean, you've got to have a talk with Dean. I feel that I should not talk to him.

EHRLICHMAN: I have talked to him.

PRESIDENT: What's he say about motive. He says it was a hush-up?

EHRLICHMAN: . . . He says he knew, he had to know that people were trying to bring that result about.

Similar discussions surround the remaining neutralizations. In each case, the rationalization is introduced in a justificatory context. The concerns are tactical: the avoidance of legal prosecution, political embarrassment, and moral blame. These concerns relate more to the consequences than to the causes of upperworld crime. However, as we noted earlier in our discussion of corporate homicide, the consequences can be important.

On the other hand, a control theory of upperworld crime may offer more in the way of a causal explanation of upperworld crime. Stated generally, from the perspective of control theory, the problem is to explain why all upperworld citizens are not criminals, or, perhaps viewed more candidly, why some of us are less criminal than others. Answers to the control theorist's question comes from within and without. Unfortunately, the first line of defense, inner constraints, is problematic in a society whose conception of upperworld morality is badly defined. Opinion data consistently indicate that the public regards white-collar crime as much less serious than other kinds of crime (Rossi, et al., 1974; Thomas, 1976). In lieu of a public morality that harshly condemns upperworld crime, the occurrence of such behaviors will depend largely on the risks and rewards (in other words, the perceived outer constraints) associated with violating public and financial trust. Watergate provides the example.

The actors involved in Watergate proved unconstrained by either moral ties or by a set of operating principles that were themselves unclear. A careful reading of the *Presidential Transcripts* reveal few references to, or considerations of, societal values. Occasional mention is made of the Nixon administration's "commitment" to "law and order"; however, the references are in passing (see p. 362), and obviously not a matter of extended consideration. Repeatedly, the rights and obligations of the executive branch (e.g., the limits of "executive privilege," the meaning of "national security," and the scope of "high crimes and misdemeanors") were debated in terms of a vague Constitution and undecided public opinion. Similarly, the situational controls operative at the time of the initial Watergate offenses were inadequate. White House aides were able to manipulate funds and personnel for criminal political purposes with little expectation of detection. One reason why there was so little expectation of detection, of course, was that the criminals in this case were people who controlled the institutions of legal control (who could have been better positioned to deviate than those who controlled the FBI, the Justice Department, etc.?). Furthermore, once "caught," punishment became problematic in an atmosphere confused by promiscuous discussions of pardons. The uncertainties surrounding these events emphasize, then, the porous nature of the controls operative in one upperworld setting.

The final irony of Watergate is that the people involved presumably had a high stake in conformity. The final costs of exposure outweighed any benefits the Watergate activities could ever have produced. Hirschi (1969, p. 21) notes, however, that if a person can calculate the costs of a line of action, he or she is also capable of *mis*calculation. Clearly, Richard Nixon miscalculated these costs over and over again.

If there is a message to the policy-minded in the Watergate experience and a control theory of upperworld crime, it is that checks and balances on power are crucial. Upperworld vocations, particularly politics and business, often carry with them a freedom to deviate unparalleled in the underworld. As control theory reminds us, unchecked freedom is a criminogenic condition.

SUMMARY AND DISCUSSION

The theories of undercontrol begin with the assumption that we are generally agreed about what is "good" and "bad" in our society. In other words, that we are in consensus about our norms and values. The question asked, then, is why some people violate laws that so many of us support. The undercontrol theories are agreed that the problem is one of regulation, or more specifically, the absence or failure of it. Durkheim anticipated this theoretical tradition with his concept of anomie, which refers to the absence of regulation, or normlessness. Each of the theories of under-control tries to account for problems of regulation in a somewhat different way.

• *Social disorganization theory* focuses on the assumed breakdown in processes that regulate lawbreaking behavior caused by the rapid growth of American cities.

• *Neutralization theory* argues that although we share norms and values in common, some of us develop ways of rationalizing, or neutralizing, the guilt that comes with their violation.

• *Control theory* argues that some of us are bound less tightly than others to society's norms and values, and that those whose ties are weakest deviate most.

We have noted weaknesses in each of these theories. A serious problem with social disorganization theory is its tendency to include crime and delinquency among other indicators of social disorganization. The problem with this is that it renders the theory circular; a description more than an explanation. However, as this perspective is moved toward the isolation of poverty, heterogeneity, and mobility as specified causes of social disorgani-zation, with crime and delinquency as its consequences, then this perspec-tive takes on more of the character of a theory. Furthermore, as this approach draws our attention to the ways in which slum and ghetto communities are distinctively ordered, it can be particularly useful.

In response to neutralization theory, we suggested that verbalizations reducing feelings of guilt may more frequently follow than precede deviant activities. In other words, neutralizations may be justifications rather than causes of criminal behavior. This does not deny, however, that rationaliza-tions help to perpetuate such behaviors.

Finally, we suggested that the implications of control theory need to be expanded into the upper regions of the class structure. The absence of decided public opinion about the seriousness of upperworld deviance, and the weakness of rules, regulations, and checks and balances on the powers and privileges of upperworld citizens, leaves members of the upperworld seductively free to deviate. To ignore this is to deny a fundamental insight of control theory.

One final way of consolidating our understanding of the theories of undercontrol is to indicate how this group of theories might collectively explain the relationship reported in Chapter 4 between social class and criminal and delinquent behavior. We noted in Chapter 4 that this relationship has been much debated and sometimes exaggerated, but that it nonetheless persists and requires explanation. Historically, the social disorganization version of undercontrol theory located the source of this relationship in the rapid growth of American cities, arguing that the circumstances of city life (poverty, heterogeneity, and mobility) were breaking down normal processes of social control. Later, control theorists noted that poverty has the effect of reducing the commitment of disadvantaged groups to conformity. The point made is that as class-linked differences in life chances are experienced, first in school and later in work, individuals' conceptions of their stakes in conformity diminish. The assumed result is a class-specific feeling of having little to lose, and much to gain, by exploring criminal and delinquent success routes. In addition, economic hardships are assumed themselves to produce a deterioration in (or at least a reordering of) family, school, and community life that weakens the control mechanisms restricting involvement in crime and delinquency. Finally, the social learning version of undercontrol theory asserts that crime and delinquency can be rewarding, particularly to those in need, and the neutralization version of undercontrol theory notes that verbalizations can play a role in perpetuating, if not actually in causing, these behaviors.

It must be emphasized that the consensually based theories of undercontrol we have reviewed represent only one possible way of understanding the class-crime relationship. The following two chapters offer alternative ways of understanding this relationship. We turn next, then, to the theories of culture, status, and opportunity.

UNDERSTANDING CRIME II: THEORIES OF CULTURE, STATUS, AND OPPORTUNITY

6

THE ISSUE: WHY DO SOME PEOPLE CHALLENGE THE STANDARDS OF THE SOCIETY IN WHICH THEY LIVE?

The theories discussed in the preceding chapter argue that people become criminal or delinquent because the bonds that constrain others do not constrain them. We noted that these theories were characterized by an assumption of consensus; an assumption that we all share values in common, with variation in *amount* rather than in *kind*. In contrast, the theories that we will consider in this chapter do not assume a weakness of values or constraints. Quite the contrary: the theories of this chapter begin to talk about differences in values and/or the means of their attainment that derive from variations in culture, status, and opportunity. These differences are seen as dividing people, pushing them to challenge the standards of the society that surrounds them. From these theoretical perspectives, then, people do not fall or drift into crime and delinquency, they are pushed. But how and by what? The three theories considered in this chapter offer three different answers.

• *Class culture* theories see crime and delinquency as the natural outgrowth of the traditions that accompany underclass life.

• *Status frustration* theories see crime and delinquency as a group response to societal expectations which the members of the group cannot fulfill and therefore choose to challenge.

• *Opportunity* theories see crime and delinquency as a product of a disparity between the goals that all of us share and the means that only some of us have for goal attainment.

What these theories have in common is that they all see forces as impelling individuals toward criminal and delinquent behavior. Before we turn to a more detailed examination of these theories and the forces they describe, we first must introduce the concept of a "subculture," a concept that is central to the theories we consider in this chapter.

The Several Meanings of Subculture

The term "subculture" is used in various ways by sociologists and anthropologists. An important distinction among these usages is noted by

Yinger (1960). He notes that a first use of the term "subculture" is simply to identify basic differences in norms and values between dominant and subordinate groups in society. The reference here, then, is to differences in values linked to hierarchically ordered groups in our society. The second usage adds something to the first: it adds a social-psychological sense of *frustration* that originates in and perpetuates the differences in norms and values. Yinger distinguishes this second usage with the term "contra-culture." However, both usages can be regarded as variations on the basic notion of a subculture. As we will see, all of the theories considered in this chapter make use of the concept of a subculture.

THE THEORIES OF CLASS CULTURE

Miller's Theory of Lower-Class Culture

The first theory of crime and delinquency we will consider in this chapter is offered by Walter Miller, who sees these activities (1958, p. 19) as a simple "by-product of . . . the lower class system." What is unique about this theory is that it sees the lower, or under, class as having its own cultural history. Indeed, Miller argues that "lower class culture is a distinctive tradition many centures old with an integrity of its own."

Miller goes on to argue that the enduring traditions of the lower class are built around six "focal concerns" (see Table 6-1). "Trouble" is the first of these concerns. Getting into and out of trouble are seen by Miller as major preoccupations of lower-class life. For lower-class men, Miller suggests that a preoccupation with trouble follows from fighting, drinking, and sexual adventures (or as R. P. Murphy succinctly describes it to the psychiatrist in *One Flew Over the Cuckoo's Nest,* "fucking and fighting").

To the concern with trouble is added a preoccupation with "toughness." The image here is of the "tough guy" of movies and television—hard, fearless, undemonstrative, and skilled in physical combat: Macho Man. It is the Clint Eastwood figure of the spaghetti westerns, the Charles Bronson antihero of urban tales of vengeance, the Tommy Lee Jones drifter of *Back Roads,* and Robert De Niro's *Raging Bull.*

Added to toughness, however, Miller suggests that there is a further concern with "smartness." This "smartness" involves the capacity to outsmart, "take," "con," or "hustle" others. The media model here is the card shark, the professional gambler, the pool hustler, the con artist, and the promoter. It is the ingenuity and humor that Burt Reynolds adds to *Smokey and the Bandit* and that Paul Newman gives to Butch Cassidy.

All the preceding qualities are combined, according to Miller, in the "search for excitement." Miller argues that this search has its origins in the extreme fluctuations that accompany the lower-class work cycle: fluctua-

TABLE 6-1
FOCAL CONCERNS OF LOWER CLASS CULTURE

Area	Perceived Alternatives (state, quality, condition)	
1. Trouble:	law-abiding behavior	law-violating behavior
2. Toughness:	physical prowess, skill; "masculinity"; fearlessness, bravery, daring	weakness, ineptitude; effeminacy; timidity, cowardice, caution
3. Smartness:	ability to outsmart, dupe, "con"; gaining money by "wits"; shrewdness, adroitness in repartee	gullibility, "con-ability"; gaining money by hard work; slowness, dull-wittedness, verbal maladroitness
4. Excitement:	thrill; risk, danger; change, activity	boredom; "deadness," safeness; sameness, passivity
5. Fate:	favored by fortune, being "lucky"	ill-omened, being "unlucky"
6. Autonomy:	freedom from external constraint; freedom from superordinate authority; independence	presence of external constraint; presence of strong authority; dependency, being "cared for"

tions between periods of exhausting and repetitive work and short weekend bursts of release, relief, and excitement. The concern is that the weekend search for "cheap thrills" leads commonly to "trouble" at the end of a "Saturday Night Special"—the cheap handguns too frequently used to resolve deadly disputes between friends and relatives.

Miller argues that a resignation to "fate" in lower-class culture leads to an acceptance of these fatal outcomes. The assumption here is that a man is not lucky at cards, horses, sex, or by extension in other areas of life, by plan or intent, but rather by chance. Good luck is not developed, it is dealt.

Finally, Miller asserts that lower-class adolescent males, for reasons we will suggest in a moment, have an ambivalent desire for "autonomy." One side of this desire is verbalized explicitly in such assertions as "No one's gonna push *me* around," in the pointed reminder that "you know where you can stick it," and in the poignant occupational refrain, "You can take your job and shove it." However, Miller (ibid., p. 13) suggests that such assertions may sometimes contain an implicit call for restraint. The argument is that, "since 'being controlled' is equated with 'being cared for,' attempts are frequently made to 'test' the severity or strictness of superordinate authority to see if it remains firm." Miller illustrates this argument by asserting that lower-class patients in mental hospitals will exercise considerable ingenuity to ensure continued commitment while persistently voicing the desire to leave, and that delinquent boys frequently will "run" from detention facilities in order to activate efforts to return them. These activities are described by Miller (ibid.) as reflecting "powerful dependency cravings," and, as we will see, these "cravings" are linked to the structure of lower-class families.

The focal concern with autonomy, along with the remaining focal concerns we have discussed, is presumed to have its basis in a type of "female-based household" disproportionately found in lower-class communities. However, the problem posed by this kind of family is not simply its weakness, as suggested in the preceding chapter, but rather its structure, in terms of the role models it provides, or more accurately, fails to provide. Miller (ibid., p. 6) estimates that about 15 percent of all North Americans make up the "hard-core" lower-class group, "defined primarily by its use of the 'female-based household' as the basic form of child-rearing." Miller is particularly concerned that males growing up in such families are deprived of appropriate role models.

It is here that group processes, emphasized in one way or another by all of the theories in this chapter, become important. It is in street-corner groups, according to Miller, that lower-class male adolescents resolve their sex-role problems. However, the individuals in these one-sex peer groups are resolving their uncertainties in the company of others facing similar sex-role difficulties. Miller submits, then, that it is not surprising that these subcultural groupings wind up emphasizing the themes of lower-class culture described above—toughness, smartness, and autonomy—that symbolize male adulthood around them. He concludes (ibid., p. 18) that simply "following . . . practices . . . of . . . lower-class culture automatically violates certain legal norms." That is, the historically rooted values of lower-class culture, particularly when exaggerated and acted out in the group context we have described, bring male adolescents into open conflict with the law. In later chapters, we will see that the group conflict theorists have linked a similar idea into a rather radical set of conclusions. However, Miller offers his conclusions without any critical comment of this kind.

Banfield and "The Unheavenly City"

An even more dismal view of lower-class culture is found in Edward Banfield's work on the plight of American cities. The pessimistic character of Banfield's perspective is signaled in his choice of an introductory quotation from Henry George to begin his discussion of crime in the city (Banfield, 1968, p. 158).

> . . . let the policeman's club be thrown down or wrested from him, and the foundations of the great deep are opened, and quicker than ever before chaos comes again. Strong as it may seem, our

civilization is evolving destructive forces. Not desert and forest, but city slums . . . are nursing the barbarians who may be to the new what Hun and Vandal were to the old.

Banfield's argument is that there are subcultural groups with varying likelihoods of crime that emerge in the city. Two factors are said to determine this "proneness" to crime: *propensity* and *incentive.* Propensity for crime is said to depend on the individual's class culture, personality, sex, and age, factors that are individually and collectively resistant to change. In other words, the propensity to crime is thought to be relatively constant. The second factor, incentive, is said to depend on situational factors, such as the number of police in an area and the availability and value of things for the taking. These situational factors are changeable, and therefore the incentive for crime is a variable. Together, propensity and incentive are said to determine an individual's proneness to crime, so that collectively "a city's *potential* for crime may be thought of as the average proneness of persons in various 'sex-age-culture-personality' groups times their number" (ibid., p. 159).

It is Banfield's discussion of propensity that is most important for our purposes, for it is the assumption of a constant propensity to crime that makes Banfield's theory subcultural. According to Banfield, five elements determine propensity: type of morality, ego strength, time horizon, taste for risk, and the willingness to inflict injury. Each of these elements involves the taking of value positions that are in conflict with the surrounding society.

For example, there are three types of morality, each referring to ways in which individuals distinguish between "right" and "wrong."

• *Preconventional morality* sees a "right" action to be one that serves one's purpose and that one can get away with; conversely, a "wrong" action is seen as one that brings failure or punishment.

• *Conventional morality* sees the "right" action as doing one's "duty" or doing what those in authority require.

• *Postconventional morality* sees the "right" action as one that is in accord with some universal (or very general) principle that is worthy of support.

The first and third of these moralities, of course, can conflict with the second, and it is the first that Banfield seems to see as creating a particularly high propensity for crime in the underclass.

The remaining elements of propensity also reflect value premises. "Ego strength" refers to the capacity for self-control; "time horizon" refers to an individual's consideration of the future; "taste for risk" refers to a person's preference for taking chances; and the "willingness to inflict injury" involves just that, the willingness of an individual to impose pain on others.

The five elements of propensity are seen by Banfield as combining to reinforce one another in various social roles. Thus males, adolescents, and persons of lower-class background are seen as most likely to adopt a "preconventional morality," to be low in "ego strength," to have a short "time horizon," an advanced "taste for risk," and a greater "willingness to inflict injury." The result (ibid., p. 165) is that "when male adolescence and lower-class culture meet in the same person, they will interact, reinforce each other and produce an extraordinarily high propensity towards crime." Furthermore, these patterns are predicted to be even more pronounced for groups than individuals. Like Miller, then, Banfield sees crime and delinquency as a normal group-linked response to the social context in which it emerges. In the end, Banfield is talking about a high subcultural propensity for crime that is located largely in the underclass and which places the affected groups in probable conflict with the prevailing societal values that surround them.

Wolfgang, Ferracuti, and the "Subculture of Violence"

The theories we have discussed to this point consider subcultural processes generally; however, this approach is also used by Wolfgang and Ferracuti (1967) to explain violent behavior more specifically. We consider Wolfgang and Ferracuti's work as a theory of class culture because its origin seems to date from Wolfgang's (1958) early research on homicide and the differences found within and between ethnic groups in rates of homicide in America. What Wolfgang found in his classic study of homicide in Philadelphia was that nonwhite males aged 20–24 had a rate of 54.6 homicides per 100,000 population, compared with only 3.8 for white males of the same ages. Beyond this, nonwhite *females* were found to have a higher homicide rate (10.2) than white males, as well as white females (0.6). These dramatic differences have endured through the years since Wolfgang's early study, and they are paralleled by pronounced patterns of violence in other parts of the world as well. For example, in Colombia *La Violencia* has claimed thousands of lives in a wave of violence that spans several decades. In Sardinia the *Vendetta Barbaricina* provides another bloody example of a long tradition characterized by deadly quarrels. And in El Salvador violence has become so commonplace as to stimulate the expression *la vida vale nada,* "life is worth nothing."

Wolfgang and Ferracuti (1967, p. 152) suggest in explanation of these cross-culturally located pockets of violence that "there should be a direct relationship between rates of homicide and the extent to which the subculture of violence represents a cluster of values around the theme of violence.'' These values include the importance attached to human life and the manner in which individuals interpret the cues of others as calling for violence in response. Where life is worth little, and where violence becomes a quick and definitive response to life's problems and frustrating circumstances, the subculture of violence thrives.

There are fascinating parallels between subcultural norms of violence and those that can exist throughout a culture during periods of war. In wartime, whole nations can become vicarious participants in acts of violence against a common enemy. Wolfgang and Ferracuti's point (1967, p. 156) is that subcultural environments can approximate the conditions of war. Thus, "Homicide . . . is often a situation not unlike that of confrontations in wartime combat, in which two individuals committed to the value of violence come together, and in which chance, prowess, or possession of a particular weapon dictates the identity of the slayer and the slain." The distinction between offender and victim becomes crucial, of course, as the subculture of violence must give way to the legal response of the surrounding culture whose values have been violated. However, Wolfgang and Ferracuti, like Miller and Banfield, do not emphasize in their analysis the role of the conflict between dominant and subordinate cultural groups. Rather, the focus is more one-sidedly on the subcultural side of the equation.

Some Critical Comments on Theories of Class Culture

A common criticism of the theories of class culture involves their tendency to *infer* values from the behaviors they seek to explain. The problem is that these theories often seem to be explaining behaviors by referring to the prevalence of the behaviors themselves. Wolfgang and Ferracuti note at one point that "some circularity of thought is obvious in the effort to specify the dependent variable (homicide), and also to infer the independent variable (the existence of a subculture of violence)." Nettler (1974, p. 152) makes the same point by noting that "it is as though one were to say that 'People are murderous because they live violently,' or 'People like to fight because they are hostile.' " It is not that such statements are false; rather, it is that they describe what we already know. These subcultural descriptions begin to be explanatory as they widen their descriptive net to include new and independent components of the phenomenon under study. To date, such efforts largely have involved the collection of survey data on attitudes and values, with results that are mixed.

Rossi et al. (1974) report in a study of the public ranking of the seriousness of crimes, discussed earlier in Chapter 2, that the subgroup least in agreement with their total sample consisted of black males with less than high school education. The main points of disagreement in the data centered around certain crimes against the person, particularly those in which the offender and victim are known to each other. For example, compared to the total sample, "beating up an acquaintance" was regarded much less seriously by poorly educated black males. Otherwise, however, Rossi et al., found considerable consensus.

Meanwhile, Ball-Rokeach (1973), in analyzing responses to the Rokeach Value Survey, found no important differences in the rankings of eighteen "terminal values" or eighteen "instrumental values" by men classified as having no, a "moderate," or a "high" degree of participation in violence at any time in their lives. Controls in this analysis for education and income, essential for the examination of a subculture which may be class-based, do not affect the findings. No control is included, however, for race.

But the best available data for a test of the subculture-of-violence hypothesis comes from a 1968 national survey supervised by Ball-Rokeach for the President's Commission on the Causes and Prevention of Violence. Respondents were asked about their general approval of the use of physical aggression in certain kinds of interpersonal interactions; those who gave general approval were then asked about four or five more specific situations. Erlanger's (1974) analysis of these data reveals an absence of major differences by race or class in approval of interpersonal violence. Typical of the findings is that for marital fighting. When approval of a husband slapping his wife is examined, 25 percent of the white and 37 percent of the black married men say that they can imagine a situation in which they would approve. There is no systematic variation by income or education. Furthermore, variation by race decreases when follow-up items are examined, and a similar pattern is found for items relating to approval of a man choking an adult male stranger. Finally, approval of punching an adult male stranger is higher among whites than blacks.

Thus, aside from the persistent patterning of criminal violence across places and groups, there is little consistent evidence to support the class-culture or subculture-of-violence approaches. Some possible sources of this inconsistency become apparent in the example we consider next.

AN EXAMPLE: MACHISMO AND CHICANO GANG VIOLENCE As we have noted, gang violence is regarded by the theories we have been considering as one expression of lower-class culture. In the Chicano barrios of East Los Angeles, this violence is seen as an expression of machismo. Howard Erlanger (1979) has analyzed the situation in some detail. He begins by noting that there are more than a million persons of Mexican heritage living in East Los Angeles, a number comparable to the population of Guadalajara or Monterey. Chicanos use the term "barrio" to refer to the many subcommunities or neighborhoods that make up East Los Angeles, and in the central, poorest barrios in this area most male youth are thought to belong to gangs. The question is what role notions of machismo play in generating violence between the barrio gangs.

Common conception sees machismo as a cultural value that predisposes men to an exaggerated sense of honor, hypersensitivity, intransigence, sexual promiscuity, callousness and cruelty toward women, physical aggression, and lack of respect for human life. Erlanger found in his initial interviews with Chicano youth that machismo meant having courage, "not backing down," and being ready to fight. However, he also found that to those interviewed, violence itself was not directly a macho trait. This point became clear in discussions of Cesar Chavez—the militant but nonviolent organizer of migrant farm workers. Although he does not use violence, respondents noted, Chavez does fight. One youth interviewed observed (ibid., p. 238),

I don't know [Chavez] personally, but from what I hear about him and what I've read about him. I don't think he'd [pause]. If somebody came up to him and slapped him, I think he'd try [pause]. He wouldn't fight back you know, but he'd fight back in words, not with fists.

Erlanger concludes from this part of his study that the core values of the Chicano subculture, then, are not directly concerned with violence, but rather with defending oneself in a more abstract sense.

Erlanger goes on to argue, in a manner that anticipates the status frustration theories we consider next, that this defense of self is a necessary response to the cultural abuse experienced in the school and community. From the time of the American conquest of the northern territories of Mexico in 1848, persons of Mexican heritage living within the United States have been subject to economic and cultural domination by Anglos. Erlanger describes the resulting feelings of powerlessness, exclusion, and absence of control over the conditions of their environment as producing a sense of "estrangement." A Chicano who has "made it" and become a teacher recalls the experiences that breed this estrangement (ibid., p. 239):

I heard teachers saying out in the field, "You goddam Mexican" to another teacher who was umpiring. . . . I heard teachers reprimand kids who were speaking Spanish in the hallways . . . and this was supposed to be a time when they were teaching Spanish in school already. I heard teachers saying, "What do you expect of these kids?"

The response to this estrangement is an identification with an alternative source of identity, the barrio gang. Erlanger's interviews indicate that this identification is equal to that with the family and is much more intense than that with religion, with political entities, or, with the exception we note in a moment, with the Chicano people as a whole. The following testimonial from one youth interviewed (ibid., p. 240) makes this point graphically:

> **Q:** What I'm trying to figure out is which was more important? What would you consider more serious-an insult to you or an insult to the barrio you were a part of at that time?
> **A:** Probably the barrio—the neighborhood.
> **Q:** The barrio was more important?
> **A:** Yeah, there's people I've seen who have given up their lives for the neighborhood. I've seen people die. . . .
> **Q:** Literally die?
> **A:** Yeah, yelling out, like "¡ Que vivas!" [Long live the neighborhood!].

Still, Erlanger notes that this intense sentiment need not necessarily lead to intergang violence. Indeed, during an interlude in the late 1960s and early 1970s in East Los Angeles, a broadly based political movement dramatically altered the established pattern. The movement itself included walkouts from the city schools, a moratorium protesting the disproportionate Chicano fatalities in the Vietnamese war, protest of allocation of Catholic church funds to construction of churches in West Los Angeles rather than to social programs in the barrios, protests against police treatment of Chicanos, and a protest of a state educational conference. During this period, Erlanger (ibid., p. 244) reports that a new focus on *carnalismo*, involving the values of brotherhood, pride, and unity, became prominent.

> The experience of one respondent well illustrates this situation. Now in his twenties and still a member of one of the toughest barrio gangs, he was never a part of the movement, does not have a clear idea of what the issues were or why the events took place, and does not feel that the movement affected his sense of being Chicano. But although his ideas and self-concept were unchanged by the movement, his lifestyle was profoundly affected. He remembered the movement period as one in which the types of actions that would otherwise be provocative did not evoke a combative response. For example, he reported that during the movement period he dated a girl whose brother was a member of a gang with which his gang has had an intense rivalry for over 30 years, but that he suffered no repercussions. Although he would have been willing to fight if challenged for this action, the challenge did not occur, and in general he reported that a high degree of freedom of movement between the two barrios existed. This is because those youths who were affiliated with the movement were playing by the new rules of carnalismo, and did not support their comrades who played by the old rules.

Erlanger's point is that there may be subcultural values that are associated with criminal violence, but these values find the form and place of their expression according to the social, economic, and political conditions that prevail. As noted above, theories of lower-class culture tend to deemphasize the latter conditions. This is less true of the theories we consider next.

THE THEORIES OF STATUS FRUSTRATION

Kobrin and the Conflict of Values

The theories we have considered thus far in this chapter see underclass crime and delinquency as developing in a world of their own, in a culture that is dominated by its own internal dynamics. In contrast, the theories of status frustration that we consider next focus on the conflicts that exist between competing value systems. An example of one of these theories is found in Solomon Kobrin's (1951) discussion of the conflict of values in delinquency areas.

Kobrin began with the observation that what we know from delinquency research discourages the easy separation of adolescents into groupings of "delinquents" and "nondelinquents." "In a real sense," Kobrin (1951, p. 657) noted, "they are neither and they are both." His point was that many adolescents move between these worlds, and that it is only over a period of time that some adolescents come to live more or less completely in one or the other of them. For Kobrin, the particular path taken depends partly on the kind of community and partly on the kind of individual experience involved. Both of these considerations are central to the theories we consider in the remainder of this chapter.

A unique feature of Kobrin's approach is the idea that criminal and conventional value systems can be integrated as well as in conflict with one another. He notes (1951, p. 657) that "the criminal culture shares with the conventional culture the goal of a large and assured money income, and like the conventional culture utilizes the flexible processes of politics to achieve this goal." The extent to which the two cultural systems are intertwined, particularly through corruption of the political process, is determinate of the kinds of delinquency that may emerge. For example, in communities where organized crime receives protection through political manipulation of the police and their enforcement activities, delinquency becomes an avenue to success in specialized kinds of adult criminal careers. Here, Kobrin argues, delinquency is a training ground for the acquisition of skills in the use of instrumental violence, concealment of offense, evasion of detection and arrest, and the purchase of immunity from punishment. Adolescents who master these skills can reasonably look forward to profitable adult criminal careers.

In contrast, where the criminal and conventional value systems achieve no integration, the prospects for adolescent delinquency are much different. Delinquency here is more expressive than instrumental, unconstrained by controls originating at any point (criminal or conventional) in the adult social structure. The result is that violent physical combat is pursued by both individuals and groups, almost as a form of recreation: "Here groups of delinquents may be seen as excluded, isolated conflict groups dedicated to an unending battle against all forms of constraint." The question that remains, though, is what motivates this violently expressive kind of activity. The answer that Kobrin gives derives from his premise that even in the circumstances described above there is a connection between criminal and conventional value systems, in the form of the status criteria set by the dominant, conventional system.

Drawing from the early writings of Albert Cohen, whose work we consider in the next section, Kobrin argues that much adolescent delinquency can be seen as a form of *defensive adaptation* to the inability to satisfy conventional status criteria. The problem, according to Cohen, is that by virtue of their underclass backgrounds many children of the lower class are relatively unequipped to move toward goals explicit in the middle-class culture of the wider society. Confronted by the inability to meet the criteria necessary to reach these goals, and faced with the assault to self-image and ego conveyed by this failure, the underclass child is left looking for a way out. The problem is the more pressing, according to Kobrin, because the child has been judged negatively not only by the surrogates of middle-class culture but by him or herself as well. Again, the problem is that conventional and unconventional value systems intersect.

Kobrin argues that the "solution" to this status problem is for the underclass child to reject the middle-class values. Kobrin uses an example of school vandalism to make this point in a graphic way.

> Nowhere is this more apparent than in the not uncommon burglaries of schools in delinquency areas in which the delinquent escapade is sometimes crowned, as it were, by defecating upon the school principal's desk. . . . In a sense, such an act is a dramatically exaggerated denial of a system of values which the delinquent has at least partially introjected, but which for the sake of preserving a tolerable self-image he must reject.

In sum, rebellion becomes an attractive way out of a situation that is insulting to the ego. Below we will note how this rebellion takes on a group form. Here it is enough to make clear that Kobrin's theory of a conflict of values is built on a social-psychological base, a base that is developed even more fully by Cohen.

Cohen's Theory of Status Deprivation

We noted above that Kobrin's theory is based in part on an early version of the work of Albert Cohen. We will now discuss Cohen's work in the greater detail provided by his book *Delinquent Boys* (1955).

Albert Cohen (ibid., pp. 88–91) sees American society as characterized by a dominant set of middle-class values, including ambition, individual responsibility, the cultivation and possession of skills, a readiness and ability to postpone gratification, rationality, personableness, the control of physical aggression and violence, wholesome recreation, and respect for property. In contrast, Cohen (ibid., p. 97) sees the working class as characterized by a rather different set of attributes: a dependence on primary groups, spontaneity, emotional irrepressibility, a freer use of aggression, and a reduced likelihood of valuing the "good appearance" and "personality" necessary to make it in a middle-class world.

It is when the working-class child enters the "middle-classified" school that middle- and working-class values come into significant conflict. It is here, according to Cohen, that the working-class child is assessed against a "middle class measuring rod." The problem of the child-cum-adolescent is clearly stated (ibid., p. 117):

> To win the favor of the people in charge he must change his habits, his values, his ambitions, his speech and his associates. Even were these things possible, the game might not be worth the candle. So, having sampled what they have to offer, he returns to the street or to his "clubhouse" in a cellar where "facilities" are meager but human relations more satisfying.

It is interesting to note that Cohen does not assume that the adolescents he describes actively want, or in other words value, what they cannot obtain. Instead, Cohen implies that middle-class values exist as *repressed* and *unrecognized* sources of status anxiety for the children of the underclass (Short and Strodtbeck, 1965, p. 53). It is not so much the denial of valued goals that hurts, but rather the more immediate degradation of classroom comparisons: "The contempt or indifference of others, particularly of . . . schoolmates and teachers, . . . is difficult . . . to shrug off" (Cohen, 1955, p. 123). The problem of the working-class adolescent, then, is one of adjusting to a status that he or she has little alternative but to accept. The attraction of the delinquent contraculture is that it facilitates this process by offering alternative criteria of status which working-class adolescents *can* meet.

The delinquent contraculture performs its role by turning disadvantage to advantage. Said sociologically, it redefines the criteria of status so that disvalued attributes become status-giving assets. It is significant to add, however, that this redefinition is conducted with a vengeance. Underclass values and norms are refashioned into "an explicit and wholesale repudiation of middle class standards" (ibid., p. 129). In sum, they "express contempt for a way of life by making its opposite a criterion of status" (ibid., p. 134). It is as if the delinquent contraculture were defiantly insisting that "we're everything you say we are and worse."

Cohen maintains that the result of all this is a delinquent contraculture that is *nonutilitarian, malicious,* and *negativisitic* in its core values. Said differently, this seems to say that members of the delinquent contraculture "raise hell for the hell of it." Cohen does not insist that all delinquency springs fully formed from the observance of contracultural norms and values. However, he does suggest (ibid., p. 315) "that for most delinquents delinquency would not be available as a response were it not socially legitimized and given a kind of respectability, albeit by a restricted community of fellow-adventurers." Within this confined community of peers, crime and delinquency become an accepted response to an unacceptable environment.

Criticism of Status Frustration Theories

One problem the status frustration theories, like other subcultural theories, have confronted is the mixed results of studies that have attempted to document the assumed value conflict between subordinate and dominant cultural groups in our society. One of the most innovative studies of this issue, by Short and Strodtbeck (1965), used detached workers as interviewers and informants to gather data on the value positions of gang delinquents and nondelinquents in Chicago. On the one hand this study finds that the acceptance of middle-class values that encourage rewarded behaviors is quite *general,* but that on the other hand middle-class norms prohibiting deviant types of behavior decline in force in the lower class. Of related interest is the finding that lower-class delinquents endorse "middle-class" views of family life (e.g., stable monogamous relationships) in private interviews, but not in the presence of peers. The implication is that the kinds of subcultural values described by Cohen and others may be the consequence of the shared misconceptions of individuals when placed in the context of the subcultural group (Matza, 1964, pp. 53–59). This finding seems to say that it is the *group process itself* which is most important to the expression and understanding of subcultural values.

There is another, perhaps related, kind of misconception that is associated with the approaches we have been considering. These accounts frequently seem to exaggerate the prevalence of gang activity. Thus many efforts to study gang behavior cast doubt on the organizational reality of gangs. For example, a classic field observation study by Yablonsky (1959) of gang life in New York City found that gangs are often loose affiliations of real, and sometimes imagined, individuals that could more accurately be described as "near groups." The conclusion of this study was that the "size" of the gangs studied was determined as much as anything else by the shifting needs of a gang's leadership. The following incident (ibid., p. 217) is indicative.

In one interview, a gang leader distorted the size and affiliations of the gang as his emotional state shifted. In an hour interview, the size of his gang varied from 100 members to 4,000, from 5 brother gangs or alliances to 60, from about 10 square blocks of territorial control to include jurisdiction over the 5 boroughs of New York City, New Jersey, and part of Philadelphia.

Yablonsky's study does not stand alone. Studies from settings as far afield as Paris (Vaz, 1962), London (Scott, 1956; Downes, 1966), Córdoba, Argentina (deFleur, 1967), as well as other American cities (Thrasher, 1937; Short and Strodtbeck, 1965; Klein and Crawford, 1967) reveal similar conclusions about gang membership and organization. Yet it may not only be a gang's leadership that distorts the public impression of its size, form, and character. This point will become clear in the example of status frustration theory that we consider next.

AN EXAMPLE: HELL'S ANGELS A unique feature of status frustration theory is its focus on group processes and their role in the adaptation of individuals to the denial or loss of status. These group processes are perhaps nowhere more dramatically described than in Hunter Thompson's (1967) journalistic account of a period he spent with the motorcyle gang Hell's Angels.

To understand Hell's Angels, it is necessary first to appreciate the stark social fact that they "are obvious losers and it bugs them" (p. 75). Indeed, Thompson (p. 332) suggests that most Angels are losers simply by birth, "sons of poor men and drifters, losers and sons of losers." What makes these losers unique, however, is that instead of submitting quietly to their collective fate, they have made their loss the basis of a full-time social vendetta. "Yeah, I guess I am [a loser]," remarks one reflective Angel to Thompson (p. 334), "But you're looking at one loser who's going to make a hell of a scene on the way out."

It is not difficult to make the description of this scene vivid. It begins with the cycles these outlaws ride (p. 127).

A chopper is often a work of art, costing as much as $3,000 to build, not counting labor. From the polished chrome spokes to the perfectly balanced super-light flywheel and the twelve coats of special paint on the gas tank, it is a beautiful, graceful machine and so nearly perfect mechanically that it is hard to conceive it screaming along some midnight highway in the hands of a drunken hoodlum only moments away from a high-speed crash into a tree or a steel guardrail.

Why this obsession with a machine? Thompson (p. 119) argues that for an Angel, "His motorcycle is the one thing in life he has absolutely mastered. It is his only valid status symbol, his equalizer."

But this "equalizer" can have real meaning only with the help of a reinforcing group. Thus Thompson (p. 102) notes that "the majority of would-be Angels are independents who suddenly feel the need for fellowship and status," and (p. 120) that "each Angel is a mirror in the mutual admiration society. They reflect and reassure each other, in strength and weakness, folly and triumph." Thompson goes on to argue that it is the lengths to which Hell's Angels will go to reinforce one another that makes them so threatening to the rest of us; and he suggests that it is this, combined with a belief in total retaliation for any offense or insult, that makes the Angels such a problem for police and so morbidly fascinating to the general public. At least within the confines of the Angel's gang, position and status are certain: ". . . in any argument a fellow Angel is *always right*. To disagree with a Hell's Angel is to be *wrong*." And, observes Thompson (p. 95), who ultimately was the victim of a beating himself, "When you get in an argument with a group of outlaw motorcyclists, your chances of emerging unmaimed depend on the number of heavy-handed allies you can muster in the time it takes to smash a beer bottle. In this league, sportsmanship is for old liberals and young fools."

In the end, though, Thompson suggests that much of what we know and think about groups like Hell's Angels is a product of exaggerated news media coverage, and the desire of many of us to consume it. The role of the media is discussed further in our consideration of labeling theory in the next chapter. Here it is enough to ask why many of us might want to read about the horrors perpetrated by the Hell's Angels. Thompson (p. 334) answers,

. . . the main reasons the Angels are such good copy is that they are acting out the day-dreams of millions of losers who don't wear any defiant insignia and who don't know how to be outlaws. The streets of every city are thronged with men who would pay all the money they could get their hands on to be transformed—even for a day—into hairy, hard-fisted brutes who walk over cops, extort free drinks from terrified bartenders and thunder out of town on big motorcycles after raping the banker's daughter. Even people who think the Angels should all be put to sleep find it easy to identify with them. They command a fascination, however reluctant, that borders on psychic masturbation.

The point this passage makes, and that we will explore further in the next chapter, is that the social audience may play a part in creating the kind of subculture we have been describing.

THE THEORIES OF OPPORTUNITY

In the preceding chapter we discussed the work of Emile Durkheim and its anticipation of the theories of undercontrol. The link was Durkheim's concept of anomie and its focus on the absence of regulation, or norm-lessness. Durkheim believed that limitations of both goals and means were required to avoid anomie. Opportunity theory as well is premised on the notion of anomie, but it is a concept of anomie refashioned by Robert Merton. Thus while Durkheim argued that the goals of individuals are infinitely *variable,* and that stability and conformity depended on the moderation of unrestricted goals, Merton asserted that these goals were constant, and the subject of societal consensus. Merton's reformulation, then, shifts our attention to the relationship between fixed goals and the *variable means* of achieving them.

Merton, Social Structure, and Anomie

Merton's (1938, 1957, 1959) reformulation of Durkheim's theory of anomie derives from a basic disagreement with the assumptions that underlie the original discussion. Rather than seeing human beings' desires as "insatiable" and "bottomless," for example, Merton (1957, p. 31) observes that "the image of man as an untamed bundle of impulses begins to look more like a caricature than a portrait." Furthermore, Merton is interested in exploring variations in crime and deviance by social class. "For whatever the role of impulses," reasons Merton (ibid., p. 131), "there still remains the further question of why it is that the frequency of deviant behavior varies within different social structures." Merton locates the answer to this question in social structures, particularly the class structure, and the pressure it places on persons located disadvantageously in society.

Merton (ibid., p. 132) focused on two features of social and cultural structure: culturally defined *goals,* and the acceptable structural *means* of achieving these goals. Merton argued that in societies like our own, goals such as financial success often are emphasized to the neglect of adequate means of achieving them. Anomie does not result simply from the unregulated goals that Durkheim discussed, then, but rather from a faulty relationship between goals and the legitimate means of access to them. The problem is a combination of shared success goals and the limited means for their attainment.

Merton went on to develop a typology of goals, means, and ways of adapting to their relationship. This typology is presented in Figure 6-1. The first type of adaptation in the figure represents what many theories of crime and deviance leave unexplained: conformity. Merton's theory asserts that conforming behavior will occur where the goals and means of society are accepted, and successfully pursued.

The second type of adaptation, called "innovation," "occurs when the individual has assimilated the cultural emphasis upon the goal without equally internalizing the institutional norms governing ways and means for its attainment" (ibid., p. 141). Merton has in mind here the most common economic and property crimes of adults and juveniles, with the particular concern that these crimes are more common in the underclass. The explanation that follows (ibid., p. 146) derives from a class-located strain between shared goals and scarce means.

> Of those located in the lower reaches of the social structure, the culture makes incompatible demands. On the one hand, they are asked to orient their conduct toward the prospect of large wealth— "Every man a king" said Marden and Carnegie and Long—and on the other, they are largely denied effective opportunities to do so institutionally. The consequence of this structural inconsistency is a high rate of deviant behavior.

Not all victims of this contradiction immediately recognize its form. However, if their consciousness is provoked, Merton warns, they may become ready candidates for the fifth type of adaptation: rebellion. We consider this possibility last.

Merton suggests that while innovation is a common adaptation of the lower class, ritualism, the third type of adaptation, is a common fate of the

Figure 6-1 Types of adaptation to the relationship between cultural goals and institutionalized means. *Note*: (+) signifies acceptance, (−) signifies elimination, and (±) signifies "rejection and substitution of new goals and standards.) (*From Robert Merton, 1957*)

	Culture Goals	Institutionalized Means
I. Conformity	+	+
II. Innovation	+	−
III. Ritualism	−	+
IV. Retreatism	−	−
V. Rebellion	±	±

lower middle class. The ritualist clings compulsively to institutional norms despite having forgone all hopes of successfully achieving societal goals. In other words, the ritualist is an obsessive follower of rules who scarcely stops to wonder why.

The fourth of the adaptations, retreatism, is the least common. Merton enumerates a list of societal dropouts in this category, including psychotics, artists, pariahs, outcasts, vagrants, tramps, alcoholics, and drug addicts. The retreatists are *in* society but not *of* it, in the sense that they have rejected both the goals and the means of society.

The last type of adaptation is rebellion. An organized struggle for social, economic, and political change is the essence of this adaptation, seeking to "introduce a social structure in which the cultural standards of success would be sharply modified and provision would be made for a closer correspondence between merit, effort, and reward" (ibid., p. 155). Above we noted that when the second type of adaptation, innovation, becomes conscious of its class basis, a progression to rebellion can occur. We will note in the following chapter that the Marxist theories of crime have as well talked about this kind of progression. Notwithstanding this possibility, however, Merton (ibid., p. 157) also notes that "it is typically members of a ruling class rather than the most depressed strata who organize the resentful and the rebellious into a revolutionary group."

In any case, socially structured adaptations to failure are the focus of Merton's theory of anomie. Problems of access to *legitimate* means of achieving the goals we all share collectively are the focus of the theory. This leaves the illegitimate means of achieving these goals still to be explored, a task taken on by Cloward and Ohlin. We turn next, then, to the theoretical consideration of socially structured *criminal* career routes.

Cloward, Ohlin, and Differential Opportunity

Cloward and Ohlin (1960; see also Cloward, 1959) note that no matter how accurately Merton might depict the pressures and motivations that can lead to crime, the particular type of crime pursued has been left unexplained. Why one form of criminal career rather than another? Cloward and Ohlin's answer (ibid., p. 147) is that to be a thief, much as to be an insurance agent or a lawyer, an individual "must have access to a learning environment and, once having been trained, must be allowed to perform his role." Their argument is that if we are going to understand criminal career choices, then we would do well to give them the same kind of detailed attention given to the pursuit of conforming success routes. Cloward and Ohlin (ibid., p. 152) suggest that to do this we "think of individuals as being located in two opportunity structures—one legitimate, the other illegitimate." Given limited access to success goals by legitimate means, they argue, the nature of the criminal or delinquent response will vary according to the illegitimate means available.

The varying kinds of illegitimate opportunities available in city slums and ghettos are seen as leading to three types of criminal subcultures: stable criminal, conflict, and retreatist. Drawing from the work of Kobrin discussed earlier in this chapter, Cloward and Ohlin observe that some linkage between persons in legitimate and illegitimate roles is necessary to the development of a stable criminal pattern. Thus the adolescent who is to move toward a stable criminal-career pattern must eventually develop connections with mature criminals, law-enforcement officials, politicians, bail underwriters, lawyers, fences, and others. These contacts lead to the kinds of experiences that can expand the potential criminal's knowledge and skills, and facilitate new opportunities for more protected and rewarding criminal activities. "The criminal, like the occupant of a conventional role, must establish relationships with other categories of persons, all of whom contribute in one way or another to the successful performance of criminal activity" (ibid., p. 165). What distinguishes this account from the earlier work of Kobrin is the emphasis on socially structured patterns of opportunity as opposed to cultural values.

Cloward and Ohlin go on to point out that violence is disruptive of both criminal and conventional activities, and therefore that the occurrence of violent conflict will be restricted where opportunities for stable criminal and conventional career patterns exist. Alternatively their point is that where neither success route is present, controls on violence are *absent,* and conflict patterns therefore will emerge. This is the problem of the disorganized slum, where criminal and conventional opportunity structures are blocked: "As long as conventional and criminal opportunity structures remain closed, violence continues unchecked" (ibid., p. 175).

There remains the final problem of those who fail in their experiences with both the criminal and the conflict opportunity structures. Competition can be intense in these spheres, as it is in the world of more conventional opportunity. Cloward and Ohlin argue that those who lose in both of the former spheres are "double failures" fated to a kind of "retreatism" that is built around a world of drugs.

At a number of points, Cloward and Ohlin seem to suggest that offenders are *conscious* participants in the direction of their fates. In a departure from Merton, then, these authors (ibid., p. 108) seem to see most deviant actors as being actively aware of the injustices of their class-linked experiences. Arguing that "the basic endowments of delinquents are the equal of or greater than those of their nondelinquent peers," Cloward and Ohlin (ibid., p. 117) characterize the criminals of the future as "persons who have been led to expect opportunities because of their potential ability to meet the formal, institutionally established criteria of evaluation." The sense of injustice emerges, however, as it becomes apparent that "ultimate success is likely to involve such criteria as race, speech, mannerisms, familial ties, and 'connections'" (ibid., p. 118). Gradually, the future criminal becomes conscious that the deck is stacked, and thus "he perceives his failure to gain access to opportunities as an injustice in the system rather than as a deficiency in himself" (ibid.). It is this view of the situation that allows the individual "to join with others in a delinquent solution to his problem without great concern about the moral validity of his actions" (ibid.). Cloward and Ohlin (ibid., p. 122) add to this the further suggestion that "the efforts of reformers to expose discriminatory practices actually furnish such persons with further justification for withdrawing sentiments in support of the legitimacy of the established norms" (cf. Banfield, 1968, p. 171; Matza, 1964, pp. 95–98).

Some Critical Comments on Anomie and Opportunity

Does the common criminal *consciously* consider the sources of his or her plight and *consciously* choose a response to it? Such explicit turning points are not easily located in most of our lives, including those of common criminals. Bordua (1961, pp. 134–135) makes the point this way: "Each generation does not meet and solve anew the problems of class structured barriers to opportunity, but begins with the solutions of its forebears." Cloward and Ohlin's account seems to demand that each potential offender think through in conscious terms the contradiction of his or her position in the class structure. Although we will discuss in a later chapter some important race and class variations in the perception of criminal injustice (Hagan and Albonetti, 1982), there is a large body of research (Stinchcombe, 1964; Reiss and Rhodes, 1967; Downes, 1966; Hirschi, 1969; Short, Rivera, and Tennyson, 1965) that fails to find evidence of the specific kind of thought process suggested by Cloward and Ohlin. There is no doubt that opportunities unjustly are denied to particular groups. Our point is simply that the historical background of this situation may blur in most people's minds its connection with immediate circumstances.

If we wish to talk of the motivations of individuals, it may be enough simply to note that in circumstances where opportunities are limited, crime may be one of the few options available. Thus, when the famous bank robber Willie Sutton was asked why he robbed banks, his well-known answer was not that this institution was a rejected part of a corporate power structure that had unjustly denied him legitimate opportunity, but rather that he had made this particular career choice "because that's where

AN EXAMPLE: A FAMILY BUSINESS AND THE BLACK MAFIA   Francis Ianni (1972, 1974) has noted that over several generations different ethnic groups have been associated with organized crime in North America. To explain the changing ethnic involvement in organized-crime activities, Ianni proposes the concept of "ethnic succession." This concept refers to the process by which successive ethnic groups have come to North America in search of a better life, but without the ready means (e.g., education, language, and job skills) to achieve it. In each of a series of cases, participation in organized crime has been a group-based response to this disparity between goals and means. Thus Ianni notes that in the United States, first the Irish, then the Jews, later the Italians, and most recently black Americans have been prominently involved in organized crime. In turn, as these groups have gained access to legitimate means of attaining success, and consequently moved up the social ladder, their involvement in organized crime has declined.

Ianni illustrates his argument most convincingly in a discussion of Italian involvement in organized crime. This discussion begins with a historical analysis of organized crime in Italy. Here Ianni notes that the roots of organized crime can be found in a collection of secret societies, of which the Mafia is only one. Furthermore, the word "Mafia" has been used in two ways: first as an adjective to describe the type of man who is known and respected because he gets things done, and second as a noun to refer to criminal organizations and societies. These meanings are often confused and may be a source of the exaggerated claims made for the existence of a single, all-powerful criminal organization. In contrast to this image of unity and omnipotence, Ianni notes, the Mafia began as a collection of local organizations in Sicily in the early nineteenth century. The emergence of the Mafia coincided with the breakdown of feudalism. In effect, the Mafia served as an intermediary, paying landowners who had fled to the cities lump-sum rents for their rural estates, and then rerenting them to peasants. In other words, the Mafia filled a vacuum between the social strata in Sicily and became a source of order within the Sicilian social system. The Mafia continued to be prominent until the time of Mussolini. Thus, the Mafia was not a single organization that could have emigrated en masse to North America.

Nonetheless, the attitudes that surrounded use of the term "Mafia" as an adjective did begin to have an impact in North America in the 1920s, notably because of prohibition, one result of which was to create an illegal industry well suited to a large new immigrant group whose other opportunities were few. Many Italians, who had traditionally produced their own wine at home, began turning their household wineries into home stills, and central organizations emerged to collect this new source of illegal profits. Later, with the coming of the depression and the repeal of prohibition, it became necessary for these organizations, or crime families, to enter new fields of illegitimate enterprise, particularly drugs and prostitution. By this time, however, second-generation members of organized-crime families were taking over the organizations, and the Italian-American involvement in organized crime was becoming more North American than Italian in character. Ianni notes that today the process of ethnic succession is working toward its logical conclusion, with declining involvement of Italians in organized crime, and the prospect of the increasing involvement of black Americans.

In fact, Ianni (1974) argues that during the 1980s we will see a systematic development of what is now a scattered and loosely organized pattern of emerging black control in organized crime, into what he calls a "Black Mafia." Today black involvement in organized crime has not effectively extended beyond the ghettos of America into the larger marketplaces that are still dominated by Italian-American crime families. Ianni notes that the same condition prevailed among the Italians in the earlier part of this century, when prohibition provided a ready source for extraghetto profits. According to Ianni, it will be necessary for the following to take place before black crime networks can be formed into larger combines like those that have characterized Italian-American involvement in organized crime: (1) greater control over sectors of organized crime (e.g., drugs) outside as well as inside the ghetto; (2) some organizing principle (e.g., ethnic consciousness) that will serve as kinship did among the Italians to bring disparate networks together into larger, monopolistic criminal organizations, and (3) better access to political power and the ability to corrupt it. Ianni leaves the clear and lasting impression that these requirements will be met, and that a full-fledged Black Mafia will emerge as part of the continuing pattern of ethnic succession he describes.

the money is" (*New York Times,* Nov. 19, 1980 p. 38). No sense of injustice is required to explain this behavior; it reflects a rational choice made among the limited options associated with disadvantaged circumstances.

Meanwhile, however, it is also important to recall that Merton's early version of opportunity theory was constructed to explain *group-based rates* of deviant behavior rather than the actions or thoughts of individuals. Where this theme has been pursued in recent work, it has generated interesting empirical results. For example, Blau and Blau (1982) have used data from America's 125 largest metropolitan areas to demonstrate that differences in income and socioeconomic status, particularly as linked to race, can explain correlations of the kind noted in Chapter 4 between race and criminal violence. The assumption that underlies their analysis is that in a democracy like the United States, which places a heavy emphasis on equal access to opportunities, socioeconomic inequalities (e.g., income) that are associated with ascribed positions (e.g., race) consolidate and reinforce ethnic and class differences, thereby producing pervasive conflict and violence. "Great economic inequalities generally foster conflict and violence," the Blaus (ibid., p. 119) observe, "but ascriptive inequalities do so particularly." That is, inequalities based on ascriptive criteria like race are particularly likely to produce criminal violence. The Blaus' analysis offers evidence to support these predictions.

Returning our focus to group-based rates, and away from individuals, in the way research like the Blaus' does, encourages us also to consider the historical roots of differential opportunity structures and their ultimate consequences for the individuals and groups caught in the resulting social and economic circumstances. This kind of focus is reflected in the opportunity-based explanation of ethnic group involvement in organized crime we consider next.

SUMMARY AND DISCUSSION

This chapter began by talking about differences in cultural values and ended by focusing on differences in socially structured patterns of opportunity. This shift in emphasis, from the cultural to the structural, is important. Cultural theories attend more to the values and attitudes of individuals and the motivations they produce. Structural theories attend more to the ways in which societies are organized to satisfy (or dissatisfy) human needs and wants, and to the group-linked advantages and disadvantages that result. In the following chapter, we will see that the structural theme in criminological theory is elaborated and extended in the theories of overcontrol.

However, cultural and structural theories are not mutually exclusive, and the theories considered in this chapter also have important features in common. They all in one way or another begin to talk about basic conflicts in our society, and these conflicts are seen as a part of the motivation or pressures that push some people to challenge the laws of the society in which they live. The push these theories provide comes in several forms.

• *Class culture* theories cite persistent and pervasive values in the culture of underclass life as an inevitable source of crime and delinquency.

• *Status frustration* theories see crime and delinquency as defensive, group-supported reactions to the problems of meeting middle-class status expectations.

• *Opportunity theories* call attention to the gap between shared success goals and the variable means of attaining them, and see crime and delinquency as a common means of closing this gap, or at least of responding to it.

All of these theories call attention to the role of subcultural groups in organizing the conflicts they identify.

We have noted difficulties with each of these theories. The class cultural theories have a tendency toward circularity, explaining behaviors in terms of themselves, or in terms of attitudes or values not far removed. Furthermore, those studies that have looked for race and/or class differences in values and attitudes have not proved very successful. Finally, insofar as a subculture of violence exists, we concluded that its expression may depend on the conditions that surround it. Thus we noted that in the barrios of East Los Angeles, gang violence has ebbed and flowed with changes in political conditions.

The status frustration theories have suffered from a similar failure of research to find predicted differences in values and attitudes, and from the finding that the emphasis this approach gives to gangs may overestimate their prevalence and importance. However, the preceding kinds of studies have suggested that shared misconceptions of individuals about their peers may influence individual behavior and the public perception of it. The status frustration theories help explain where these shared misconceptions come from and why they are consequential.

The opportunity theories draw attention to the structural inequalities that can lead to group-linked variations in rates of crime and delinquency. While in the hands of Cloward and Ohlin this theory may predict a greater consciousness and understanding of the inequalities of opportunity, and their connection to crime and delinquency, than research can confirm, the emphasis on opportunity structures has proved productive in explaining race and class differences in criminal violence and variations in ethnic participation in organized crime.

A final way of consolidating our understanding of the theories of class, status, and opportunity is to summarize how this group of theories might collectively explain the relationship reported in Chapter 4 between social class and criminal and delinquent behavior. All of these theories see crime and delinquency as a response to inequalities. The theories vary in the mechanisms they see as mediating the impact of inequalities on crime and delinquency: the class-cultural theories focus on long-standing cultural values, the status frustration theories concentrate on patterns of defensive adaptation, and the opportunity theories emphasize the structuring of the means of goal attainment. Each of these approaches identifies a channel through which the pressure toward crime and delinquency may flow. It is this pressure and the inequality from which it derives that these theories use to explain the relationship between crime and class. As we have noted, the latter two theories are more optimistic than the first about the prospects of changing this relationship.

UNDERSTANDING CRIME III: THE THEORIES OF OVERCONTROL

7

THE ISSUE: WHY DO WE REACT TO CRIME THE WAY WE DO?

The theories of crime we will consider in this chapter often seem to turn the study of crime on its head. Instead of asking why some persons behave in ways we call "criminal," the theories of overcontrol more often ask why we respond to these persons in the ways we do. That is, they ask why it is that we single out such persons to be called "criminals." These theories, then, are very concerned with "criminalization," the process by which particular kinds of persons and behaviors are designated as criminal.

Underlying the study of criminalization is an awareness that the dividing line between what is and is not called "criminal" is changeable, and frequently subject to *conflict*. Thus unlike the theories of undercontrol, which assume a basic societal consensus about the definition of crime, the theories of overcontrol make the conflicts that may underlie these definitions a starting point for their work. The importance of this difference is expressed in a change of focus that characterizes much modern criminological work. The new focus is on how behaviors become valued or disvalued by and within particular groups, and on how such evaluations may in turn influence future behaviors. In other words, the theories of overcontrol focus not simply on criminal *behaviors* but on the criminal *status* of these behaviors. The causes and consequences of criminal status are of particular interest.

Another salient feature of the theories of overcontrol is their tendency to be *critical* of the processes they describe and seek to explain. These theories all note the role of the state in determining definitions of crime, and tend to see the state as too zealous in the exercise of its definitional powers, at least in response to crimes of the underclass. While the theories of undercontrol may see the state as merely compensating for the inadequacies of the family, school, and community, the theories of overcontrol are more likely to see state crime-control activities as intrusions or as instances of repression.

The theories of overcontrol we consider in this chapter are:

• *Labeling theories,* which are often credited with providing the first concentrated look at the societal response to crime.

• *Group conflict theories,* which link the labeling of crime to socially and economically dominant groups in society.

• *Marxist theories,* which have made economic forces *the* focal point in the understanding of crime-control activities.

Of course, there is much more to each of the theories than these summary statements indicate. These statements suggest, however, the emphasis placed by these theories on the role of conflict in the process of criminalization. Our task in this chapter is to examine each of the theories in greater detail. As we do so, the themes of conflict and criminalization will form a recurring backdrop to our discussion.

LABELING THEORY

In the previous chapter we noted that criminal and delinquent activities may often be a normal part of the subcultural environment from which they emerge. Whether these activities become the subjects of criminal disrepute may depend, therefore, on their discovery by representatives of the surrounding society. A prominent concern of labeling theory is that defining subcultural or other behaviors as criminal may increase the problems posed by these behaviors, resulting in the maintenance or even escalation of the behavior patterns involved. Kitsuse and Dietrick (1959) put the problem this way: ". . . the delinquent subculture persists because, once established, it creates for those who participate in it, the very problems which were the bases for its emergence." The striking implication of this line of thought is that many of these problems could be avoided by modifying the societal response to these subcultural activities; in other words, by avoiding the labels that define these behaviors as criminal.

Tannenbaum and the "Dramatization of Evil"

An early version of labeling theory appears in the historian Franklin Tannenbaum's textbook *Crime and the Community*. Tannenbaum (1938, p. 17) was struck by the fact that initial acts of juvenile delinquency can be a normal part of adolescent street life: "Breaking windows, annoying people, running around porches, climbing over roofs, stealing from push carts, playing truant—all are items of play, adventure, [and] excitement." On the other hand, the larger community, including merchants and others, may see such activities as a nuisance, evil, or delinquency. Sounding a theme that will echo throughout this chapter, Tannenbaum (ibid., p. 17) explains that "this conflict . . . is one that arises out of a divergence of values." He then focuses on the translation of this value conflict into an official response to the individual at hand. This translation is of particular concern because "there is a gradual shift from the definition of the specific acts as evil to a definition of the individual as evil, so that all his acts come to be looked upon with suspicion" (ibid., p. 17). One particular step in this process is singled out as crucial by Tannenbaum (ibid., p. 19), for "the first dramatization of 'evil' which separates the child out of his group for specialized treatment plays a greater role in making the criminal than perhaps any other experience." In other words, first impressions count, and it is therefore the first application of a criminal label that may have the biggest impact on the individual.

It is the impact of this initial "dramatization of evil" on the individual's self-concept that is of particular concern. The individual, Tannenbaum contends (ibid., pp. 17–18), is overwhelmed by the response to his or her acts and begins to think of him or herself as the "type of person"—a delinquent or criminal—who would do such things. Over time, "the young delinquent becomes bad because he is defined as bad and because he is not believed if he is good." This is thought to be the case in spite of the fact that officials involved in this process may intend to "reform" the individual. Tannenbaum's point is that these very efforts may intensify the problem by calling more attention to it. "The way out," he suggests (ibid., p. 20), "is through a refusal to dramatize the evil. The less said about it the better."

Lemert and Primary and Secondary Deviance

Tannenbaum's discussion of the dramatization of evil is elaborated by Edwin Lemert's (1951, 1967) suggestion of specific terms to distinguish acts that occur before and after the initial societal response. *Primary deviation,* on the one hand, refers to the initial acts of the individual which call out the societal reaction. Lemert notes that primary acts may happen at random or be stimulated by a broad diversity of initiating factors. What is theoretically significant, however, is that the initial acts have little impact on the individual's self-concept: "Primary deviation . . . has only marginal implications for the psychic structure of the individual" (Lemert, 1967, p. 17).

On the other hand, *secondary deviation* consists of the behaviors that follow from the societal reaction to primary acts of deviance. At least in part, the cause of secondary behaviors is a traumatization of self-concept that results from the first dramatization of evil, "altering the psychic structure, producing specialized organization of social roles and self-regarding attitudes" (ibid., pp. 40–41). Of greatest concern, however, is that secondary deviation often involves the stabilization of the deviant behavior pattern. "Objective evidences of this change will be found in the symbolic appurtenances of the new role, in clothes, speech, posture, and mannerisms, which in some cases heighten social visibility, and which in some cases serve as symbolic cues to professionalization" (Lemert, 1951, p. 76). This version of labeling theory again implies that a "refusal to respond" might diminish or even eliminate some of the problems.

A classic example of secondary deviation, which may or may not involve criminal consequences, is found in Lemert's (1962) discussion of paranoia. People who are called "paranoid" are conventionally assumed to engage in defensive or vengeful acts in response to inaccurate perceptions that the individuals and/or groups that surround them are conspiring against them. Lemert's provocative point (ibid., p. 3) is that in the end these perceptions very often turn out to be accurate, even if they may have been exaggerated or inaccurate in the beginning. The problem is that "while the paranoid person reacts differentially to his social environment, it is also true that 'others' react differentially to him and this reaction commonly if not typically involves covertly organized action and conspiratorial behavior in a very real sense." For example (ibid., p. 8), as the peers or even the family members of a person become aware of "problems" in his or her behaviors, the pattern of social interaction begins to subtly change: ". . . it becomes *spurious,* distinguished by patronizing, evasion, 'humoring,' guiding conversation on to selected topics, under-reaction, and silence, all calculated either to prevent intense interaction or to protect individual and group values by restricting access to them." These changes will be perceived, probably accurately, by the person involved, producing a *new* set of communication problems for him or her. Lemert's concern is that the result is a spiraling pattern of secondary deviation that is very difficult to reverse, and, alternatively, very likely to end in exclusion from the group or individual relationship involved. This provides the ultimate ratification of the "paranoid" person's initial, and now fulfilled, expectations. This is a pattern that can lead away from conforming, and into nonconforming, groups.

Becker's "Outsiders"

In his volume *The Outsiders,* Howard Becker (1963; see also 1964) notes that society creates "outsiders" by generating the rules that define crime and other kinds of deviance. Becker (1963, p. 2) also notes, however, that the persons who are so defined may have a quite different view of the matter. Thus "the rule-breaker may feel his judges are outsiders." It is the two-sided character of the conflict that makes the rule-making process political; and it is through this political process that "social groups create deviance by making the rules whose infraction constitutes deviance" (ibid., p. 9). Perhaps the most important distinction that emerges from this view of crime and deviance is that drawn between rule-breaking *behavior* on the one hand and the disreputable *status* of being called "criminal" or "deviant" on the other.

With the above point in mind, Becker (ibid., p. 14) suggests that "it might be worthwhile to refer to such behavior as *rule-breaking behavior* and reserve the term *deviant* for those labelled as deviant by some segment of society." The inevitable question that this distinction raises is that of "who makes the rules?" Becker's answer (ibid., p. 18)—"those groups whose social position gives them weapons and power"—is pursued in greater detail by the group conflict and Marxist theorists that we consider below. Becker's more immediate interest, however, is in the individuals who are on the receiving end of the labeling process.

Becker suggests that we understand these processes as unfolding in careerlike progressions. Thus a parallel is drawn with more conventional occupational careers and the sequence of movements they involve from one position to another. Each movement, it is noted, involves a "career contingency" that includes both objective facts of social structure and changes in the perspectives, motivations, and desires of the individual. The most consequential career contingency in Becker's description of the deviant career is the imposition of a disvalued label. Thus (ibid., p. 31), "one of the most crucial steps in the process of building a stable pattern of deviant behavior is likely to be the experience of being caught and publically labelled as deviant." Behind this assertion lies an assumption that the imposition of a disvalued label begins a process through which the individual's self-concept is stigmatized (cf. Goffman, 1961, 1963) or degraded (Garfinkel, 1956), so that she or he becomes what the label implies. Said differently (Becker, 1963, p. 34), the labeling process is a self-fulfilling prophecy which "sets in motion several mechanisms which conspire to shape the person in the image people have of him."

Cicourel and the Ethnomethodology of Juvenile Justice

If labels do indeed have the kinds of effects suggested above, it is important to know how individuals are singled out to receive them. Stereotypes may in various ways play a role in the process. This possibility is explored in the ethnomethodological work of Aaron Cicourel (1968), who introduces his research by noting (p. 24) that "following an ethno-methodological perspective . . . directs the researcher's attention . . . particularly to theories employed by police, probation, and court officials when describing the existence of delinquency." The purpose of this emphasis is to try to understand how official "theories" held by police and others may influence the process of labeling delinquents. These official decision-makers, according to Cicourel, develop stereotyped views of the causes of delinquency, and therefore of what types of adolescents are likely to be delinquents. Cicourel (ibid., p. 40) calls this a process of "typification" in which "the language and physical behavior employed by different types of adolescents provide law enforcement officials with the 'evidence' or 'data' for employing a typology of typical delinquents and 'good kids' whereby juveniles are labelled, and categorized for further action."

The danger of this type of decision-making, of course, is that it bypasses traditional safeguards involving standards of due process and associated presumptions of innocence. In their place, a presumption of guilt is introduced for certain types of suspects: "Thus the officer's preconstituted typifications and stock of knowledge at hand leads him to prejudge much of what he encounters" (ibid., p. 67). More specifically, Cicourel (ibid.) suggests that this typification process is based on class-linked commonsense assumptions of the police about where delinquency is most frequently to be found.

> My observations suggest police and probation perspectives follow community typifications in organizing the city into areas where they expect to receive the most difficulty from deviant or "difficult" elements to areas where little trouble is expected and where more care should be taken in dealing with the populace because of socioeconomic and political influence.

What is at issue from this perspective is the extent to which these assumptions, or typifications, are accurate or inaccurate, and therefore justified or unjustified. To the extent that the stereotypes are false, the imposition of legal labels will be biased.

Some Critical Comments on Labeling Theory

Perhaps the most important contribution of labeling theory has been the stimulus it has provided for research on the societal response to crime and other kinds of deviance (see, for example, Spector, 1976; Wellford, 1975; Hagan, 1973; Gove, 1975). There are at least three research traditions that derive from labeling theory: research of the kind reviewed in Chapter 3 on the social and historical origins of legal labels; research of the kind to be reviewed in Chapter 8 on the role of agents of the criminal-justice system in selecting and processing criminal offenders; and research to be considered here on the effects of labels on individuals' future behaviors.

From the outset, labeling theory has included an assumption that the application of a disvalued label involves a general stigmatizing effect that can spill over into other aspects of the subject's life. The argument is that labels often initiate typification processes that result in self-fulfilling prophecies. Two studies that are of importance in assessing these arguments are an examination by Fisher (1972) of the effects of being placed on court probation on future school behavior, and an exploration by Wiatrowski et al. (1982) of the effects of being tracked or streamed in school on later delinquent behavior. A crucial feature these studies share is their attention to behavior that precedes as well as succeeds the imposition of a label. There is a tendency for labeling theory to portray the deviant as a passive victim of one-sided societal abuse; to see deviance as all societal response and no deviant stimulus (Bordua, 1969). However, labels frequently may identify *preexisting* and *enduring* behavioral differences correctly, and in this sense be the *consequence* rather than the *cause* of the behaviors of concern.

Fisher's study utilized junior high school students of two types: students placed on probation (an "experimental" group) and others without such experience (a "control" group). Drawing from labeling theory, Fisher (1972, p. 79) hypothesized that "if definition as a deviant leads to increased imputation of negative attributes, and thus to increased deviance, this should be reflected in a comparison of performance of 'deviants' and 'non-deviants' in the school system." Test comparisons were made on the basis of academic (i.e., grades in academic courses) and nonacademic (i.e., grades given for work habits, character, personality factors, etc.) criteria.

What makes Fisher's study an important test of labeling theory is the inclusion of both "before-probation" and "after-probation" data (i.e., measures before and after the imposition of the label), and his effort to control for prelabeling measurements of academic ability. Fisher initially reports findings supportive of labeling theory in the form of a theoretically expected relationship between being placed on probation and lower academic and nonacademic performance. Subsequent analysis, however, shows differences between experimentals (i.e., the labeled) and controls (i.e., the nonlabeled) *prior* to probation that were nearly as great as those found after the probation label was acquired. Furthermore, in three out of four statistical controls for academic ability in the postprobationary data, the initial relationship between probationary status and school performance is eliminated. As Fisher (ibid., p. 82) notes, "This means that the essential differences between the two groups may not begin with the label but may have to do with school adaptation prior to this label."

A more recent study by Wiatrowski et al. (1982) produced results that are consistent with the above study by Fisher. Focusing on a national sample of high school students who were interviewed at four points in their schooling, the authors of this study are able to test an explicit causal model of the effects of curriculum-track placement on delinquent behavior during the subjects' senior year and one year after high school. The assumption is that low track placement has a stigmatizing effect. However, contrary to the expectations generated by prior work (Polk and Schafer, 1972; Kelly, 1976), this study finds that curriculum tracking did not significantly contribute to the prediction of delinquent behavior in the senior year or after high school. Interestingly, Wiatrowski et al. also report that 87 percent of the respondents in their study were satisfied with their curriculum at the end of their junior year. They conclude (ibid., p. 158) that "the absence of major effects of tracking on delinquency in this study may reflect the fact that students eventually accept their placement in a given curriculum."

The results of the above research should not be taken to deny that there is considerable importance to the labeling viewpoint. Rather, our point is that in the future we will want to be particularly attentive to the issue of *which* labels, in *what* situations, may actually *cause* the particular effects with which we are concerned. As Wiatrowski et al. note, some of the most important future research will need to examine the possibility that labeling effects occur very early in the schooling process with initial tracking or streaming decisions. In any case, the obvious importance of the labeling approach is that it emphasizes the need to study the societal response to deviance as a topic in its own right. We go on next to consider a very different example of how this may be done.

AN EXAMPLE: THE STUDY OF CRIME WAVES   To this point we have focused primarily on the consequences for individuals of being labeled. However, we have also noted that labeling theory is concerned with how particular kinds of individuals, in other words identifiable *groups* of individuals, are singled out to receive labels. There are several interesting studies in the labeling tradition that address this issue by examining the social forces that generate "crime waves." The common assumption derived from the labeling tradition that these studies share is that crime waves do not simply consist of increases in criminal behavior, but rather that they follow from increased sensitivities to the kinds of behaviors involved. Two studies, one by Kai Erikson (1966) of the Massachusetts Bay Colony in the seventeenth century, and another by Mark Fishman (1978) of New York City in the mid-1970s, will help to clarify the labeling perspective on the occurrence of crime waves.

Erikson's work draws from Durkheim the notion that crime and deviance can actually be a natural and beneficial part of social life. This view argues that the societal response to what is called "criminal" and "deviant" is a way of distinguishing publicly between acceptable and unacceptable behaviors. Erikson refers to this labeling process as fulfilling a "boundary maintaining function," and he argues that it can only be accomplished by open confrontations between "deviants" and agents of social control. He then suggests that a society will encounter the largest amounts of what it calls "crime" or "deviance" at precisely those points regarded as most distinctive and important in that society, again, as a way of emphasizing the society's distinctive social and normative boundaries. For example, the implication is that because in our society we regard private property as such a fundamental institution, we should expect to have a great deal of property crime. The societal response to such crimes reaffirms the boundaries of the concept of private property and the consequences of their violation.

Erikson goes on to reason that when a society is confronted by a challenge to its boundaries, as a result of realignment of power within the society or the appearance of new adversaries from outside it, the challenge and the crisis it provokes can be perceived by the members and leaders of the society as something akin to what we now call a crime wave. In his book *The Wayward Puritans*, Erikson identifies three such crime waves that occurred in the Puritan settlement of the Massachusetts Bay Colony: (1) the Antinomian controversy of 1636; (2) the Quaker persecutions of the late 1650s; and (3) the Salem witchcraft hysteria of 1692. The Bay Colony was for the Puritans an experimental proving ground in which the orthodox principles of their religion could be tested as the framework for a new way of living. Erikson argues that the above crime waves were the result of perceived threats and challenges to this experiment.

For example, the Antinomian controversy of 1636 centered around the person of Anne Hutchinson, who came to the colony after its founding and began to question subtle changes that the leadership of the colony had made in the basic tenets of Puritan thought. Hutchinson shortly captured a large following, so that she became a threat to the established patterns and leadership of the colony. The eventual outcome was a prolonged trial in which Anne Hutchinson and her followers were banished from the colony and excommunicated from the church.

The Quaker persecutions began in 1656 after a group of Quaker missionaries visited the colony. While there were few real differences between the Puritans and the Quakers, their very presence in the colony presented a challenge by raising the issue of religious toleration in the midst of a community founded on the notion of religious orthodoxy. Since England had just embarked on an era of religious toleration at the time of the original Puritan settlement, this left the exclusive character of the Puritan experiment in doubt. The Puritans reacted strongly to the activities of the Quaker missionaries, first by banishing them from the colony, then by subjecting them to corporal and eventually to capital punishment. Finally, the king of

England intervened, forbidding further violence against the Quakers. The Puritans continued to harass the Quakers with vagrancy laws, but from this point on, as a labeling theorist would ironically predict, the Quakers gradually diminished their activities in the colony.

In the period between the Quaker invasion and the Salem witch-hunt, several disturbing events occurred: the legal basis for the colony's charter was questioned in England, and disputes over land claims became rampant. Again, the coherence of the Puritan experiment seemed threatened.

The witchcraft hysteria began in the home of the Reverend Samuel Parris in Salem. Several young girls who were cared for in the Parris home by a woman slave named Tituba developed an unusual set of symptoms: screaming unaccountably, falling into grotesque convulsions, and sometimes scampering along on their hands and knees making noises like the barking of a dog. A local doctor diagnosed the girls as bewitched, and the local ministry concluded that the solution was for the girls to identify the witches who were tormenting them.

Three people, including Tituba, were initially named. Tituba in turn confessed in court and suggested that there were many additional witches in the colony. More and more persons were named as witches, as the witch-hunt spread outwards and upwards through the social structure of the colony. Eventually the pastor of Boston's First Church and the president of Harvard College were named, and people began to question the evidence being applied in the witch-hunt. By 1692 the Puritan experiment was coming to an end: the sense of mission had gone from the movement, and crime waves could no longer revive it.

Are modern crime waves any more real in the sense of changes in the behaviors they seek to control? Mark Fishman (1978) argues that they are not in a study of a crime wave against the elderly that was reported by the media in New York City in 1976. Late in that year the city's three daily newspapers and five local television stations reported a surge of violence against the elderly that lasted approximately seven weeks and eventually received national attention. However, Fishman notes that New York Police Department statistics do not substantiate that such a crime wave occurred. Homicide statistics show an actual 19 percent drop over the previous year's rate of elderly persons murdered. More generally, the police statistics indicate that there was a continuing increase in victimization of the elderly, as well as of the general population, but not that old people were singled out in particular.

Fishman seeks to explain this disparity by looking at the way news coverage is organized. His point with regard to the specific coverage of crime news is that something becomes a "serious type of crime" more on the basis of what is going on *inside* newsrooms than *outside*. For example, Fishman notes that newsworkers make crime news by seeing "themes" in the news, that is, by seeing specific incidents as instances of larger trends. Thus the mugging of an 80-year-old woman is reported as "the latest instance of the continuing trend in crimes against the elderly." For this to happen, however, incidents must be seen in a way that effectively ties them together.

To make the above point more concretely, Fishman reports how the above incident was tied into a larger story at the beginning of the New York crime wave. At about ten o'clock in the morning at the television station in question, the assignment editor saw that in the 113th Precinct in Queens an elderly person had been mugged and that one perpetrator had been shot. As he was clipping this dispatch, he also heard over the all-news radio that the police were holding a crime prevention meeting with senior citizens in the 112th Precinct in Queens.

The assignment editor now knew what his lead stories for the evening news would be and what he had to do to line them up: (1) he would send a reporter to the 113th Precinct to get on film whatever he could about the mugging; (2) the reporter would then go over to the 112th Precinct to get on film the police meeting with senior citizens; and (3) these two reports would then be followed by a pretaped feature on a Senior Citizens Robbery Unit that had been established in the police department. Separately, these stories might not have generated much attention; however, seen collectively, Fishman observes, they constituted a news theme that would receive considerable attention. Eishman goes on to note how police officials can make or break such stories by controlling the quality and quantity of the information they release. In the end, the conclusion of this study is that officials can use their positions to encourage fledgling crime themes that are initially identified by journalists, or, alternatively, that they can use their positions to deny the reality of potential crime themes. Either way, news people and public officials can influence and distort our impressions of when increases and decreases in crime are occurring. There is more to the perception of crime than the particular behaviors involved.

GROUP CONFLICT THEORY

As labeling theory has focused its attention on the application of labels by some groups to others, it has moved increasingly toward a group conflict theory of crime. What group conflict theory most conspicuously adds to the labeling theorist's interest in the application of labels is a greater emphasis on the role of self-interested groups in the development of legal labels. A key feature of this approach is its assumption that various groups have specific interests in laws that mandate the imposition of labels, and that these groups therefore play a central role in guiding particular legal labels through the lawmaking and law-enforcing process. Dominant societal groups are seen as imposing criminality on subordinate groups by making and enforcing laws that make criminals of them.

Vold's Group Conflict Theory of Crime

Probably the first North American social scientist to write explicitly about a group conflict theory of crime was the political scientist George Vold (1958). Vold saw crime as having two components: human behaviors (i.e., acts) and the judgments or definitions (i.e., mores, customs, or laws) of others as to whether specific behaviors are acceptable. Vold regarded the judgmental component as more significant, and his primary interest was therefore in the influence of groups in imposing their value judgments by defining the behaviors of others as criminal.

One of Vold's most interesting suggestions was that crime and delinquency are "minority group" behaviors. He proposed (1958, p. 211), for example, that "the juvenile gang . . . is nearly always a 'minority group,' out of sympathy with and in more or less direct opposition to the rules and regulations of the dominant majority, that is, the established world of adult values and power." The police defend the values of the adult world in this struggle, while the juvenile gang is seen as seeking the material and symbolic advantages that it is not permitted under the adult code. Intergenerational value conflict is the root of the problem, Vold argues, with adults destined to prevail through their control of the legal process.

Although Vold (ibid., p. 219) held that his theory was relevant to a "considerable amount of crime," he also cautioned that "the group conflict hypothesis should not be stretched too far." In the end, he suggested that his approach was most appropriately applied to four kinds of crime.

Political protest movements underlie the first type of crime Vold considered. Here he notes that while a successful revolution makes criminals out of the government officials previously in power, an unsuccessful revolution makes its own leaders into traitors. The former point is well-illustrated by the fall of the Shah of Iran and the waves of corporal and capital punishment that followed. The latter point is illustrated by the fates of members of the Puerto Rican F.A.L.N. in the United States.

Clashes between company and labor interests during strikes and lockouts result in the second type of crime considered by Vold. The conflict here (ibid., p. 216) is that "participants on either side of a labor dispute condone whatever criminal behavior is deemed 'necessary' for the maintenance of their side of the struggle." Thus the history of American labor relations has often been a bloody one, with strikers particularly likely to feel the heavy hand of the law.

A third type of crime included within Vold's theory involves disputes between and within competing unions. "Such disputes often involve intimidation and personal violence," Vold (ibid., p. 217) notes, "and sometimes they become entangled with the 'rackets' and gang warfare of the criminal underworld."

Racial and ethnic clashes are the basis of the final type of crime considered under Vold's theory. Vold (ibid.) observes here that "numerous kinds of crimes result from the clashes incidental to attempts to change, or to upset the caste system of racial segregation in various parts of the world." Nat Turner's rebellion in the American south (see Styron, 1967) is an example of this kind of conflict being called "criminal."

Although Vold narrowed his focus to the four kinds of crimes described above, more recent efforts have broadened the range of attention of group conflict theory. Austin Turk has offered what is probably the most systematic of these efforts.

Turk's Theory of Crime and the Legal Order

For Austin Turk (1969, p. 25), criminality is first and foremost a status that is defined and conferred by others: ". . . criminality is not a biological, psychological, or even behavioral phenomenon, but a social status defined by the way in which an individual is perceived, evaluated, and treated by legal authorities." Who, then, defines this criminal status? Turk (ibid., p. 33) answers that there are basically two kinds of people in society: "There are those . . . who constitute the dominant, decision-making category—the authorities—and those who make up the subordinate category, who are affected by but scarcely affect law—the subjects." Authorities make laws that make criminals out of subjects. There remains the question of how this is accomplished.

The foundation of this state of affairs, according to Turk (ibid., pp. 41–42), is a learning process in which "both eventual authorities and eventual subjects learn and continually relearn to interact with one another as, respectively, occupants of superior and inferior statuses and performers of dominating and submitting roles." The key to this process is that authorities learn "social norms of domination," while subjects learn "social norms of deference." However, it is also the case that there can never be complete agreement on the normative lessons to be learned, with the significant consequence that the resulting conflict can become a challenge to authority. Thus, "*lawbreaking* is taken to be an indicator of the failure or lack of authority; it is a measure of the extent to which rulers and ruled . . . are not bound together in a perfectly stable authority relationship" (ibid., p. 48). Turk then notes particular conditions in which the conflict can become most intense. These are the conditions in which crime rates are expected to be highest. For example, among the conditions considered is the relative power of the persons involved. It is the poor and nonwhite who are assumed to have the least power, and it is therefore persons with these status characteristics who are expected to have the highest rates of criminalization. Much of the work in the conflict theory tradition has focused on the process by which this "differential criminalization" occurs.

Chambliss and Seidman's Perspective on Differential Criminalization

William Chambliss and Robert Seidman (1971) begin by noting that our society is made up of groups with widely varying norms and values. They do not assume, however, that all societies have always been like our own in this respect. Some societies that are less complex and less stratified may resolve internal differences through compromise and reconciliation, allowing a condition of relative consensus. However, reconciliation becomes progressively more difficult as societies become more complex and highly stratified, and they argue that in such societies rule enforcement becomes increasingly common. The issue then becomes one of whose rules will be enforced and how. Chambliss and Seidman (1971, p. 474) observe that bureaucratically structured agencies take on such responsibilities in societies like our own. A consequence of this bureaucratic rule is that "rule creation and rule enforcement will take place when such creation or enforcement increases the rewards for the agencies and their officials, and they will not take place when they are conducive to organizational strain." Thus the guiding principle of legal bureaucracy is to maximize organizational gains and minimize organizational strains.

Chambliss and Seidman (ibid., p. 268) go on to argue that the effect of the above principle is to operationalize a consequential "rule of law": "The rule is that discretion at every level . . . will be so exercised as to bring mainly those who are politically powerless (i.e., the poor) into the purview of the law." The reason for this is that the poor are unlikely to have the resources necessary to generate organizational strains, and therefore they become attractive targets for organizational activities. It follows also, Chambliss and Seidman (ibid., p. 475) reason, that "those laws which prohibit certain types of behavior popular among lower-class persons are more likely to be enforced." From this perspective, then, there is little surprise that the poor form such a large component of our official crime statistics. Rather than seeing this as resulting from the behavior of the poor themselves, Chambliss and Seidman base their explanation in the dynamics of our bureaucratic legal system and in the class bias of our society.

Quinney's Social Reality of Crime

The early work of Richard Quinney goes on to link the above focus on the formulation and application of criminal definitions with the occurrence of criminal behaviors. Quinney (1970, p. 21) cites several sources of such behavior, including (1) structured opportunities, (2) learning experiences, (3) interpersonal associations and identifications, and (4) self-conceptions. The attention to structured opportunities and learning experiences reflects the assumption in Quinney's work that *prior* to the legal response there *are* class-based differences in behaviors that are later called "criminal." This is because "persons in the segments of society whose behavior patterns are not represented in formulating and applying criminal definitions are more likely to act in ways that will be defined as criminal than those in the segments that formulate and apply criminal definitions" (ibid., p. 21). Said differently, the rich typically criminalize the behavior patterns that are learned, often in response to differential opportunities and learning experiences, by the poor.

On the other hand, the second set of factors discussed by Quinney, interpersonal associations, identifications, and self-conceptions, suggest that class-based behavior patterns called "criminal" exist as a *response* to encounters with the law. Drawing here from the labeling theories we considered above, Quinney (ibid., pp. 21–22) argues that "those who have been defined as criminal begin to conceive of themselves as criminal; as they adjust to the definitions imposed upon them, they learn to play the role of criminal."

All of the above factors are brought together in Quinney's early work by a focus on the *conceptions* of crime held by powerful segments of society. Of instrumental concern here are the conceptions of crime portrayed in personal and mass communications, particularly as these conceptions represent the interests of the socially and economically powerful. Quinney's point is that the conceptions of crime held by the powerful (i.e., their definitions of the "crime problem") become *real* in their consequences; it is these conceptions, Quinney argues, that ultimately determine "the social reality of crime." Quinney (ibid., p. 23) summarizes his formulation this way:

In general . . . the more the power segments are concerned about crime, the greater the probability that criminal definitions will be created and that behavior patterns will develop in opposition to criminal definitions. The formulation and application of criminal definitions and the development of behavior patterns related to criminal definitions are thus joined in full circle by the construction of criminal conceptions.

A summary diagram of Quinney's theory is presented in Figure 7-1.

Some Critical Comments on Group Conflict Theory

George Vold (1958) anticipated much of the modern criticism of group conflict theory when he urged that the conflict hypothesis "not be taken too far." His concern was that this viewpoint applied to some forms of crime and deviance better than others. We made a related point in Chapter 2, and we will do so in a somewhat different way again below, by separating the consensus crimes (e.g., premeditated murder, kidnapping, etc.) from the conflict crimes. The point is that most people, most of the time, across several centuries, and in most nations, rather consistently have called at least some behaviors "criminal." In other words, there is relative consensus about *some* forms of behavior. Group conflict theory fares best in explaining other types of crime about which less consensus exists.

It is also important in assessing group conflict theory to take note of Austin Turk's warning (1976*b*, p. 292) that "conflict-coercion theory does not imply that most accused persons are innocent, nor that more and less powerful people engage in conventional deviations to the same extent. It does not even imply that legal officials . . . discriminate against less powerful and on behalf of more powerful people." This warning is significant because it acknowledges two kinds of findings too often ignored in conflict analyses: that there *are* class-linked differences in criminal-behavior patterns (see Chapter 4), and that patterns of differential treatment by legal officials are smaller than frequently assumed (see Chapter 8). However, having made these somewhat critical points, it is important that we also reaffirm (see Chapter 3) a more fundamental

Figure 7-1 Model of the social reality of crime. (*Source: Quinney, 1970:24*)

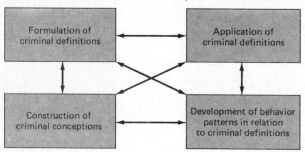

assumption of group conflict theory: that activities common among the socially and economically disadvantaged are more likely to be designated criminally disreputable than activities more common among the socially and economically powerful. It is this truth that makes group conflict theory particularly important in the study of crime. This point is pursued further below in our consideration of the Marxian theories of crime. We turn first, however, to two recent studies that illustrate the significant role group conflict theory increasingly is playing in stimulating important criminological research.

AN EXAMPLE: CRIME AROUND THE WORLD Two social scientists, Lynn McDonald (1976) and Ted Robert Gurr (1977; see also Gurr et al., 1977), have recently used conflict theory as a starting point for the comparative study of crime in different parts of the world. Each focuses on the early work of Richard Quinney as most representative of the conflict tradition. As noted above, Quinney very explicitly assigns a causal role to agencies of law creation and enforcement in determining the amount and type of crime recorded in a society. Both McDonald and Gurr attempt to bring data to bear on this provocative hypothesis. Significantly, their results tell us different things.

McDonald's analysis is conducted primarily with the nation-state as the unit of analysis. The first set of data comes from two sources: the International Criminal Police Organization (Interpol), providing crime statistics for forty countries and 38 percent of the world's population, and United Nations' statistics on juvenile delinquency, providing information for thirty-one countries and 25 percent of the world's population. In preparing these data for use in testing Quinney's version of conflict theory, McDonald (1976, p. 152) concludes that across nation-states "the most direct indicator of the means of formal control was the size of the police force. The greater the number of police per population the higher the official sanctions rate was hypothesized to be." Thus indicators of police-force size and expenditures are given particular emphasis among other variables in the analyses that follow. What McDonald (ibid., pp. 154–155) finds is that these variables have the expected effects: "the variables most successful at explaining rates of official crime and sanctions were the indicators of the means for formal control, and economic and social resources for it." Only one notable exception to this pattern is indicated: more traditional variables, such as unemployment, are somewhat successful in explaining murder rates.

Two additional points should be made in closing this selective review of McDonald's wide-ranging study. First, McDonald makes very clear the conflict position that official crime figures can be taken as no more than indicators of "recorded crime." Second, the relationship between police-force expenditure and size on the one hand, and recorded crime rates and sanctioning on the other, is regarded as one of cause and effect. However, the issue remains whether the police actually cause increases in crime rates and sanctioning, or whether the causal arrow points (as more conventionally assumed) in the opposite direction. This issue, and that of "real crime," are addressed again in the work of Gurr, which we consider next.

Gurr's research is concerned with "crime and civil strife," or with what he more generally calls "public disorder," in four major cities of the world—London, Stockholm, Sydney, and Calcutta—during the past century and a half. In this account, particular attention is given again to the evolution of public policies and institutions that define and control disorder. However, from the beginning Gurr assumes a rather different view of the problem than McDonald, a view that combines consensual and conflict themes. For example, Gurr (1977, p. 14) begins with the expectation that although the law sometimes may be used selectively to criminalize and thereby repress social movements that threaten elites, nonetheless in other circumstances the law is also used (albeit usually ineffectively) in response to widely supported demands for the control of behavior that threatens the safety of all or most of us.

Gurr finds substantial evidence that criminal legislation is used to protect class interests (i.e., by defining threatening collective behaviors as criminal) and that urban police forces have grown most frequently and dramatically in response to civil strife. However, this is only half the story. Other types of criminal law, particularly those dealing with "common crimes," are found to have a more consensual base, and increases in common crimes are found to precede rather than succeed police expansions. Thus Gurr (ibid., p. 130) notes that "in virtually every instance of correlation between increased disorder and an increase in police, disorder came first. In the case of strife there is typically a year's lag between a major episode and police expansion; the indicators for crime usually register increases for *five* years or more before police expansion." In other words, Gurr finds a causal sequence opposite to that implied by McDonald.

The task that remains is to make sense of these sometimes divergent findings. Much of the difference between McDonald and Gurr seems to be of degree rather than kind. For example, McDonald acknowledges that at least one crime—murder—is better explained with traditional consensus-based theories than group conflict theory, and Gurr acknowledges that the elite-motivated interests emphasized by conflict theory explain much of the criminalization of civil discontent. Thus, at a minimum, these authors seem to agree that some selection among the crimes to be considered is necessary if group conflict theory is to be used to maximum advantage. Put differently, there seems to be a base of agreement that the more traditional theories work best in explaining crimes like murder, and that the newer conflict theories work best in explaining responses to collective protest. The issue still to be resolved is the extent to which the different theories succeed in explaining the range of behaviors between the two extremes, and how the range of behaviors might best be divided with reference to the different theories (see

Hagan et al., 1977). Unfortunately, little has yet been accomplished along these lines, and as we note below, there is hostility to an eclectic approach of this kind among some Marxist criminologists.

MARXIST THEORIES

The debate that exists between consensus and conflict-based theories of crime is long-standing, and for some years most criminologists remained agnostic with regard to its underlying issues. (For discussion of this debate, see Chambliss and Seidman, 1971: Hills, 1971; Chambliss, 1973.) Thus in the late 1960s, William Chambliss (1969, pp. 8, 10) expressed a common view when he observed that "a resolution of this debate . . . would be premature"; that "in many cases there is no conflict"; and that "the influence of interest groups . . . is but one aspect of the processes which determine the emergence and focus of the legal norms." However, in the early 1970s, this view began to change. For example, two years after the above observations, Chambliss and Seidman (1971, p. 19) offered a far more definitive conclusion: "Indeed, the empirical studies . . . make it quite clear that the value-consensus model is . . . incapable of accounting for the shape and character of the legal system."

Similarly, Quinney's (1969, 1970) early work (reviewed above) talked about a variety of interest groups and contained a restrained optimism about legal change. Quinney (1969, p. 5) optimistically noted that criminal prosecutions emerged in Athens in the sixth century B.C., and that "this step protected . . . the lower class of Athens from aggression by the rich and powerful." Furthermore, Quinney (1970, p. 41) conceded that "groups . . . similar in power may well check each other's interests," and that "interest groups receive their individual claims in return for allowing other groups to press for their interests." As we have noted, at this stage Quinney was still a group conflict theorist, denying the assumption that a diversity of interests typically is resolved through compromise, but acknowledging that a plurality of interests operate, and clinging to the Poundian hope that "the public interest may become an ideal fulfilled" (Quinney, 1970, p. 42; cf. Pound, 1943).

However, the English "new criminologists" (Taylor et al., 1973, pp. 265–266) soon challenged the work of Quinney and other group conflict theorists by asserting that "the view of law as . . . in the hands of 'powerful interest groups,' does not take us far enough." Quinney (1975*b*, p. 193) soon agreed that "from the evidence of radical scholarship, government and business are inseparable." Thus (ibid., p. 194), "whilst pluralists may suggest that there are diverse and conflicting interests among groups in the upper class, what is ignored is the fact that members of the ruling class work within a common framework." Speaking for the new criminologists, Taylor et al. (1975, p. 3) have endorsed Quinney's new position as a "move to a Marxist economism." We turn next to a consideration of this new Marxist approach to the study of crime.

The New Criminology

The use of Marxist theory to understand crime is not entirely new (e.g., Bonger, 1916; Rusche and Kirchheimer, 1939). However, until recently this perspective was rarely applied, and underdeveloped. Ian Taylor, Paul Walton, and Jock Young (1973) ended the period of dormancy with their call for a new criminology. The two key features of their work for our purposes are a reconstituted perspective on the evolution of criminal laws and a revised image of criminal offenders.

As noted above, Taylor et al. see the group conflict theorists as having erred in regarding the criminal law as the outcome of a plurality of interest groups. There is only one prevailing interest in the view of the new criminologists: that formed in an alliance of capitalists and the state. This is possible, it is argued, because the institutions of capitalism have ensured their interests by masterminding the victory of "an ethic of individualism." This ethic holds *individuals* responsible for their acts, and at the same time diverts attention from the *environmental* structures in which these acts emerge. Even more significantly, however, this ethic has its primary effect on the *under*class, for it is "the labour forces of the industrial society" that are bound by the ethic of individualism, through the criminal law and its penal sanctions. The latter, of course, are premised on the ethic of individualism. Meanwhile, "the state and the owners of labour will be bound only by a civil law which regulates their competition between each other" (Taylor et al., 1973, p. 264). Two kinds of citizenship and responsibility are formed by this societal arrangement, the more advantaged of which is "beyond incrimination" and therefore beyond criminal sanction.

A second key feature of the new criminology is its attack on the group conflict theorists for maintaining "a conception of the criminal man as pathological" (ibid., p. 267). Taylor et al. acknowledge that the character of the "pathologies" is more likely in modern theories to be economic or political than psychological or biological. Still, they note (ibid.) that the picture is one of determination and "the overwhelming impression is one of determination at the expense of *purpose* and *integrity*" (emphasis in original). The "new criminal" is a "purposive creator and innovator of action," according to the new criminologists, and the crimes of these offenders are said (ibid.) to be the product of "individual or collective action taken to resolve . . . inequalities of power and interest." The new criminal, then, is the product of an informed "class consciousness."

The new criminology is ultimately a call to arms, exhorting its followers that "the retreat from theory is over, and the politicization of crime and criminology is imminent" (ibid., p. 281). This call for action includes references to "direct action revolutionaries," exemplified by the work of activist Scandinavian criminologists (ibid.).

The normative prescription of the new Scandinavian criminology led to the formation of the K.R.U.M., a trade union for inmates of Scandinavian prisons, and a union which was able, two years ago, to cordinate a prison strike across three national boundaries and across several prison walls.

Among other things, the new criminology is therefore also a strident call for action.

Spitzer's Marxian Theory of Crime and Deviance

The tendency of the new criminology to see all or most criminals as conscious catalysts for a classless society strains the credibility of the perspective presented. This tendency may be as naive, in another direction, as the tendency of labeling theory earlier to suggest that crime and deviance are simple products of societal attempts to control them; that is, all societal response and no deviant stimulus. Steven Spitzer's development of a Marxian theory of deviance deals with both of these problems in interesting ways.

Spitzer (1975, p. 640) begins by arguing that we must account not only for the status of labeled criminals but for criminal acts. Thus, "We must not only ask why specific members of the underclass are selected for official processing, but also why they behave as they do." Spitzer's answer lies in the historical and structural characteristics of capitalism. More specifically, Spitzer (ibid., p. 642) suggests that "problem populations" are produced because their behavior, personal qualities, and/or position threaten the *social relations of production* in capitalist societies.

These threats may take various forms as they disturb, hinder, or call into question any of the following key components of a capitalist society:

1 Capitalist modes of appropriating the product of human labor (e.g., when the poor "steal" from the rich).

2 The social conditions under which capitalist production takes place (e.g., those who refuse or are unable to perform wage labor).

3 Patterns of distribution and consumption in capitalist society (e.g., those who use drugs for escape and transcendence rather than sociability and adjustment).

4 The process of socialization for productive and nonproductive roles (e.g., youth who refuse to be schooled or those who deny the validity of "family life," such as gays).

5 The ideology which supports the functioning of capitalist society (e.g., proponents of alternative forms of social organization).

In turn, these threats are thought to derive from two sources: directly from fundamental contradictions in the capitalist mode of production (e.g., the emergence of "surplus populations"—the unemployed), and indirectly from disturbances in the system of class rule (e.g., the critical attitudes that educational institutions may produce in the form, for example, of dropouts and student radicals).

Spitzer goes on to suggest that the above processes may result in two distinct kinds of problem populations. On the one hand, there is "social junk," which, from the point of view of the dominant class, is a costly yet relatively harmless burden to society. Examples of this category include the officially administered aged, handicapped, mentally ill, and retarded, as well as some kinds of alcohol and drug offenders. In contrast to social junk, there is also a category that is described as "social dynamite." The distinctive feature of this category of persons is "its potential actively to call into question established relationships, especially relations of production and domination" (ibid., p. 645). Correspondingly, Spitzer notes that social dynamite tends to be more youthful, alienated, and politically volatile than social junk.

Finally, Spitzer suggests that there are two basic strategies followed in controlling the above kinds of criminals and deviants. The first strategy is referred to as "integrative," the latter as "segregative." The first approach involves control measures applied in the community, such as probation and parole, while the latter relies more on the use of institutions. For reasons that Andrew Scull outlines in greater detail below, it is argued that integrative controls will increasingly replace segregative controls in modern capitalist societies. We turn next, then, to a discussion of how the trend toward integrative control may occur.

Scull's Theory of Decarceration

To understand the work of Andrew Scull it is necessary first to define the term "decarceration." This term refers to a policy of dealing with offenders in and by the community by screening cases out of the criminal-justice system, settling cases prior to trial, and/or using sanctions other than imprisonment. More starkly, Scull (1977, p. 1) suggests that decarceration

> is shorthand for a state-sponsored policy of closing down asylums, prisons, and reformatories. Mad people, criminals, and delinquents are being discharged or refused admission to the dumps in which they have been traditionally housed. Instead, they are to be left at large, to be coped with "in the community."

Scull's purpose is to explain why this kind of change in the structural form of punishment might be occurring in capitalist societies. His answer builds on what Marxists (e.g., O'Connor, 1973) call "the fiscal crisis of the state."

The argument is that in modern capitalist societies, the state must try to fulfill two important but contradictory functions: accumulation and legitimation. The continual use of coercion in the interest of accumulation threatens the legitimacy of the state. To promote accumulation and legitimation, the state uses two major forms of expenditure: *social capital,* involving services and projects which increase the productivity of the labor force (e.g., health, housing, education) and *social expenses,* involving outlays necessary to maintain social harmony (e.g., welfare payments). The problem is that both of the above kinds of expenditures are increasingly being taken over by the state, while profits continue to be privately appropriated. This continuing "socialization of capital costs" has resulted in a fiscal crisis for the state. Meanwhile, the argument is that as the costs of institutionalization increase, and therefore contribute to the fiscal crisis, community alternatives become increasingly attractive. These alternative forms of treatment, outside of institutions, appear to be cheaper and more humane.

Scull, of course, does not see the decarceration movement as actually being humane. Rather, he sees this movement as resulting in the neglect of criminal and other kinds of dependent populations (i.e., "social junk" in Spitzer's terms) who are dumped into "deviant ghettos" with little or no concern for their care. Scull (ibid., p. 142) writes:

> As if they are industrial wastes which can without risk be left to decompose in some well-contained dump, these problem populations have increasingly been dealt with by a resort to their ecological separation and isolation in areas where they may be left to safely prey on one another.

This is a provocative view of a movement that has otherwise been understood in more sanguine terms.

Some Critical Comments on the Marxist Theories

A serious problem that has plagued Marxist theories of crime is their tendency to offer propositions that are difficult, if not impossible, to test. For example, a key proposition for many Marxist criminologists asserts that "the criminal law is . . . first and foremost a reflection of the interests and ideologies of the governing class" (Chambliss, 1974, p. 37; see also Quinney, 1976*b*, p. 192). However, little guidance is offered as to what exactly is the membership of this governing class. Thus Chambliss (1974, p. 37) is ultimately unable to decide "whether that class is private industry or state bureaucracy" and instead winds up reaching the contradictory conclusion (ibid., p. 27) that "government bureaucracies may, in the last analysis, be controlled by those who influence the society's economic resources . . . , but they also have a life and a force of their own." Assuming these two possibilities were not mutually exclusive, which they would seem to be and which would undermine the notion of a *single* ruling class, some significant questions remain unanswered. For example, how much of private industry and state bureaucracy is to be included within the "ruling class"? How diverse and extensive can these groupings be and still be considered a single "ruling class"? To what extent is there conflict within and between private industries and state bureaucracies? And, under what conditions do various industrial or bureaucratic groups prevail?

A response of the Marxist criminologist Richard Quinney (1975*b*, p. 194) to such questions is to suggest that "in contrast to pluralist theory, radical theory notes that the *basic interests,* in spite of *concrete differences,* place the elite into a distinct ruling class" (emphasis added). However, a difficulty with this formulation is that these "basic interests" are nowhere specifically identified, and it is therefore difficult to know what these class interests would predict in terms of legal control strategies. Thus the arguments of Spitzer (e.g., 1975, pp. 647–649) and Scull indicate that even direct *release* of offenders can be taken as evidence of the use of "integrative controls" to perpetuate the interests of a ruling class and state capitalism. This does not make the theory wrong or untrue, it simply makes it weak in predictive terms and difficult to disconfirm. This problem is partially addressed in the following discussion of an example of Marxist research. This study also introduces an important distinction between "instrumental" and "structural" Marxism.

AN EXAMPLE: BLACK REBELS BEFORE THE AMERICAN COURTS　The example of Marxian theory we will consider involves a study by Isaac Balbus (1973) of the legal response to several black ghetto riots: the 1965 Watts revolt, the 1967 Detroit rebellion, and the 1968 Chicago revolt. To begin with, Balbus notes that in each of these cities the "fires in the street" made court authorities acutely aware of their interest in aiding political authorities in stopping the street violence that had engulfed their cities. Put simply, authorities in all three cities were united in their desire to reestablish *order*. However, these revolts were also, of course, very *public* events that required *formal rationality,* or an attention to legal rules and procedures, for their effective control. Finally, it is clear that in each of the cities the results of the riots put overwhelming volume pressures on court organizations, in terms of the numbers of offenders handled, so that some attention to *organizational maintenance* was also necessary. Balbus argues that the need to be mindful of order, formal rationality, and organizational maintenance produced a remarkably similar court response in all three cities.

Thus during the initial phase in each city the processes of arrest, charging, and bail-setting were characterized by serious and widespread abrogations of the dictates of formal rationality and organizational maintenance. For example, in each city bail was set in amounts high enough to ensure that those arrested would be "kept off the streets" at least for the duration of the revolt, and in each city both judges and prosecutors publicly acknowledged this policy of preventive detention. Still, even during this phase of the court response, Balbus (p. 234) notes that formal legal rationality was not completely abandoned: "Although the police and military response was often brutal and led to considerable destruction of life, there was no wholesale slaughter of the riot participants. Martial law was *not* declared, and *some* concern for the legality of the arrests was exhibited." Balbus regards the latter as very important in that the effect of this policy was to treat these events and activities as far as possible as "ordinary crimes" rather than as acts of political protest and revolt.

Meanwhile, Balbus goes on to note that in all three cities the efforts of court authorities to "keep rioters off the streets" led to an unprecedented influx of prisoners into already overburdened detention facilities. However, this influx and the end of riot activity led ultimately to a dramatic shift in priorities among order, formal rationality, and organizational maintenance. The end of the revolts, a consequent decline in court interest in maintaining order, the overwhelming threat to organizational maintenance (created by the "keep them off the streets" policies), and a new concern for reestablishing full formal rationality led to a new effort to "clear the jails." In each city, therefore, while bail releases were far less frequent than normal during the first few days following arrest, releases subsequent to this initial period were dramatically *more* frequent than normal.

As well, postrevolt sanctioning policy, like postrevolt bail policy, was characterized by leniency. Thus whereas during the revolt the overriding interest in order led court authorities to prosecute virtually all those arrested and to do so on serious charges, in the weeks and months following the revolts the combined dictates of formal rationality and organizational maintenance produced convictions on less serious charges and sentences which Balbus describes as minimal. Note that in ordinary circumstances it becomes progressively more difficult with each step into the criminal-justice system to escape unscathed. However, what Balbus finds with rioters (p. 238) is just the opposite.

> . . . we found . . . a striking reversal of the standard model of the criminal process which posits a series of screens whose holes progressively diminish in size and from which the defendants thus find it increasingly difficult to escape; following the Los Angeles and Detroit major revolts, in contrast, the "holes" became progressively larger, and it was much easier to "escape" at the preliminary hearing and trial stages than it was at the earlier prosecution stage.

It is through the above means, Balbus concludes, that the American courts were able to put down the black ghetto revolts of the 1960s. Thus the revolts were repressed speedily and effectively, a semblance of legality prevailed (despite serious abrogations in the initial stages), and the equilibrium of the court organization was not seriously or permanently disrupted.

A key feature of the above analysis is its attention to the use of formal rationality. This emphasis distinguishes the analysis as an example of "structural" as opposed to "instrumental" Marxism (see also Greenberg, 1981). Instrumental Marxists tend to see the state and legal system as instruments which can be manipulated, almost at will, by the capitalist class as a whole or, in certain moments, by particular parts of this class. On the other hand, structural Marxists have argued that state apparatuses exercise a "relative" autonomy in their relationship with the capitalist class: "This means that in its basic struggle with the working class, the capitalist class cannot manipulate state institutions at will" (Bierne, 1979, p. 379). This is why, according to Balbus, the courts paid at least *some* attention to the law in dealing with ghetto rioters. More generally, the task remains to predict in advance, and with accuracy, when the law will be more and less autonomous from the class interests that seek to control it (Jacobs, 1980). It is this problem of prediction that presents the greatest challenge to the useful development of a Marxian theory of crime.

SUMMARY AND DISCUSSION

This chapter continued the structural theme of Chapter 6, but with a difference: the focus has here been on the way society is organized to control crime. Each kind of theory considered in this chapter does this in a somewhat different way.

* *Labeling theories* provided the lead in considering the ways in which society *responds* to crime and deviance as a topic in its own right.
* *Group conflict theories* focused in a more specific way on the role of different kinds of interest groups in making and enforcing the law.

• *Marxist theories* narrowed attention further by emphasizing the influence of economic forces in producing what are regarded as the crime problems of capitalist societies.

The above kinds of theories also share features in common. All are concerned with the process of criminalization, through which behaviors come to be considered criminal. As well, in considering the criminalization process, all of these theories are attentive to the role of conflict in determining outcomes. It is the exercise of power through conflict that is assumed to determine much of the patterning of crime. Finally, all of the theories we have considered in this chapter adopt a somewhat critical position with regard to the process of criminalization. That is, processes and patterns of criminalization are not taken for granted, but rather are examined in terms of the social and economic forces that produce them, and questioned in terms of the purpose and necessity of these forces, operating as they do. It is in large part this critical attitude that has led us to group the theories considered in this chapter as theories of overcontrol.

The theories of this chapter, like those of preceding chapters, have been subjected to criticism. A basic issue raised with regard to labeling theory is the extent to which behaviors assumed to result from the imposition of labels may actually precede them. Several studies using before-and-after longitudinal data were reviewed, with the resulting conclusion that labels often accurately identify preexisting behavioral differences. The challenge for labeling theory is to identify the kinds of situations where criminal labels consistently result in further criminality than would otherwise have occurred.

A related kind of concern was expressed for the group conflict theories. Early theoretical work emphasized the point that while some kinds of crime are effectively examined in conflict terms, others are not. Yet we have not progressed very far in our efforts to draw this kind of distinction. The discussion of consensus and conflict crimes in Chapter 2 is one attempt to do so, and in our discussion of McDonald's and Gurr's work we have noted that there is additional research that encourages this kind of division.

The most common complaint about the Marxist theories of crime involves their tendency to be nonfalsifiable. This problem has become particularly apparent in the shift from instrumental to structural Marxism. Recall that instead of seeing economic forces as always, or even usually, determining crime-control patterns in capitalist societies, the structural Marxists instead acknowledge some autonomy in legal behavior. Similarly, structural Marxists note that attempts to control crime may be "integrative" as well as "segregative," resulting in policies as apparently benign as direct release without trial or conviction. The problem is that all possibilities are allowed for within the purview of the theory; and insofar as the theory does not provide explicit predictions, it becomes difficult to test. Thus there may be a tendency to accept this theory more on the basis of faith than on the basis of data. Alternatively, as Marxist theory is developed, it may be possible to specify those conditions, for example, when the law is and is not expected to be autonomous from the class interests that seek to control it. We have reviewed in this chapter interesting research by Balbus, on the use of criminal law to control ghetto revolts, that is consistent with this goal. Additional research relevant to the Marxian theories will be considered in following chapters, particularly Chapter 8 which focuses on the operations of criminal-justice agencies.

A final way of bringing together our understanding of the theories of overcontrol is to summarize how they collectively explain the finding in Chapter 4 of a relationship between social class and criminal and delinquent behavior. The labeling theories early on made us aware of the role police and court bias can play in inflating this relationship, particularly in the form of official statistics gathered and published by crime-control agencies. These theories, then, call attention to the role of the societal response in generating this relationship. The group conflict and Marxist theories have gone on to note that sources of these differences include bureaucratic mechanisms that are involved in crime control, group interests that exercise their influence in the definition of crime, and the kinds of property relations that generate surplus populations in capitalist societies. All of these theories imply that our society experiences more crime than is necessary, and that much of this crime results from governmental overreactions to it.

RESPONDING TO CRIME: THE INJUSTICES OF CRIMINAL JUSTICE

8

THE ISSUE: RACE, CLASS, AND CRIMINAL INJUSTICE

Do the poor and minorities receive discriminatory treatment from the criminal-justice system? This is the issue that has animated research on the activities of criminal-justice agencies and the work that they do. With the emergence and development of the theories of overcontrol we discussed in Chapter 7, research on criminal-justice agencies has become a very central part of modern criminological work. The theories of overcontrol traditionally have predicted that the activities of criminal-justice agencies are discriminatory, in the sense noted above, and much recent criminological work has sought to test the validity of this prediction. However, it should not be assumed that the issue is as simple as it may initially seem.

The issue is complex, in part, because the meaning of "criminal justice," like the meaning of "crime," discussed in Chapter 1, is symbolic and variable (Hagan and Abonetti, 1982). The meaning of "criminal justice" is *symbolic* in that the criminal law and its enforcement by criminal-justice agencies are expected to embody fundamental principles, for example, "equality before the law," that are thought to define the very kind of society in which we live. At the same time, the meaning of "criminal justice" is *variable* in that these symbols and principles are subject to change, as well as to alternative understandings. Philosophers from Plato and Aristotle to Rawls (1971) have resisted these fundamental facts by seeking and suggesting principles that could give the idea of justice an absolute and fixed meaning. These efforts have failed (Nettler, 1979, pp. 28–31) because conceptions and perceptions of justice are determined in substantial part by the times, places, and locations in the social structure from which they derive. This does not mean that there are no standards by which criminal justice can be measured, or that criminal justice itself is standardless. What it does mean is that our standards of criminal justice, such as equality'before the law, are neither as certain nor as constant as commonly assumed.

For example, Nettler (1979, p. 30) is able to identify three common meanings of equality (numerical, proportional, and subjective equality), all of which are important in determining patterns of legal behavior.

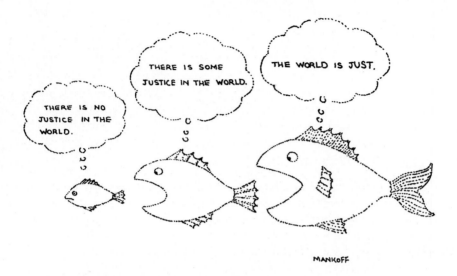

MANKOFF

"Numerical equality" refers to efforts to make punishments correspond in invariant ways to offenses. This meaning of equality is as old as the desire for "an eye for an eye," and as new as calls for determinate sentencing laws which require judges to give exactly the same sentences to offenders convicted of the same crimes. "Proportional equality," on the other hand, seeks to vary the punishment in proportion to some characteristic of the offender; for example, if the punishment is a fine, in proportion to the person's income. "Subjective equality," or equity, attempts to take more subjective considerations into account; for example, by judging that embezzlement is more serious when committed by an elected public official than when committed by a private citizen, and by varying penalties accordingly. The variable meanings of "equality" frequently come into conflict, making it difficult, and sometimes impossible, to conclude whether discrimination has occurred.

Nettler goes on to draw an important connection between social change and criminal justice by noting that the specific meaning of "equality" as applied in the pursuit of justice often varies with the vantage point considered. Thus in an earlier era when laws involving the crimes of women and children developed in this country, an *assumption* of subjective equality (or equity) dictated that unequal treatment be mandated by legislation for what were then regarded as *un*equal members of society. Although these laws often encouraged differential leniency, and although they were justified as "protective," they perpetuated symbolically an unequal status for women and children. Today as women, and sometimes children, are recognized as equals, equal treatment (numerical equality) is also demanded, and the older laws in turn are now more likely to be regarded as "discriminatory."

In this chapter we will use the various meanings of "equality" to consider the activities of criminal-justice agencies and the work that they do. While the multiple meanings of "equality" may complicate the moral judgments we can reach about the injustices of criminal justice, they will not prevent us from saying a great deal about what these agencies do, and about the perceptions of their activities by some very significant parts of the public. As we will see, the multiple meanings we have considered are a key part of the conflict that pervades criminal-justice activities today.

UNDERSTANDING THE CRIMINAL-JUSTICE SYSTEM

Two terms recur in writings about the police and courts: the first makes reference to a criminal-justice *process,* the second to a criminal-justice *system.* When talking about the criminal-justice process, criminologists generally have in mind the sequence of decisions that confront an accused person moving through the stages that lead from the discovery to the punishment of a crime; including arrest, charging, pleading, the setting of bail, conviction, and sentencing. The interconnections between these decision points and the actors and agencies that make them are often taken as constituting a criminal-justice system. This system has some of the characteristics of a hierarchy in that the organizations which comprise it can be roughly ranked in their final authority to review decisions made by others; but as Albert Reiss (1974, p. 680) notes, the flow of people and information in the system does not correspond altogether with the hierarchical arrangements.

Reiss goes on to identify seven major parts of what many call the "criminal-justice system."

1 The citizen law-enforcement system, made up of individual and corporate actors who report cases as victims, complainants, and witnesses.

2 The public law-enforcement, or police, system, which controls decisions about discovering crimes, investigating complaints, making arrests, pressing warrants, and booking offenders.

3 The defendant system, made up of citizens accused of crimes and their defense counsel.

4 The public prosecution system, which controls decisions about filing the information, making the charge, securing the evidence, plea bargaining, and forming the strategy for prosecution.

5 The misdemeanor and felony courts, where substantive and procedural questions of law and adjudication must first be resolved.

6 The correctional system, consisting of the organizations responsible for the custody and rehabilitation of convicted offenders.

7 The appellate judicial system, which has the power to stay the actions of others pending review, and the sole power to grant or deny appeals.

We will refer to the above as a "loosely coupled system" (see also Hagan et al., 1979). Leaving aside for the moment the precise meaning attached to this concept, we can note that there is considerable precedent for a conception of looseness in the American criminal-justice system. Reiss (1974, p. 690) speaks of American criminal justice as a "loosely articulated hierarchical network." Eisenstein and Jacob (1977, p. 37) note of this same system that even "the judge does not rule or govern, at most, he manages, and often he is managed by others." Jack Gibbs (1978) is perhaps most pessimistic in calling the American criminal-justice system an "ungoverned mishmash." Meanwhile, Reiss suggests that "the major means of control among the subsystems is *internal* to each," with the significant consequence that "each subsystem creates its own system of justice." The loosely coupled character of the American criminal-justice system facilitates this tendency toward internal control.

We can now offer a connotative definition of "loose coupling": it is meant to evoke the image of entities, in this case court subsystems, that, although somewhat responsive to one another, still maintain independent identities with considerable evidence of physical and social separateness (Weick, 1976). This tendency toward loose coupling is found, of course, not only in the criminal-justice system, but also in the educational system and other large bureaucracies. Meyer and Rowan (1979) have noted the following characteristics that loosely coupled systems share in common: structural elements (e.g., the representatives of subsystems) are only loosely linked to one another and to activities; rules often are violated; decisions often go unimplemented, or if implemented have uncertain consequences; techniques are often of uncertain efficacy; and evaluation and inspection systems are often subverted or rendered so vague as to provide little coordination.

Below we will discuss some specific consequences of loose coupling in the criminal-justice system, and of occasional attempts to tighten the links. Here we will note a more general point. A salient advantage of loosely coupled systems (whether they be the courts, the educational system, or some other bureaucracy) is that they can easily incorporate changes demanded by the external environment (e.g., the community) and at the same time selectively ignore the purposes of the changes. (Attempts to abolish plea bargaining are a common example, and are discussed below). The importance of this capability is that the organization is able to maintain and often increase its institutional legitimacy by giving the impression of reforming itself, without dramatically changing its day-to-day practices. Thus the more such organizations change, the more, for many practical purposes, they remain the same. All of this is very useful in serving the symbolic goals of criminal justice noted above, although, as we will note below, is frequently lends a ceremonial or mythical quality to criminal-justice operations that frustrates more instrumental goals of reform.

We turn now to a more specific discussion of some of the important components of the loosely coupled system we have thus far described in very general terms.

THE POLICE

From Idea to Reality

As central as police forces are to modern conceptions of the city, they are a relatively recent innovation. The Metropolitan Police of London was created in 1829 and served as a model for police forces in the United States, which were established in every major American city between about 1840 and 1870. Prior to this, Richardson (1970) notes, an extremely broad conception of the police prevailed. For example, the term "police" was used early in the nineteenth century to refer to the general state of public order and health of the city. The "police" of a city was considered good if the streets were clean and public order was maintained.

Police services as we now conceive them were provided by a number of groups prior to the formation of a full-time force in New York City: a salaried night watch kept a lookout for fires and disorderly youth, there was a small group of elected constables, and 100 marshals were appointed by the mayor. The constables and marshals received their pay in the form of fees for services and, in criminal matters, acted only when engaged by the victim of a theft to recover stolen property. To accomplish the latter goal, officers cultivated extensive contacts among professional criminals. The corruption involved in such relationships, combined with the absence of service where no reward was forthcoming, encouraged the search for another form of police organization.

However, Richardson (1974) notes that these were not the only factors involved. Urban riots were common in cities like Boston, New York, and Philadelphia in the 1830s and 1840s. The riots involved ethnic, religious, and political rivals, and later labor conflicts. The idea of a civilian police force under military discipline was attractive as a means of containing such conflicts. The idea of a police force also spoke to a concern about "unseemly public behavior," particularly public drunkenness. The early nineteenth century represented a high point in the per capita consumption of alcohol in the United States, and, as Richardson (ibid., p. 213) points out, "prior to the establishment of bureaucratic police departments, sober citizens could do nothing about drunken ones except to avoid them or step over them." These several factors combined to provide American police departments with a broad mandate to prevent and detect crime, maintain public order, and suppress unseemly behavior in public places.

However, what is perhaps most interesting about the development of this mandate in American cities is that it very early on involved a form of organization that facilitated the loosely coupled system of internal control described above. This point is well made by a comparison of the early London and New York City police.

The Police of Two Cities

The New York City police force was established in 1845, sixteen years after the London force. From the beginning, the two forces were very different. London officers were clothed in a long "blue-tailored coat, blue trousers . . . and a glazed black top-hat . . . with a leather crown" (Critchley, 1967, p. 51). They carried no weapons other than short batons hidden under the long tails of their coats. In contrast, the New York City police did not wear a distinguishing blue uniform until 1853, and although not formally authorized, by the end of the 1860s revolvers were standard equipment. These outward differences in appearance reflected more fundamental differences in the organization of the forces and the ways in which they operated (Miller, 1975).

London's first police commissioners, Charles Rowan and Richard Mayne, along with the founder of the force, Sir Robert Peel, were faced with the task of creating a police strategy to contain very explicit forms of class conflict. To achieve public acceptance, Rowan and Mayne sought to identify police practices as closely as possible with the legal system, drawing on the authority of national sovereignty, the restraints of procedural rules, and guarantees of civil liberties. Their purpose was to make the police a tightly disciplined body of professionals, subject to summary dismissal for misconduct and divorced from the politics of the localities they served. Miller (1975, p. 317) acknowledges that "while the laws of England were hardly a pure realm of justice above contemporary social inequality, they were the broadest available source of external legitimation for the police." Nineteenth-century observers noted the ironic effectiveness of this symbolism in containing the class conflicts in London during this period.

> The mob quails before the simple baton of the police officer, and flies before it, well knowing the moral as well as physical force of the Nation whose will, as embodied in law, it represents. And take any man from that mob, place a baton in his hand and a blue coat on his back, put him forward as the representative of the law, and he too will be found équally ready to face the mob from which he was taken, and exhibit the same steadfastness and courage in defense of constituted order (cited in Silver, 1967, p. 14).

Alternatively, New York City of the mid-nineteenth century was characterized more by ethnic than class conflict. This is not to say that class conflicts were unimportant in New York or that the police played no role in them. By the 1880s and 1890s, American police were playing a prominent role in controlling labor unrest (see Harring, 1977). However, Miller (1974, p. 316) notes that in the 1860s, "America's propertied and working class alike saw a political order they valued threatened by irresponsible foreigners who did not appreciate democracy." Here the police were supporting a political order that was threatened by an alien minority rather than a native majority. Thus there was no need in New York City to use the legal system to rise above social conflict. The new police instead drew on the ideals of democracy and the representation of a local political community. The authority of the New York City police officer was personal rather than institutional. The London police were too authoritarian for democratic America.

The most important consequence of the American reliance on personal rather than impersonal authority was that it granted much greater discretionary authority to the individual officer. We see in this one historical source the kind of looseness we have associated with American criminal justice. An important manifestation of this looseness, or increased discretionary power, was the freedom it granted police officers in the use of force. While the London commissioners were known for their careful supervision of the use of force by the city's "bobbies," Miller (1974, p. 319) notes that by the end of the 1860s,

> The New York Times complained that shooting was becoming a substitute for arrest and described the patrolman as "an absolute monarch, within his beat, with complete power of life and death over all within his range . . . without the forms of trial or legal inquiry of any kind." Amidst a vicious cycle of criminal and police

violence, the patrolman was free to exercise much greater physical force than his London colleague.

In sum, New York police officers were both less regulated and less restrained than their London counterparts. The implication is that historically American police have had a form of low visibility and wide-ranging discretion that encourages abuse. That is, the police do much of their work out of public view and with considerable freedom to shape their own decisions. How has this discretion been used? What exactly do the police do with their time? Is it systematically used to the disadvantage of the poor and minorities? To answer these questions, we turn to contemporary studies of the use of discretion in the context of what we have characterized as a loosely coupled criminal-justice system.

Police Work

There is no doubt that modern police work is a diversified task. It has been variously suggested that we consider the police as an "omnibus service agency" (Clark and Sykes, 1974, p. 462), that we understand the police officer in his or her correlated roles as "philosopher, guide, and friend" (Cumming, Cumming, and Edell, 1965), and that we examine the activities of the police officer as a "peace keeper" (Bittner, 1967). Each in its own way, these proposals all note that the police do many other things in addition to catching criminals. One criminologist who traded his armchair *temporarily* for a badge observes, "As a police officer myself, I found that society demands too much of its police: not only are they expected to enforce the law but to be curbside psychiatrists, marriage counselors, social workers and even ministers and doctors" (Kirkham, 1974).

When in doubt or desperation, it seems, we frequently call the police. This makes the police the key decision-makers, or gate-keepers, into the worlds of juvenile and criminal justice. There are at least two factors that keep the police in this role. The first factor is that the variety of tasks helps the police to avoid an exclusively oppressive role. Instead, they are able to serve a social service role as well. The second factor is that the police often are the only agency available on a twenty-four-hour emergency basis. Thus in addition to occasional incidents of crime, the police must deal with everything from unexpected childbirths to bag ladies, skid row residents, drug addicts, psychiatric cases, domestic disputes, landlord-tenant disputes, and traffic violations. "Perceived through time-and-motion studies," Clark and Sykes (1974, p. 462) conclude, "the vast majority of what police personnel do must be categorized as omnibus service that, on the surface at least, *could* be provided by a nonpolice organization." The varied demands on police time are significant, in part, because as we will see, the public gets, to a surprising extent, much of what it asks for.

The Encounter of Police with Citizens

Albert Reiss and Donald Black (Black and Reiss, 1970; Reiss, 1971*b*) have conducted some of the most important research on police-citizen encounters. Theirs was one of the first studies to use trained field observers to study police behavior. Thirty-six persons with law and social science backgrounds rode in patrol cars and walked with police officers in three of North America's largest cities. Covering all shifts, all days of the week, for seven consecutive weeks, the observers reported on 5,713 incidents. The results inform us about a variety of important issues.

Above we noted the theme of democracy in the historical understanding of American policing. A very basic insight of the Reiss and Black research echoes this democratic theme in noting that most police work is "reactive" rather than "proactive." Their point is that the police in large American cities usually do not *seek out* deviant behavior, but rather respond to complaints about such behavior. They make this point by distinguishing two basic types of mobilization of the police in terms of who makes the initial decision that police action is appropriate: "reactive mobilizations" are citizen-initiated, while "proactive mobilizations" are police-initiated. Most of the incidents Black and Reiss observed were reactive, that is, citizen-initiated. Interestingly, the historical roots of this pattern go back to the period between 1880 and 1890—to the advent of the patrol wagon and signal system, based on alarm boxes spread throughout large American cities. This system was invented in Chicago in 1881 and was employed in more than 100 cities by 1900. The modern analogue, of course, is the radio-dispatched patrol car. The point is that these technologies allowed the police to organize their work "reactively" around citizen calls for assistance, rather than "proactively," as the older "watch" system implied (Harring, 1977, p. 294–5).

So it is the citizens of the community, and not the police, who assume the initiating role in much modern police work. Once past this initiating stage, however, the police officer assumes a more central role in the unfolding social drama. It is his or her role to make sense of and/or reorder the situation in question. Reiss and Bordua (1967) argue that the basic tactic for accomplishing these goals is to "take charge." Often, the intent is to "freeze" the situation and avoid escalation of the incident involved. Verbal and physical expressions of authority are the principal instruments used in this "take-charge" strategy. This strategy becomes most important when it fails, because, as we see next, it is in these circumstances that unnecessary arrests and brutality are most likely to occur.

The Use and Abuse of Force

Slippage in the amount of respect they are receiving in police-citizen encounters may be perceived by officers as a warning signal that they are losing their authoritative edge, and the outcome of such a situation may be the unnecessary use of force. Alarmed at the apparent willingness of Chicago police to resort to the use of violence, William Westley (1970) designed a study to determine just how extensive police rationalizations of the use of brutality were. Westley found in the course of his research that the police regard the public as their enemy, feeling that the demands of their occupation set them in conflict with the community. Skolnick (1966) has noted that the requirement that police enforce unpopular morality and traffic laws further distances then from the public, while the danger of the potentially more violent aspects of policing leads them to treat large parts of the public as "symbolic assailants." Taylor Buckner (1970) summarizes the situation when he describes the relationship of the police to society as one of "antagonistic symbiosis." The problem is that most societal institutions need the police to carry out their "dirty work" but seldom value police services. Meanwhile, the police must rely on the support of these social institutions but can never satisfy their range of conflicting demands.

Westley goes on to note additional pressures that complicate the police officer's work, including the competition between patrol officers and detectives for important arrests, the publicity value associated with *solved* cases, and public demands for strict control of certain offenses (e.g., sexual assaults and drug abuse). All of these factors encourage or pressure officers to enlarge on the areas of their work where the use of violence will be legally justified. Westley finds that the results of these pressures are tendencies toward police secrecy, attempts to coerce respect from the public, and a belief that almost any means are legitimate in completing an important arrest.

Westley (1953, p. 39) uses the results of a survey conducted with the Chicago police to support his thesis, for his data indicate that "37% of the men believed that it was legitimate to coerce respect." The point, of course, is that police officers who believe this are likely to resort to violence to obtain respect from the public. Reiss (1971b) goes on to suggest that as the kinds of factors we have discussed accumulate, and as they are combined with a perception that the courts are not proceeding in agreement with police views, levels of police brutality will increase. In such circumstances, Reiss suggests, a "police subculture" with its own standards of justice may emerge. Skolnick regards this subculture as a logical extension of the police officer's "working personality." The implications are ominous.

Using records on 1,500 civilians killed by the police across the United States up to 1970, Kobler (1980) has recently dramatized just how ominous the police use of force can be. This research begins by noting that the police are the only representatives of governmental authority who in the ordinary course of events legally are permitted to use force against citizens. Other agencies of the state must rely upon requests, persuasion, public opinion, custody, and legal and judicial processes to gain compliance with rules and laws. One might expect, then, that the police access to force would be closely monitored. However, this is not the case, despite the fact that the ratio of citizens to police killed in these deadly encounters is on the order of 5:1. In fact, only 3 of the 1,500 killings resulted in criminal punishments. At the same time, there is considerable evidence that a sizable percentage of the killings were of questionable necessity and justifiability. This point is made most effectively by noting that when some threat of death or severe injury to a person is used as the criterion for the justifiability of a police homicide, it is estimated that about 40 percent of the deaths were justifiable, 20 percent questionable, and 40 percent unjustifiable. Just how academic such a calculation is becomes apparent, however, when it is recalled that less than 1 percent of the police homicides were legally judged unjustifiable. "Defense of life" and "fleeing felon" rules regularly and leniently are used to justify such killings. Indeed, in some states "reasonable suspicion" that the victim is carrying out a felony, or simply the act of fleeing itself, is justifiable grounds for the police use of deadly force. Kobler notes that the "fleeing felon" rule seems to derive from the time when all felonies were punishable by death. However, given that today many nonviolent offenses (e.g., statutory rape, larceny, sodomy, perjury, adultery) are accorded felony status, and that today the death penalty is rare, the fleeing felon rule seems rather incongruous. In any case, such laws and the above findings make clear the great significance of the police use of discretion in relations with the public.

The Role of Suspect Demeanor

One hypothesis implied by the above findings is that it would be suspects who do not show respect in their interactions with the police who would be most likely to be subjected to arrest and conviction. Piliavin and Briar (1964) set out to test this hypothesis. Their expectation was that the "demeanor" of juveniles constitutes a basic set of cues used by the police to make their decisions in juvenile cases. Consistent with this expectation, Piliavin and Briar found that other than previous record, it was the juvenile's general demeanor that was the most crucial determinant of both decisions on the street (i.e., whether to take the juvenile in) and the decision made in the station (i.e., whether to release or detain). More specifically, Piliavin and Briar found that the degree of "contriteness" projected by juveniles influences their legal fate. Their conclusion is that the official delinquent is the product of a social as well as a legal judgment made by the police.

Implicit in the Piliavin and Briar study is an explanation for higher arrest rates among juveniles from minority groups. The explanation is that juveniles from minority groups are more frequently arrested because their demeanor elicits a punitive police response (Ferdinand and Luchterhand, 1970; Black, 1971). A fascinating test of a hypothesis of this kind is found in a study by Sykes and Clark (1975). They note that in general an "asymmetrical status norm" characterizes police-citizen encounters. This norm requires that the police receive more deference than they give; for example, in the form of being addressed as "officer," while the citizen is addressed by given name. This asymmetry exists in part because the police represent the authority of the law, and also because the police are often of higher occupational and socioeconomic status than the suspects they confront. All of this becomes more complicated and problematic when elements of race and ethnicity are present in the situation. For example, an entirely unprejudiced officer, in expecting general deference, may be interpreted by a minority citizen as indicating the officer's own ethnic group's superordination. On the other hand, the minority citizen's refusal to express deference may be viewed by the officer as a refusal to acknowledge the normal social obligations of all citizens and the officer's symbolic status. In sum, observation of the asymmetrical status norm can convey double meanings, placing both the officer and the minority civilian in a double bind. Sykes and Clark are able to show with their data that this can lead to the more punitive treatment of minorities.

We are therefore back to the issue with which we started this chapter: what role do the racial and class positions of citizens play in determining the outcomes of their encounters with police? An increasing number of studies have sought to answer this very question.

The Role of Police Bias

One of the first systematic efforts to summarize research on class bias in the use of police discretion is provided by David Bordua (1969). Four studies are emphasized in this review. Each of the studies examines factors associated with police decision-making in juvenile cases. Their purpose is to answer the following question, "What determinants operate in police decisions regarding the handling of juveniles taken into custody?"

The studies Bordua cites were conducted by Goldman (1963), McEachern and Bauzer (1967), Bodine (1964), and Terry (1965). In three of the four studies, Bordua (1969, p. 158) finds that the following factors influence the disposition of juvenile cases: "If we put together the findings of McEachern and Bauzer and Bodine we find that offense type, arrest record, probation status, age, department, and officer all seem to affect disposition; of the factors common to these studies, and also in Goldman's, offense and previous record seem the most securely established." What stands out in this summary is that class and race achieve *no consensual recognition* as determinants of police dispositions in juvenile cases.

Robert Terry's (1965) study of police work in a midwestern city is the last piece of research considered in Bordua's review, and it is this study that is most central to his conclusions. What Terry found was that offense, prior record, and age held up as correlates of disposition of decision. When twelve factors were considered, "Terry points out that his results imply a rather 'legalistic' handling of juveniles and also that the much claimed socio-economic bias of the police simply does not appear" (Bordua, 1969, p. 158). Although, as we note further below, not all studies confirm Terry's legalistic viewpoint (e.g., Ferdinand and Luchterhand, 1970; Smith, 1982), there are recent assessments that reach similar conclusions (e.g., Green, 1970; Hirschi, 1975). The implication is that if race and class biases exist in police decision-making, they apparently are not as pervasive as was once believed.

Bordua offers a compelling explanation for the failure of a more substantial class bias to show up in police statistics. The police are constrained in the number of juveniles that they can refer to court, and beyond court, there is limited institutional space for juveniles. The great majority of juveniles must be returned to the community, and the police know this. Thus in Terry's study nearly 90 percent of the juveniles were returned to the community without a court appearance, with court referrals reserved for only the most severe cases. Bordua (1969, p. 158) concludes that we should therefore not be surprised at the absence of substantial class bias in police studies: ". . . in order for socio-economic bias to appear, it would have to be monumental since after all the police must pay *some* attention to the law."

The important research of Albert Reiss and Donald Black (Black and Reiss, 1970; Reiss, 1971*b*) was designed so as to allow examination of racial differences in the police treatment of suspects and offenders in several large American cities. At the outset, this research revealed a disparity between the proportion of black and white juveniles taken into custody and later arrested: only 8 percent of the whites were eventually arrested, as compared to 21 percent of the blacks. The disparity was explained partly by the fact that black juveniles were disproportionately involved in more serious offenses. However, a second factor was also found to account for the disparity: the preferences of *black complainants*.

The point that Black and Reiss make with these data is that a complainant in search of justice can make direct demands with which the police officer has little choice but to comply. In the cases of complaints about black juveniles in these data, the complainants seeking more severe dispositions are themselves black. On the other hand, the white officer acting without a black complainant is considerably more lenient; and when no complainant is involved in the police-juvenile encounter, the racial difference in arrest rates nearly disappears (14 percent for blacks, 10 percent for whites). The conclusion Black and Reiss (1970, p. 72) reach is that, "Given the prominent role of the . . . [black] complainant in the race differential . . . , it may be inappropriate to consider this pattern as an instance of discrimination on the part of police."

However, if the police did not exercise racial prejudice in the kinds of decisions that Black and Reiss studied, there is nonetheless plenty of evidence that they held prejudicial attitudes toward blacks, as reflected in verbal expressions of hostility. Thus an earlier report by Black and Reiss (1967) indicates that over the course of the observations, a large majority of the police expressed antiblack attitudes. The implication is that there is a disparity between words and deeds. Another part of the above study offers interesting evidence on this point. Here Reiss (1968) looked at incidents of police brutality, taking into account whether the officer involved was black or white. The results indicated that white officers inflicted less than half as much of their brutality on black citizens as did black officers. Reiss (ibid., p. 17) uses these findings to reflect on the words and deeds issue, concluding, "though no precise estimates are possible, the facts just given suggest that white policemen, even though they are prejudiced . . . , do not discriminate . . . in the excessive use of force."

In this section we have given considerable attention to the research of Reiss and Black. Two recent studies that yield somewhat different findings should also be considered. The first is a study done by Ericson (1982) in a suburban Canadian jurisdiction. Of 1,323 encounters between citizens and officers observed in Ericson's study, 47.4 percent were characterized as proactive mobilizations, and only 52.6 percent as reactive mobilizations. "On the surface," Ericson (ibid., p. 74) notes, "our data reveal that patrol officers are much more assertive in producing encounters with citizens than the figures provided by Reiss, Black and others would lead us to believe." Still, when only "major incidents" are looked at in the Canadian data, Ericson reports that more than 82 percent result from reactive mobilizations. In these incidents, complainants may still loom large in the decision-making process.

A second study by Smith (1982), based on 742 suspect contacts with police in twenty-four American departments, confirms the influence of complainants but also points to the impact of suspect characteristics. Thus this study reports that antagonistic suspects are much more likely to be taken into custody than suspects who display deference. Furthermore, black suspects are more likely to be arrested. Smith explains that *part* of this race effect can be accounted for by the fact that black suspects are significantly more likely to act toward the police in a hostile or antagonistic manner. Nonetheless, and apart from suspect behavior and victim demands, it remains the case that in Smith's data black suspects are somewhat more likely than white suspects to be arrested.

The Social Organization of Police Work

The inconsistency of findings on such issues as race and class bias in police decision-making encourages the search for factors, such as the way in which police work is variously organized within and between departments, that might increase or decrease the occurrence of discrimination. For example, we know that very different kinds of police organizations have developed across the cities of America. One distinguishing feature that may be relevant to the occurrence of discrimination in policing is the degree to which different departments have become professionalized. By the 1930s, Richardson (1974) notes, a model of the police as professional had come to dominate the literature on police work. A department was considered professional to the extent that it freed itself from political interference, had long-term leadership, employed the latest technology, and emphasized its crime-fighting capabilities. The development of the *Uniform Crime Reports* (*UCR*) and the National Police Academy under the auspices of the FBI both played a role in furthering the goal of professionalism. The major crime index and the clearance ratio of the *UCR* gave a measure to evaluate departments in the pursuit of professional standards, and the National Police Academy provided an institutionalized form of certification for police administrators. Some argued that the worst of two worlds was coming into being, in that American departments still lacked the careful administrative controls characteristic of English and European police, while now the tradition of control by local elected political officials was being dismantled as well (Berkley, 1969). Nonetheless, the hope was that the "new police officer," a well-educated and extensively trained public servant, working in a highly organized and technologically proficient department, would be less prone to brutality and other patterns of decision-making that produce disparity in enforcement.

James Q. Wilson (1968*a*; see also 1968*b*) provides a classic evaluation of this "new look" in the organization of police work. Wilson begins by noting that the considerable discretion given officers in their handling of juveniles allows the organization of a department to make a large difference in the disposition of juvenile cases. Two cities are considered by Wilson, one in a western city and another in an eastern city, and compared in their respective ways of dealing with juvenile cases. "Western City" is characterized as having a "professional" department. The department is highly organized and centralized; its officers are recruited on the basis of their achievement as contrasted with their ascribed characteristics, with education playing a particularly important role in hiring decisions.

On the other hand, "Eastern City" is characterized as having a "fraternal" department. Decentralization is a distinguishing feature of the department. Here officers are chosen primarily on the basis of their ascribed rather than achieved characteristics. Special significance is attached to their residence and recognition in the community. Rather than formal training, the focus in the department is on learning "how to get along." The difference between the cities is well expressed by the expectation in the fraternal type of setting that "it's not what you know, but who you know that counts."

A comparison of the official statistics generated by the departments in the two cities is revealing. The "professional" officers in Western City, operating within the framework of their impersonal standards, apparently arrest a relatively larger share of the juveniles they encounter. In other words, the professional department of Western City follows a more punitive policy.

Where this pattern becomes most interesting, however, is as it involves black neighborhoods. Blacks are referred to court in Eastern City at a higher rate than whites, while blacks and whites are referred at about the same rate in Western City. In other words, a disparity occurs in the fraternal department, but not in the professional department. The absence of statistical controls for the kinds of variables considered above (victim demands, suspect demeanor) makes it difficult to call this disparity "discrimination." What is intriguing, however, is that the disparity in referrals vanishes in the professional department not by way of a reduction in arrests but through an increased arrest rate. Put differently, professionalization reduces or eliminates discrimination, but at the cost of increasing arrests overall.

Wilson has an explanation for the higher arrest rate that characterizes the more professional department. This explanation focuses on the in-depth, personalized knowledge that officers in fraternal departments have of the communities in which they work. Other than through patrol assignments, officers in professional departments tend to know little of the communities in which they work. In fraternal departments, officers are often picked from the community and for their relationship to it. The significance of this difference is that officers in a fraternal department, such as Eastern City, may often be aware of means other than arrest for resolving cases involving juveniles. Knowing the family, the neighborhood, and the kinds of problems that regularly disturb it, officers may often be able to find personalized solutions that avoid the need for arrests.

Not only the kind of department, but also the work done within it, may influence the use made of police discretion. We have already noted the important distinction between reactive and proactive mobilizations of the police. Some crimes, particularly what are often called "victimless crimes" (e.g., drugs, prostitution, gambling, etc.), nearly always require a pro-active form of police work, because there are no complainants to initiate cases and provide information. Whole areas of police work, for example, the work done by agents of the Drug Enforcement Administration, are organized around the problems of such investigations (Wilson, 1978). In this kind of police work, and, as we will see later, in the resulting prosecutions, it is often necessary, by improvising on the forms of discretion available, to find means of *tightening* the links in an otherwise loosely coupled criminal-justice system. The links are tightened as a means of successfully pursuing what are otherwise usually unprosecutable cases. Jerome Skolnick's (1975) classic study, *Justice Without Trial*, illustrates this point.

Skolnick's observations of a middle-sized American police force lead him to conclude that there are important differences between the kinds of work done by what are called "peace officers" (ordinary patrol personnel) and "law officers" (specialists, including detectives, members of the vice and fraud squads, etc.) The key difference is that the latter kinds of police work are more punitive and inquisitory in nature, relying heavily on the use of offenders or persons who can supply information about offenses. Thus Skolnick notes that because reports of crimes of vice do not arise from citizen complaints, law officers must use informers to lead them to potential offenders. The result is a gamelike pattern of activities that is at its peak in the area of narcotics. Narcotics enforcement encourages, and often may require, the expansion of discretion into undelegated areas. Narcotics officers must cultivate networks of informers, develop entrap-ment techniques, evade or circumvent search-and-seizure restrictions, become knowledgeable about the use of various drugs, and become skilled interrogators. The need for informers is the most serious of these potentially corrupting requirements. Officers must cultivate and coerce their informers to extract necessary information, as illustrated in such films as *Prince of the City*. This may require not only the unauthorized use of drugs and money, and therefore access to them, but the negotiation and manipulation of police reports, plea bargaining, and charging practices as well. At the same time, officers with well-developed informer networks can become very central persons in police and court operations, because the information they obtain can be crucial to convictions not only in narcotics but in other kinds of cases. In an otherwise loosely coupled system, then, law officers and prosecutors may have resources to exchange: law officers have and can get information needed for convictions, while prosecutors control the plea bargaining that can be used to further develop these information sources. The end result may, in these circumstances, be a more tightly coupled set of operations than is characteristically the case. We pursue these points, as they relate to the courts, below.

In the end, Skolnick concludes that the narcotics division of a department can be a source of the widespread abuse of discretion. By focusing on this proactive form of police work, Skolnick provides a different picture of policing than Reiss and Black. The implication is that while reactive police work may be more common, proactive police work is more corrupt. Neither picture of police work is the more correct; they are, in effect, two sides of the same coin. As we will see below, the reactive/proactive distinction can be crucial to the understanding of court operations as well.

THE COURTS

Police apprehension is, of course, only a first and tentative step into the worlds of juvenile and criminal justice. In this section, we will be concerned with the steps that can lead from apprehension to institutionalization. We will consider first the related roles of the prosecutor in securing convictions and the defense counsel in representing the accused; second, the role of the probation officer in the preparation of presentence reports; and third the role of the judge in finalizing sentencing decisions. We will introduce our consideration of these interrelated roles by discussing the history of plea bargaining. We do so because more than any other practice, it is plea bargaining that has influenced the forms American criminal justice has taken in this century.

The Historical Roots of Plea Bargaining

Although it has sometimes been suggested that plea bargaining has "ancient antecedents" (e.g., *Buffalo Law Review*, 1974), this view seems to represent so loose a definition of plea bargaining as to be misleading. We begin, then, with a definition suggested by Alschuler (1979, p. 213): ". . . plea bargaining consists of the exchange of official concessions for the act of self-conviction." The official concessions offered in exchange for a plea of guilty may include a reduction in sentence, a reduction in charges, or other inducements. Participants in such exchanges include the police, prosecutor, and defense counsel as well as the judge. It is not always easy to recognize all the elements of plea bargaining in the official records that must form the basis of much historical research. For example, Newman's (1966, pp. 91–92) early description of plea bargaining in Kansas includes situations where prosecutors negotiated with defendants after the arrest but before the filing of charges. The records in these cases showed defendants pleading guilty to charges that had already been reduced before being officially filed.

Similarly, Milton Heumann (1975; see also Alschuler, 1975) uses the phrase "implicit plea bargaining" to describe situations where defendants realize they will be better off if they plead guilty, and do so without actual negotiation ever taking place. These defendants may avoid a heavy sentence, even though no word of a "deal" has been spoken. It is difficult to know from official records what the inducements to plead may have been in any particular situation. Nevertheless, Heumann argues convincingly that a high percentage of guilty pleas in a court is a sure sign of plea bargaining, whether explicit or implicit.

By this measure, there is little evidence that plea bargaining was common until the latter part of the nineteenth century. Ferdinand's (1973, table 2) study of the Boston Police Court in 1824 reveals only 11 percent of over 2,000 defendants pleading guilty. A study of prosecution practices in New York State beginning in 1839 reports that only 25 percent of all felony convictions were in that year a result of guilty pleas. The same study reveals that in Manhattan and Brooklyn only 15 percent of all felony convictions were by guilty plea in 1839, but that the figures increased steadily at decade intervals to 45, 70, 75, and 80 percent (Moley, 1928, p. 108, cited in Alschuler, 1979). It was not until after the mid-nineteenth century, then, that plea bargaining became common.

The first United States Supreme Court decision taking note of plea bargaining occurred in the Whiskey Cases of 1878 (Alschuler, 1979). This, and evidence like that presented above, leads Alschuler to conclude that plea bargaining only became a significant practice after the American Civil

War. Consistent with this, Friedman (1979) presents data on the processing of felony cases in the Superior Court of Alameda County, California, from 1880 to 1974. These data indicate that most cases have ended with some kind of guilty plea since the early twentieth century, and that the number has risen steadily.

Friedman does not regard Alameda County as unique, and goes on to suggest that the ninety years between 1880 and 1970 can be divided into three distinct periods. The first period lasts through the turn of the century and involves a mixed pattern in which many defendants took a chance on trial by jury, while others either plea bargained or simply pleaded guilty in hope of leniency. In the second period, lasting until about 1950, the guilty plea was much more common, perhaps because it looked like the one chance for leniency, and the only chance for probation. In the most recent period, plea bargaining has taken center stage. Defendants rely less on "understandings" and more on outright negotiation. On the other hand, prosecutors regularly "overcharge" to strengthen their bargaining positions. Alschuler (1968, p. 85) confirms this depiction of the latter period with his description of prosecutors who "throw everything in . . . down to and including spitting on the sidewalk." He goes on (ibid., p. 88) to quote an Oakland prosecutor as speculating that "if a robber forced his victim to move from a front room to a back room, I would probably file a kidnapping charge."

There is considerable speculation as to why and how plea bargaining became common. One point is clear: by the turn of the century the practice was widespread, despite its condemnation by the appellate courts. The corrupt character of urban courts during this period was certainly a factor. By 1914, Alschuler (1979, pp. 227–228) notes, there was a New York defense attorney whose financial arrangements with a magistrate enabled him to "stand out on the street in front of the Night Court and dicker away sentences in this form: $300 for ten days, $200 for twenty days, $150 for thirty days." The dean of the University of Illinois Law School described a similar situation during this era in Chicago (Harno, 1928, p. 103, cited in Alschuler, 1979, p. 228).

> When the plea of guilty is found in records it is almost certain to have in the background, particularly in Cook County, a session of bargaining with the State's Attorney. . . . These approaches . . . are frequently made through another person called a "fixer." This sort of person is an abomination and it is a serious indictment against our system of criminal administration that such a leech not only can exist but thrive. The "fixer" is just what the word indicates.

In Manhattan, the role of the "plea getter" is described by Arthur Train (1924, pp. 223–224, cited in Alschuler, 1979, p. 228).

> Court officers often win fame in accordance with their ability as "plea getters." They are anxious that the particular Part [courtroom] to which they are assigned shall make as good a showing as possible in the number of cases disposed of. Accordingly each morning some of them visit the pens on the floor below the courtroom and negotiate with the prisoners for pleas. . . . The writer has known of the entire population of a prison pen pleading guilty one after another under the persuasion of an eloquent bluecoat.

However, probably the most striking description of these turn-of-the century prosecution practices and their consequences is provided by Haller (1979, p. 277).

> A knowledgeable offender, once arrested, might start by attempting to bribe the arresting officer. If he failed, he could make further such attempts in the precinct station. Beyond that, a number of strategies remained. He or his friends might call on a politically influential attorney, saloonkeeper, or the bailbondsman to approach the prosecutor or judge for a favor. Or a friend might offer the victim restitution in return for an agreement to drop the charges. Even if the defendant was eventually convicted and incarcerated, he was not likely to perceive this as the triumph of legal norms; rather, he would feel that he had somehow failed to find the right levers for manipulating the system.

Nonetheless, Haller does not argue that corruption alone was at work here. He also cites structural changes that encouraged and facilitated the growth of plea bargaining. These changes included the creation of modern police departments and full-time prosecutors to bring defendants into the system, and the development of incarceration as a standard penalty for crime. We have already noted in Chapter 1 that by this time victims were becoming quite peripheral to the system, so that now the "new professionals" were left to determine charges and sentences based upon the needs of the new organizational units and the larger system rather than the interests of victims.

It is in this context that the courts became a loosely coupled system of processing agencies standing between an expanding caseload over which they exercised minimal control and a relatively rigid prison system that could not admit all who might be eligible. Haller argues that high rates of dismissals and plea bargaining were two likely responses to the situation.

But how could they occur in the face of appeals-court disapproval of plea bargaining? The answer is that the criminal-justice system simply was not very legally oriented in most urban jurisdictions. We noted in the previous section the local, highly politicized character of early American policing. Recruits usually were of blue-collar background, often with no formal schooling beyond the age of 13 or 14, and they typically started on the street with no formal training. Police officers were, therefore, expected to know little law (Haller, 1976). Beyond this, the justices in the lower courts were mostly nonlawyers, and defendants often appeared in court without attorneys. It is little wonder that the elite bar scorned such courts and chose to ignore them. Public-defender offices did not emerge until much later in the twentieth century. A result was that the appellate review of criminal cases was rare during the period when plea bargaining became common, leaving the practice beyond any meaningful supervision. Finally, late-nineteenth-century cities, and therefore their courts, were dominated by political machines which were based upon the exchange of favors for votes. Plea bargaining fit well with this political culture.

To these factors which encouraged and facilitated the growth of plea bargaining, Lynn Mather (1979) has added two more. In Chapter 1 we noted that at the end of the nineteenth century a new "positive" school of criminology, and ultimately a "new penology," emerged. This evolving school of thought was based on a philosophy of "individualized sanctions" whose purpose was to reform the offender. Plea bargaining provided a means for judges and prosecutors to reach a sentence that, in their view, would be more appropriate for the needs of the individual offender.

In the late nineteenth and early twentieth century, there was also a tremendous growth of the criminal law, particularly to criminalize what we have come to call "victimless crimes." In Chapter 3 we noted the range of the lawmaking efforts associated with the progressive era in American political history. Pound (1930, p. 23, cited in Alschuler, 1979, p. 234) observed that "of one hundred thousand persons arrested in Chicago in 1912, more than one half were held for violation of legal precepts which did not exist twenty-five years before." Whether for reasons of caseload volume or because of uncertainty that these offenses really warranted penal sanctions, they were frequently plea bargained. As the following quotation (National Commission on Law Observance and Enforcement, 1931, p. 56, cited in Alschuler, 1979, p. 235) indicates, this was nowhere more clear than in the case of prohibition.

> . . . federal prosecutions under the Prohibition Act terminated in 1930 had become nearly eight times as many as the total number of all pending federal prosecutions in 1914. In a number of urban

districts the enforcement agencies maintain that the only practicable way of meeting this situation with the existing machinery of the federal courts . . . is for the United States Attorneys to make bargains with defendants.

Mather (1973) makes the further point that if drug offenses are substituted for liquor offenses, there is an interesting similarity in the kinds of cases settled by plea bargains then and now. However, as we noted above and will discuss further below, this area of plea bargaining can also involve elements of coercion. We turn next, then, to a discussion of research on the prosecution and defense of criminal cases in contemporary settings.

Decisions to Prosecute

The unique feature of the decision to prosecute a criminal case is that it officially makes private "trouble" public (Emerson and Messinger, 1977). In effect, this decision changes what is often a dyadic relationship between suspect(s) and victim(s) into a triadic relationship that includes, as third parties, official agents of the court (Gulliver, 1969). The salient feature of a triad, of course, is asymmetry: the third party can take sides (Simmel, 1950). The criminal law encourages this possibility (Turk, 1976a), because it emphasizes a determination of guilt and innocence—what Chambliss and Seidman (1971) call the "winner takes all" method of dispute settlement.

Criminal prosecutors have virtually complete discretionary power to determine when the above-described consequences follow from the trouble brought to them (Blumberg, 1967b; Cox, 1976). In so doing, they use their discretion to determine which kinds of private trouble will receive public attention and therefore require expenditures of scarce court resources. In this sense, initial prosecutorial decisions, usually called "early" or "preliminary screening" decisions, are allocational: with respect to the amount and type of office resources to be used in disposing cases (Emerson, 1969; Bottomly, 1973). Cases for which no or few further resources will be committed are distinguished from those for which extensive resources are needed to arrive at the proper label and/or sanction. Officials relinquish jurisdiction over the former set of cases either at the time the decision is made or shortly thereafter. The latter set of cases continues under official jurisdiction, and receives more individualized treatment.

How, then, are the initial allocational decisions made? Myers and Hagan (1979) suggest that prosecutors "typify" (Cicourel, 1968) private trouble in terms of their prior experience with cases that have been pursued successfully to conviction and sentencing. They refer to this process as "strong-cases typification"—a process of allocating prosecutorial resources so as to maximize the ratio of convictions (and some times harsh sentences) to personnel effort invested. Features of cases that reduce the ratio are typified as weaknesses; they justify or require a plea bargain or dismissal. Features that enhance the ratio are typified as strengths; they increase the probability that prosecutors will proceed with the case and neither offer nor accept a plea bargain. The strong case consists in part, then, of abstract and generalized evaluations of case-specific characteristics, for example, as to whether the victim is a credible witness.

Since a large number of features characterize each case and can be interpreted as strengths or weaknesses, the strong case functions as an ideal that is seldom encountered. However, as a standard, the strong case expresses the prosecutor's concern with legally relevant features of the case. Prominent among these are the amount and quality of evidence that pertains to the defendant's guilt (Miller, 1970; Mather, 1973; Neubauer, 1974; Eisenstein and Jacob, 1977). In addition to evidence, prosecutors tend to couch other elements of the strong case in legally relevant terms. For example, they note and evaluate victims and defendants with reference to their probable credibility as witnesses (Miller, 1970; Hall, 1975; Stanko, 1977). Prosecutors also speak of the legal seriousness of the offense (Blumberg, 1967b; Mather, 1973; Neubauer, 1974). These elements, while legalistic in tone, are underlain in actual practice by a subtle mixture of social and legal considerations. Assessments of victim credibility, for example, depend in part on the victim's socioeconomic status and behavior prior to the crime, such as provocation of the defendant (Miller, 1970). For a variety of reasons, black victims of black defendants tend to be considered less credible witnesses than white victims of black defendants (Newman, 1966; Miller, 1970). On these grounds, their cases appear to move less frequently from the status of private to public trouble. The key to understanding public processing decisions, then, involves combined consideration of a variety of variables traditionally separated into "social" and "legal" categories.

The Role of Defense Counsel

Of course, as a criminal case progresses the defense counsel will also usually become a part of the decision-making process. However, in a provocative description of this role, Abraham Blumberg (1967a, 1967b) suggests that much defense work amounts to "the practice of law as a confidence game." The core of this argument is the observation that over time court officials, prosecutors, *and* defense lawyers develop working relationships that place the defendant in the role of a potentially disruptive outsider. Several factors are said to encourage this situation. The limitations of court resources put court officials and prosecutors under a strain to move cases through the court system as efficiently as possible. Meanwhile, defense lawyers will often gain financially if they handle as many cases as possible in the shortest period of time. The result is a common desire to resolve cases quickly, and Blumberg therefore suggests that prosecutors, judges, and defense attorneys may covertly conspire to encourage the defendant to plead guilty.

Blumberg goes on to suggest that the defense counsel may adopt a number of strategies to stimulate the guilty plea and to assure the payment of his or her legal fees. One of these strategies involves bringing the defendant's family into the case. Often with the help of adjournments offered by an accommodating judge, the defense attorney is able to convince the family of the financial and practical wisdom of the defendant's "pleading guilty for considerations." Donald Newman (1956, 1966) estimates from his research that in about a third of such cases the result is an alteration in charges, while in about two-thirds of the cases the expectation is a reduced sentence. There is some uncertainty that reduced sentences always follow such pleas, an uncertainty that fits well with the analogy to a confidence game. The suspicions that give rise to this analogy are further encouraged by Blumberg's finding that it is usually the lawyer for the defense who first suggests to the defendant that it would be best to plead guilty.

Blumberg's research focuses on private defense counsel, but much criminal-defense work today is done by public defenders. Does plea bargaining characterize their cases as well? The classic research of David Sudnow (1965) in a midwestern public defender's office provides an affirmative answer. Sudnow concentrates on providing an in-depth description of the procedures used in bargaining for reduced charges. The reduction of charges focuses on two types of offenses: "necessarily included offenses" and "situationally included offenses." The former occur by association with one another in their legal definition; for example, "homicide" cannot occur without "intent to commit murder." In contrast, the latter occur together by convention; for example, "public drunkenness" often, but not by necessity, occurs in conjunction with "creating a public disturbance." The general premise in bargaining for charge reductions involves reducing the initial charge to a lesser necessarily or situationally included offense.

The fascinating point that Sudnow's research makes is that the procedural rules to be followed in deciding what sort of reduction is appropriate are not set out exclusively by the law. These rules evolve out of lawyers' and prosecutors' working conceptions of what they regard as "normal crimes": ". . . the typical manner in which offenses of given classes are committed, the social characteristics of the persons who regularly commit them, the features of the settings in which they occur, the types of victims often involved, and the like" (Sudnow, 1965, p. 259). On the basis of these working conceptions of "normal crimes" an initial legal categorization can be established, and attention can then be directed to determining which (*possibly* necessarily or situationally included) lesser offenses constitute the appropriate reduction. Thus Sudnow reports that in the jurisdiction he observed a burglary charge is routinely reduced to petty theft. The point, however, is that "the propriety of proposing petty theft as a reduction does not derive from its . . . existence in the present case, but is warranted . . . [instead] by the relation of the present burglary to 'burglaries,' normally conceived" (ibid., p. 263). Sudnow does note, however, that there must be a balance between the sentence the defendant might have received for the original charge and that which will probably be received for the lesser charge. This balance is greatly assisted by the fact that criminal codes generally allow the judge so much discretion in sentencing that the likelihood is substantial of the defendant's receiving the same sentence for *either* the greater or the lesser charge.

Are the Bargains Biased?

What types of defendants benefit most and least from the bargaining practices we have considered? Chambliss and Seidman (1971, p. 412) assert that "how favorable a 'bargain' one can strike with the prosecutor in the pretrial confrontations is a direct function of how politically and economically powerful the defendant is." Yet data collected by Donald Newman (1956) through interviews with convicted felons cast doubt on such assertions. Newman reports that when his defendants are compared in terms of their initial pleas, no significant differences are found by education, occupation, and residence. Similarly, his "analysis of the sample of offenders showed no clear-cut categories separating bargained from non-bargained convictions" (ibid., p. 780). Still, Newman does conclude with the assertion (ibid., p. 790) that "the way bargaining now works, the more experienced criminals can manipulate legal processes to obtain light sentences and better official records."

A study of criminal prosecution in a western Canadian province (Hagan, 1975*b*) focuses more specifically on charge alterations and their impact on the final disposition imposed. This study emphasizes the crucial role of defense counsel and the presence of multiple charges in generating a charge alteration. The latter is a reference to the fact that many offenders may be systematically "overcharged" to set the bargaining process in motion. However, no clear evidence is found that experienced offenders receive more or better "bargains," and the proportions of white and nonwhite offenders retaining counsel, pleading guilty, and receiving charge alterations are approximately equal. Probably the most intriguing finding of this study is that charge alterations have no substantial impact on final disposition unless the charges are completely dropped: "This finding suggests that 'considerations' won in early stages of the legal process may ultimately prove illusionary, a finding that fits well with Blumberg's characterization of the bargaining process as a 'confidence game' " (ibid., p. 544).

Other studies have questioned the advantages at sentencing provided by plea bargaining. Eisenstein and Jacob (1977, p. 270) report from their study of criminal courts in three cities that "the effect of dispositional mode [is] insignificant in accounting for the variance in sentence length." Similarly, a major study of plea bargaining in the District of Columbia concludes that "contrary to expectations, sentence concessions were not routinely awarded to suspects entering guilty pleas" (Rhodes, 1978). Some studies do find sentencing benefits following from guilty pleas (Uhlman and Walker, 1979, 1980; Brereton and Casper, 1981–82; Zatz and Hagan, 1984), but the issue remains unresolved. Until this issue is resolved, it will be impossible to answer the question of whether some bargainers benefit more than others. Meanwhile, we can only speculate. LaFree (1980) reports the interesting finding that in rape cases black defendants are more likely to be tried in court than plead guilty. Yet even here there is uncertainty, for LaFree (ibid., p. 839) observes that he "could not determine from [his] observations whether black defendants were more reluctant to plead guilty than white defendants or whether the prosecution was less willing to plea bargain when the defendant was black." In either case, it is unlikely that such pleas work to the advantage of black offenders, but it is impossible to say much more.

The Social Organization of Plea Bargaining

It is clear that the *form* if not the substance of plea bargaining varies by characteristics of offenders. Earlier in this chapter we noted how the proactive character of police work in areas such as drug enforcement has notable consequences for the way police work is organized. Related conclusions emerge from research done on the prosecution of drug and white-collar crimes, two groups of offenses usually thought of as unrelated. What is similar about them is the absence of complainants. Most white-collar crimes are so diffuse in character (e.g., price-fixing) that the victims (consumers) are not aware of their victimization. Meanwhile, drug offenders are in effect "consensual" victims, and are therefore unlikely to complain of their own "victimizations." A result is that for both of these types of crimes information and evidence must be developed in a proactive fashion.

Plea bargaining is a major means of successfully building such cases proactively. In exchange for lenient penalties, key informants and witnesses are encouraged to provide the evidence necessary for the successful prosecution of others (Cloyd, 1979). The problem is how to get the leverage required to "turn witnesses," and the key to obtaining the leverage is to forge a connection between plea negotiations and concessions and coercion ultimately in sentencing. In other words, it is necessary to tighten the links between prosecutors and sentencing judges, making these parts of the criminal-justice system more tightly coupled than is usually the case. Even when this is accomplished, Chein et al. (1964, p. 331) observe that "going after higher levels of the narcotics business pyramid, to say nothing of the apexes, is a long, hazardous, and at best uncertain affair."

To determine more specifically how prosecutors proactively pursue these goals, Hagan and Bernstein (1979, p. 471) interviewed assistant U.S. attorneys about their work on white-collar cases (see also Katz, 1979). The techniques used by prosecutors in these cases are suggested candidly in the following interview.

Q. How do you urge cooperation from defendants?

A. We threaten to send them to jail. It's the most effective way we've ever done it. We make a good, solid case on them and hang it over their head like a hammer.

Q. And what are the mechanics of doing that, how exactly do you present it to the defendant?

A. We tell them "if you don't cooperate, we will convict you. And we will do it in a way that will make you look—we'll do it so well that you would get really good jail time, a solid big chunk of time."

Q. At what stage do you do this?

A. Well, we are willing to make deals with people in a whole host of ways running all the way from giving them a "pass" to they just don't get anything at all in return for testifying.

Q. Do you usually indict them first?

A. We make deals at all stages. . . . We talk to them before indictment in the very big cases. Then we have all kinds of pleas like a guy has committed a felony. We'll let him plead to a misdemeanor and won't prosecute . . . a whole range of things

all the way 'till he pleads to the principal count . . . to charging
him with exactly what he did and saying nice things about him
at sentencing.

The possibilities this interview reveals are as coercive as they are numerous.

We have already noted that essential to generating cooperation and
establishing credibility is a shared understanding between the prosecutor
and the judge that negotiated agreements will be ratified and expectations
fulfilled. Hagan and Bernstein's (1979, p. 472) interviews suggest that this
link exists on a very practical level. For example, they quote an assistant
U.S. attorney to the effect that "judges understand that in order to expose
official corruption you do have to give some concessions to people who are
involved. Again, because only those people who are involved know and
can testify about it."

This kind of research establishes that there are a number of ways of
eliciting cooperation from defendants, and that negotiations using a mix of
promised concessions and threatened coercion are very important to
proactive prosecution. In later sections, we will note the impact of reactive
and proactive prosecutorial patterns on the sentencing of white-collar
offenders. Next we consider efforts to alter experimentally the bargaining
policies of criminal courts.

Plea Bargaining Experiments

Citizens are understandably concerned about plea bargaining. It raises the
specter of a kind of criminal justice that is hidden from public view,
operated by careless lawyers who are preoccupied with their caseloads,
resulting in outcomes that may be either too lenient or too severe, as well
as inconsistent and coercive. It is not surprising, then, that there have been
a number of efforts to reform or eliminate plea bargaining. Social scientists
have been skeptical that most of these reforms can accomplish their goals.
Malcolm Feeley (1979, p. 204) articulates this view:

I do not want to claim that efforts to alter the guilty plea process
are foredoomed. I only wish to reiterate what students of mandatory and determinate sentencing schemes have long maintained:
eliminating discretion at one stage of the process fosters it at
others (Alschuler, 1978). Proscribing any post-indictment modification of charges may simply result in increased pre-indictment
"plea adjustment." Reforms that focus exclusively on a narrow
problem without seeing it in the context of the entire system may

generate unanticipated consequences even less desirable than the status quo.

Nonetheless, a number of such reforms have been attempted on an experimental basis.

Plea bargaining related to charges and sentencing was banned across the state of Alaska by a newly elected attorney general in 1975. An evaluation of this ban by Rubinstein and White (1979) reports that explicit plea bargaining was substantially reduced, with no noticeable increase in implicit bargaining. The most interesting effect, however, was on sentencing. The severity of sentences for the white-collar crimes of fraud and forgery increased 117 percent, and for drug crimes 233 percent. An explanation of these findings is that the ban on plea bargaining made the proactive prosecution of the cases described above impossible. More generally, Rubinstein and White conclude that the ban on bargaining increased the number of trials modestly, but also increased the productivity of the criminal-justice system, for example, by contributing to a decline in disposition time. Rubenstein and White speculate that the success of this ban may result from the fact that prosecutors and defense counsel were simply wasting less time on negotiations. Whether these results could be generalized to other jurisdictions, particularly jurisdictions with larger caseloads, is unclear.

Detroit is an example of a larger jurisdiction that attempted to abolish plea bargaining in selected cases. The Wayne County (Detroit) prosecutor's subordinates were prohibited from plea bargaining in any case in which a recently enacted state firearms statute warranted a mandatory sentence. This statute imposed an additional two-year prison term if a defendant possessed a firearm while committing a felony. Heumann and Loftin (1979) report in an evaluation of this experiment that, although there is some evidence that the law and the prohibition on plea bargaining may have selectively increased the severity of sentences for certain classes of defendants, for the most part disposition patterns appear not to have been altered dramatically. Furthermore, in many serious cases sentences for the primary felony were adjusted downward to take into account the additional two-year penalty; and in "equity" cases in which defendants had not previously received prison time, other mechanisms, such as abbreviated bench trials, were often employed to circumvent the mandatory sentencing provision. These are the kinds of "rearrangements" that Feeley warns about above.

A final experiment, conducted in Dade County, Florida, suggests that some modest goals can be accomplished through plea bargaining reform. Here a pretrial settlement conference was used as a means of restructuring plea negotiations. Heinz and Kerstetter (1979) report that these negotiations took place in front of a judge, with the defendant, victim, and arresting officer invited to attend. Although the conferences were brief, they usually reached at least an outline of a settlement. Heinz and Kerstetter suggest that the change in structure of these bargaining situations reduced the time involved in processing cases by lowering the information and decision-making costs to the judges and attorneys. No significant changes were observed in the settlement rate or in the imposition of criminal sanctions. Nonetheless, there was some evidence that police and victims who attended the sessions obtained more information and developed more positive attitudes about the way their cases were handled.

The Causes and Consequences of Plea Bargaining

In the end, it must be acknowledged that we know much less about plea bargaining than we need to. What we do know makes it doubtful that plea bargaining is merely the result of heavy caseloads, the oppressiveness of pretrial detention, the low quality of public defenders, the financial incentives of private attorneys, the laziness of prosecutors, or the stupidity of judges (Feeley, 1975, 1979; Heumann, 1975). The historical work that we considered above suggests that there are other factors, more enduring and less tractable, at work—most notably the rise of specialization and professionalism (Heumann, 1978; Alschuler, 1979; Friedman, 1979). Criminal law has become increasingly complicated and open to challenge, while the emergence of court professionals has provided the personnel to press these points outside the trial setting. Thus Feeley notes (1979, p. 201) that the "defendant who, lacking an attorney, might once have sat passively through a ritual trial is now likely to be represented by counsel capable of challenging evidence in a host of pretrial proceedings, who will resort to trial only if the client's interests cannot otherwise be secured." At the same time, prosecutors are now better prepared to sort out cases and charges at early stages of the court process. From this perspective, there may be benefits as well as liabilities to plea bargaining.

Clearly, someone must be benefiting from plea bargaining. If not, it is unlikely that such practices would have grown to their current dimensions. The task remains to establish how the benefits and liabilities of these practices are distributed. Meanwhile, the practice persists.

The Role of the Probation Officer

In addition to the prosecutor and the judge, the probation officer also plays a role in determining dispositions. Wheeler et al. (1968) demonstrate in a juvenile court study that the probation officer sustains strategic contact with, and communicates crucial information between, all participants in the court process. The background to this aspect of the probation officer's role is described in part by Everett Hughes's (1951, 1962) concept of "dirty work"—occupational activities that are socially necessary but in some significant sense "unclean." In a graphic description of court work, Hughes (1958, p. 71) notes that "what the learned lawyers argue before an Appellate Court . . . is but a purified distillate of some human mess." But who undertakes, and by what means, the process of "purification"? It has been argued that an important part of the task falls to the probation officer.

Although probation has been called "the growth industry of corrections" (Wallace, 1974), the role of the probation officer originated with religious sponsorship. The history is discussed in greater detail in the following chapter. However, we note here that the Church of England Temperance Society appointed the first probation officers as "court missionaries" in 1876 (Chute and Bell, 1956; Timasheff, 1941; Madley, 1965). Their initial responsibilities were to provide lay supervision. However, as the role of the probation officer became professionalized, much of its identity was drawn from the field of social work. The result was to add a methodology to a vocation.

The method of the probation officer follows from the principles of casework (Diana, 1960; Towle, 1973). These principles outline techniques for objectifying (i.e., "purifying") the circumstances of "persons in trouble" (Cicourel, 1968). The primary step involves "observing, gathering, and recording" the social, legal, and historical facts of the case. These "social facts" are then assembled in the form of a probation report. Gradually, jurists recognized the potential of such reports for informing the sentencing process (Chute and Bell, 1956, pp. 136–151). From here it was a small step to the elevation of the probation officer to an advisory role in the sentencing process: probation reports became presentence reports, and diagnostic evaluations became prognostic recommendations. Thus, research by Wahl and Glaser (1963) indicates that as early as twenty years ago probation officers were spending nearly as much time on presentence work as on supervision. This arrangement is viewed by many observers as an efficient and rational division of court labor.

The work of Everett Hughes suggests another view of this process. Hughes notes that occupations within institutions often maintain symbiotic (i.e., mutually rewarding) status relationships. Thus, the judiciary reinforces its status by delegating to probation officers the "dirty work" of collecting information for sentencing. Senior probation officers, in turn, can enhance their own status by turning over to less experienced probation officers increasing responsibilities for case supervision. A consequence is that senior probation officers spend more time in office and court activities. Most importantly, however, the court activities of probation officers now involve prestige-conferring opportunities to offer presentence recommendations. The results of these organizational rearrangements, then, may be socially rewarding for both groups.

Hughes (1958, p. 77) warns, however, that such organizational innovations may often have unanticipated consequences. One of the consequences is suggested by Carter and Wilkins (1967), who cite the close and apparently causal relationship between recommendations and dispositions, and suggest the hypothesis that probation officers are a source of disparities in judicial sentencing. A study by Hagan (1975c; see also Myers, 1979) examines this hypothesis by comparing cases where probation officers' recommendations are explicitly requested to cases where they are not. In the former cases, particularly in rural jurisdictions (Hagan, 1977a), it is found that the recommendations are influenced by a succession of variables, beginning with the offender's ethnic background, following with the probation officer's perception of the offender's demeanor, and culminating in the probation officer's perception of the offender's prospects for success on probation. More specifically, nonwhite offenders whose demeanor was perceived unfavorably by probation officers were evaluated as having poorer prospects for success on probation, and were less likely to receive a lenient recommendation for sentence.

Recall, however, that the above research focuses on cases where recommendations are explicitly requested from probation officers. Often "evaluations" are requested instead of recommendations, or the recommendations are requested in writing and are not presented formally in court. A recent study (Hagan, Hewitt, and Alwin, 1979) argues that the latter kind of arrangement often functions to make the participation of the probation officer in criminal cases seem more consequential than it is. Prosecutors, as we noted above, can also have a strong interest in sentencing, particularly as a means of ratifying plea bargaining, and judges are sensitive to this. The data analyzed indicate that prosecutors actually are much more influential in their recommendations for sentences than are probation officers. The set of arrangements described above, then, allows the courts, in effect, to have it both ways: the involvement of probation officers in the presentencing process helps to legitimize court decisions, while limiting their involvement to evaluation or undisclosed recommendations allows prosecutors to maintain their influence—all without the appearance of overt conflict or contradiction. In terms that we used earlier, probation officers may be only loosely coupled to the decision-making process, or actually decoupled from it, while the link between prosecutors and judges is strengthened. Hagan et al. refer to this as a form of "ceremonial justice," in that it may be the appearance of justice, more than anything else, that is most clearly served by the involvement of probation officers in sentencing.

The Role of the Judiciary

Judges must bear the ultimate responsibility for sentencing decisions, and it is these decisions, more than any of the others made in the criminal-justice system, that have attracted social scientific attention. This should not be surprising. As Thurman Arnold (1967, p. 23) observes, "The center of ideals of every western government is in its judicial system." Sentencing decisions are a very visible product of this system. However, we noted at the outset of this chapter that despite the strength with which fundamental ideals like "equality before the law" are held, such ideals are ambiguously operationalized. This has become particularly apparent in the study of sentencing decisions, as researchers have tried to distinguish, for example, between "legal" and "extralegal" sources of inequality in these decisions. As we will see below, this issue, and others related to it, have made it difficult to reach meaningful conclusions about the issue of discrimination in sentencing.

A distinction frequently drawn in the 1960s and early 1970s was that offense seriousness (as indicated by the maximum sentence allowed by law) and prior conviction record (often written into the law as a basis for more severe sentences) were "legal" influences on sentencing, while the race, sex, age, and other characteristics of offenders not included in the law were "extralegal." Difficulties with this distinction cut in at least two directions.

On one hand, it has been noted that what are called "legal variables" differ from jurisdiction to jurisdiction (i.e., rankings of offense seriousness vary among states), that what is legal at one stage of decision-making may not be at another (e.g., community ties may be considered relevant for bail decisions and irrelevant at sentencing), and that what is legal at the sentencing stage (e.g., prior record) may be the product of discrimination at earlier stages (e.g., by the police) (see Bernstein et al., 1977). On the other hand, it can also be noted that what are called "extralegal variables" are directly or indirectly built into some parts of the criminal law. For example, probation statutes often encourage consideration of the offender's age, and there remain some state statutes (e.g., many prostitution laws) that justify differential treatment by sex. Many statutes encourage judicial consideration of an offender's employment record at various stages of the criminal-justice process (see, for example, the language of the criminal-code bill that passed the Senate Judiciary Committee in the first session of the Nineteenth Congress), a factor that works disproportionately against black offenders. Thus even though the Fourteenth Amendment to the U.S. Constitution provides that "no state shall . . . deny to any person within its jurisdiction the equal protection of the laws," the law seems to provide judges and other decision-makers with plenty of latitude to do just that. In sum, the law is an ambiguous guide as to the factors that may legitimately influence sentencing.

To acknowledge the uncertain nature of what influences on sentencing are acceptable, we can speak of "legitimized" and "nonlegitimized" rather than legal and extralegal influences on sentencing. Legitimized and nonlegitimized influences are those that within a given *structural context* the public thinks should and should not affect sentencing. Although there is no method for unambiguously sorting all influences on sentencing into these two categories, social survey data do provide one important source of information about what influences are and are not regarded as legitimate by the public at any given time and place. Such surveys make it clear that the American public regards prior convictions and type of offense as legitimate influences on sentencing, and that it does not regard economic and ethnic characteristics as legitimate influences on sentencing. Much sentencing research has sought to determine whether the latter factors exercise an influence when the former factors are taken fully into account (see, for example, Hagan, 1974; Kleck, 1981; Hagan and Bumiller, 1983).

These studies usually incorporate either an "individual-processual" or a "structural-contextual" approach to the study of sentencing. The first of these approaches emphasizes the premise that sentencing is the end result of a decision-making process involving many stages (e.g., Farrell and Swigert, 1978b). The latter approach adds a second premise: that both the individuals and the system occupy variable positions or locations within a social structure. The point of the latter approach is that sentencing patterns will vary by social context. Several recent studies incorporate the second premise of the structural-contextual approach. Using data sets from several jurisdictions, Balbus (1973), Eisenstein and Jacob (1977), and Levin (1977) have linked variations in political environments to sentencing behavior. Within single jurisdictions, Lizotte (1978) and LaFree (1980) have linked individuals' relational positions in the social structure to sentencing outcomes, while Hagan (1982) has examined the consequences when corporate entities, as compared to individuals, act as victim-complainants in the criminal-justice process. Each of these studies adds some feature of structural and contextual variation to its consideration of the individual processing that leads to sentencing decisions.

Consideration of the structural contexts in which sentencing studies have been done helps to make sense of some otherwise puzzling results. For example, while Peterson and Hagan (1984) report that sentencing studies reveal a gradual tendency toward the equal treatment of whites and blacks during this century in America, they also note studies that reveal differential severity as well as leniency in the treatment of blacks. The general tendency toward equality is explained by noting that the legal structure of race relations in America, however slowly and imperfectly, has improved over the last half-century. But there are important exceptions to this trend that can also be understood in terms of structural context. Early in this century in the south, blacks convicted of offenses against white victims were particularly likely to receive severe sentences, especially in rape cases (Wolfgang and Riedel, 1973), and there is evidence that this pattern continues today (LaFree, 1980). We should perhaps not be surprised by the persistence of this pattern: interracial crimes represent intense conflict across important structural divisions in our racially stratified society. Rape, as Eldridge Cleaver graphically noted in *Soul on Ice,* is a crime that symbolizes these conflicts. On the other hand, homicide is less likely than rape to be an *inter*racial crime, and in fact more often is *intra*racial, involving blacks victimizing blacks. Studies focusing on homicide have sometimes found blacks receiving more lenient treatment than whites (Garfinkel, 1949; Bowers and Pearce, 1980). To the extent that blacks occupy less-valued structural positions in our society, we should not be surprised to find the cases of black victims receiving lenient treatment. Furthermore, a more general tendency to see some kinds of black offenders, for example black drug offenders (Peterson and Hagan, 1983), as victims may partially explain the trend toward equality noted above, as well as the anomaly of black offenders (see Kleck, 1981) sometimes receiving more lenient sentences than whites. Further attention is given in the chapter that follows to the role of structural context in determining the sentencing of white collar offenders. Here it is enough to note that sentencing varies across structural contexts, as offender and offense characteristics take on different meanings in these variable settings.

CONCLUSIONS

We began this chapter with a question: do the poor and minorities receive discriminatory treatment from the criminal-justice system? Criminologists as far apart as Richard Quinney (1970:142) and Travis Hirschi (1980, p. 284) have answered this question affirmatively. The issue that remains is that of determining the structural contexts in which discrimination becomes more or less acute. Unfortunately, we have noted from the outset that the issue of discrimination is more complex than it may initially seem. The complexity derives from the uncertain meaning of such key concepts as "equality before the law." To establish in what contexts equality before the law does or does not exist, it is necessary to know unambiguously what the legal standards of criminal justice decisions are. We have seen with each of the decisions we have considered that no such certainty exists. Instead, factors that may or may not have legal justification can influence all of them: for example, the demeanor of a suspect can influence decisions to arrest, the credibility of a witness can influence decisions to prosecute, and the employment status of a convicted offender can influence decisions to sentence. Since minority and underclass persons are more likely to be perceived as poor in demeanor, evaluated as less-credible witnesses, and unemployed, these factors often can account for the more severe treatment that poor and minority offenders sometimes receive. It is important that research continue to determine how such factors mediate the effects of race and class position on criminal-justice decision-making. However, whether such mediated effects are designated as discriminatory is an issue that is often open to interpretation, and therefore to variation in public perception.

Using data gathered in a national survey, Hagan and Albonetti (1982) have looked at how two structural cleavages in North American society, race and class, influence perceptions of criminal justice. Ten aspects of criminal justice are considered in this research: two involving law-enforcement officials/police, four involving the courts, two involving juries, and one each involving lawyers and judges. All of the areas considered relate directly or indirectly to the justness of decisions reached in the criminal-justice system, with special attention given to the experiences of economic and ethnic minorities with problems of equality before the law. Items taping the preceding issues are combined to form a scale of perceived criminal injustice. The analysis of the national survey data including this scale and its component parts produced three major findings: (1) that black Americans are considerably more likely than white Americans to perceive criminal injustice; (2) that regardless of race, members of the surplus population (i.e., the unemployed) are significantly more likely than members of other classes to perceive criminal injustice; and (3) that class position conditions the relationship of race to the perception of criminal injustice, with the division between the races in these perceptions being most acute in the professional managerial class.

Various interpretations can be given to the above findings, and further research will be required to choose among them. Regardless of which interpretations prevail, however, it is clear that sharp conflicts do exist in American perceptions of criminal-justice activities. These conflicts may be as important as the conflicts that underlie the activities themselves.

UNDERSTANDING THE "NEW CRIMES": THE UNEXPLAINED CRIMES OF CLASS AND GENDER

9

THE ISSUE: CAN OLD THEORIES EXPLAIN NEW CRIMES?

Modern criminality often seems an embarrassment to modern criminology. The source of the embarrassment is that, while the public has been much concerned in recent years about apparent increases in the crimes of women, persons of high occupational position, and corporations, existing theories of crime have had relatively little to say about these crimes (Harris, 1977; Wheeler, 1976). Nonetheless, modern criminologists have in other ways begun to take notice of such crimes and the public response to them. For example, Freda Adler (1977, p. 101) writes that today's women are

> no longer satisfied with their traditional limitation to the typewriter, the mimeograph machine, and the coffee-maker, they are increasingly taking a more active role. . . . So aggressive did their activities become that on 28 December 1968 the females of the United States reached a criminal landmark when the first one of them was admitted to the infamous Federal Bureau of Investigation "Ten Most Wanted" list. Since that time the inclusion of women for murder, robbery, kidnapping, and violent revolutionary acts has become quite common.

Equally striking is Clinard and Yeager's (1980, p. 14) description of the widespread publicity given to corporate criminality in recent years.

> For example, widespread publicity has been given to the Watergate investigations and illegal Nixon political contributions; the questionable or illegal foreign payments by more than 300 large corporations; the apparent role of ITT in heading off federal antitrust action by donating heavily for the 1972 Republican National Convention; the political contributions of the Associated Milk Producers to obtain an increase in milk price supports; the flagrant violations of Equity Funding; the conviction of Allied Chemical for polluting the James River; the recalls and suits involving Ford Pintos; and Firestone's recall of more than 10 million defective tires. These cases in particular have led to greater

public concern and increasingly negative attitudes towards the corporations, as has been shown in public opinion polls.

Against this background, existing theories seem curiously preoccupied with the more common street crimes of underclass men.

Can existing theories explain the new crimes? We believe that to do so existing theories must be less exclusive in their conceptual boundaries, and more comparative and historical in their methods. To do otherwise is to miss what the changing circumstances of class, gender, and work can tell us about crime, and vice versa, what the changing character of crime can tell us about the social organization of class, gender, and work.

Modern criminologists characteristically organize their thinking in one of two ways: (1) around informal processes of social control that involve institutions such as the school and family (see, for example, the theories of undercontrol discussed in Chapter 5), or (2) around formal processes of social control that involve institutions such as the juvenile and criminal law, and occasionally the civil law (see, for example, the theories of overcontrol discussed in Chapter 7). The first kind of thinking has been primarily concerned with the causes of delinquent and criminal behavior, the second with reactions to such behavior. We argue below that it is no longer useful to preserve these divisions; that to understand the unexplained crimes of class and gender it is necessary to think simultaneously about informal and formal controls; and that it is important to think about the variable ways in which these controls operate on men and women, and on persons in various kinds of occupational positions, particularly in large corporations. The thread that will tie the following discussion together is a focus on the social organization of work and the stratification system that derives from it. It is the world of work that makes the divisions of class and gender particularly acute, and indirectly explains much of the variation in the kinds of crime we will attempt to understand.

GENDER, WORK, AND CRIME

When it comes to criminal forms of deviance, men clearly exceed women (Hindelang, 1979; Nettler, 1978). This does not mean that the relationship between gender and criminality is a simple one: the disparity between the sexes varies with the class of crime, time, and social setting. We make this variation a part of our account below. Nonetheless, we can begin secure in the assumption that today men in North America are significantly more likely to be involved in the more serious forms of crime (the evidence for this conclusion is summarized in Chapter 4). The association between gender and crime is largely unexplored in existing theories of crime. Our argument is that an explanation for the strong but neglected association between gender and crime is to be found in the social organization of the world of work, the stratification system, and the different means used to control men and women.

We note first that the most fundamental aspect of the stratification system is not *how* actors are allocated to social classes or *how* rewards (e.g., prestige and income) are distributed. Instead, the most fundamental aspect is *who* is eligible in the first place to compete for the rewards and outcomes distributed in the system. Clearly, women are far more restricted than men in their access to the rewards of the stratification system. This is not simply a matter of overt economic discrimination in, or exclusion from, the world of work; it is a matter of men more generally being ascribed to the public arena (i.e., the world of work) and women to the private sphere (i.e., the home). It is of special significance to us that one consequence of the restriction of women to the private space is to make them less available for the public ascription of criminal and delinquent statuses (Stinchcombe, 1963). However, a better understanding of this situation requires an awareness of its historical precedents.

Crime *and* work are sexually stratified. This pattern of stratification is linked historically to the removal of men's work from the home and the emergence of the formal segregative agencies of social control that we recognize today as the criminal-justice system. With the rise of large-scale trade and commerce, and later of industrialization, there emerged a growing differentiation between formal and informal structures of social control. Scull (1976, p. 346) makes this point when he notes that "the development of national and international markets produced a diminution, if not a destruction, of the influence traditionally exerted by local groups (especially kinship groups)," leading eventually "to the development of a state sponsored system of segregative control."

The historical differentiation noted by Scull between the constraints imposed at one end of a continuum by the family, and at the other end by the state, is reflected conceptually in the sociological concept of social control (Black, 1983; Gibbs, 1977; Janowitz, 1975). Operationally, social control is recognized in formally and informally organized acts of surveillance, supervision, and sanctioning. Scull's historical concern is that, in conjunction with advancing capitalism and the movement of work away from the home, surveillance, supervision, and sanctioning activities have shifted increasingly in their locus of organization from family and kinship groups to the state. In brief, the new form of work brought a new form of social control, now called "crime control," as operationalized in modern systems of criminal justice. Our point is that this linkage between the control of crime and work had much more to do with the legal control of men than women—for it was the former who were moving most rapidly into the new and more public places of work (Huber, 1976, pp. 371–388). The result was to subject men increasingly to the formal social control of the emerging criminal-justice system, while leaving women to the informal social control of the family.

It is therefore our argument that two well-established statistical regularities—the exclusion of women from the "race" for stratification outcomes *and* less crime among women—have as a common source patterns of informal social controls involving women, which are established and perpetuated within the family. An adequate understanding of this point, and a more complete explanation of patterns of crime and delinquency among *both* men and women, requires that we give combined attention to differing types of social-control processes. As we have noted, such processes usually have been considered independently.

Thus in the formative years of American criminology, researchers were concerned most conspicuously with informal processes of social control (e.g., Ross, 1901; Park, 1921; see also Schwendiger and Schwendiger, 1974). These early explanations of crime gave considerable attention to the role of the *family* and *community* in accounting for increasing rates of crime and delinquency in changing urban environments (e.g., Park, 1915; Thomas, 1923; Thrasher, 1927; Shaw and McKay, 1931; see also Wilkinson, 1974).

Gradually, interest shifted to socially structured patterns of opportunity (e.g., Merton, 1938; Cloward and Ohlin, 1960), then to the growing impact of *formal* agencies of social control (e.g., the police, courts, and corrections) on individuals (e.g., Tannenbaum, 1938; Lemert, 1951; Becker, 1963), and finally to such agencies as institutions worthy of study in and of themselves (e.g., Wheeler, 1968; Skolnick, 1975; Reiss, 1971*b*). Thus the question asked most commonly today is how such agencies come, historically and organizationally, to seek out as their customary targets young, poor, urban males, and how this selection corresponds to the wishes of dominant interest groups (e.g., Taylor, Walton, and Young, 1973; Chambliss and Seidman, 1971; Quinney, 1970).

However, it is our contention that the question of differential treatment cannot be answered effectively without simultaneous consideration of both formal *and* informal structures of social control, and their linkages into the stratification system. Underlying this combined consideration is the fundamental assumption that formal social controls are inversely related to informal social controls. Identifying law and its application with formal social control, and family and kinship group activity with informal social control, Donald Black (1976) applies this proposition at two levels: across collectivities (e.g., nations, corporations, status groups) and across indviduals. It is postulated that the less informal social control there is in a collectivity, the more law will be generated. Below we argue that this is a source of the modern urgency to do something about the legal control of corporations, and the greater formal social control imposed on men than women. Similarly, the less informal social control *individuals* are subject to, the more law to which they will be subjected. Black's theory implies that a shifting balance exists between the two types of social control, with one type growing in compensation for a decline in the other. To this we might add that the balance shifts toward more formal social control as the behaviors involved become more public and diverse in their character. Scull's argument is that the advance of capitalism makes this shift inexorable. Whether the causal agent is capitalism, industrialization, urbanization, or all of the preceding, the trend seems apparent.

It is important to add here that formal social controls extend beyond the law, and that informal social controls extend beyond the family. For example, rules of the workplace, sometimes enforced by private security personnel, exist in greater and lesser degrees of formality (Spitzer and Scull, 1977; Shearing and Stenning, 1983). As well, activities of peer and work groups can constitute informal social controls. These aspects of social control are considered in relation to corporate criminality below.

In terms of our immediate interest in gender and crime, we can begin to make the argument we are developing more formal by offering the following general proposition:

1 Formal legal controls are inversely related to informal familial controls.
The logic of this proposition is that as the surveillance and supervisory activities of the family diminish in their influence, the application of the law and its sanctions will increase.

This proposed relationship between formal legal controls and informal social controls is made particularly significant for our purposes by the further proposition that these control structures are sexually stratified. For example, when it comes to the care of children:

2 Females more than males are the *instruments* and the *objects* of informal familial controls.

More specifically,

2.1 Mothers more than fathers are the instruments of informal familial controls over children.

2.2 Daughters more than sons are the objects of informal familial controls.

Together, the above propositions form the basis of female assignment to an instrument-object relationship in the socialization process—what Rosabeth Kanter (1974; see also Millman, 1975) calls the "intimate oppression" of informal social control. Chowdrow (1971) observes the same process when she notes that "women are the primary socializers. Men may also help in child care, but their 'work' is elsewhere; for women it is the reverse." A result is that "young girls, used to relying on older siblings and adults ('seeking help'), soon give this help ('offer help and support') to younger children." Cummings (1977) reports that this instrument-object cycle persists among working women who come to believe in "Horatia Alger as a feminist Model"—the model of a woman who *makes* time to be both the primary socializer of her children *and* the architect of a career. The point is that even among more liberated women, the instrument-object realtionship may be perpetuated.

Children are not insensitive to the sexually stratified relationship between the instruments and objects of informal familial controls: "As the child's social perception becomes more sophisticated, (s)he is able to discriminate between the behavior of . . . father and . . . mother and decipher from an abundance of clues that people are divided into two categories—male and female—and that (s)he and one parent belong to one category, and the other parent belongs to the other" (Udry, 1974, p. 53). Further, Udry (ibid., p. 54) observes that "by age three, the boy will begin to perceive that some new requirements go with being male. Males are not supposed to be passive, compliant, and dependent, but on the contrary, are expected to be aggressive, independent, and self-assertive." Although Udry designates these socialized signals of masculinity as "requirements," the reader likely will agree that aggressiveness, independence, and assertiveness connote freeness (or the absence of control) more than restriction. Beyond this, our point is that it is mothers more than fathers who are held responsible for socializing "passivity, compliance, and dependence" into their daughters more than their sons.

Our primary interest, of course, is in the implications of this instrument-object relationship for the patterning of crime and delinquency. To understand the connection we are postulating, it is useful to regard criminal and delinquent behavior as pleasurable, if not liberating. Crime and delinquency can be *fun* (Bordua, 1961; Hagan, 1977c; Greenberg, 1981)—and perhaps even more important, a type of fun that is infrequently allowed to women. One reason why delinquency is fun is that it anticipates a range of activities, some having to do with criminal and others with more conventional occupations, that are more open to males than females. It is the sexually stratified socialization process described above that cultivates this awareness, with results that include the following:

2.2.1 Women define risk-taking less positively than men.

2.2.2 Women define involvement in crime and delinquency less positively than men.

2.2.3 Women are therefore less likely to have been involved in criminal and delinquent behavior than men.

However, the above propositions are not the end of the story. The sexual stratification of social control is made complete with the formal ascription of deviant status. That men more than women are engaged *instrumentally* in this ascriptive process is as obvious as the visibility of one's local constabulary: police, court, and correctional workers are overwhelmingly male (e.g., Milton, 1972). Meanwhile, Pollak (1951; see also Simon, 1975; Nagel and Hagan, 1983) argues that women are underrepresented as the *objects* of official crime statistics because they are underdetected, underreported, and underpunished. Our final propositions are therefore that:

3 Men more than women are the instruments of formal social control, and,

3.1 Offensive behavior held constant, men more than women are the objects of formal social controls.

Summarizing, the above propositions tie the concern of the early deviance theorists with informal processes of social control to the more recent interest in processes of formal social control. Our coordinating hypothesis is that the two control processes are inversely related. Underlying both processes is a gender-based system of sexual stratification that characterizes the world of crime and delinquency as it does the world of work. We believe that there is considerable evidence to support this perspective.

For example, using a survey design with 611 students in four suburban Canadian schools, Hagan, Simpson, and Gillis (1979) have attempted to test each of the above propositions. Items drawn from Hirschi's (1969) formulation of control theory are used to measure maternal and paternal familial controls, scales are developed for the measurement of "taste for risk" and the "perception of delinquency as fun," and measures are provided of official police contacts and self-reported delinquency. The results of the analysis are summarized in the causal model presented in Figure 9-1. This model provides initial support for the proposition that when it comes to child care, females more than males are made the instruments and the objects of *informal* social control. Thus it is found that *both* mothers and fathers control their daughters more than their sons (in terms of knowing where they are and who they are with), but that mothers

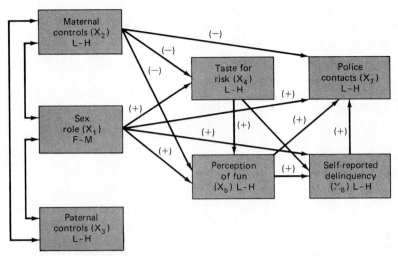

Figure 9-1 A gender-based model of deviance and control. (*Source: Hagan, Simpson, and Gillis, 1979:coefficients deleted*)

control their daughters even more than do their fathers. Furthermore, elsewhere in the model, the causal influences of paternal controls disappear, while the causal effects of maternal controls persist. The consequences of this instrument-object relationship are recognized in the direct effects of maternal controls and sex role on the socially acquired taste for risk, and the effect of all three of these variables on the perception of delinquent pursuits as fun. Said differently, these findings strongly suggest that it is the instrument-object relationship established between mothers and daughters that denies delinquency as a fun and liberating pursuit for girls; meanwhile, it is adolescent boys who disproportionately are allowed delinquency as an outlet, at least to the point of encountering the police. Finally, the object status of males in the formal control process is indicated by the direct effect of sex role on police contacts: all other variables taken into account, including the amount of delinquent behavior, it is boys more than girls who are most likely to be picked up by the police.

What these findings seem to suggest is that women are systematically "oversocialized." It has been argued (Wrong, 1981) that the perspectives of an earlier era presented an oversocialized conception of the human being. Perhaps part of the problem was that these perspectives focused so exclusively on men, for our findings suggest that women *are* oversocialized. The point of the gender-based propositions presented above is to place this finding within the context of a larger stratification system—a system which makes women the instruments and objects of informal social controls, and men the instruments and objects of formal social controls. Thus, we have argued that in the world of crime and delinquency, as in the world of work, women are denied full access to the public sphere through a socialization sequence that moves from mother to daughter in a cycle that is self-renewing.

It is interesting to speculate about the prospects for change in these structural arrangements. Adler (1975) has argued that there is a rising new breed of violent, aggressive female offender (but see Steffensmeier, 1978), and a recent review by Smith and Visher (1980) argues that behavioral differences between the sexes are diminishing. Similarly, Rita Simon (1975) suggests that as occupational opportunities for women expand, and as formal control agents become less chivalrous, male-female patterns of crime should become increasingly alike. However, Simon also acknowledges that to date such changes are limited in scope, and Huber (1976, p. 361; see also Lorber, 1975) emphasizes more generally that "the problem is not only women's invisibility in market and political institutions but also men's invisibility in the home."

Huber's point is that it is easier to get women some new types of work than it is to relieve them of responsibilities for child-care. An increasingly common consequence is a *double* burden for women. Furthermore, when middle- and upper-class women are relieved of child-care, it is commonly through the employment of underclass women to act as their surrogates. In either case, the instrument-object relationship of women in the informal process of social control is preserved. Thus, while women may be employed in instrumental roles with increasing frequency by formal agencies of social control (e.g., as police officers), and while women may increasingly receive an equality of object status from these agencies, it seems *less* likely that the home-based instrument-object relationship of women and its enduring consequences will change as quickly. Male and female rates of criminality therefore are likely to remain quite different for some time to come.

CLASS, CRIME, AND CORPORATIONS

Our interest turns next to crimes committed through and on behalf of corporations. The involvement of corporations in crime has been recognized at least since E. A. Ross (1907, p. 7) wrote of a new type of criminal "who picks pockets with a 'rake-off' instead of a jimmy, cheats with a company prospectus instead of a deck of cards, or scuttles his town instead of his ship." These new criminals earned a lasting label with Edwin Sutherland's (1940) presidential address on the topic of "white-collar crime" to the American Sociological Society. Sutherland (ibid., p. 9) proposed that white-collar crime be defined "as a crime committed by a person of respectability and high social status in the course of his occupation."

From this point on, Wheeler and Rothman (1982, p. 1404) note, there has been continuing confusion about the role of *occupation* and *organization* in the study of white-collar crime (see also Shapiro, 1980). For example, they note that two influential works, Clinard's and Hartung's research on black-market activities during World War II, defined white-collar crime in two rather different ways. Clinard (1952, p. 8) defined white-collar crime occupationally, as "illegal activities among business and professional men," while Hartung (1950, p. 25) included an organizational component, defining such crimes as "a violation of law regulating business, which is committed for a firm by the firm or its agents in the conduct of its business." The problem, of course, is that the occupational and organizational components of many white-collar crimes cannot be easily separated. Clinard and Yeager (1980, p. 19) has recently made this point with the example of a Firestone official who aided his corporation in securing and administering illegal political contributions benefiting the corporation, but then embezzled much of the funds for himself. We will concern ourselves here with both the occupational and the organizational aspects of corporate crime.

It is increasingly recognized that the organizational form of the corporation is crucial to understanding most white-collar crime (Reiss, 1980; Schrager and Short, 1978; Wheeler, 1976; Ermann and Lundman, 1978). As Wheeler and Rothman (1982, p. 1406) note, the corporation "is for white collar criminals what the gun or knife is for the common criminal—a tool to obtain money from victims." Of course, the importance of the corporation is not unique to the world of crime. From the industrial revolution on it has become increasingly apparent that "among the variety of interests that men have, those interests that have been successfully collected to create corporate actors are the interests that dominate the society" (Coleman, 1974, p. 49). The above reference to men is not accidental. It forms the connection between the first and second parts of this chapter, for,

4 Corporate entities are disproportionately male in employment, ownership, and control.

What makes the above proposition interesting is its connection into the control structure of western industrial societies, because, while we have already argued that men are less likely than women to be instruments and objects of informal familial controls, we now propose that

"You've shown great corporate potential, Ms Cranmore. You're deceptive, conniving, manipulative—without sacrificing your femininity."

5 Corporate entities (dominated by men) are less likely than individual actors to be the instruments and objects of informal social control.

There are two aspects of the above proposition that require further comment. The first has to do with differences between corporate and individual actors, the second with the role of individual actors within corporate entities. Any discussion of corporate entities must be clear in acknowledging that the corporation itself is a "legal fiction," with, as H. L. Mencken aptly observed, "no pants to kick or soul to damn." Thus corporations are "juristic persons" that the law chooses to treat, for many practical purposes, like "natural persons." The limits of this legal analogy in terms of formal social controls, including the impossibility of imprisoning or executing corporations, are considered below. Here we focus on differences between corporate and individual actors with regard to informal social controls.

We have noted earlier the role of maternal and paternal controls in generating gender differences in crime. These controls are conventionally understood to induce in human beings feelings of guilt, shame, and a sense of responsibility that discourage criminality. Yet the old legal saw tells us that the corporation has no conscience or soul. Stone (1975, p. 35) describes the problem well:

> When individuals are placed in an organizational structure, some of the ordinary internalized restraints seem to lose their hold. And if we decide to look beyond the individual employees and find an organizational "mind" to work with, a "corporate conscience" distinct from the consciences of particular individuals, it is not readily apparent where we would begin—much less what we would be talking about.

Stone goes on to suggest interesting ways in which the "corporate conscience" and "corporate responsibility" could be increased; however, our need here is to recognize fully the problems caused by the present weakness of these controls.

The problem is in part one of the absence of cultural beliefs to discourage corporate criminality (see Geis, 1961). C. Wright Mills (1956, p. 95) captured part of the problem in his observation that "it is better, so the image runs, to take one dime from each of ten million people at the point of a corporation than $100,000 from each of ten banks at the point of a gun." However, even if condemnatory beliefs about corporate crime were strong, there would be no mechanisms in place to assure their controlling influence. Indeed, the internal structure of the modern corporation often seems at odds with the control of corporate crime.

Consider for a moment the internal structure of a typical modern corporation, as illustrated by Woodmansee's description of the General Electric Corporation of 1975 (cited in Clinard and Yeager, 1980, pp. 24–25), noting the complexity of this enterprise and its sexual stratification.

> We begin by describing the way GE's employees are officially organized into separate layers of authority. The corporation is like a pyramid. The great majority of the company's workers form the base of this pyramid; they take orders coming down from above but do not give orders to anyone else. If you were hired by GE for one of these lowest-level positions, you might find yourself working on an assembly line, installing a motor in a certain type of refrigerator. You would be in a group of 5 to 50 workers who all take orders from one supervisor, or foreman, or manager. Your supervisor is on the second step of the pyramid; she or he, and the

other supervisors who specialize in this type of refrigerator, all take orders from a General Manager.

There are about 180 of these General Managers at GE; each one heads a Department with one or two thousand employees. The General Manager of your Department, and the General Managers of the one or two other Departments which produce GE's other types of refrigerators, are in turn supervised by the Vice President/ General Manager of the Refrigerator Division. This man (there are only men at this level and above) is one of the 50 men at GE responsible for heading GE's Divisions. He, and the heads of several other Divisions which produce major applicances, look up to the next step of the pyramid and see, towering above, the Vice President/Group Executive who heads the entire Major Appliance Group. While there are over 300,000 workers at the base of the pyramid, there are only 10 men on this Group Executive level. Responsibility for overseeing all of GE's product lines is divided between the ten. At about the same level of authority in the company are the executives of GE's Corporate Staff; these men are concerned not with particular products but with general corporate matters such as accounting, planning, legal affairs, and relations with employees, with the public and with government.

And now the four men at the top of the pyramid come into view; the three Vice Chairmen of the Board of Directors, and standing above them, GE's Chief Executive. . . . Usually, these four men confer alone, but once a month, 15 other men join them for a meeting. The 15 other members of the Board of Directors are not called up from lower levels of the GE pyramid; they drift in sideways from the heights of neighboring pyramids. Thirteen of them are chairmen or presidents of other corporations, the four-teenth is a former corporate chairman, and the fifteenth is a university president.

Could or should the board of directors of the above corporation exercise the kind of control over its employees that individual actors are expected to exercise over their dependents? Indeed, is there any analogy at all? Stone (1975, p. 62) points out that top officers and directors theoretically are liable to suit by the corporation itself (via a shareholders' action) if they through negligence allow a law violation to occur. However, Stone then cites an Allis-Chalmers antitrust case to make the point that legally little is expected from corporations in the way of control over their individual actors. In dismissing the claim made in this case, the Delaware Supreme

Court (*Graham v. Allis-Chalmers Mfg. Co.*, 188 A.2d 125, 130 [Del. 1963]) said:

> The precise charge made against these director defendants is that, even though they had no knowledge or any suspicion of wrongdoing on the part of the company's employees, they still should have put into effect a system of watchfulness which would have brought such misconduct to their attention in ample time to have brought it to an end. . . . On the contrary, it appears that directors are entitled to rely on the honesty and integrity of their subordinates until something occurs to put them on suspicion that something is wrong. If such occurs and goes unheeded, then liability of the directors might well follow, but *absent cause for suspicion there is no duty upon the directors to install and operate a corporate system of espionage to ferret out wrongdoing which they have no reason to suspect exists.*
>
> The duties of the Allis-Chalmers Directors were fixed by the nature of the enterprise which employed in excess of 30,000 persons, and extended over a large geographical area. By force of necessity, the company's Directors could not know personally all the company's employees. The very magnitude of the enterprise required them to confine their control to the broad policy decisions.

The effect of this kind of decision is to reinforce the practice of top management keeping itself uninformed about the very details of illegal activities that the public interest requires they know.

How widespread is this executive disengagement from the details of corporate criminality? Two intriguing studies (Baumhart, 1961; Brenner and Molander, 1977) published in the *Harvard Business Review* suggest that the problem is large and growing. The latter of these studies reports that the percentage of executives who have reported an inability to be honest in providing information to top management has nearly doubled since the earlier research, done in the 1950s. About half of those surveyed in the latter study thought that their superiors frequently did not wish to know how results were obtained, as long as the desired outcome was accomplished. Furthermore, the executives surveyed "frequently complained of superiors' pressure to support incorrect viewpoints, sign false documents, overlook superiors' wrongdoing, and do business with superiors' friends" (Brenner and Molander, 1977).

The last set of findings suggests not only the absence of controls within the workplace, but the presence as well of pressures from the top of an industry downward that generate corporate criminality. Farberman (1975) has referred to such pressures in the automotive industry, and in other highly concentrated corporate sectors, as constituting a "criminogenic market structure." The crime-generating feature of these markets is their domination by a relatively small number of manufacturers who insist that their dealers sell in high volume and at a small per unit profit. Dealerships that fail to perform risk the loss of their franchises in an industry where the alternatives are few. A result is high pressure to maximize sales and minimize service. More specifically, Farberman suggests that dealers in the car industry are induced by the short profit margins on new cars to compensate through fraudulent warranty work and repair rackets. The connection between these findings and those noted above is that the executives of the automotive industry can distance themselves from the criminal consequences of the "forcing model" (high volume/low per unit profit) they impose. The result is an absence of control over repair and warranty frauds within the industry.

We have now made the case that corporate entities are less likely than individual actors to be the instruments and objects of informal social controls; and furthermore that individual actors acting within corporate entities are also less bound by such controls than would otherwise be the case. The question that follows is whether formal legal controls compensate for this imbalance. Although we will argue below that there may be a historical trend in this direction, we propose first that this is not currently the case. Thus,

6 Corporate actors are less *liable* than individual actors to the risk of being the objects of formal social control.

7 Corporate actors are therefore less likely than individual actors to be the objects of formal legal control.

Furthermore,

8 Corporate actors are more likely than individual actors to be the instruments of formal social control.

Each of these propositions requires clarification and elaboration.

"We have arranged things," writes Christopher Stone (1975, p. 46), "so that the people who call the shots do not have to bear the full risks." This, in a nutshell, is the consequence of the limited liabilities borne by modern corporate actors.

Take, for example, a small corporation involved in shipping dynamite. The shareholders of such a company, who are typically also the managers, do not *want* their dynamite-laden truck to blow up.

But if it does, they know that those injured cannot, except in rare cases, sue them as individuals to recover their full damages if the amount left in the corporation's bank account is inadequate to make full compensation (which it will be if the explosion has, say, leveled downtown Portland). What this means is that in deciding how much money to spend on safety devices, and whether or not to allow trucks to drive through major cities, the calculations are skewed toward higher risks than suggested by the "rational economic corporation/free market" model that is dreamily put forth in textbooks. If no accident results, the shareholders will reap the profits of skimping on safety measures. If a truck blows up, the underlying human interests will be shielded from fully bearing the harm that they have caused. And then, there is nothing to prevent the same men from setting up a new dynamite shipping corporation the next day; all it takes is the imagination to think up a new name, and some $50 in filing fees (Stone, 1975, pp. 46–47).

It is conceded that large corporations are not quite so free to dissolve and reconstitute their operations. However, there is a related problem of liability in the separation of shareholder and management interests. Given that corporate officers gain their primary rewards through salaries, the effects of damage judgments are indirect, and judging from experience, limited. Stone (ibid., p. 47) reminds us that in 1972, for example, the Ford Motor Company suffered fines and penalties of approximately $7 million for a violation of the Environmental Protection Act. Yet the salaries of the chief executives of this company increased dramatically in following years. There is no record of shareholders successfully altering such patterns by changing management in the wake of lawsuits.

Probably the most disconcerting instances of limited liability, however, involve job-induced illness and death. It is estimated that annually about 100,000 Americans die because of occupational diseases, while about 390,000 workers are disabled (*U.S. News and World Report,* Feb. 5, 1979, p. 39). Simon and Eitzen (1982, p. 110) offer the following examples of the specific risks of continued exposure in certain industries.

• Workers in the dyestuffs industry (working with aromatic hydrocarbons) have about thirty times the risk of the general population of dying from bladder cancer.

• The wives of men who work with vinyl chloride are twice as likely as other women to have miscarriages or stillbirths.

• In 1978, Occidental Chemical Company workers handling the pesticide DBCP were found to be sterile as a result of the exposure, substantiating a 1961 study by Dow Chemical which indicated that DBCP caused sterility in rats.

• A 1976 government study determined that if 129,00 workers were exposed to the current *legal* level.of cotton-dust exposure, over a period of time 23,497 would likely become byssinotics (victims of "brown lung").

• Starting with 632 asbestos workers in 1943, one researcher determined each of their fates after twenty years of employment. By 1973, 444 were dead, a rate 50 percent greater than for the average white male. The rate for lung cancer was 700 percent greater than expected, and the rate for all types of cancer was four times as great.

Swartz (1975) has argued that at least some of these deaths and illnesses should be considered as criminal in origin; indeed, that some should be considered murders. "By any legitimate criteria," writes Swartz (ibid., p. 18), "corporate executives who willfully make a decision to expose workers to a dangerous substance which eventually causes the death of some of the workers, should be considered murderers." A recent film about Karen Silkwood provides a compelling example. Yet Swartz observes that no executive has ever served a day in jail for such a practice, while most are probably well rewarded for saving the company money.

But what of the corporate actors who are held criminally liable and processed through the criminal-justice system? Are they liable to as severe sanctioning as individual actors? Notions of "equality before the law" are perhaps nowhere more subjective in meaning than in their application to the sentencing of white-collar offenders. This is reflected in at least two kinds of comments made by judges about the sentences they impose for white-collar crimes. It is reflected first in the suggestion that white-collar offenders experience sanctions differently than other kinds of offenders, and second in the assertion that different kinds of sanctions are appropriate in white-collar cases.

The view, common among judges, that white-collar offenders experience sanctions differently than other kinds of offenders is well summarized by Mann, Wheeler, and Sarat's (1980, pp. 483–484) conclusions after interviewing a sample of American federal district court judges: "Most judges have a widespread belief that the suffering experienced by a white-collar person as a result of apprehension, public indictment and conviction, and the collateral disabilities incident to conviction—loss of job, professional licenses, and status in the community—completely satisfies the need to punish the individual." The argument for white-collar leniency is therefore clear: the defendant, having suffered enough from the acts of prosecution and conviction, does not require a severe sentence.

What kinds of sentences therefore are appropriate for white-collar offenders? In white-collar cases judges seem to face a recurring problem:

how to accomplish the goal of general deterrence without doing a perceived injustice to the individual offender. A judge interviewed by Mann et al. (ibid., p. 499) suggests the mental conflict this dilemma stimulates.

> The problem is the tension between use of incarceration for its deterrent factors, and the inclination not to use it because it is too excessive given the non-criminal record of the [white-collar] offender. From the individual standpoint there are good arguments against sentencing; from the societal interest of deterring crime there are some good arguments for using the sentence. . . . the tension between those two values is very acute.

Mann et al. (ibid.) conclude that most judges seek a compromise in resolving this dilemma. "The weekend sentence, the very short jail term, and the relatively frequent use of amended sentences (where a judge imposes a prison term and later reduces it) are evidence of this search for a compromise."

It is important also to acknowledge the disputed role of fines in sentencing white-collar offenders. Posner (1980, p. 409) asserts that "the white-collar criminal . . . should be punished only by monetary penalties." His argument is that if fines are suitably large they are an equally effective deterrent, cheaper to administer, and therefore socially preferable to imprisonment and other "afflictive" punishments. We have already noted that corporate entities are liable to little else than fines. However, Mann et al. find federal judges to be skeptical of the effectiveness of fines. They report (1980, p. 496),

> . . . a conspicuous absence of responses by judges that a fine was the appropriate sanction to be imposed on a defendant. . . . Where fines were used in conjunction with another sentence it was generally the other sentence . . . that was thought to have the intended deterrent effect. Where the fine was used alone, the idea that the commencement of the criminal process against the defendant was the punishment seemed to be the more important in the judges' minds than the fine itself.

The sense that emerges is that judges are acutely aware of the issues of deterrence, disparity, and discrimination in the sentencing of white-collar offenders, and that they attempt to respond to these issues by fashioning sentences that combine sanctions in a compromise fashion. Consistent with this view, Hagan and Nagel (1982) find, in a sentencing study covering the period from 1963 to 1976 in the federal court for the Southern District of New York, that judges attempted to compensate for shorter prison terms

given white-collar offenders by adding probation or fines to their sentences. Similarly, fines were most frequently used in conjunction with prison
and probation sentences. Finally, white-collar offenders in this district
were more likely than other offenders to receive amended or shortened
sentences. While we will have reason to consider some recent and
interesting changes in these patterns below, here we can simply note that
the above findings support the proposition that white-collar offenders are
advantaged by the specific types and combinations of formal sanctions that
are imposed on them.

We turn now to the proposition that corporate actors are more likely
than individual actors to be instruments of formal social control. Given
that in Anglo-American systems of criminal law it is almost always a
state-supported prosecutor who pursues cases through the criminal-justice
system, individual actors have little opportunity to be instruments of
formal legal control. Individual victims effectively are decoupled from the
criminal-justice process. Beyond this, however, Hagan (1982) has shown
that corporate actors play a disproportionate role in bringing cases to the
law (see Tables in Chapter 4). Using victimization data on burglary and
robbery collected in thirteen American cities, it is shown (as might be
expected, given the opportunities and benefits of crimes against corporate
actors), that for both burglary and robbery, the per capita rates of
victimization are higher for commercial establishments than for individuals
and households. More to the point, however, for both burglary and
robbery, commercial establishments are more likely than individual
households to report the victimizations they experience to the police.
Undoubtedly, this difference is influenced by types and amounts of
corporate insurance coverage. Nonetheless, it remains significant that on a
per capita basis, corporate actors are much more likely than individual
actors to require and make use of the formal legal system. Beyond this,
Hagan finds, using Canadian data, that corporate actors are more likely
than individuals to obtain convictions, and that the likelihood of conviction
increases with the size of the organization. A more general conclusion of
this study is that corporate actors not only have proven themselves
successful in avoiding large-scale criminal prosecutions, they also have
demonstrated themselves effective in using criminal prosecutions to penalize individual actors who offend against them.

Given all that precedes, our next proposition should not surprise.

9 Corporate actors profit more from, and perpetrate larger, crimes than
individual actors.

The evidence for this proposition comes from an intriguing study by
Wheeler and Rothman (1982). Using data gathered from presentence

reports completed from 1976 to 1978 in American federal courts, Wheeler and Rothman categorized white-collar offenders into three groups: those who committed offenses alone or with affiliated others using neither an occupational nor an organizational role (individual offenders); those who committed offenses alone or with affiliated others using an occupational role (occupational offenders); and those who committed offenses in which both organization and occupation were ingredients (organizational offenders). The results of this study indicate in a variety of ways the enormous advantages accruing to those who use formal organizations in their crimes. For example, across a subset of four offenses, the "median take" for individual offenders was $5,279, for occupational offenders $17,106, and for organizational offenders $117,392. Why the organizational edge? Wheeler and Rothman (ibid., p. 1417) answer with an example.

> Represented by its president, a corporation entered into a factoring agreement with a leading New York commercial bank, presenting it with $1.2 million in false billings over the course of seven months; the company's statements were either inflated to reflect much more business than was actually being done, or were simply made up. Would the bank have done this for an individual? Whether we conclude that organizations are trusted more than individuals, or that they simply operate on a much larger scale, it is clear that the havoc caused when organizations are used outside the law far exceeds anything produced by unaffiliated actors.

The point is that just as the organizational form has facilitated economic and technological development on a scale far beyond that achieved by individuals, so too has this form allowed criminal gains of a magnitude that men and women acting alone would find hard to attain.

We turn finally to our last proposition:

10 Formal legal controls are growing faster for corporate actors than for individual actors.

This proposition corresponds to the first proposition we offered at the beginning of the chapter, namely, that formal legal controls are inversely related to informal social controls. We have already noted the relative weakness of both formal and informal controls as they affect corporate as compared to individual actors. The point of our last proposition is to observe that while the history of the modern corporation is relatively short, there is an apparent trend toward the compensation of weak informal controls through the expansion of formal legal controls. This trend is recognized in a variety of ways, but perhaps most dramatically in the events of the post-Watergate period.

Prior to Watergate, but especially immediately after it, the resources of the American federal courts were increasingly used to prosecute and punish various kinds of white-collar and corporate criminals. Katz (1980) has described the emergence of this new enforcement priority, and it is reflected in the "proactive" prosecutorial polices of several U.S. attorneys described by Hagan and Nagel (1982). Wheeler et al. (1982) have even sought to demonstrate that such policies have led to the more severe sentencing of high-status white-collar offenders. Hagan and Palloni (1983) concur in reporting an increased use of imprisonment with white-collar offenders after Watergate, but also indicate that the length of the prison sentences is unusually short. In any case, the prosecution, if not the sentencing, of white-collar offenders did increase after Watergate.

Of course, the need for increasing control of corporate actors was recognized much earlier in this century. Berg (1982, p. 176) speaks of "the drift toward public controls since the Pujo committee's investigations of the armaments industry; the old post–World War I investigations of the armaments industry; the TNEC explorations . . . ; the New, the Fair, and other Deals; and the logic behind interventions by New Frontiersmen and Great Society Builders." An interesting question is whether the Reagan and later administrations will dismantle the embodiments of this trend. However, Berg notes that the Reagan administration today speaks less and less about *de*regulation, and more and more about *self*-regulation. The point is that the need for regulation is acknowledged; the difference is in the optimism attached to public and private sources of regulation.

Meanwhile, the division between the public and private spheres becomes increasingly obscure.

Private airlines operate out of public airports to serve passengers who arrive in public buses or private taxis (the latter with publicly controlled medallions), that use public parkways. Steelmakers' sales are often facilitated by publicly accorded "trigger prices"; these are set by public leaders in response to competition from private overseas firms whose managers, in turn, enjoy public support from their home governments. . . . Scientists in universities—some state, some private—collect royalties from licenses to patents on discoveries that emanate from publicly supported research. . . . New York City's government is currently "selling" the depreciation allowances on its buses to a private profit-making syndicate in need of tax offsets. It was President Dwight Eisenhower, finally, who cautioned Americans about the most visible of the public/private partnerships, the so-called military-industrial complex (Berg, 1982, p. 179).

Where such partnerships will lead us is unclear. That they will require new and undeveloped mechanisms of control is a lesson of our changing corporate as well as individual experience.

CONCLUSIONS

The instrument and object relationships established by and through formal and informal structures of social control are more taken for granted than studied in western societies. Yet we have argued that these structural relationships are central to the explanation of the variable participation of men and women, and corporations and individuals, in crime. Like the grammar that comes subconsciously to organize our writing and speech, these instrument-object relationships, we have argued, play a powerful role in organizing our involvement in work as well as in crime. Thus we argued that women are characteristically denied full access to the public sphere through a socialization process that moves from mother to daughter in a cycle that is self-renewing, as well as self-denying, in terms of the experience of work as well as crime. Women are more likely than men to be the instruments and objects of the informal social controls that dominate childhood socialization, while men are more likely than women to be the instruments and objects of the formal legal controls that dominate adolescent and adult criminality. Meanwhile, the corporate forms that dominate the world of work, and that are dominated by men, are less likely to be objects of both formal and informal social control than are individual actors. The absence of more formal legal control of corporate crime means that we know less about this kind of crime than we could, while the relative absence of informal social control leads us to expect that there is much more corporate criminality than is officially recognized. Of course, all of the above is subject to change, and it is the prospect of change that is beginning to raise some of these structural relationships to new levels of public awareness.

For example, we are as a society today much more self-conscious about the sex-role socialization of our children, and we similarly are more critically aware of the need to channel constructively the growth and development of corporate power. This kind of critical awareness inevitably raises questions about the ways in which formal and informal structures of control operate. Analyses of these instrument-object relationships can be informed by modern criminological theory. This implies a theory of crime that is sensitive to the larger social structure in which controls exercise their influence.

LIVING WITH CRIME: THE FAILURES AND FUTURES OF PUNISHMENT, TREATMENT, AND PREVENTION

10

THE ISSUE: HOW TO RESPOND TO CRIME

How could and should we best respond to crime? There are two very different questions here. The first question—how *could* we best respond to crime?—is at least in part empirical. That is, assuming agreement that our common goal is to reduce crime, we can go about the task, empirically, of measuring what kinds of responses to crime produce what kinds of outcomes. We will explore the results of research on this topic in this chapter. However, the second question—how *should* we best respond to crime?—cannot be answered by any amount of empirical research. It is a moral question; a question of values. Empirical research can inform moral issues, but empirical research cannot finally resolve these issues. When it attempts to do so, as in debates about capital punishment, the results are disappointing. Thus whether capital punishment does or does not deter crime cannot in any definitive way tell us whether capital punishment should or should not be imposed. Some believe capital punishment is a just desert, a suitable form of retribution, for some crimes regardless of its effect(s) on the incidence of crime. Hannah Arendt (1964, p. 254) offers such a view when she writes of the hanging of Adolf Eichmann, the Nazi war criminal, "What good does it do? . . . It will do justice." On the other side of the ledger, there are those, including Karl Marx (1853), who believe there is no absolute moral right to punish, even if and when it may deter further crimes: ". . . what right have you to punish me for the amelioration or intimidation of others?" We do not attempt to resolve such moral issues in this chapter. However, we do note the importance of such issues, and we will attempt to inform them by reviewing historical and empirical aspects of efforts to punish, treat, and prevent criminal behavior.

THE PURPOSES OF CRIMINAL SANCTIONS

Criminal sanctions can have nonpunitive as well as punitive purposes. Seven purposes of criminal sanctions are noted frequently: (1) *restraint or incapacitation:* to stop the behavior in question; (2) *individual or specific deterrence:* the use of a punishment to reduce the likelihood that the person who receives it will offend again in the future; (3) *general deterrence:* punishing one person to reduce the likelihood that others will pursue the same kind of behavior; (4) *reform or rehabilitation:* imposing a punishment, usually in this case called a "treatment," to correct what went wrong in the person who committed the crime; (5) *moral affirmation or symbolism:* a punishment intended to reaffirm the moral norm that has been violated, by making the offender a symbol of the consequences of violation, and by in this way drawing "moral boundaries" between the "good" and "bad" in society; (6) *retribution:* the use of a punishment to balance the harm done—in effect, to return the offense in kind; and (7) *restitution or compensation:* the imposition of a sanction that also seeks to reestablish balance, but now usually with the currency of money.

Although the above goals may sometimes overlap, they are not necessarily consistent, and they often seem in conflict. To cite only the most obvious example, it would seem doubtful that one could achieve the goals of retribution and rehabilitation at the same time. This point will become particularly apparent when we consider below the problems of administering prisons, which often are expected to reconcile such goals. It is significant to note here, however, that crime-control agents apparently have come to believe that such conflicting goals can be reconciled. Hogarth (1971, p. 77) reports that among criminal-court judges a belief in reformation is associated with a belief in the efficacy of most penal measures, including institutional measures. Similarly, Wheeler et al. (1968, p. 56) report that among juvenile-court judges a belief in social welfare ideology is associated with taking what is commonly regarded as the most severe actions regarding delinquents, again including institutional measures. In drawing conclusions from both studies it is noted that judges are often confronted with having to use institutions in spite of their nonpunitive goals. Hogarth (1971, p. 77) reasons that "the easiest way out of the dilemma is to see prisons as therapeutic institutions." Wheeler et al. (1968, p. 50) trace a similar line of thought in noting: "Clearly, if a person thinks of the institutions to which these youths are sent as benign, humane, and therapeutic, rather than existing as a last resort for punishment and community protection, then he may more easily be persuaded that it is in the youth's behalf that he is sent there."

We have introduced the above research because it anticipates a theme that will recur in this chapter. The theme is that we often conceal from ourselves, as individuals and as a society, the punishments we impose on others. This is not a new theme in social science. It is, for example, the essence of Evert Hughes's (1962) discussion of "Good People and Dirty Work," and an explanation of how otherwise well-informed publics can ignore atrocities that sometimes occur at close physical and/or social distances from them. The capacity to do this forms a backdrop to a debate about trends in the punishment of criminals in western societies. Ted Robert Gurr (1980, p. 46) has written recently that "the contemporary offender, even when found guilty, is likely to suffer only a small personal fraction of the retribution which fell on his nineteenth-century counterpart." Gurr attributes this assumed improvement to a more general "humanization of interpersonal relations" in western societies. However, others, while agreeing that the forms of punishment have changed, are not so quick to conclude that the severity of punishment has diminished. Below we will discuss the decline of corporal and capital punishment, the shift to imprisonment, and the rise of probation and parole. As we do so, it is worthwhile to keep in mind the observation of David Rothman (1980, p. 152) that "lacking a calculus for pain, it is not always easy to measure one kind of punishment against another. . . . [for example] in no simple sense can the substitution of solitary [confinement] for the whip be automatically considered a 'reform.' " We will have reason to reflect further on this point below.

THE DECLINE OF CORPORAL AND CAPITAL PUNISHMENT

Thorsten Sellin (1976, p. 133) has noted that "it was only natural that those who established settlements in the New World would bring with them not only their possessions and skills, but also their social and legal institutions, including the traditional penal methods of their homelands—Spain, Portugal, France, and England." Included among these methods were the whipping post, the stocks, the pillory, the stake, the wheel, the gallows, the gibbet, the branding iron, and instruments of torture and mutilation. Several of these methods, the whipping post and the gallows, survived into the mid-twentieth century. The colonists also revived forms of penal slavery, a set of punishments long since abandoned in the mother country.

Clearly, however, public forms of corporal and capital punishment are not as popular today as they were in earlier periods of our history. Particularly graphic is the modern decline in the use of the death penalty in America, although there are threats of its resurgence (Bowers and Pierce, 1976). Thus in America between 1930 and 1967 there were 3,859 executions. There were no executions over the next decade, but there have been a number of executions since, and more than a thousand persons are under current sentences of death. Only time will tell whether executions will again become common in America. There is new evidence that use of the death penalty is discriminatory (Radelet, 1981), and this may again raise the issue of the constitutionality of the death penalty.

Nonetheless, current debate about a possible limited return to the death penalty should not obscure what is a clear long-term shift from the *public* punishment of the criminal *body* to the more *private* punishment of the criminal *mind*. One way to emphasize this point is to remind ourselves of just how torturous the former kinds of punishment regularly were. Michel Foucault (1979, p. 3) provides a graphic example:

> On 2 March 1757 Damiens the regicide was condemned "to make the [amende honorable] before the main door of the Church of Paris," where he was to be "taken and conveyed in a cart, wearing nothing but a shirt, holding a torch of burning wax weighing two pounds"; then, "in the said cart, to the Place de Greve, where, on a scaffold that will be erected there, the flesh will be torn from his breasts, arms, thighs and calves with red-hot pincers, his right hand, holding the knife with which he committed the said parricide, burnt with sulphur, and, on those places where the flesh will be torn away, poured molten lead, boiling oil, burning resin, wax sulphur melted together and then his body drawn and quartered by four horses and his limbs and body consumed by fire, reduced to ashes and his ashes thrown to the winds."

The task is to explain why we no longer do such things, and why, when we do contemplate, for example, a return to the death penalty, we do so in a far different way.

Foucault's answer begins with the observation that such punishments did not accomplish their intended results. Their purpose was to display the crime, its confession, and its consequences in the tortured form of the offender. However, a problem was that on such occasions, "if the crowd gathered round the scaffold, it was not simply to witness the sufferings of the condemned man or to excite the anger of the executioner: it was also to hear an individual who had nothing more to lose curse the judges, the laws, the government and religion" (p. 60). The reformers of the eighteenth and nineteenth centuries (including the classical criminologists discussed in Chapter 1) were able to note not only that these punishments were so severe that they seldom were used, but also that public tortures and executions did not, as intended, frighten people. Indeed, they often made their sufferers into folk heroes. Corporal and capital punishment, at least as applied, did not accomplish their goals.

This perhaps also does something to explain why capital punishment, when it has endured in western capitalist societies, has taken a decidedly different form. John Lofland (1977, p. 283) notes that "to contrast English and American state executions circa 1950 with those circa 1700 is virtually to contrast pure strategies of dramaturgical concealment and openness." Lofland's point is that when we do use the death penalty today we go to great lengths to avert attention from the execution itself. Access to the condemned is restricted, an inconspicuous time for the execution is selected, removal of the condemned to the place of execution is accomplished with dispatch, the place of execution is private, few witnesses are allowed, the executioner is kept impersonal, the condemned is allowed little expression, the technique of execution is "clean" and quick, the corpse is quickly removed, and media attention is restricted. A comparison of open and concealed strategies is summarized in Table 10-1. The comfortable assumption is that strategies of concealment are more humane to the condemned. It may be so. But it may also be the case that such strategies make the dealing of death more acceptable to the public, allowing a punishment to persist when it might not otherwise. Lofland (ibid., p. 321) adds to this the irony that "however raucous or crude historic executions may have been, they did provide the condemned with opportunity for dying with a display of courage and dignity utterly denied in modern executions."

THE SHIFT TO IMPRISONMENT

The nineteenth century brought to Europe and America a curtailment of hanging, the abolition of branding and the stocks, and the widespread adoption of the penitentiary as the punishment of first choice for serious crimes (Ignatieff, 1978, p. 154). Thus most accounts locate a revolutionary change in the preferred form of criminal punishment, a shift to the use of imprisonment, as having occurred between 1780 and 1850 (Rothman, 1971; Foucault, 1977; Ignatieff, 1978). More specifically, Ignatieff (1977, p. 160) suggests that "it was only after 1776 in America and after 1789 in France that imprisonment began to replace hanging as *the* penalty appropriate to modern enlightened republics."

John Howard (1726–1790) is the Englishman whose name is most frequently associated with prison reform and the beginning of the penitentiary system. Howard began his reform work as a county sheriff who took seriously the task of inspecting prisons. The result was the inevitable discovery of abuses. However, Ignatieff (1978, p. 52) notes that Howard's denunciation of these abuses was not novel. What was novel was the "scientific" form of the critique. Indeed, "Howard was one of the first philanthropists to attempt a systematic description of a social problem." The implication is that the mantle of science, as much as the humanitarian goals of these reforms, was the force behind Howard's success.

In England, the first national penitentiary, Milbank, was opened in 1816. Although this prison proved a health hazard and experienced lengthy

TABLE 10-1
OPEN AND CONCEALED DRAMATURGY OF STATE EXECUTIONS

	Open	Concealed
Death wait	Long	Short
Death confinement	Many, self-chosen visitors Diverse activities allowed Exhorted about death Exposed to death preparations	Few, regulated visitors Few activities allowed Left alone about death Insulated from death preparations
Execution time	Socially conspicuous day and hour	Socially inconspicuous day and hour
Death trip	Long Elaborate and specialized transport devices Large cortege Dramatic events en route Complicated, public route	Short No transport devices Tiny cortege, if any No events en route Simple, private route
Death Place	Public, outdoors Large, open, visible Multiple and dispersed locations Specialized decoration	Private, indoors Small, enclosed, buffered Centralized location Neutral decoration
Death witnesses	Unlimited number Socially diverse Perform personal and diverse activities	Small, controlled number Socially homogeneous Perform impersonal and restricted activities
Executioner	Professional Publicly known Performance discretionary Strong, colorful, deviant personal style Personal contact with condemned	Part-time Publicly anonymous Performance drilled Bland, conformist, quiet personal style Impersonal, limited contact with condemned
Condemned	Self-chosen, diverse accoutrements Diverse acts and speech	Narrowly restricted accoutrements Narrow range of acts and speech
Death technique	Unreliable, long-acting, noisy, painful, scream-provoking, mutilating, struggle-inducing, odor-causing, highly visible	Reliable, fast-acting, quiet, painless, non-scream-provoking, non-mutilating, non-struggle-inducing, odorless, concealed

TABLE 10-1 *(cont'd)*
OPEN AND CONCEALED DRAMATURGY OF STATE EXECUTIONS

	Open	Concealed
Death wait	Long	Short
Corpse disposal	Public display Prolonged Marked grave	No display Quick Anonymous grave
Death announcement	Unrestricted media Suspension of institutional activities and other symbols	Restricted media No suspension of institutional activities or other symbols

periods of open revolt among its inmates, lessons were learned, and a more successful regime was established with the opening of Pentonville in 1842. This institution, built on the principles of solitude, hard labor, and religious indoctrination, became a model for many of the prisons that followed.

As early as 1776, the Commonwealth of Pennsylvania's first constitution instructed that "houses ought to be provided for punishing by hard labour those convicted of crimes not capital" (cited in Sellin, 1976, p. 139). To this end, a small "penitentiary" section was added to the Walnut Street Jail in Philadelphia in 1790. This section of the jail allowed for the solitary confinement of convicts, and in 1794 the death penalty was abolished except for first-degree murder. The Walnut Street Jail subsequently became a model for the construction of other state prisons or penitentiaries. A number of important institutions were constructed between 1820 and 1830—Auburn, 1819–1823; Ossining, 1825; Pittsburgh, 1826; Philadelphia, 1829 (Rothman, 1971). In the separate system at Philadelphia, prisoners were kept completely isolated in their cells and were forbidden to communicate or otherwise associate with fellow prisoners. The theory of the silent regime, common by the 1840s, was that it would eliminate a criminal subculture that was assumed to cause much crime. Although prisoners were allowed to work together, they were not allowed to communicate in any way. As Ignatieff (1981, p. 164) notes, "the penitentiary was something new and unprecedented and was understood as such by the great observers of the age, Alexis de Tocqueville, Charles Dickens, and Thomas Carlyle."

Gradually, the penitentiary system gave way in popularity to the reformatory system, as represented by the Elmira Reformatory, established in 1876. This institution was the culmination of efforts by the National Prison Association, led by the penologist Enoch Wines. What distinguished the reformatory from the penitentiary, at least in principle,

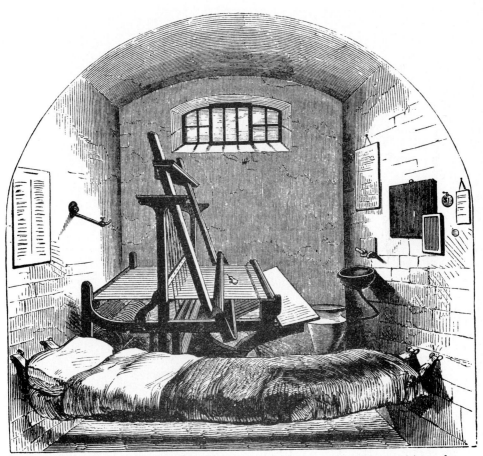

Separate cell in Pentonville Prison with hammock slung for sleeping and loom for daywork. (*Source: Ignatieff's A Just Measure of Pain*)

was a greater emphasis on education and preparation for a trade. Elmira was from the beginning thought to have as much or more relevance for young offenders as for adults. Thus its inmates consisted of first-time felons between the ages of 16 and 30 who, in the estimation of the sentencing judge, were thought capable of reformation (Rothman, 1980, p. 33). Although it cannot be said that Elmira itself was a particularly dramatic breakthrough in the design and operation of prisons, it did signal a new and more modern emphasis on the goal of rehabilitation in penology (Platt, 1969). We consider next some of the problems of accommodating such goals within contemporary penal settings.

The chapel, on the "separate system," in Pentonville Prison, during divine service. (Source: Ignatieff's *A Just Measure of Pain*)

Prisoners picking oakum under the silent system at the Middlesex House of Correction, Coldbath Fields. (*Source: Ignatieff's A Just Measure of Pain*)

THE SOCIAL ORGANIZATION OF PRISONS

Much criminological research has focused on prisons, attempting to determine how they are organized in structural and cultural terms. A classic early example of this tradition was Donald Clemmer's (1940) study, *The Prison Community*. Clemmer stimulated an enduring interest in three aspects of prison life: (1) the "inmate code": the norms that are presumed to rule prison relations; (2) "argot roles": the social roles that are described by prison slang and are assumed to organize the responses of prisoners to the problems of prison life; and (3) "prisonization": the socialization experience that accompanies time spent in prison. This tradition of research saw the prison experience as determined primarily by the structure of the prison itself. Sometimes called the "indigenous origin" model, this tradition attached great importance to the existence of a prisoner subculture. Sykes and Messinger (1960) identified five major components of the inmate code that organized this subculture: (1) don't interfere with inmate interests, be loyal to your class—the cons; (2) don't lose your head; play it cool and do your own time; (3) don't exploit inmates; be right; (4) don't weaken; be a man; (5) don't be a sucker; be sharp.

The most important research in this tradition is Gresham Sykes's *The Society of Captives* (1958). Sykes begins with the premise that prisons are self-contained institutions that generate their own unique kind of social order. Fundamental to the social organization of these institutions are the conflicting tasks they are expected to accomplish. Prison administrators are expected to maintain the custody of their inmates, to establish and maintain order within the prison, to make the prison as self-sufficient in meeting subsistence needs as possible, to provide a punishing experience, and simultaneously to provide for the rehabilitation of the inmates. The attempt to accommodate these conflicting tasks inevitably imposes deprivations on inmates, the response to which is the emergence of argot roles (e.g., rats, center men, gorillas, merchants, wolves, punks, fags, ball busters, real men, toughs, and hipsters). Some of these roles—for example the "ball buster," who challenges authorities at every turn, and the "merchant," who sells contraband goods and services—are "alienating" in the sense that they generate discontent and unrest. However, the "real man"—who simply wants to "pull his own time" without the kinds of provocations that may lead to a longer sentence—is a "cohesive" social role. Most of the time, prison officials and guards reach accommodations with inmates who occupy such cohesive roles, in the interests of prison stability and order. However, occasional efforts to reorganize or reform prisons may challenge these arrangements and destabilize the balance among the roles.

More recent research challenges the "indigenous origin" model of the prison, often with what is now called the "importation hypothesis." This hypothesis suggests that the prison subculture derives less from the structure of the prison itself than from the criminal and conventional subcultures outside the prison. Work in this latter tradition (Irwin and Cressey, 1962; Irwin, 1970) increasingly emphasizes the role of race and ethnicity in establishing the social organization of prison life (Jacobs, 1977).

A benchmark in prison race relations occurred in the late 1950s as blacks began to protest segregation and discrimination in prisons (Jacobs, 1979). Central to this protest was the Black Muslim movement. The Black Muslims took an active role in organizing inmates, bringing the spirit of "black nationalism" into prisons and making possible a collective challenge to the authority of white prison officials. The American Correctional Association officially fought the Muslims by denouncing their activities. To the extent that the Muslims took their grievances about religious and racial discrimination to the courts, they frequently won. Ironically, Jacobs (1979, p. 10) suggests that "after their religious grievances were redressed, the Muslims became a quiescent and stabilizing force in many prisons, which began to be racked by new cohorts of violent and disorganized ghetto youth." Minorities often dominated the prisons, even when they were not dominant in numbers. For example, Bartollas et al. (1976) report that in an Ohio juvenile facility characterized by numerical racial equality, lower-class blacks were the dominant group, followed by middle-class blacks, lower-class whites, and middle-class whites. They go on to note two distinct sets of inmate norms. The black inmate norms were: exploit whites, do not force sex on blacks, and defend your brother; white norms encouraged universal distrust, and each man for himself. More striking still is a finding by Carroll (1974) that in a Rhode Island institution that was only 25 percent black, 75 percent of the homosexual rapes involved blacks raping whites.

Jacobs (1979, p. 17) offers a convincing explanation of the dominance of minorities in contemporary American prison settings.

The key to black dominance is their greater solidarity and ability to intimidate whites. As the distinct minority in the larger society, blacks have long experienced racial discrimination. They have necessarily defined themselves in terms of their racial identity and have linked their opportunities in the larger society to the fate of their race. Whites, especially outside the south, have had almost no experience in grouping together on the basis of being white. Ethnicity has been a more important basis for social interaction. . . . Consequently, whites face imprisonment alone or in small cliques based on outside friendships, neighborhood, or ethnic background.

What is clear from the new prison research is that prisons are no longer, if ever they were, characterized by homogeneous subcultures or inmate codes. It is also clear from this research that prisons remain dangerous and punishing places.

THE RISE OF PROBATION AND PAROLE

It is not difficult to see why modern reformers were anxious to find alternatives to prison. Probation and parole represented the attractive prospect of avoiding prison in the first place, or failing this, the prospect of shortening the duration of prison terms.

The earliest notions of probation can be traced to the reign of Henry II in thirteenth-century England, and the introduction of the "benefit of clergy," a practice that usually resulted in the removal of an offender from the jurisdiction of the court (Timasheff, 1941*a*, 1941*b*). However, the first use of the term "probation" is American and can be traced to early voluntary activities in the courts of Boston by John Augustus. This work led ultimately to passage of the first probation law by the Massachusetts legislature in 1878. It was twenty years before another American state passed such a law, and longer still until much was done in terms of implementing the idea of probation. A key figure in advancing the idea was Charles Chute, general secretary and executive director of the National Probation Association from 1915 to 1947 (Hagan, 1977*b*). Chute was both a product of the American probation movement and a spokesman for it.

The NPA organized its work in various ways. Juvenile court and adult probation statutes were drafted for a number of states. Most significantly, however, the association began, with its inception in 1909, a sixteen-year campaign to obtain passage of a federal probation law in the United States. For many years, the efforts of the NPA to have a federal probation law passed were complicated by the strategically located chairman of the House Judiciary Committee, Congressman Andrew J. Volstead.

In the beginning, the absence of a probation law was much more a concern for the NPA than it was for the courts. The courts proceeded through "judge-made law" to claim a common law power to suspend or "set aside" prison sentences. However, in 1915 the attorney general of the United States began a campaign to prevent suspended sentences, claiming that this practice was an infringement on the executive pardoning power, and therefore unconstitutional. In 1916, the issue was placed before the

Supreme Court in the Killits case, with a resulting decision that no inherent power existed in the federal courts to suspend sentences permanently.

The result was a court crisis (cf. Lemert, 1970) that accompanied the onset of the national prohibition of alcohol. As one judge wrote to Chute, "I am at this time, and have been for the past two months, trying large criminal dockets for violations of the liquor laws. . . . I find myself seriously embarrassed in knowing how to deal with them under the federal statutes and the decision of the Supreme Court in the Killits case" (cited in Hagan, 1977*b*, pp. 301–302). For several years, Representative Volstead chaired the House Judiciary Committee and blocked efforts to get a probation bill passed. However, Volstead's term of office finally ended in 1923. A probation bill was reported favorably in both the House and the Senate in 1924, and passed into law in 1925.

Court statistics indicate that the slow assent of probation was linked to the decline of prohibition. The legal propriety of using probation in prohibition cases was questioned several times during this period, with the legality of the practice each time upheld. In the last year of prohibition, 16,907 persons were placed on probation by the courts, 13,537 of whom were convicted under the National Prohibition Act. There is considerable evidence that during this period probation was an instrumental resource used in plea bargaining prohibition cases. In this way, probation may actually have helped to conceal the unenforceable character of prohibition.

We come, then, to an issue that has confronted both probation and parole: have they actually decreased imprisonment? There is no clear evidence that they have. As Rothman (1980, p. 9) has noted, "innovations that appeared to be substitutes for incarceration became supplements to incarceration." For example, it is highly unlikely that all the prohibition violators prosecuted in the federal courts could ever have been sentenced to jail. There were not jails enough to hold them. Probation has always been used primarily with young and first offenders who otherwise are unlikely to be imprisoned. Similarly, parole was largely a refinement in the way sentences were set. Until about 1900, judges set the precise term of incarceration for adult offenders. With the turn of the century, judges began to use minimum and maximum terms, leaving it for parole boards to decide upon the moment of release and the conditions of postrelease supervision. Rothman (1980, p. 44) notes that "by 1923, almost half of all inmates sentenced to state prisons were under an indeterminate sentence, and a little over half of all releases were under parole." But there is little in the history of parole that encourages the assumption that it reduced imprisonment. "Parole is not leniency," concluded the Wickersham Commission in 1939 (cited in Rothman, 1980, pp. 193–194), "It adds to the period of imprisonment a further period involving months or even years of supervision." The desire to punish, it seems, endured unabated.

THE DETERRENT EFFECTS OF CRIMINAL SANCTIONS

One of the most frequently asked questions about criminal sanctions is, Do they deter crime? Questions of this type always seem to be more complicated than they first appear. This question is no exception. What most people seem to have in mind when they inquire about deterrence is whether punishment has preventive effects. However, as Gibbs (1975, p. 2) has noted, deterrence ideally refers more narrowly to the prevention of crime that results from the *fear* of punishment: "the omission of an act as a response to the perceived risk and fear of punishment for *contrary* behavior" (emphasis in original). To this fine distinction are added others. We have already noted the distinction between *specific* (or individual or special) deterrence and *general deterrence*. The former deals with the future behavior of the individual being punished, the latter with the effects on the population more generally. A distinction is also drawn between *absolute* and *restrictive deterrence*. The former refers to the absence throughout a lifetime of criminal behavior, while the latter refers only to a degree of restraint effected in the amount of a person's criminal behavior that would otherwise have been greater. Finally, a distinction is drawn between deterrence and *incapacitation:* the reduction in criminal behavior that is accomplished simply as a result of keeping offenders "off the street" for a particular period of time (see, for example, Geerken and Gove, 1977).

Deterrence has been studied in three major ways: through experiements, quasi experiments, and analyses of natural variation (Blumstein, Cohen, and Nagin, 1978). The latter approach is most common and involves the use of surveys as well as official records. Surveys focus on *individual* perceptions and actual experiences of criminal sanctions, and then look for their correlations with criminal behavior. Official records of sanctioning and crime are collected and again examined for correlation, in this case usually by *state*. The standard deterrence hypotheses hold that perceived and actual risks of apprehension, conviction, imprisonment, and execution are negatively correlated with criminal behavior. That is, as rates of apprehension, conviction, imprisonment, and execution go up, criminal behavior should go down. These hypotheses follow from assumptions that the certainty, celerity (i.e., quickness), and severity of punishment are negatively correlated with criminal behavior. Celerity of punishment is seldom studied, but rates of apprehension and conviction are often taken to reflect certainty of punishment, while imprisonment and execution rates are assumed to reflect severity.

"Taken as a whole," concludes a recent National Academy of Science Panel on Deterrence and Incapacitation (Blumstein, Cohen, and Nagin, 1978, p. 4), "the reported evidence consistently finds a negative association between crime rates and the risks of apprehension, conviction or imprisonment." We will examine the basis for such a conclusion in more detail below. Meanwhile, there is another issue: Is this negative relationship causal? Or in other words, is the association found between sanctions and crime *because* the higher sanction levels reduce the amount of crime committed? One alternative explanation for the observed association is that the moral climate of the context in which the research is done may be causing *both* more sanctions *and* less crime, rather than the sanctions themselves affecting criminal behavior. In other words, are areas that are very sensitive to moral issues more likely to have both high sanctioning rates and less crime? Ideally, the question of causality is dealt with by a research design that experimentally manipulates the causal variable, in this case the criminal sanction. Experimental research on deterrence is limited because of the obvious ethical problems involved in experimentally manipulating punishments. Nonetheless, some interesting experimental work has been done on deterrence. We review this work before going on to consider survey and official record research on the issue of deterrence.

Two fascinating experiments have been done with taxpayers and the Internal Revenue Service, and with college students in classrooms. In the IRS experiment, Schwartz and Orleans (1967) randomly designated subjects to be (1) interviewed and made aware of the penalties for tax evasion, (2) interviewed and reminded of their moral obligation to pay taxes, (3) interviewed with neither the warning nor reminder, and (4) an uninterviewed control group. Both the moral reminder and the prospect of sanctions were found to increase the payment of taxes, with the moral reminder having the bigger effect. In the college classroom experiment, Tittle and Rowe (1973) allowed students to grade their own exams. A moral appeal was issued first to the effect that students were obliged to mark their exams honestly. The appeal had no effect. However, a later warning that spot-checks for accuracy would be followed by punishments for inaccuracies did reduce cheating. These studies are at least consistent in indicating a causal effect of threatened sanctions.

Survey research also provides some support for deterrence hypotheses. This research has been particularly concerned with the impact of the perception of sanctions. For example, Jensen et al. (1978, p. 58) identify perception as the key element of deterrence and argue that "the more members of a population perceive the punishment for a type of offense as being certain, severe and celeritous, the lower the [crime] rate for that population." The research of Jensen et al. and others (e.g., Jensen, 1969; Waldo and Chiricos, 1972; Grasmich and Milligan, 1976; Silberman, 1976; Tittle, 1977; Teevan, 1976a,b, 1977) rather consistently supports the argument that among surveyed subjects, the more *certain* sanctions are perceived to be, the lower the levels of reported crime are. Findings of survey studies are less convincing with regard to *severity* of sanctions. We have more to say about this below. Meanwhile, the issue of causal order has most recently concerned survey researchers in this area. The concern is to demonstrate that, as measured in social surveys, the perceived certainty of punishment varies in advance of, rather than in response to involvement in crime and delinquency. The evidence on this issue is only beginning to accumulate (Jensen and Stitt, 1982; Paternoster et al., 1982), with mixed results.

What further knowledge we have about deterrence comes largely from research based on official records. The two areas in which the natural variation in sanctions and criminal behavior have been most closely studied are with regard to capital punishment and drunken driving. Historically, deterrence studies involving capital punishment have been conducted in three ways: (1) comparing homicide rates in contiguous jurisdictions, some of which had abolished capital punishment; (2) examining time series data on homicide rates within a jurisdiction during the years before and after the abolition of capital punishment; and (3) comparing homicide rates in a jurisdiction before and after the imposition of a death sentence or execution. Although methodologically flawed in various ways, these studies have generally failed to show a deterrent effect of the death penalty (e.g., Bowers, 1974; Schuessler, 1952; Sellin, 1967; Savitz, 1958). An exception to this pattern of findings is the recent research of Isaac Ehrlich (1975), which claims to identify a deterrent effect in a time series that runs from 1933 to 1969. Erhlich's findings are made particularly provocative by an inference that each additional execution in these data prevented seven or eight murders. However, subsequent reanalyses do not confirm Ehrlich's conclusions (see Zeisel, 1976). A major problem with Ehrlich's analysis is that it is particularly sensitive to the time period 1962 to 1969, when executions ceased and homicides increased. The problem is, as we saw in Chapter 4, that this was a time when most other crimes were increasing as well. This broader time-bound pattern makes doubtful the significance attached by Ehrlich to the death penalty. The only safe conclusion seems to be the one reached by the Panel on Deterrence and Incapacitation (Blumstein, Cohen, and Nagin, 1978, p. 9):

In summary, the flaws in the earlier analyses finding no effect and the sensitivity of the more recent analysis to minor variations in model specification and the serious temporal instability of the results lead the Panel to conclude that the available studies provide no useful evidence on the deterrent effect of capital punishment.

More revealing are time series studies of the deterrence of drinking and driving. H. Laurence Ross (1982) has noted that the literature on drinking, driving, and deterrence is unique in its relatively good measures of effect, involving time series of fatal crashes gathered by hospitals and health departments, and by the availability of relatively strong quasi-experimental designs, based on efforts cross-nationally.to redefine and reinforce laws dealing with drinking and driving. The result is a set of conditions that often meet the criteria for the utilization of an interrupted time series design. That is, there is an independent variable (change in law and/or enforcement) that changes abruptly at a single point in time, along with dependent variables (e.g., crash series) that are expected to shift sharply and simultaneously, and that are measured reliably over an extended period of time. Beginning in Norway in 1936, several Scandinavian countries and later Britain (in 1967) imposed strict drinking-and-driving laws that since have been adopted in many western nations. These efforts form the basis of a review by Ross (1982) of the deterrent effects of such laws. Although deterrence theory usually predicts abrupt declines in behavior that are preferably permanent, Figure 10-1 outlines the alternative possibilities. What Ross (1982) finds when he looks at the cross-national findings is that "in all cases in which deterrent effectiveness was noted, it proved to be temporary, disappearing within months of its attainment." In other words, cracking down on drunk drivers may produce deterrent effects, but they are of limited duration.

Where does this leave us? In 1973 Tittle and Logan ended an influential review of empirical research on deterrence with the necessarily modest conclusion that "sanctions apparently have some deterrent effect under some circumstances." There was not enough systematic research to say much more. Seven years and fifty studies later, Tittle (1980, p. 4) concludes that it still is impossible to specify with clarity and certainty the precise conditions under which sanctions are likely to be important influences on behavior. The research that will do so remains to be done. Lacking this research we can only conclude that the burden of evidence at least supports the deterrence hypothesis that *certainty* of criminal sanctioning is causally related to criminal behavior.

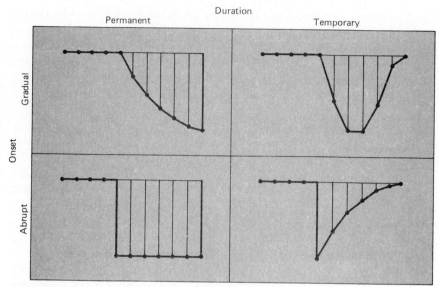

Figure 10-1 Impact models of deterrent effects. (*Source: Ross, 1982:73*)

TREATMENT AND PREVENTION OF CRIME

Thus far our discussion of responses to crime has failed to disclose much societal interest in the treatment and prevention of crime other than through the threat of sanctions. If we have demonstrated anything, it is that the inclination to punish is still very much with us, despite a succession of reform efforts to modify the punishments, and considerable doubt as to the deterrent effects of severe punishments. Yet, efforts are made at treatment and prevention other than by punishment, especially with young offenders, and some attention to the successes and failures of these efforts is in order. It is in these efforts that our more optimistic societal sentiments are revealed. We discuss such efforts under two headings: individual treatment and social reform.

INDIVIDUAL TREATMENT

There is something very American about the time-honored approach to nonpunitive crime prevention: individual treatment. Treatment of the individual fits well with the emphasis traditionally placed on individual initiative and responsibility in our society. The emphasis in this approach to crime prevention is placed on the social-psychological development of the criminal, with particular attention to the experiences of adolescence. The assumption that characterizes this approach is that much juvenile and adult crime could be prevented if only the delinquent or predelinquent could be identified and corrective therapy applied. A variety of important treatment programs have been initiated on the basis of this assumption, often with efforts to evaluate the results.

Among the earliest and most ambitious treatment programs was the Cambridge-Somerville Youth Study (Powers and Witmer, 1951; McCord and McCord, 1959). Teachers, police officers, social workers, and a psychiatrist were asked in this project to identify future delinquents; the selected individuals were then assigned either to an intensive counseling program or to a comparison (i.e., "control") group that received no treatment at all. Unfortunately, no positive effects of the counseling program were revealed in a follow-up evaluation based on subsequent contacts of the adolescents with local police.

A less rigorously evaluated program that *seemed* to be more successful was the Highfields experiment (Weeks, 1958). Based in a progressive institutional setting, this experiment utilized an intensive program of guided group interaction with 16- to 17-year-old youths. Inmates from a more typical reformatory setting were later compared in terms of rates of reconviction. The results of this comparison indicated that "for every hundred boys who complete residence, . . . the Highfields program rehabilitates twenty-eight more than does the traditional program of caring for such boys" (ibid., p. 120). However, the comparison was flawed. Highfields youths tended to be younger, better-educated, first-time offenders. In commonsense language, the Highfields boys were probably "better bets" in the first place. Meanwhile, it has also been noted that simply *being* in a special program can induce a "policy effect" on the part of police and others, with the result that control agents respond more favorably to the subjects involved. This official reluctance to arrest or otherwise sanction may often be confused with presumed "treatment effects" (Lerman, 1968).

A more stringently evaluated program based on guided group interaction was the Provo Project (Empey and Erickson, 1972). Young "habitual offenders" were assigned in this program to community-based group therapy, probation, or institutionalization. A six-month follow-up after "release" indicated rates of success (i.e., absence of arrests) of 84, 77, and 42 percent respectively. The implication is that while the community-based effort was more successful than incarceration, it was about equal in success to a period of probation involving almost no treatment at all. In a second study, the Silverlake Experiment, Empey and Lubeck (1971) compared a residential community-treatment program with a private training school program. This study also failed to find much evidence that the experimental program was superior to the control program.

The Opportunities for Youth Project was an experimentally designed effort to prevent delinquency using employment and teaching machines (Hackler, 1966). The treatment design involved an effort to improve subjects' self-concepts by convincing them that (1) they were capable of working successfully, and (2) they were competent to assess the adequacy of teaching machines. Data were gathered on police contacts four years after the project began. These data indicated that boys involved in the work program were slightly *more* delinquent than those in the comparison group, while boys in the teaching machine program were slightly *less* so. These perplexing findings leave "only faint optimism with regard to uncovering effective 'cures' for the ills of delinquency" (Hackler and Hagan, 1975, p. 105).

We noted above that one of the earliest and most ambitious treatment programs was the Cambridge-Somerville Youth Study. Recently Joan McCord (1978) completed a thirty-year follow-up of the effects of this program. Despite the fact that thirty years after the termination of the program many of the subjects still remembered their counselors favorably —"sometimes recalling particular acts of kindness and sometimes noting the general support they felt in having someone available with whom to discuss their problems" (1978, p. 288)—almost no objective evidence could be found that treatment had improved the lives of those in the treatment group. Indeed, it is reported that men who had been in the treatment program were more likely than those in the control group to commit a second crime. Among other things, this follow-up also revealed that men in the treatment group were more likely to evidence signs of alcoholism and die younger. McCord (1978, p. 289) reaches the chilling conclusion that "intervention programs risk damaging the individuals they are designed to assist."

One might by now reasonably wonder where this brief introduction to individualized treatment is leading us. It leads to a much noted conclusion, based on a review of 231 evaluations of treatment programs and reported by Robert Martinson (1974), that "with few and isolated exceptions, the rehabilitative efforts that have been reported so far have had no appreciable effect on recidivism" (p. 25). Although this conclusion has been challenged, it also reflects a general consensus about the evidence of success in such programs. Previous reviews by Hood and Sparks (1970) and Bailey (1966) reached similar conclusions, as have subsequent assessments by Greenberg (1977), Brody (1976), and Fienberg and Grambsch (1979).

The most noteworthy exception to these conclusions is taken by Palmer (1975, 1978), who argues for the success of the Community Treatment Program (CTP) of the California Youth Authority. However, a subsequent and independent assessment of this program by Paul Lerman (1975, p. 67) concludes that "the CTP did not have an impact on youth behavior that differed significantly from the impact of the control program."

There remain the interesting possibilities that particular kinds of offenders (e.g., particularly "amenable" offenders), and particular kinds of treatment programs (e.g., those providing extensive supervision), evaluated in new and/or different ways (e.g., focusing on amount and/or seriousness of offenses, rather than their simple presence or absence), might reveal better evidence of success (see, for example, Murray and Cox, 1979; Wilson, 1980). It is also important not to misinterpret the lack of success so far found (see Question and Answer dialogue within box). Perhaps the soundest conclusion is that drawn by the Panel on Research on Rehabilitative Techniques (1979):

> . . . the Panel believes that there is not now in the scientific literature any basis for any policy or recommendations regarding rehabilitation of criminal offenders. The data available do not present any consistent evidence of efficacy that would lead to such recommendations. . . . On the basis of its review, the Panel believes that the magnitude of the task of reforming criminal offenders has been consistently underestimated. It is clear that far more intensive and extensive interventions will be required if rehabilitation is to be possible; even then, there is no guarantee of success.

MARTINSON RESPONDS TO QUESTIONS ABOUT HIS RE-VIEW OF TREATMENT PROGRAMS **Question:** Doesn't this study conclusively prove that our criminal justice system is a failure?

Answer: No. Only that the weight of the evidence is that the *addition* of treatment elements ("programs" of the kind evaluated) to the system has no appreciable effect in changing offenders into non-offenders. The system may still deter *potential* offenders or temporarily incapacitate those who are incarcerated. These, and many other aspects of criminal justice remain to be evaluated.

Question: Doesn't the survey show that probation and parole are ineffective and should be abandoned?

Answer: Not in the least! Indeed, it indicates that those placed on probation *do no worse* than those imprisoned and may do slightly better. It does indicate that *small caseloads* on probation do no better than standard caseloads, and that probation *supervision* (as currently practiced) is not an effective "treatment," i.e., does not substantially improve the behavior of those supervised over what would be expected.

Question: Wouldn't treatment work if it were accomplished in the community rather than in the prison?

Answer: A large number of these treatment programs took place outside of prison, and the burden of the evidence is not encouraging. Also, in figuring the relative costs of probation and confinement, we must include the possible cost to the public of having a larger number of potential offenders at large, and not rest our case simply on a comparison of recidivism rates.

Question: Does the survey recommend that we abolish or reduce programs such as vocational training, prison education, counseling, or group therapy that are found to be ineffective?

Answer: If the sole justification for a "program" is that it will reduce recidivism among those who receive it, then the survey will provide evidence as to whether this is achieved, and may therefore call many such programs into question. My own position is that we should cease demanding from our criminal justice networks what they are unable to accomplish, thus freeing them to justify their activities in a proper way. For example, if a prison needs facilities to reduce inmate idleness, a law library, weightlifting equipment, or a television set might accomplish this somewhat better than an additional counselor or psychiatrist. After all, do we vary the food or clothing or visits given to inmates on the grounds of rehabilitation or on the grounds that we believe in a minimum standard of human decency in criminal justice?

Question: If rehabilitation is ultimately shown to be a "myth," must we then "get tough" with offenders?

Answer: Why must we reel from pillar to post in our reactions, substituting rhetoric for the search for more effective policies? We have spent 3.2 billion dollars since the Safe Streets Act and only now has Congress insisted that this effort be evaluated. I am now involved in research on deterrence through the Crime Control and Offender Career project. Preliminary findings indicate that deterrence "works," but we do not know within what limits or with what costs. After all, there are various ways of "getting tough," and our planning agencies need to know whether we need milder and more certain penalties or more severe penalties for those we now convict and incarcerate. In addition, almost nothing is known about crime prevention other than deterrence. Knowledge that we have had over-inflated expectations about "treatment" should lead one to demand evidence of the effectiveness of these alternate proposals. Otherwise we may simply go galloping down another blind alley.

Source: Criminal Justice Newsletter, National Council on Crime and Delinquency, 5(21), November 18, 1974, pp. 4–5.

PREVENTION THROUGH SOCIAL REFORM

Social reform programs begin with a more sociological assumption than the individual treatment programs, namely, that it is the environmental influences of the peer group, or the social structure of the surrounding community, rather than the individual, that must be changed. The time-honored tools of this approach are "detached workers" and "community organization."

The oldest of the social reform programs, the Chicago Area Project (CAP), was organized and operated by David McKay and Clifford Shaw (Kobrin, 1959). The key feature of this program involved the enlistment of community members and leaders in organizations through which welfare programs were then developed and administered. A useful description of these efforts is provided by Burgess, Lohman, and Shaw (1937, p. 8).

The Chicago Area Project is a program which seeks to discover by actual demonstration and measurement a procedure for the treatment of delinquents and the prevention of delinquency. . . . the distinctive emphasis in the Project is to achieve the fullest possible neighborhood participation. . . . All of the activities in the program are carried on with a view to making the *neighborhood* conscious of the problems of delinquency, *collectively* interested in the welfare of its children, and active in promoting programs for such improvements of the *community environment* as will develop in the children interests and habits of a constructive and socially desirable character (emphasis added).

In intent as well as accomplishment, the Chicago Area Project was an important challenge to the individualistic emphases of programs operated by psychologists and psychiatrists in the early part of this century. However, its contributions to crime and delinquency prevention have been a matter of some uncertainty. Shaw and his colleagues were increasingly reluctant to assess the success of CAP in quantitative terms. Thus, although there was evidence that rates of delinquency did decline in areas served by the project, and that the character of the communities themselves was altered, Clifford Shaw in particular became increasingly reluctant to draw strong inferences from these findings. This cautious attitude and its consequences are considered further below.

A more recent program, the Midcity Youth Project, also aimed its efforts at the larger community, largely through the medium of detached street workers (Miller, 1962). In this program, seven street workers concentrated their efforts on approximately 400 members of twenty-one gangs over a three-year period. The best hopes of this project rested on the stabilizing influence of the street workers acting as middle-class role models. Unfortunately, the results were not encouraging, "All major measures of violative behavior—disapproved actions, illegal actions, during-contact court appearances, before-during-after appearances, and project-control group appearances—provide consistent support for a finding of 'negligible impact' " (ibid., p. 187).

The most expensive and dramatic of modern social reform programs aimed at delinquency prevention are described by Daniel Patrick Moynihan in his book *Maximum Feasible Misunderstanding* (1969). Although this book is more generally concerned with the American "War on Poverty," Moynihan points out that an important model for these programs was a New York–based delinquency prevention effort, the Mobilization for Youth Project (MFY). This project focused initially on the problem of juvenile delinquency, using Cloward and Ohlin's differential opportunity theory of delinquency as its guide. As noted in Chapter 6, Cloward and Ohlin's central thesis is that delinquents use desperately deviant measures in an effort to achieve the success goals widely shared in the larger society. The burden of the theory is that opportunities must be expanded so that lower-class youth can achieve success goals by legitimate means. The initial MFY project was therefore organized around three priorities: (1) jobs for young people; (2) education for young people; and (3) community organization. The project was designed as a social experiment: "From the outset it was understood that what came to pass in the 13 census tracts on the lower east side would have national significance" (Moynihan, 1969, p. 59).

However, much was to happen between the design of the MFY project and the appearance of its results. Juvenile delinquency, and its links to the problems of employment and race, became a priority of the Kennedy administration. Following Kennedy's death, Lyndon Johnson picked up this priority and the pace of its implementation. Thus before the MFY project could be completed, much less evaluated, its translation of differential opportunity theory into social policy became a basis for national legislation.

However, even before the resulting War on Poverty legislation could begin to take effect, the *New York Daily News* declared that the Mobilization for Youth project had become "infested with subversives." Significantly, it was not the employment or education programs of MFY that drew the wrath of the *News;* it was the community organization program, and its confrontational tactics. Moynihan (ibid., p. 107) offers this analysis:

> If [MFY] started out to create cooperative arrangements that would open the neighborhood opportunity structures to deviant or potentially deviant youth; in short order the opportunity structure

was being defined as a power structure, and itself accused of deviance in the largest social sense of good and bad behavior. . . . Reform inched toward revolution. Right or wrong, MFY did not very long remain the carefully calibrated experiment it had set out to be.

Moynihan (ibid., p. 112) goes on to suggest that "men such as Cloward moved fairly rapidly from the effort to integrate the poor into the system to an effort to use the poor to bring down the whole rotten structure."

What is significant about the events in New York City is that they were predictive of problems that were to beset the War on Poverty. Education and job programs, as in the MFY project, received less emphasis than the community organization efforts guided through Community Action Programs. Moynihan suggests that a four-stage sequence characterized such programs:

1 A period of organizing, with much publicity and great expectations.

2 The beginning of operations, with the onset of conflict between the agency and local government institutions, followed by even greater publicity.

3 A period of counterattack from local government.

4 Victory for the established institutions, followed by the ultimate disappearance of the professional reformers.

Moynihan (ibid., p. 170) offers a cryptic synopsis of this unique period in American government: "This is the essential fact: the government did not know what it was doing. . . . The U.S. government at this time was no more in possession of confident knowledge as to how to prevent delinquency . . . than it was the possessor of a dependable formula for motivating Vietnamese villagers to fight Communism."

One clear difference between the community organization efforts that often characterized the War on Poverty and those of the Chicago Area Project we discussed earlier was the deemphasis in the latter program on confrontational tactics. This difference became particularly apparent in the focus of the objections of one of the Chicago Area Project's most aggressive young street workers, Saul Alinsky. Alinsky's experiences in this project became part of the basis for a famous book on community organization, *Reveille for Radicals* (1969). In this book and in his conflicts with the leadership of the project, Alinsky consistently insisted that "confrontational tactics . . . were the only viable means of alleviating the 'social disorganization' which Shaw and the Chicago School of Sociology so eloquently described" (Schlossman and Sedlak, 1983, p. 101). Shaw and McKay adopted a much more pragmatic attitude.

A recent reanalysis by Schlossman and Sedlak (1983) of materials from the Chicago Area Project suggests that this program may, in retrospect, deserve greater appreciation than it has received. Schlossman and Sedlak focus particularly on the project's work in the Russell Square neighborhood of South Chicago in the 1930s and early 1940s. Between 1932 and 1937, the Russell Square delinquency arrest rate was more than halved, while in a comparable South Chicago neighborhood which the project did not serve, juvenile arrests did not decline at all. While at first Shaw and McKay thought these findings conclusive evidence of success, they later adopted a much more cautious attitude that eventually led them to eschew any quantitative measures of impact at all. In doing so, Shaw and McKay adopted a rather modern skepticism about official statistics. The following statement by Shaw reflects this new, for Shaw and for 1954, attitude (cited in Schlossman and Sedlak, 1983, p. 115).

> Conclusive statistical proof to sustain any conclusion regarding the effectiveness of this work in reducing the volume of delinquency is difficult to secure for many reasons. Trends in rates of delinquents for small areas are affected by variations in the definition of what constitutes delinquent behavior, changes in the composition of the population, and changes in administrative procedures in law enforcement agencies. We know from our experiences in the inner city areas that there are a large number of unofficial cases of unlawful behavior, and the extent to which these unofficial cases become apprehended and dealt with as official delinquents depends upon a wide variety of influences and pressures which vary from one community to another.

Yet, as Schlossman and Sedlak are able to show in their detailed reanalysis of archival materials, something does seem to have happened in the Russell Square community. Shaw and McKay were able to generate an impressive level of public participation in community organization and delinquency prevention efforts, and they sustained a set of programs that consistently directed attention to the problems of seriously delinquent youth, all while avoiding the kinds of confrontations and conflicts that disrupted and often destroyed federally sponsored programs for delinquency prevention during the 1970s. With such points in mind, Schlossman and Sedlak (1983, p. 122) suggest that "it seems prudent not to dismiss out of hand the initial statistical picture that Shaw presented of unique achievement in Russell Square; that picture may well have captured social reality to some degree." As we survey the disappointing history of delinquency treatment and prevention programs, this reanalysis suggests one kind of program that may have achieved some level of success.

CONCLUSIONS

Although criminological research on the deterrent effects of criminal sanctions and the evaluation of treatment and reform programs have developed separately, there is no clear conceptual reason why this need be the case. All constitute societal reactions to criminal behavior, and their results can be considered in common. Doing so allows us to answer the broader questions posed at the outset of this chapter.

How, then, could we best respond to crime? Ideally, our review would seem to encourage attempts to make criminal sanctions more certain, and to make community organization programs more pragmatic and sustained. However, both suggestions are tentative and imprecise. Taking the findings of recent research even this far strains its credibility, for we know little about the conditions under which they apply, or the limits to which they can be generalized. This is a common frustration in mixing the needs to form social policy with the constraints of social research (Schlegal, 1979).

However, as we noted at the outset of this volume, modern criminology is likely to prove more satisfying when it seeks to understand the role of crime in our society and societal reactions to it than when it seeks to predict and control criminal behavior. The research we have considered in this chapter speaks to the former issues as well as the latter. Indeed, capital punishment and social reform programs do much to define two ends of a continuum in the societal response to crime. Both represent responses that in the extreme might ultimately have substantial deterrent/preventive effects on criminal behavior. That is, a *much* more draconian criminal-justice system and/or a *much* less stratified social structure would seem likely to produce notable changes in levels of crime. However, what is perhaps more interesting and revealing is that we are unlikely to move very far in either direction. To do so would be to redefine the kind of society in which we live: a society that prides itself on avoiding totalitarian governmental restraints, and simultaneously accepts high levels of social and economic inequality. Such a society seems likely to endure much crime, and we do. Meanwhile, we look for modest revisions in the social order, including the use of penal sanctions, individual treatment, and social reform, that will produce marginal reductions in crime. It is unclear how much of this kind of knowledge we can generate, and how great the marginal gains in reduced crime might be. Meanwhile, however, we are learning much about the society that subsidizes our research.

BIBLIOGRAPHY

Abel, Richard L.
1973 "Law Books and Books About Law." *Stanford Law Review* 26:175–228.
Addams, Jane
1912 *A New Conscience and an Ancient Evil.* New York: MacMillan.
Adler, Freda
1975 *Sisters in Crime.* New York: McGraw-Hill.
1977 "The Interaction Between Women's Emancipation and Female Criminality: A Cross-Cultural Perspective." *International Journal of Criminology and Penology* 5:101–112.
1980 "The Interaction Between Women's Emancipation and Female Criminality: A Cross-Cultural Perspective." In Susan Datesman and Frank Scarpitti (eds.), *Women, Crime and Justice.* New York: Oxford University Press.
Akers, Ronald
1977 *Deviant Behavior: A Social Learning Approach.* Belmont, Calif.: Wadsworth.
Akman, D. D., A. Normandeau, and S. Turner
1967 "The Measurement of Delinquency in Canada." *Journal of Criminal Law, Criminology and Police Science* 58:330–337.
Allen, Francis
1964 *The Borderland of Criminal Justice.* Chicago: University of Chicago Press.
Alinsky, Saul
1969 *Reveille for Radicals.* New York: Vintage Books.
Allen, Francis
1960 "Raffaele Garofalo." In H. Mannheim (ed.), *Pioneers in Criminology.* London: Stevens.
Almy, Frederic
1902 "Juvenile Courts in Buffalo." *Annals of the American Academy of Political and Social Science* 20:279–285.
Alschuler, Albert
1968 "The Prosecutor's Role in Plea Bargaining." *University of Chicago Law Review* 36:50–112.
1975 "The Defense Attorney's Role in Plea Bargaining." *Yale Law Journal* 84:1179–1314.
1979 "Plea Bargaining and Its History." *Law and Society Review* 13:211–246.

Anderson, Eric
1974 "Prostitution and Social Justice: Chicago, 1910–15." *Social Science Review* 49:203.
Arendt, H.
1964 *Eichmann in Jerusalem: A Report of the Banality of Evil.* New York: Viking Press.
Arnold, Thurman
1967 "The Criminal Trial." In Herbert Jacob (ed.), *Law Politics and the Federal Courts.* Boston: Little Brown.
Arnold, W. R.
1965 "Continuities in Research: Scaling Delinquent Behavior." *Social Problems* 13:59–66.
Bachman, G., P. O'Malley, and J. Johnston
1978 *Youth in Transition*, vol. VI: *Adolescence to Adulthood: Change and Stability in the Lives of Young Men.* Ann Arbor: University of Michigan, Institute for Social Research.
Bailey, W. C.
1966 "Correctional Outcome: An Evaluation of 100 Reports." *Journal of Criminal Law, Criminology and Police Science* 57:153–160.
Balbus, Isasac
1973 *The Dialectics of Legal Repression.* New York: Russell Sage.
Balkin, Steven
1979 "Victimization Rates, Safety and Fear of Crime." *Social Problems* 26:343–358.
Ball-Rokeach, Sandra J.
1973 "Values and Violence: A Test of the Subculture of Violence Thesis." *American Sociological Review* 38(6):736–749.
Banfield, Edward
1968 *The Unheavenly City.* Boston: Little, Brown.
Barter, James, George Mizner, and Paul Werme
1970 "Patterns of Drug Use Among College Students: An Epidemiological and Demographic Survey of Student Attitudes and Practices." Department of Psychiatry, University of Colorado Medical School, unpublished.
Bartollas, C., S. Miller, and S. Dinitz
1976 *Juvenile Victimization: The Institutional Paradox.* Beverly Hills, Calif.:Sage.
Baumhart, Raymond C.
1961 "How Ethical Are Businessmen?" *Harvard Business Review* 39:5–176.
Beattie, J. M.
1974 "The Pattern of Crime in England, 1660–1800." *Past and Present* 62:47–95.
Beccaria, Cesare
1764 *An Essay on Crimes and Punishments.* Philadelphia: Nicklin.
Becker, Howard
1963 *Outsiders: Studies in the Sociology of Deviance.* New York: Free Press.
1964 *The Other Side: Perspectives on Deviance.* New York: Free Press.

Becker, Theodore
1974 "The Place of Private Police in Society: An Area of Research for the Social Sciences." *Social Problems* 21(3):438–455.
Bentham, Jeremy
1892 *Introduction to the Principals of Morals and Legislation.* Oxford: Clarendon Press.
Berg, Ivar
1982 "Social Control and the Economy: In Quest of Common Denominators." In Jack Gibbs (ed.), *Social Control: Views from the Social Sciences.* Beverly Hills, Calif.: Sage.
Berk, Richard, Harold Brackman, and Selma Lesser
1977 *A Measure of Justice: An Empirical Study of Changes in the California Penal Code, 1955–1971.* New York: Academic Press.
Berkley, George
1969 "Europe and America: How the Police Work." *New Republic.* August:15–18.
Bernstein, Ilene Nagel, Edward Kick, Jan Leung, and Barbara Schulz
1977 "Charge Reduction: An Intermediary Stage in the Process of Labelling. Criminal Defendants." *Social Forces* 56(2):362–384.
Biderman, Albert
1981 "Sources of Data for Victimology." *Journal of Criminal Law and Criminology* 72:789–817.
Biderman, A. D., et al.
1967 *Report of a Pilot Study in the District of Columbia on Victimization and Attitudes Toward Law Enforcement.* Washington: U.S. Government Printing Office.
Bierne, Piers
1979 "Empiricism and the Critique of Marxism on Law and Crime." *Social Problems* 26:373–385.
Birket-Smith, Kaj
1959 *The Eskimos.* London: Methuen.
Bittner, E.
1967 "The Police on Skid Row: A Study of Peace Keeping." *American Sociological Review* 32:699–715.
Black, Donald
1970 "Production of Crime Rates." *American Sociological Review* 35:733–748.
1971 "The Social Organization of Arrest." *Stanford Law Review* 23:1087–1111.
1976 *The Behavior of Law.* New York: Academic Press.
1983 "Crime as Social Control." *American Sociological Review* 48(1):34–45.
Black, Donald, and Albert Reiss
1967 *Studies in Crime and Law Enforcement in Major Metropolitan Areas.* Washington, D.C.: U.S. Government Printing Office.
1970 "Police Control of Juveniles." *American Sociological Review* 35:63–77.
Blackstone, Sir William
1765 *Commentaries on the Laws of England.* Oxford: Clarendon Press.

Blau, Judith, and Peter Blau
1982   "The Cost of Inequality: Metropolitan Structure and Violent Crime."
American Sociological Review 47:114–129.
Block, Alan
1977   "Aw—Your Mother's in the Mafia: Women Criminals in Progressive New
York." *Contemporary Crisis* 1:5–22.
Blum, Richard H.
1969   *Students and Drugs.* San Francisco: Jossey-Bass.
Blum, Richard, and Mary Lou Funkhauser
1965   "Legislators on Social Scientists and a Social Issue." *Journal of Applied
Behavioral Science* 1:84–112.
Blumberg, Abraham S.
1967a   "The Practice of Law as a Confidence Game." *Law and Society Review*
1967b   *Criminal Justice.* Chicago: Quadrangle Books.
1:15–39.
Blumstein, Alfred, and Jacqueline Cohen
1980   "Sentencing of Convicted Offenders: An Analysis of the Public's View."
Law and Society Review 14:223–262.
Blumstein, Alfred, Jacqueline Cohen, and Daniel Nagin
1978   "Summary." In *Deterrence and Incapacitation: Estimating the Effects of
Criminal Sanctions on Crime Rates.* Washington: National Academy of Sciences.
Bodine, George E.
1964   *Factors Related to Police Dispositions of Juvenile Offenders.* Syracuse:
University Youth Development Center.
Bohannan, Paul
1965   "The Differing Realms of the Law." *American Anthropologist* 67(6) (pt.
2):33 (Special Publication).
Bonger, William
1916   *Criminality and Economic Conditions.* Boston: Little, Brown.
Bonnie, Richard J., and Charles H. Whitebread
1974   *The Marihuana Conviction.* Charlottesville: University of Virginia Press.
Bordua, David
1958–59   "Juvenile Delinquency and 'Anomie': An Attempt at Replication."
Social Problems 6:230–238.
1961   "Delinquent Subcultures: Sociological Interpretations of Gang Delinquency." *Annals of the American Academy of Political and Social Science* 338:119–
136.
1969   "Recent Trends: Deviant Behavior and Social Control." *Annals of the
American Academy of Political and Social Science* 369:149–163.
Bottomley, A. K.
1973   *Decisions in the Penal Process.* South Hackensack, N.J.: Rothman.
Bowers, W. J.
1974   *Executions in America.* Lexington, Mass.: Heath.
Bowers, William and Glenn Pierce

1980 "Arbitrariness and Discrimination in Post-Furman Capital Cases." *Crime and Delinquency* 26:563–635.

Bowring, Sir John
1962
(1843) *The Works of Jeremy Bentham.* Published under the superintendance of his executor, John Bowring. New York: Russell & Russell.

Boyd, Neil
1978 "An Examination of Probation." *Criminal Law Quarterly* 355–381.

Braithwaite, John
1981 "The Myth of Social Class and Criminality Reconsidered." *American Sociological Review* 46:36–57.

Brenner, B.
1967 "Alcoholism and Fatal Accidents." *Quarterly Journal of Studies on Alcohol* 28:517–526.

Brenner, S. N., and E. A. Molander
1977 "Is the Ethics of Business Changing?" *Harvard Business Review* 55:57–71.

Brereton, David and Jonathan Casper
1981-82 "Does it Pay to Plead Guilty? Differential Sentencing and the Functioning of Criminal Courts." *Law and Society Review.* 16:45–70.

Brody, S. R.
1976 *The Effectiveness of Sentencing: A Review of the Literature.* Home Office Research Report 35. London: H. M. Stationery Office.

Bryant, Keith L.
1968 "The Juvenile Court Movement: Oklahoma as a Case Study." *Social Science Quarterly* 49:368–376.

Buckner, H. Taylor
1970 "Transformations of Reality in the Legal Process." *Social Research* 37(Spring):88–101.

Buffalo Law Review
1974 "Comment: The Plea Bargain in Historical Perspective." 23:499.

Burgess, Ernest
1928 "Factors Determining Success or Failure on Parole." In A.A. Bruce (ed.), *The Workings of the Indeterminate-Sentence Law and the Parole System in Illinois.* Springfield, Ill.: State of Illinois.
1931 *Children's Behavior Problems.* Chicago: University of Chicago Press.

Burgess, Ernest, Joseph Lohman, and Clifford Shaw
1937 "The Chicago Area Project." *National Probation Association Yearbook.*

Burgess, Robert L., and Ronald Akers
1966 "A Differential Association–Reinforcement Theory of Criminal Behavior." *Social Problems* 14:128–147.

Byrnes, Thomas
1969 *1886 Professional Criminals of America.* New York: Chelsea House.

Cameron, Mary Owen
1964 *The Booster and the Snitch: Department Store Shoplifting.* New York: Free Press.

Campbell, D. T.
1969 "Reforms as Experiments." *American Psychologist* 24:409–429.
Campbell, D. T., and D. Fiske
1959 "Convergent and Discriminant Validation by the Multitrait–Multimethod Matrix." *Psychological Bulletin* 56:81–105.
Carroll, Leo
1974 *Hacks, Blacks and Cons*: *Race Relations in a Maximum Security Prison.* Lexington, Mass.: Lexington Books.
Carter, Robert, and Leslie Wilkins
1967 "Some Factors in Sentencing Policy." *Journal of Criminal Law, Criminology and Police Science* 58:503–514.
Casparis, J., and E. W. Vaz
1973 "Social Class and Self-Reported Delinquent Acts Among Swiss Boys." *International Journal of Comparative Sociology* 14:47–58.
Cavan, Ruth
1968 *Delinquency and Crime*: *Cross Cultural Perspectives.* Philadelphia: J.B. Lippincott, Company.
Cernkovich, Stephen, and Peggy Giordano
1979 "A Comparative Analysis of Male and Female Delinquency." *Sociological Quarterly* 20:131–145.
Chambliss, William
1964 "A Sociological Analysis of the Law of Vagrancy." *Social Problems* 12:67–77.
1969 *Crime and the Legal Process.* New York: McGraw-Hill.
1973 "Functional and Conflict Theories of Crime." *MSS Modular Publications* 17:1–23.
1974 "The State, the Law and the Definition of Behavior as Criminal or Delinquent." In Daniel Glaser (ed.), *Handbook of Criminology.* Indianapolis: Bobbs-Merrill.
1976 "Functional and Conflict Theories of Crime: The Heritage of Emile Durkheim and Karl Marx." In William J. Chambliss and Milton Mankoff (eds.), *Whose Law, What Order?* New York: Wiley.
Chambliss, William, and R. H. Nagasawa
1969 "On the Validity of Official Statistics: A Comparative Study of White, Black, and Japanese High-School Boys." *Journal of Research in Crime and Delinquency* 6:71–77.
Chambliss, William, and Robert Seidman
1971 *Law, Order and Power.* Reading, Mass.: Addison-Wesley.
Chapin, Bradley
1964 *The American Law of Treason*: *Revolutionary and Early National Origins.* Seattle: University of Washington Press.
Chein, I., D. Gerard, R. Lee and E. Rosenfeld
1964 *The Road to H*: *Narcotics, Delinquency and Social Policy.* New York: Basic Books.

Chell, Eugene P.
1958   "Sunday Blue Laws: An Analysis of Their Position in Our Society." *Rutgers Law Review* 12:505–521.
Chilton, Roland J.
1964   "Continuity in Delinquency Area Research: A Comparison of Studies for Baltimore, Detroit and Indianapolis." *American Sociological Review* 29:71–83.
1970   "Social Control through Welfare Legislation: The Impact of a State 'Suitable Home Law'." *Law and Society Review* 5:205–224.
Chowdrow, N.
1971   "Being and Doing: A Cross-Cultural Examination of the Socialization of Males and Females." In Gornick and Moran (eds.), *Women in Sexist Society*. New York: Basic Books.
Chute, Charles, and Marjorie Bell
1956   *Crime, Courts and Probation*. New York: Macmillan.
Cicourel, Aaron
1968   *The Social Organization of Juvenile Justice*. New York: John Wiley and Sons.
Clairmont, Donald H.
1963   *Deviance Among Indians and Eskimos in Aklavik, N.W.T.* Ottawa, Ontario: Northern Coordination and Research Centre, Department of Northern Affairs and National Resources.
1974   "The Development of a Deviance Service Centre." In Jack Haas and Bill Shaffir (eds.), *Decency and Deviance*. Toronto: McClelland & Stewart.
Clark, and Marshall
1967   *A Treatise on the Law of Crimes*. 7th ed. New York: Holt.
Clark, J. P., and E. P. Wenninger
1962   "Socio-Economic Class and Area as Correlates of Illegal Behavior Among Juveniles." *American Sociological Review* 27:826–834.
Clark, J. P., and L. L. Tift
1966   "Polygraph and Interview Validation of Self-Reported Deviant Behavior." *American Sociological Review* 31:516–523.
Clark, John, and Richard Sykes
1974   "Some Determinants of Police Organization and Practice in a Modern Industrial Bureaucracy." In Daniel Glaser (ed.), *Handbook of Criminology*. Chicago: Rand McNally.
Clelland, Donald, and Timothy Carter
1980   "The New Myth of Class and Crime." *Criminology* 18:319–336.
Clemmer, Donald
1940   *The Prison Community*. New York: Holt, Rinehart & Winston.
Clinard, Marshall
1952   *The Black Market: A Study of White Collar Crime*. New York: Holt, Rinehart.
1951   "Criminology as a field in American Sociology." *Journal of Criminal Law, Criminology and Police Science*. 41:549–577.

Clinard, Marshall, and Peter Yeager
1980   *Corporate Crime*. New York: Free Press.
Cloward, Richard
1959   "Illegitimate Means, Anomie, and Deviant Behavior." *American Sociological Review* 24:164–176.
Cloward, Richard, and Lloyd Ohlin
1960   *Delinquency and Opportunity*: *A Theory of Delinquent Gangs*. New York: Free Press.
Cloyd, Jerald W.
1979   "Prosecution's Power, Procedural Rights, and Pleading Guilty: The Problem of Coercion in Plea Bargaining Drug Cases." *Social Problems* 26:452–466.
Cohen, Albert
1955   *Delinquent Boys*. New York: Free Press.
Cohen, Lawrence, Marcus Felson, and Kenneth Land
1980   "Property Crime Rates in the United States: A Macrodynamic Analysis, 1949–77, with Ex Ante Forecasts for the Mid-1980s." *American Journal of Sociology* 86:90–118.
Cohen, Stanley
1974   "Criminology and the Sociology of Deviance in Britain: A Recent History and a Current Report." In P. Rock and M. McIntosh (eds.), *Deviance and Social Control*. London: Tavistock.
Cohn, S. F., and J. E. Gallagher
1977   "Crime and the Creation of Criminal Law: A Partial Model." *British Journal of Law and Society* 4:220.
Coleman, James
1974   *Power and the Structure of Society*. New York: Norton.
Committee on Homosexual Offences and Prostitution
1957   Home Office Report. London: H. M. Stationery Office.
Cook, Beverly B.
1977   "Public Opinion and Federal Judicial Policy." *American Journal of Political Science* 21:567–600.
Cook, Shirley
1969   "Canadian Narcotics Legislation, 1908–23: A Conflict Model Interpretation." *Canadian Review of Sociology and Anthropology* 6:36–46.
1970   *Variations in Response to Illegal Drug Use*. Toronto: Alcoholism and Drug Addiction Research Foundation. Unpublished manuscript.
Courtis, M. C.
1970   *Attitudes to Crime and the Police in Toronto*: *A Report on Some Survey Findings*. Toronto: University of Toronto, Centre of Criminology.
Cox, Sarah
1976   "Prosecutorial Discretion: An Overview." *American Criminal Law Review* 13:383–434.
Cressey, Donald
1971   *Other People's Money*: *A Study of the Social Psychology of Embezzlement*. (1953) Glencoe, Ill.: Free Press.

1965 "The Respectable Criminal: Why Some of Our Best Friends Are Crooks." *Transaction* 2:12–15.
Crime in Eight American Cities
1974 National Criminal Justice Information and Statistics Service. Washington, D.C.: Law Enforcement Assistance Administration.
Critchley, Thomas
1967 *A History of Police in England and Wales*. London: Constable.
Cumming, Elaine, Ian Cumming, and Laura Edell
1965 "Policeman as Philosopher, Guide and Friend." *Social Problems* 12:276–286.
Cummings, L. D.
1977 "Value Stretch in Definitions of Career among College Women: Horatio Alger as Feminist Model." *Social Problems* 25(1):65–74.
Currie, Elliot P.
1968 "The Control of Witchcraft in Renaissance Europe." *Law and Society Review* 3:355.
Cuskey, Walter, T. Premkumar, and Lois Sigel
1979 "Survey of Opiate Addiction Among Females in the United States Between 1850 and 1970." In Freda Adler and Rita Simon (eds.), *The Criminology of Deviant Women*. Boston: Houghton Mifflin.
Davis, Arthur
1944 "Veblen's Study of Modern Germany." *American Sociological Review* 9:603–609.
Davis, Kingsley
1966 "Sexual Behavior." In Robert K. Merton and Robert A. Nisbet (eds.), *Contemporary Social Problems*. New York: Harcourt, Brace & World.
de Fleur, L. B.
1967 "Delinquent Gangs in Cross-Cultural Perspective: The Case of Cordoba." *Journal of Research in Crime and Delinquency* 4:132–141.
Devlin, Lord Patrick
1965 *The Enforcement of Morals*. London: Oxford University Press.
Diana, Lewis
1960 "What Is Probation." *Journal of Criminal Law, Criminology and Police Science*. 51:189–208.
Dickson, Donald T.
1968 "Bureaucracy and Morality: An Organizational Perspective on a Moral Crusade." *Social Problems* 16:143–156.
Dinitz, Simon, Frank R. Scarpitti, and Walter Reckless
1962 "Delinquency Vulnerability: A Cross Group and Longitudinal Analysis." *American Sociological Review* 27:515–517.
Downes, David
1966 *The Delinquent Solution: A Study in Subcultural Theory*. London: Routledge & Kegan Paul.
1978 "Promise and Performance in British Criminology." *British Journal of Sociology* 29:483–502.

Durkheim, Emile
1951
(1897) *Suicide*. Translated by John A. Spaulding and George Simpson. Glencoe, Ill.: Free Press.
1949 *The Division of Labor in Society*. Translated by George Simpson. Glencoe, Ill.: Free Press.
Duster, Troy
1970 *The Legislation of Morality: Law, Drugs and Moral Judgment*. New York: Free Press.
Ehrlich, I.
1975 "The Deterrent Effect of Capital Punishment: A Question of Life and Death." *American Economic Review* 65:397.
Eisenstein, James, and Herbert Jacob
1977 *Felony Justice*. Boston: Little, Brown.
Elliot, D. S., and S. S. Ageton
1980 "Reconciling Race and Class Differences in Self-Reported and Official Estimates of Delinquency." *American Sociological Review* 45:95–110.
Elliott, Mabel
1952 *Crime in Modern Society*. New York: Harper.
Emerson, Robert M.
1969 *Judging Delinquents: Context and Process in Juvenile Court*. Chicago: Aldine.
Emerson, Robert, and Sheldon Messinger
1977 "The Micro-Politics of Trouble." *Social Problems* 25:121–134.
Empey, LeMar, and Maynard Erickson
1972 *The Provo Experiment*. Lexington, Mass.: Lexington.
Empey, LeMar, and Steven Lubeck
1971 *The Silverlake Experiment*. Chicago: Aldine.
Ennis, P.H.
1967 *Criminal Victimization in the United States: A Report of a National Survey*. Washington, D.C.: U.S. Government Printing Office.
Ericson, Richard
1982 *Reproducing Order: A Study of Police Patrol Work*. Toronto: University of Toronto Press.
Erikson, Kai
1966 *Wayward Puritans: A Study in the Sociology of Deviance*. New York: Wiley.
Erlanger, Howard
1974 "The Empirical Status of the Subculture of Violence Thesis." *Social Problems* 22:280–292.
1979 "Estrangement, Machismo and Gang Violence." *Social Science Quarterly* 60(2):235–248.
Ermann, M. David, and Richard J. Lundman
1978 *Corporate and Governmental Deviance: Problems of Organizational Behavior in Contemporary Society*. New York: Oxford University Press.
1980 *Corporate Deviance*. New York: Holt, Rinehart & Winston.

Erskine, H.
1974 "The Polls: Fear of Violence and Crime." *Public Opinion Quarterly* 38:131–145.

Eysenck, Hans
1964 *Crime and Personality*. Boston: Houghton Mifflin.

Farberman, Harvey A.
1975 "A Criminogenic Market Structure: The Automobile Industry." *Sociological Quarterly* 16:438–457.

Farington, D. P.
1973 "Self-Reports of Delinquent Behavior: Predictive and Stable?" *Journal of Criminal Law and Criminology* 64:99–110.

Feeley, Malcolm
1975 "The Effects of Heavy Caseloads." Paper presented at the annual meeting of the American Political Science Association, San Francisco.
1979 *The Prc ℓss Is the Punishment*. New York: Russell Sage.

Feldman, Egal
1967 "Prostitution, the Alien Woman, and Progressive Imagination: 1910–15." *American Quarterly* 19:192–206.

Ferdinand, Theodore
1967 "The Criminal Patterns of Boston Since 1849." *American Journal of Sociology* 73:84–99.
1972 "Politics, the Police, and Arresting Practices in Salem, Massachusetts since the Civil War." *Social Problems* 19:572–588.
1973 "Criminality, the Courts, and the Constabulary in Boston: 1703–1967." Unpublished manuscript.

Ferdinand, Theodore, and Elmer Luchterhand
1970 "Inner-City Youth, the Police, the Juvenile Court, and Justice." *Social Problems* 17:510–527.

Ferri, Enrica
1915, 1917
1929 *Criminal Sociology*. New York: Appleton.

Feurverger, A. and C. Shearing
1982 "An Analysis of the Prosecution of Shoplifting," *Criminology* 20(2):273–289.

Feyerherm, William
1981 "Gender Differences in Delinquency: Quantity and Quality," In Lee H. Bowker (ed.), *Women and Crime in America*. New York: Macmillan.

Fienberg, Stephen, and Patricia Grambsch
1979 "An Assessment of the Accuracy of 'The Effectiveness of Correctional Treatment'," In L. Sechrest, S. O. White, and E. D. Brown (eds.), *The Rehabilitation of Criminal Offenders: Problems and Prospects*. Washington, D.C.: National Academy of Sciences.

Filler, Louis
1950 *Crusaders for American Liberalism*. Yellow Springs, Ohio: Antioch Press.

Fisher, Sethard
1972 "Stigma and Deviant Careers in Schools." *Social Problems* 20:78–83.

Fishman, Mark
1978 "Crime Waves as Ideology." *Social Problems* 25:531–543.
Foote, Caleb
1956 "Vagrancy-Type Law and Its Administration." *University of Pennsylvania Law Review* 104:603–650.
Foucault, Michel
1977 *Discipline and Punish: The Birth of the Prison.* Translated by Alan Sheridan. New York: Pantheon.
Fox, Sanford
1970 "Juvenile Justice Reform: An Historical Perspective." *Stanford Law Review* 22:1187–1239.
Franklin, Alice
1979 "Criminality in the Work Place: A Comparison of Male and Female Offenders." In Freda Adler and Rita Simon (eds.), *The Criminology of Deviant Women.* Boston: Houghton Mifflin.
Friedman, Lawrence
1979 "Plea Bargaining in Historical Perspective." *Law and Society Review* 13:247–259.
Friedmann, Wolfgang
1959 *Law in a Changing Society.* London: Stevens.
1967 *Legal Theory.* London: Stevens.
Galliher, John F., James L. McCartney, and Barabara Baum
1974 "Nebraska's Marijuana Law: A Case of Unexpected Legislative Innovation." *Law and Society Review* 8:441–456.
Galliher, John F., and Allyn Walker
1977 "The Puzzle of the Social Origins of the Marijuana Tax Act of 1937." *Social Problems* 24:367–376.
Garfinkel, Harold
1949 "Research Note on Inter- and Intra-Racial Homicides." *Social Forces* 27:369–381.
1956 "Conditions of Successful Degradation Ceremonies." *American Journal of Sociology* 61:420–424.
Garofalo, Raffaele
1914 *Criminology.* Boston: Little, Brown.
Geerken, Michael, and Walter Gove
1977 "Deterrence, Overload and Incapacitation: An Empirical Evaluation." *Social Forces* 56:424–447.
Geis, Gilbert
1960 "Jeremy Bentham." In H. Mannheim (ed.), *Pioneers in Criminology.* London: Stevens.
1962 "Toward a Delineation of White-Collar Offenses." *Sociological Inquiry* 32:160–171.
Gibbons, Don
1974 "Say, Whatever Became of Maurice Parmelee, Anyway?" *Sociological Quarterly* 15:405–416.

1979   *The Criminological Enterprise*: *Theories and Perspectives*. Englewood Cliffs, N.J.: Prentice-Hall.
Gibbons, Don, and Manzer Griswold
1957   "Sex Differences among Juvenile Court Referrals." *Sociology and Social Research* 42:106–110.
Gibbs, Jack
1975   *Crime, Punishment and Deterrence*. New York: Elsevier.
1977   "Social Control, Deterrence and Perspectives on Social Order." *Social Forces* 56(2):
1978   "Deterrence, Penal Policy, and the Sociology of Law." In Rita Simon (ed.), *Research in Law and Sociology*. Greenwich, Conn.: JAI Press.
Gibbs, Jack, and Maynard Erickson
1976   "Crime Rates of American Cities in an Ecological Context." *American Journal of Sociology* 82:605–620.
Gillin, John L.
1926   *Criminology and Penology*. New York: Century.
Giordano, Peggy
1978   "Guys, Girls and Gangs: The Changing Social Context of Female Delinquency." *Journal of Criminal Law and Criminology* 69(1):126–132.
Giordano, Peggy, Sandra Kerbel, and Sandra Dudley
1981   "The Economics of Female Criminality: An Analysis of Police Blotters, 1890–1975." In Lee H. Bowker (ed.), *Women and Crime in America*. New York: Macmillan.
Glass, G. V., V. L. Willson, and J. Gottman
1975   *The Design and Analysis of Time Series Experiments*. Boulder: Colorado Associated University Press.
Glueck, S., and E. Glueck
1930   *500 Criminal Careers*. New York: Knopf.
1950   *Unraveling Juvenile Delinquency*. Cambridge, Mass.: Harvard.
Goffman, I.
1961   *Asylums*. Chicago: Aldine-Atherton.
1963   *Stigma*: *Notes on the Management of Spoiled Identity*. Englewood Cliffs, N.J.: Prentice-Hall.
Gold, M.
1970   *Delinquent Behavior in an American City*. Belmont, Calif.: Brooks/Cole.
Goldman, Nathan
1963   *The Differential Selection of Offenders for Court Appearance*. New York: National Council on Crime and Delinquency.
Gordon, Robert
1967   "Issues in the Ecological Study of Delinquency." *American Sociological Review* 32:927–944.
Gove, Walter
1975   "Labelling and Mental Illness: A Critique." In Walter Gove (ed.), *The Labelling of Deviance*: *Evaluating a Perspective*. New York: Sage.

Graham, Hugh Davis, and Ted Robert Gurr
1969 *The History of Violence in America*: *Historical and Comparative Perspectives*. New York: Praeger.
Graham, James M.
1972 "Amphetamine Politics on Capitol Hill." *Transaction* 9:14.
Grasmich, H. G., and H. Milligan
1976 "Deterrence Theory Approach to Socioeconomic Demographic Correlates of Crime." *Social Science Quarterly* 57:608–617.
Green, Edward
1970 "Race, Social Status and Criminal Arrest." *American Sociological Review* 35:476–490.
Greenberg, David
1976 "On One-Dimensional Criminology." *Theory and Society* 3(4):611–621.
1977 "The Correctional Effects of Corrections: A Survey of Evaluations." In D. F. Greenberg (ed.), *Corrections and Punishment*. Beverly Hills, Calif.: Sage.
1981 *Crime and Capitalism*. Palo Alto, Calif.: Mayfield.
Gulliver, P. H.
1969 "Introduction to Case Studies of Law in Non-Western Societies." In Laura Nader (ed.), *Law in Culture and Society*. Chicago: Aldine.
Gurr, Ted Robert
1977 "Crime Trends in Modern Democracies since 1945." *International Annals of Criminology* 16:41–85.
1979 "On the History of Violent Crime in Europe and America." In Hugh D. Graham and Ted R. Gurr (eds.), *Violence in America: Historical and Comparative Perspectives*. Beverly Hills: Sage.
1980 Development and Decay: Their Impact on Public Order in Western History". In James A. Inciardi and Charles E. Faupel (eds.), *History and Crime*. Beverly Hills, Calif.:Sage.
1981 "Historical Trends in Violent Crimes: A Critical Review of the Evidence." In M. Toary and N. Morris (eds.), *Crime and Justice: Annual Review of Research*. 3:295–353.
Gurr, Ted Robert, Peter Grabosky, and Richard Hula
1977 *The Politics of Crime and Conflict*: *A Comparative History of Four Cities*. Beverly Hills, Calif.: Sage.
Gusfield, Joseph R.
1963 *Symbolic Crusade: Status Politics and the American Temperance Movement*. Urbana: University of Illinois Press.
Guyot, D.
1976 "What Productivity? What Bargain?" *Public Administration Review* 36:341.
Hackler, James
1966 "Boys, Blisters and Behavior—The Impact of a Work Program in an Urban Central Area." *Journal of Research in Crime and Delinquency* 3:155–164.
1971 "A Developmental Theory of Delinquency." *Canadian Review of Sociology and Anthropology* 8(2):61–75.

Hackler, James, and John Hagan
1975   "Work and Teaching Machines as Delinquency Prevention Tools: A Four-Year Follow-up." *Social Sciences Review* 49(1):92–106.
Hagan, John
1973   "Labelling and Deviance: A Case Study in the 'Sociology of the Interesting.'" *Social Problems* 20(4):448–458.
1974   "Extra-Legal Attributes and Criminal Sentencing: An Assessment of a Sociological Viewpoint." *Law and Society Review* 8(3):357–383.
1975*a*   "Explaining Watergate: Toward a Control Theory of Upperworld Crime." In Nicholas Kittrie and Jackwell Susman (eds.), *Legality, Morality, and Ethics in Criminal Justice*. New York: Praeger.
1975*b*   "Parameters of Criminal Prosecution: An Application of Path Analysis to a Problem of Criminal Justice." *Journal of Criminal Law, Criminology and Police Science* 65:536–544.
1975*c*   "The Social and Legal Construction of Criminal Justice: A Study of the Pre-Sentencing Process." *Social Problems* 22:620–637.
1977*a*   "Criminal Justice in Rural and Urban Communities: A Study of the Bureaucratization of Justice." *Social Forces* 55:597–612.
1977*b*   "Symbolic Justice: The Status Politics of the American Probation Movement." *Sociological Focus* 12:295–309.
1977*c*   *The Disreputable Pleasures*. Toronto: McGraw-Hill Ryerson.
1980   "The Legislation of Crime and Delinquency: A Review of Theory, Method and Research." *Law and Society Review* 14(3):603–628.
1982   "The Corporate Advantage: The Involvement of Individual and Organizational Victims in the Criminal Justice Process." *Social Forces* 60(4):993-1022.
1983   *Victims Before the Law*. Toronto: Butterworth.
Hagan, John, and Celesta Albonetti
1982   "Race, Class and the Perception of Criminal Injustice in America." *American Journal of Sociology* 88:329–355.
Hagan, John, and Ilene Bernstein
1979   "The Sentence Bargaining of Upperworld and Underworld Crime in Ten Federal District Courts." *Law and Society Review* 13:467–478.
Hagan, John, and Kristen Bumiller
1983   "Making Sense of Sentencing: A Review and Critique of Sentencing Research." In Alfred Blumstein, Jacqueline Cohen, Susan Martin, and Michael Tonry (eds.), *Research on Sentencing: The Search for Reform*. Washington, D.C.: National Academy Press.
Hagan, John, Ron Gillis and John Simpson
1984   "The Class Structure of Gender and Delinquency: Toward a Power-Control Theory of Delinquent Behavior." Unpublished manuscript.
Hagan, John, John Hewitt, and Duane Alwin
1979   "Ceremonial Justice: Crime and Punishment in a Loosely Coupled System." *Social Forces* 58:506–527.
Hagan, John, and Jeffrey Leon
1977   "Rediscovering Delinquency: Social History, Political Ideology and the Sociology of Law." *American Sociological Review* 42:587–598.

Hagan, John, and Ilene Nagel
1982 "White Collar Crime, White Collar Time: The Sentencing of White Collar Criminals in the Southern District of New York." *American Criminal Law Review* 20(2)259–301.
Hagan, John, Ilene Nagel, and Celesta Albonetti
1980 "The Differential Sentencing of White Collar Offenders in Ten Federal District Courts." *American Sociological Review* 45:802–820.
Hagan, John, and Alberto Palloni
1983 "The Sentencing of White Collar Offenders Before and After Watergate." Paper presented at the American Sociological Association meetings, Detroit.
Hagan, John, Edward Silva, and John Simpson
1977 "Conflict and Consensus in the Designation of Deviance." *Social Forces* 56(2):320–340.
Hagan, John, and John Simpson
1977 "Ties That Bind: Conformity and the Social Control of Student Discontent." *Sociology and Social Research* 61:520–538.
Hagan, John, John Simpson, and A. R. Gillis
1979 "The Sexual Stratification of Social Control: A Gender-Based Perspective on Crime and Delinquency." *British Journal of Sociology* 30(1):25–38.
Halevy, Elie
1955 *The Growth of Philosophic Radicalism.* Translated by Mary Morris. 3 vols. Boston: Beacon.
Hall, Jerome
1952 *Theft, Law and Society.* Indianapolis: Bobbs-Merrill.
1960 *General Principles of Criminal Law.* Indianapolis: Bobbs-Merrill.
1963 *Comparative Law and Social Theory.* Baton Rouge: Louisiana State University press.
1975 "Role of the Victim in the Prosecution and Disposition of a Criminal Case." *Vanderbilt Law Review* 28(October):931–985.
Haller, Mark
1970 "Urban Crime and Criminal Justice: The Chicago Case." *Journal of American History* 57:619–635.
1976 "Historical Roots of Police Behavior: Chicago, 1890–1925." *Law and Society Review* 10:303–323.
1979 "Plea Bargaining: The Nineteenth Century Context." *Law and Society Review* 13:273–279.
Hannan, M.
1971 *Aggregation and Disaggregation in Sociology.* Lexington, Mass.: Lexington Books.
Harding, Alan
1966 *A Social History of English Law.* Harmondsworth, England: Penguin.
Harno, Albert J.
1928 "The Workings of the Parole Board and Its Relation to the Courts." *Journal of the American Institute of Criminal Law and Criminology* 19:83.

Harring, Sidney
1977 "Class Conflict and the Suppression of Tramps in Buffalo, 1892–1894." *Law and Society Review* 11:873–911.
Harris, Anthony R.
1977 "Sex and Theories of Deviance: Toward a Functional Theory of Deviant Type-Scripts." *American Sociological Review* 42:3–16.
Harris, George E.
1892 *A Treatise on Sunday Laws*. Rochester, N.Y.: Lawyers' Cooperative Publishing Co.
Hart, H. L. A.
1963 *Law, Liberty and Morality*. Stanford: Stanford University Press.
Hartung, Frank E.
1950 "White-Collar Offenses in the Wholesale Meat Industry in Detroit." *American Journal of Sociology* 56:25–34.
Haskins, George Lee
1960 *Law and Authority in Early Massachusetts*. New York: Macmillan.
Hay, Douglas, Peter Linebaugh, John G. Rule, E. P. Thompson, and Cal Winslow
1975 *Albion's Fatal Tree*. London: A. Lane.
Healy, William
1915 *The Individual Delinquent*. Boston: Little, Brown.
Heinz, Anne, and Wayne Kerstetter
1979 "Pretrial Settlement Conference: Evaluation of a Reform in Plea Bargaining." *Law and Society Review* 13:349–366.
Heumann, Milton
1975 "A Note on Plea Bargaining and Case Pressure." *Law and Society Review* 9:515–528.
1978 *Plea Bargaining: The Experience of Prosecutors, Judges and Defense Attorneys*. Chicago: University of Chicago Press.
Heumann, Milton, and Colin Loftin
1979 "Mandatory Sentencing and the Abolition of Plea Bargaining: The Michigan Felony Firearm Statute." *Law and Society Review* 13:393–430.
Heyl, Barbara
1979 "Prostitution: An Extreme Case of Sex Stratification." In Freda Adler and Rita Simon (eds.), *The Criminology of Deviant Women*. Boston: Houghton Mifflin.
Hibbert, Christopher
1963 *The Roots of Evil: A Social History of Crime and Punishment*. Boston: Little, Brown.
Hill, Gary D., and Anthony R. Harris
1981 "Changes in the Gender Patterning of Crime, 1953-77: Opportunity v. Identity." *Social Science Quarterly* 62(4):658–671.
Hills, S. L.
1971 *Crime, Power and Morality*. Scranton: Chandler.

Hindelang, M. J.

1971 "Age, Sex and Versatility of Delinquent Involvement." *Social Problems* 18:522–535.

1973 "Causes of Delinquency: A Partial Replication and Extension." *Social Problems* 20(4):471–487.

1974a "Decisions of Shoplifting Victims to Invoke the Criminal Justice Process." *Social Problems* 21:580–593.

1974b "The Uniform Crime Reports Revisited." *Journal of Criminal Justice* 2(1):1–17.

1978 "Race and Involvement in Common Law Personal Crimes." *American Sociological Review* 43:93–109.

1979 "Sex Differences in Criminal Activity." *Social Problems* 27(2):143–156.

Hindelang, Michael, Travis Hirschi, and Joseph Weis

1981 *Measuring Delinquency*. Beverly Hills, Calif.: Sage.

Hirschi, Travis

1969 *Causes of Delinquency*. Berkeley: University of California Press.

1973 "Procedural Rules and the Study of Deviant Behavior." *Social Problems* 21:159–173.

1975 "Labelling Theory and Juvenile Delinquency: An Assessment of the Evidence." In Walter Gove (ed.), *The Labelling of Deviance*: *Evaluating a Perspective*. Beverly Hills, Calif.: Sage.

1980 "Postscript to Labelling Theory and Juvenile Delinquency." In W. R. Gove (ed.), *The Labelling of Deviance*. Beverly Hills, Calif.: Sage.

Hirschi, Travis, and Hanan Selvin

1967 *Delinquency Research*: *An Appraisal of Analytic Methods*. New York: Free Press.

Hogarth, John

1971 *Sentencing as a Human Process*. Toronto: University of Toronto Press.

Holmes, Kay Ann

1972 "Reflections by Gaslight: Prostitution in Another Age." *Issues in Criminology* 7:83–101.

Hood, Roger, and Richard Sparks

1970 *Key Issues in Criminology*. New York: McGraw-Hill.

Hopkins, Andrew

1975 "On the Sociology of Criminal Law." *Social Problems* 22:608–619.

Horning, Donald N.

1970 "Blue-Collar Theft: Conceptions of Property, Attitudes Toward Pilfering, and Work Group Norms in a Modern Industrial Plant." In Erwin O. Smigel and H. Laurence Ross (eds.), *Crimes Against Bureaucracy*. New York: Van Nostrand Reinhold.

Horowitz, Irving, and Lee Rainwater

1970 "Journalistic Moralizers." *Transaction* 7(7):5.

Huber, Joan

1976 "Toward a Socio-Technological Theory of the Women's Movement." *Social Problems* 23(4):371–388.

Hughes, Everett
1951 "Work and the Self." In John H. Rohrer and M. Sherif (eds.), *Social Psychology at the Crossroads*. New York: Harper & Brothers.
1958 *Men and their Work*. Glencoe, Ill.: Free Press
1962 "Good People and Dirty Work." *Social Problems* 10(1):3–11.
Humphreys, Laud
1970 *Tearoom Trade*. Chicago: Aldine.
Hurst, J. Willard
1950 *The Growth of American Law: The Law Makers*. Boston: Little, Brown.
Ianni, Francis
1972 *A Family Business*. New York: Russell Sage.
1974 *Black Mafia*. New York: Simon & Schuster.
Ignatieff, Michael
1978 *A Just Measure of Pain: The Penitentiary in the Industrial Revolution, 1750–1850*. New York: Pantheon.
1981 "State, Civil Society, and Total Institutions: A Critique of Recent Social Histories of Punishment." In Norval Morris and Michael Tonry (eds.), *Crime and Justice*, vol. III.
International Prison Commission
1904 *Children's Courts in the United States: Their Origin, Development and Results*. H.R. Doc. no. 701, 58th Cong., 2d sess.
Irwin, John
1970 *The Felon*. Englewood Cliffs, N.J.: Prentice-Hall.
Irwin, John, and Donald Cressey
1962 "Thieves, Convicts and the Inmate Culture." *Social Problems* 10:142–155.
Jackson, B.
1969 *A Thief's Primer*. New York: Macmillan.
Jacobs, David
1980 "Marxism and the Critique of Empiricism: A Comment on Beirne." *Social Problems* 27:467–470.
Jacobs, James
1977 *Stateville: The Penitentiary in Mass Society*. Chicago: University of Chicago Press.
1979 "Race Relations and the Prison Subculture." In Norval Morris and Michael Tonry (eds.), *Crime and Justice*, vol. I. Chicago: University of Chicago Press.
Janowitz, Morris
1975 "Sociological Theory and Social Control." *American Journal of Sociology* 81:82–108.
Jaspan, Norman, and Hillel Black
1960 *The Thief in the White Collar*. Philadelphia: J. B. Lippincott.
Jeffrey, Clarence R.
1957 "The Development of Crime in Early English Society." *Journal of Criminal Law, Criminology and Police Science* 47(6):647–666.
Jensen, Gary
1969 "'Crime Doesn't Pay': Correlates of Shared Misunderstanding." *Social Problems* 17:189–201.

Jensen, G. F., M. L. Erickson, and J. P. Gibbs
1978 "Perceived Risk of Punishment and Self-Reported Delinquency." *Social Forces* 57:57–78.

Jensen, Gary, and Raymond Eve
1976 "Sex Differences in Delinquency: An Examination of Popular Sociological Explanations." *Criminology* 13:427–448.

Jensen, Gary, and B. Grant Stitt
1982 "Words and Misdeeds: Hypothetical Choices versus Past Behavior as Measures of Deviance." In John Hagan (ed.), *Deterrence Reconsidered: Methodological Innovations*. Beverly Hills, Calif.: Sage.

Johnson, Alvin W.
1934 "Sunday Legislation." *Kentucky Law Journal* 23:131–166.

Johnson, R. E.
1980 "Social Class and Delinquent Behavior: A New Test." *Criminology* 18:86–43.

Kanter, Rosabeth Moss
1974 "Intimate Oppression." *Sociological Quarterly* 15(2):302–314.

Katz, Jack
1979 "Legality and Equality: Plea Bargaining in the Prosecution of White-Collar and Common Crimes." *Law and Society Review* 13:431–460.
1980 "The Social Movement Against White-Collar Crime." In Egon Bittner and Sheldon Messinger (eds.), *Criminology Review Yearbook,* Vol. 2. Beverly Hills, Calif.: Sage.

Kelly, Delos
1976 "Track Position, School Misconduct, and Youth Deviance." *Urban Education* 10:379–388.

Kelly, D. H., and W. T. Pink
1975 "Status Origins, Youth Rebellion and Delinquency: A Reexamination of the Class Issue." *Journal of Youth and Adolescence* 4:339–347.

Kirkham, George L.
1974 "What a Professor Learned When He Became a 'Cop.'" *U.S. News and World Report* 76:70–72.

Kitsuse, John, and Aaron Cicourel
1963 "A Note on the Uses of Official Statistics." *Social Problems* 11:131–139.

Kitsuse, John, and David Dietrick
1959 "Delinquent Boys: A Critique." *American Sociological Review* 24:208–215.

Kleck, Gary
1981 "Racial Discrimination in Criminal Sentencing: A Critical Evaluation of the Evidence with Additional Evidence on the Death Penalty." *American Sociological Review* 46:783–805.

Klein, Malcolm, and L. Y. Crawford
1967 "Groups, Gangs and Cohesiveness." *Journal of Research in Crime and Delinquency* 4:63–75.

Kobler, Arthur
1980 "Police Homicide in a Democracy." In Richard Lundman (ed.), *Police Behavior*. New York: Oxford University Press.

Kobrin, Solomon
1951 "The Conflicts of Values in Delinquency Areas." *American Sociological Review* 16:657–662.
1959 "The Chicago Area Project—A 25-Year Assessment." *Annals of the American Academy of Political and Social Science* 322:19–29.
Kornhauser, Ruth
1978 *Social Sources of Delinquency*. Chicago: University of Chicago Press.
Kratcoski, Peter, and J. Kratcoski
1975 "Changing Patterns in the Delinquent Activities of Boys and Girls: A Self Reported Delinquency Analysis." *Adolescence* 10:83–91.
Kraut, R. E.
1976 "Deterrent and Definitional Influences on Shoplifting." *Social Problems* 23:358–368.
Krisberg, Barry
1972 Review of *Tearoom Trade*. *Issues of Criminology* 7:126–127.
Lacey, Forrest W.
1953 "Vagrancy and Other Crimes of Personal Condition." *Harvard Law Review* 66:1203–1226.
LaFree, Gary
1980 "The Effect of Sexual Stratification by Race on Official Reactions to Rape." *American Sociological Review* 45:842–854.
Lander, Bernard
1954 *Towards an Understanding of Juvenile Delinquency*. New York: Columbia.
Lane, Roger
1968 "Crime and Criminal Statistics in Nineteenth Century Massachusetts." *Journal of Social History* 2:156–163.
1974 "Crime and the Industrial Revolution: British and American Views." *Journal of Social History* 7:287–303.
1980 "Urban Police and Crime in Nineteenth-Century America." *Crime and Justice* 2:1–44.
Lemert, Edwin
1951 *Social Pathology*. New York: McGraw-Hill.
1962 "Paranoia and the Dynamics of Exclusion." *Sociometry* 25:2–20.
1967 *Human Deviance, Social Problems and Social Control*. Englewood Cliffs, N.J.: Prentice-Hall.
1970 *Social Action and Legal Change: Revolution Within the Juvenile Court*. Chicago: Aldine.
Leon, Jeffrey
1975 *Drug Related Deaths in Metropolitan Toronto*. Toronto: Addiction Research Foundation.
Lerman, Paul
1968 "Evaluative Studies in Institutions for Delinquency: Implications for Research and Social Policy." *Social Work* 13:55–64.
1975 *Community Treatment and Social Control*. Chicago: University of Chicago Press.
Letkemann, Peter
1973 *Crime as Work*. Englewood Cliffs, N.J.: Prentice-Hall.

Levin, Martin A.
1977   *Urban Politics and the Criminal Courts*. Chicago: University of Chicago Press.
Levy, Leonard W.
1963   *Freedom of Speech and Press in Early American History*: *Legacy of Suppression*. New York: Harper & Row.
Lewis, Abram
1888   *A Critical History of Sunday Legislation from 321 to 1888 A.D.* New York: Appleton.
Liebow, Elliot
1967   *Tally's Corner*. Boston: Little, Brown
Linden, Eric
1976   "Religiosity and Drug Use: A Test of Social Control Theory." Paper presented at Canadian Sociology and Anthropology Association meetings, Quebec City, May.
Linden, Eric, and James Hackler
1973   "Affective Ties and Delinquency." *Pacific Sociological Review* 16:27–46.
Lindesmith, Alfred R.
1947   *Opiate Addiction*. Bloomington, Ind.: Principia Press.
1957   "The British System of Narcotics Control." *Law and Contemporary Problems* 5:138.
1959   "Federal Law and Drug Addiction." *Social Problems* 7:48–57.
1967   *The Addict and the Law*. New York: Vintage Books.
1968   *Addiction and Opiates*. Chicago: Aldine.
Lindesmith A., and Y. Levin
1937   "The Lombrosian Myth in Criminology." *American Journal of Sociology* 42:653–671.
Lizotte, Alan J.
1978   "Extra-Legal Factors in Chicago's Criminal Courts: Testing the Conflict Model of Criminal Justice." *Social Problems* 25:564–580.
Lizotte, Alan, and David Bordua
1980   "Firearms Ownership for Sport and Protection: Two Divergent Models." *American Sociological Review* 45:229–244.
Lofland, John
1977   *The Dramaturgy of State Executions*. Montclair, N.J.: Patterson Smith.
Lombroso, Cesare
1911   *Criminal Man, According to the Classification of Cesare Lombroso*. Summarized by Gina Lombroso-Ferrero. New York: Putnam's.
1918   *Crime, Its Causes and Remedies*. Boston: Little, Brown.
Lorber, J.
1975   "Beyond Equality of the Sexes: The Question of the Children." *Family Coordinator* 24:465–472.
Lou, Herbert H.
1927   *Juvenile Courts in the United States*. Chapel Hill: University of North Carolina Press.

Lubove, Roy
1962 "The Progressives and the Prostitute." *Historian* 24:308–330.
Lucas, Netley
1926 *Crook Janes: A Study of the Women Criminals in the World Over.* London: Stanley Paul.
McCall, George, and J. L. Simmons
1969 *Issues in Participant Observation: A Text and Reader.* Reading, Mass.: Addison-Wesley.
McCleary, R., B. C. Nienstedt, and J. M. Erven
1982 "Uniform Crime Reports as Organizational Outcomes: Three Time Series Quasi-Experiments." *Social Problems* 29:361–372. McClure Magazine.
McCord, Joan
1978 "A Thirty-Year Follow-Up of Treatment Effects." *American Psychologist* 33:284–289.
McCord, J. and W. McCord
1959 "A Follow Up Report on the Cambridge-Somerville Youth Study." *Annals of the American Academy of Political and Social Science.* 322:89–96.
McCord, William, Joan McCord, with Irving Zola
1959 *Origins of Crime.* New York: Columbia.
McDonald, Lyn
1976 *The Sociology of Law and Order.* London: Faber & Faber.
McEachern, A. W., and Riva Bauzer
1967 "Factors Related to Disposition in Juvenile Police Contacts." In Malcolm W. Klein (ed.), *Juvenile Gangs in Context: Research, Theory and Action.* Englewood Cliffs, N.J.: Prentice-Hall.
McFarlane, George C.
1966 *The Development of Probation Services in Ontario.* Toronto: Queen's Printer.
McGaghy, Charles H., and Serge Denisoff
1973 "Pirates and Politics: An Analysis of Interest Group Conflict." In R. Serge Denisoff and Charles H. McGaghy (eds.), *Deviance, Conflict and Criminality.* Chicago: Rand McNally.
Madley, John
1965 "Probation." In W. T. McGrath (ed.), *Crime and Its Treatment in Canada.* Toronto: Macmillan.
Maine, (Sir) Henry James Sumner
1960 *Ancient Law.* London: Dent.
Mann, Kenneth, Stanton Wheeler, and Austin Sarat
1980 "Sentencing the White Collar Offender." *American Criminal Law Review* 17(4):479.
Mannheim, H., and L. T. Wilkins
1955 *Prediction Methods in Relation to Borstal Training.* London: H. M. Stationery Office.
Martinson, Robert
1974 "What Works?—Questions and Answers About Prison Reform." *The Public Interest* 35:22–54.

Marx, Karl
1853   "Capital Punishment." *New York Daily Tribune,* reprinted in T.B. Bottomure and M. Rubel (eds.), *Karl Marx; Selected Writings in Sociology and Social Philosophy.* Harmondsworth, England: Penguin.
Mather, Lynn
1973   "Some Determinants of the Method of Case Disposition: Decision-Making by Public Defenders in Los Angeles." *Law and Society Review* 8:187–216.
1979   *Plea Bargaining or Trial? The Process of Criminal Case Disposition.* Lexington, Mass.: Lexington Books.
Matza, David
1964   *Delinquency and Drift.* New York: Wiley.
Mayhew, Henry
1862   *London Labor and the London Poor.* London: Griffin, Bohn.
Mead, George Herbert
1918   "The Psychology of Punitive Justice." *American Journal of Sociology* 23:577–602.
Mennel, Robert M.
1973   *Thorns and Thistles: Juvenile Delinquents in the United States, 1825–1940.* Hanover, N.H.: University Press of New England.
Merton, Robert
1938   "Social Structure and Anomie." *American Sociological Review* 3:672–682.
1957   *Social Theory and Social Structure.* Glencoe, Ill.: Free Press.
1959   "Social Conformity, Deviation, and Opportunity Structures: A Comment on the Contributions of Dubin and Cloward." *American Sociological Review* 24:177–189.
Meyer, J. W., and B. Rowan
1979   "Institutionalized Organizations: Formal Structure as Myth and Ceremony." *American Journal of Sociology* 83:340–363.
Mill, John Stuart
1859   "On Liberty." In Max Lerner (ed.), *Essential Works of John Stuart Mill.* New York: Bantam Books, 1961.
Miller, Walter
1958   "Lower Class Culture as a Generating Milieu of Gang Delinquency." *Journal of Social Issues* 14(3):5–19.
1962   "The Impact of a 'Total Community' Delinquency Control Project." *Social Problems* 10:168–191.
1973   "The Molls." *Society* 11:32–35.
Miller, Wilbur
1975   "Police Authority in London and New York City 1830–1870." *Journal of Social History* 8:81–101.
Millman, M.
1975   "She Did It All for Love: A Feminist View of the Sociology of Deviance." In M. Millman and R. M. Kanter (eds.), *Another Voice: Feminist Perspectives on Social Life and Social Science.* Garden City, New York: Anchor Press.
Mills, C. Wright
1943   "The Professional Ideology of Social Pathologists." *American Journal of Sociology* 49:165–180.

1956   *The Power Elite*. New York: Oxford University Press.
Milton, Catherine H.
1972   *Women in Policing*. Washington: Police Foundation.
Moley, Raymond
1928   "The Vanishing Jury." *Southern California Law Review* 2:97.
Monachesi, Elio
1960   "Cesare Beccaria." In H. Mannheim (ed.), *Pioneers in Criminology*. London: Stevens.
Monkkonen, Eric
1975   *The Dangerous Class*: *Crime and Poverty in Columbus, Ohio, 1860–1920*. New York: Cambridge University Press.
1981   *Police in Urban America, 1860–1920*. New York: Cambridge.
Morris, Norval, and Gordon Hawkins
1969   *The Honest Politician's Guide to Crime Control*. Chicago: University of Chicago Press.
Morris, Richard B.
1959   *Studies in the History of American Law*. Philadelphia: Mitchell.
Moynihan, Daniel P.
1969   *Maximum Feasible Misunderstanding*. New York: Free Press.
Mueller, Gerhard O. W.
1961   *Legal Regulation of Sexual Conduct*. New York: Oceana.
Murray, Charles A., and Louis A. Cox
1979   *Beyond Probation*: *Juvenile Corrections and the Chronic Delinquent*. Beverly Hills, Calif.: Sage.
Musto, David F.
1973   *The American Disease*: *Origins of Narcotic Control*. New Haven: Yale.
Myers, Martha
1979   "Offended Parties and Official Reactions: Victims and the Sentencing of Criminal Defendants." *Sociological Quarterly* 20:529–540.
Myers, Martha, and John Hagan
1979   "Private and Public Trouble: Prosecutors and the Allocation of Court Resources." *Social Problems* 26:439–451.
Nagel, Ilene, and John Hagan
1983   "Gender and Crime: Offense Patterns and Criminal Court Sanctions." *Crime and Justice*: *Annual Review of Research* 4:91–144.
National Research Council
1976   *Surveying Crime*. Panel for the Evaluation of Crime Surveys. Washington: National Academy of Sciences.
Nelson, Harold L.
1959   "Seditious Libel in Colonial America." *American Journal of Legal History* 3:160–172.
Nelson, William E.
1967   "Emerging Notions of Modern Criminal Law in the Revolutionary Era: An Historical Perspective." *New York University Law Review* 42:450–482.
Nettler, Gwynn
1974   "Embezzlement Without Problems." *British Journal of Criminology* 14(1):70–77.

1978   *Explaining Crime.* New York: McGraw-Hill.
1979   "Criminal Justice." *Annual Review of Sociology* 5:27–52.
Neubauer, David
1974   *Criminal Justice in Middle America.* Morristown, N.J.: General Learning Press.
Newman, Donald J.
1956   "Pleading Guilty for Considerations: A Study of Bargain Justice." *Journal of Criminal Law, Criminology and Police* Science 46:780–790.
1966   *Conviction: The Determination of Guilt or Innocence without Trial.* Boston: American Bar Association.
Newman, Gramae
1976   *Comparative Deviance.* New York: Elsevier.
Noblet, George, and Janie Burcart
1976   "Women and Crime: 1960–70." *Social Science Quarterly* 56:650–657.
Normandeau, A.
1966   "The Measurement of Delinquency in Montreal." *Journal of Criminal Law, Criminology and Police Science* 57:172–177.
Nye, F. Ivan
1958   *Family Relationships and Delinquent Behavior.* New York: Wiley.
Nye, F. I., and J. F. Short
1957   "Scaling Delinquent Behavior." *American Sociological Review* 22:326–331.
O'Connor, James R.
1973   *The Fiscal Crisis of the State.* New York: St. Martin's Press.
Odegard, Peter H.
1928   *Pressure Politics.* New York: Columbia.
Packer, Herbert
1968   *The Limits of the Criminal Sanction.* Stanford: Stanford University Press.
Palmer, Ted
1975   "Martinson Revisited." *Journal of Research in Crime and Delinquency* 12(2):133–152.
1978   *Correctional Intervention and Research.* Lexington, Mass.: Lexington Books.
Panel on Research in Rehabilitive Techniques
1979   National Research Council. Washington: National Academy of Sciences.
Park, R.
1915   "The City: Suggestions for the Investigation of Human Behavior in the City Environment." *American Journal of Sociology* 20:577–612.
1921   *Introduction to the Science of Sociology.* Chicago: University of Chicago Press.
Parmelee, Maurice
1918   *Criminology.* New York: Macmillan.
Parker, Graham
1976a   "The Juvenile Court Movement." *University of Toronto Law Journal* 26:140–172.
1976b   "The Juvenile Court Movement: The Illinois Experience." *University of Toronto Law Journal* 26:253–306.

Parsons, Talcott
1951   *The Social System*. Glencoe, Ill.: Free Press.
1966   *Societies*: *Evolutionary and Comparative Perspectives*. Englewood Cliffs, N.J.: Prentice-Hall.
Paternoster, R., L. E. Saltzman, G. P. Waldo, and T. G. Chiricos
1982   "Estimating Perceptual Stability and Deterrent Effects: The Role of Perceived Legal Punishment in the Inhibition of Criminal Involvement." *Journal of Criminal Law and Criminology* 74(1):270–297.
Peterson, Ruth, and John Hagan
1984   "Changing Conceptions of Race: Towards an Account of Anomalous Findings of Sentencing Research." *American Sociological Review*. 49:56–71.
Piliavin, Irving, and Scott Briar
1964   "Police Encounters with Juveniles." *American Journal of Sociology* 70:206–214.
Pivar, David J.
1973   *Purity Crusade*: *Sexual Morality and Social Control, 1868–1900*. Westport, Conn.: Greenwood Press.
Platt, Anthony M.
1969   *The Child Savers*: *The Invention of Delinquency*. Chicago: University of Chicago Press.
1974   "The Triumph of Benevolence: The Origins of the Juvenile Justice System in the United States." In Richard Quinney (ed.), *Criminal Justice in America*. Boston: Little, Brown.
1975   "Prospects for a Radical Criminology in the U.S.A." In Ian Taylor, Paul Walton, and Jock Young (eds.), *Critical Criminology*. London: Routledge & Kegan Paul.
Ploscowe, Morris
1960   "Sex Offenses: The American Legal Context." *Law and Contemporary Problems* 25:217–224.
Polk, Kenneth
1957–58   "Juvenile Delinquency and Social Areas." *Social Problems* 5:214–217.
1983   "Curriculum Tracking and Delinquency: Some Observations." *American Sociological Review* 48:282–284.
Polk, Kenneth, and Walter Schafer
1972   *Schools and Delinquency*. Englewood Cliffs, N.J.: Prentice-Hall.
Pollak, Otto
1961   *The Criminality of Women*. New York: A.S. Barnes.
Polsky, Ned
1969   *Hustlers, Beats and Others*. New York: Anchor Books.
Porter, John
1965   *The Vertical Mosaic*. Toronto: University of Toronto Press.
Porterfield, Austin
1943   "Delinquency and Its Outcome in Court and College." *American Journal of Sociology* 49:199–208.
1946   *Youth in Trouble*. Fort Worth, Tex.: Leo Potisham Foundation.

Posner, Richard A.
1980 "Optimal Sentences for White Collar Criminals." *American Criminal Law Review* 409–418.
Pound, Roscoe
1930 *Criminal Justice in America*. New York: Henry Holt.
1943 "A Survey of Social Interests." *Harvard Law Review* 57:1–39.
Powers, Edwin
1966 *Crime and Punishment in Early Massachusetts*. Boston: Beacon Press.
Powers, Edwin, and Helen Witmer
1951 *An Experiment in the Prevention of Delinquency*. New York: Columbia University Press.
Presidential Transcripts
1974 *The White House Transcripts*. New York: Viking Press.
Price, J. E.
1966 "A Test of the Accuracy of Crime Statistics." *Social Problems* 14:214–221.
Priestly, Phillip, Denise Fears, and Roger Fuller
1977 *Justice for Juveniles: The 1969 Children and Young Persons Act*: London: Routledge & Kegan Paul.
Quetelet, Adolphe
1842 *A Treatise on Man*. A facsimile reproduction of English translation of 1842 by Solomon Diamond. Gainesville, Fla.: Scholars' Facsimiles and Reprints, 1969.
Quinney, Richard
1964 "Crime, Delinquency, and Social Areas." *Journal of Research in Crime and Delinquency* 1:149–154.
1969 *Crime and Justice in Society*. Boston: Little, Brown.
1970 *The Social Reality of Crime*. New York: Little, Brown.
1974 *Critique of Legal Order*. Boston: Little, Brown.
1975a "Crime Control in Capitalist Society: A Critical Philosophy." In Ian Taylor, Paul Walton, and Jock Young (eds.), *Critical Criminology*. London: Routledge & Kegan Paul.
1975b *Criminology*. Boston: Little, Brown.
Radelet, Michael
1981 "Racial Characteristics and the Imposition of the Death Penalty." *American Sociological Review* 46:918–927.
Radzinowicz, Leon
1937 "Variability of the Sex Ratio of Criminality." *Sociological Review* 29:76–102.
1948 *A History of English Criminal Law and Its Administration from 1750*. London: Stevens.
Rainwater, Lee
1970 *Behind Ghetto Walls: Black Families in a Federal Slum*. Chicago: Aldine.
Rawls, J.
1971 *A Theory of Justice*. Cambridge, Mass.: Harvard.

Reasons, Charles
1974 "The Politics of Drugs: An Inquiry in the Sociology of Social Problems." *Sociological Quarterly* 15:381–404.
Reckless, Walter C.
1961 "A New Theory of Delinquency and Crime." *Federal Probation* 25:42–46.
1973 *The Crime Problem*. New York: Appleton-Century-Crofts.
Reiss, Albert J.
1951 "Unraveling Juvenile Delinquency." *American Journal of Sociology* 57:115–120.
1968 "How Common Is Police Brutality?" *Transaction* July/August 10–19.
1971a "Systematic Observation of Natural Social Phenomena." In Herbert Costner (ed.), *Sociological Methodology*. San Francisco: Jossey-Bass.
1971b *The Police and the Public*. New Haven: Yale University Press.
1974 "Discretionary Justice." In Daniel Glaser (ed.), *Handbook of Criminology*. Chicago: Rand McNally.
1975 "Inappropriate Theories and Inadequate Methods as Policy Plagues: Self-Reported Delinquency and the Law." In N. J. Demerath III et al. (eds.), *Social Policy and Sociology*. New York: Academic Press.
1981 "Foreword: Towards a Revitalization of Theory and Research on Victimization by Crime." *Journal of Criminal Law and Criminology* 72:704–713.
Reiss, Albert, and Albert Biderman
1980 *Data Sources on White Collar Law Breaking*. Washington: National Institute of Justice.
Reiss, Albert, and David Bordua
1967 "Organization and Environment: A Perspective on the Municipal Police." In David J. Bordua (ed.), *The Police: Six Sociological Essays*. New York: Wiley.
Reiss, Albert, and Albert Rhodes
1967 "The Distribution of Juvenile Delinquency in the Social Class Structure." *American Sociological Review* 26:720–732.
Reitman, B.
1937 *Sister of the Road: The Autobiography of Box-Car Bertha*. New York: Macaulay.
Rhodes, William
1978 *Plea Bargaining: Who Gains? Who Loses?* Promis Research Project No. 14. Washington, D.C.: Institute for Law and Social Research.
Richardson, James
1970 *The New York Police: Colonial Times to 1901*. New York: Oxford University Press.
1974 *Urban Police in the United States*. Port Washington, N.Y.: Kennikat Press.
Roby, Pamela A.
1969 "Politics and Criminal Law: Revision of the New York State Penal Law on Prostitution." *Social Problems* 17:83–109.
1972 "Politics and Prostitution: A Case Study of the Revision, Enforcement and

Administration of the New York State Penal Laws on Prostitution." *Criminology* 9:425–447.

Ross, E. A.
1901   *Social Control* New York: Macmillan.
1907   *Sin and Society*. Boston: Houghton Mifflin.

Ross, H. Laurence
1982   "Interrupted Time Series Studies of Deterrence of Drinking and Driving." In John Hagan (ed.), *Deterrence Reconsidered: Methodological Innovations*. Beverly Hills, Calif.: Sage.

Ross, H., R. McCleary, and T. Epperlein
1982   "Deterrence of Drinking and Driving in France: An Evaluation of the Law of July 12, 1978." *Law and Society Review* 16:345–374.

Rossi, Peter, Emily Waite, Christine Bose, and Richard Berk
1974   "The Seriousness of Crimes: Normative Structure and Individual Differences." *American Sociological Review* 39:224–237.

Rothman, David
1971   *The Discovery of the Asylum*. Boston: Little, Brown.
1980   *Conscience and Convenience: The Asylum and Its Alternatives in Progressive America*. Boston: Little, Brown.

Rubinstein, Michael, and Teresa White
1979   "Alaska's Ban on Plea Bargaining." *Law and Society Review* 13:367–383.

Rusche, Georg, and Otto Kirchheimer
1939   *Punishment and Social Structure*. New York: Columbia.

Sagarin, Edward
1973   "The Research Setting and the Right Not to Be Researched." *Social Problems* 21(1):52–64.

Savitz, L.
1958   "A Study in Capital Punishment." *Journal of Criminal Law, Criminology and Police Science* 49:338–341.

Schafer, Stephen
1977   *Victimology: The Victim and His Criminal*. Reston, Va.: Reston.

Schauffler, Richard
1974   "Criminology at Berkeley: Resisting Academic Repression." *Crime and Social Justice* 1:58–61.

Schauffler, Richard, and Michael Hannigan
1974   "Criminology at Berkeley: Resisting Academic Repression, Part 2." *Crime and Social Justice* 2:42–47.

Schlapp, Max, and E. H. Smith
1928   *The New Criminology*. New York: Boni & Liveright.

Schlegel, Henry
1979   "American Legal Realism and Empirical Social Science: From the Yale Experience." *Buffalo Law Review* 28:459–.

Schlossman, Steven
1977   *Love and the American Delinquent*. Chicago: University of Chicago Press.

Schlossman, Steven, and Michael Sedlak

1983 *The Chicago Area Project Revisited*. Santa Monica, Calif.: Rand.
Schmeiser, Douglas
1972 "Indians, Eskimos and the Law." Unpublished manuscript, Saskatoon: University of Saskatoon.
Schmid, C. F.
1960a "Urban Crime Areas: Part I." *American Sociological Review* 25:527–542.
1960b "Urban Crime Areas Part II." *American Sociological Review* 25:655–678.
Schrager, Laura S., and James F. Short
1978 "Toward a Sociology of Organizational Crime." *Social Problems* 25(4):407–419.
Schuessler, K. F.
1952 "The Deterrent Influence of the Death Penalty." *Annals of the American Academy of Political and Social Science* 284:54–62.
Schultz, J. L.
1973 "The Cycle of Juvenile Court History." *Crime and Delinquency* 19:457–476.
Schur, Edwin M.
1962 *Narcotic Addiction in Britain and America: The Impact of Public Policy*. Bloomington: Indiana University Press.
1965 *Crimes Without Victims*. Englewood Cliffs, N.J.: Prentice-Hall.
Schwartz, R. D., and S. Orleans
1967 "On Legal Sanctions." *University of Chicago Law Review* 34:274–300.
Schwartz, Richard, and Jerome Skolnick
1964 "Two Studies of Legal Stigma." In Howard Becker (ed.), *The Other Side: Perspectives on Deviance*. New York: Free Press.
Schwendinger, Herman, and Julia Schwendinger
1967 "Delinquent Stereotypes of Probable Victims." In M. W. Klein and B. Meyerhoff (eds.), *Juvenile Gangs in Context*. Englewood Cliffs, N.J.: Prentice-Hall.
1974 *The Sociologists of the Chair*. New York: Basic Books.
Scott, P. D.
1975 "Defenders of Order or Guardians of Human Rights?" In I. Taylor, P. Walton, and J. Young (eds.), *Critical Criminology*. London: Routledge & Kegan Paul.
1956 "Gangs and Delinquent Groups in London." *British Journal of Delinquency* 7:4–26.
Scull, Andrew
1976 "Madness and Segregative Controls: The Rise of the Insane Asylum." *Social Problems* 24(3):337–351.
1977 *Decarceration: Community Treatment and the Deviant—A Radical View*. Englewood Cliffs, N.J.: Prentice-Hall.
Seagle, William
1941 *The Quest for Law*. New York: Knopf.

Seidman, D.
1975 "The Urban Arms Race: A Quantitative Analysis of Private Arming." Ph.D. thesis, Yale University.

Seidman, David and Michael Couzens
1974 "Getting the Crime Rate Down: Political Pressure and Crime Reporting." *Law and Society Review* 8:457–493.

Sellin, Thorsten
1937 *Research Memorandum on Crime in the Depression*. New York: Social Science Research Council, Bulletin 27.
1938 *Culture Conflict and Crime*. New York: Social Science Research Council.
1960 "Enrico Ferri." In H. Mannheim (ed.), *Pioneers in Criminology*. London: Stevens.
1967 *Capital Punishment*. New York: Harper & Row.
1976 *Slavery and the Penal System*. New York: Elsevier.

Sellin, Thorsten, and Marvin Wolfgang
1964 *The Measurement of Delinquency*. New York: Wiley.

Shallo, J. P.
1933 *Private Police*. Philadelphia: American Academy of Political and Social Science.

Shapiro, Susan
1980 "Thinking About White-Collar Crime: Matters of Conceptualization and Research." In *Research on White Collar Crime*. Washington, D.C.: National Institute of Justice.

Shaw, Clifford
1929 *Delinquency Areas*. Chicago: University of Chicago Press.
1930 *The Jack-Roller*. Chicago: University of Chicago Press.
1938 *Brothers in Crime*. Chicago: University of Chicago Press.

Shaw, C., and H. McKay
1931 *Social Factors in Juvenile Delinquency*. National Commission of Law Observance and Enforcement. Washington.
1942 *Juvenile Delinquency and Urban Areas*. Chicago: University of Chicago Press.
1969 *Juvenile Delinquency and Urban Areas*. Rev. ed. Chicago: University of Chicago Press.

Shaw, C., and Moore, M. E.
1931 *Natural History of a Delinquent Career*. Chicago: University of Chicago Press.

Shearing, Clifford, and Philip Stenning
1983 "Private Security: Implications for Social Control." *Social Problems* 30(5):493–506.

Sherry, Arthur
1960 "Vagrants, Rogues and Vagabonds—Old Concepts in Need of Revision." *California Law Review* 48:557–573.

Short, James, Ramona Rivera, and Ray Tennyson
1965 "Perceived Opportunities, Gang Membership, and Delinquency." *American Sociological Review* February:56–67.

Short, James, and Fred Strodtbeck
1965 *Group Process and Gang Delinquency.* Chicago: University of Chicago Press.
Silberman, M.
1976 "Toward a Theory of Criminal Deterrence." *American Sociological Review* 41:442–461.
Silver, A.
1967 "The Demand for Order in Civil Society: A Review of Some Themes in the History of Urban Crime, Police, and Riot." In David Bordua (ed.), *The Police: Six Sociological Essays.* New York: Wiley.
Sinclair, Andrew
1962 *Prohibition: The Era of Excess.* Boston, Little, Brown.
Simmel, Georg
1950 "Quantitative Aspects of the Group." In Kurt H. Wolff (ed.), *The Sociology of Georg Simmel.* New York: Free Press.
Simon, David, and D. Stanley Eitzen
1982 *Elite Deviance.* Boston: Allyn & Bacon.
Simon, Rita
1975 *Women and Crime.* Lexington, Mass.:
1976 "American Women and Crime." *Annals AAPSS* 423:31–46.
Skogan, Wesley
1975 "Measurement Problems in Official and Survey Crime Rates." *Journal of Criminal Justice* 3:17–32.
Skolnick, Jerome
1975 *Justice Without Trial: Law Enforcement in a Democratic Society.* New York: Wiley.
Smart, C.
1976 *Women, Crime and Criminology.* London: Routledge & Kegan Paul.
Smigel, E. O., and H. L. Ross
1970 *Crimes Against Bureaucracy.* New York: Van Nostrand Reinhold.
Smith, Douglas, and Christy Visher
1980 "Sex and Involvement in Deviance/Crime: A Quantitative Review of the Empirical Literature." *American Sociological Review* 45(4):691–701.
1982 "Street Level Justice: Situational Determinants of Police Arrest Decisions." *Social Problems* 29:167–177.
Spector, Malcolm
1976 "Labeling Theory in *Social Problems*: A Young Journal Launches a New Theory." *Social Problems* 24:69–75.
Spitzer, Steven
1975 "Toward a Marxian Theory of Deviance." *Social Problems* 22:638–651.
Spitzer, Steven, and Andrew Scull
1977 "Privatization and Capitalist Development: The Case of the Private Police. *Social Problems* 25(1):18–29.
Stanko, Elizabeth
1977 "These Are the Cases That Try Themselves." Unpublished doctoral dissertation, Graduate School, City University of New York.

Stapleton, Vaughn, David Aday, and Jeanne Ito
1982 "An Empirical Typology of American Metropolitan Juvenile Courts."
American Journal of Sociology 88:549–564.
Stark, R.
1979 "Whose Status Counts? Comment on Tittle, Villemez and Smith." *American Sociological Review* 44:668–669.
Steffensmeier, D.
1978 "Crime and the Contemporary Woman: An Analysis of Changing Levels of Female Property Crime, 1969–75." *Social Forces* 57:566–584.
1980 "Sex Differences in Patterns of Adult Crimes, 1965–77: A Review and Assessment." *Social Forces* 58:1080–1108.
Stephen, James Fitzjames
1883 *A History of the Criminal Law of England*. London.
Stinchombe, Arthur
1963 "Institutions of Privacy in the Determination of Police Administrative Practice." *American Journal of Sociology* 69:150–160.
1964 *Rebellion in a High School*. Chicago: Quadrangle Books.
Stone, Christopher
1975 *Where the Law Ends: The Social Control of Corporate Behavior*. New York: Harper & Row.
Stone, Julius
1950 *The Province and Function of Law*. Cambridge, Mass.: Harvard.
Styron, William
1967 *The Confessions of Nat Turner*. New York: Random.
Suchman, Edward
1968 "The Hang-Loose Ethic and the Spirit of Drug Use." *Journal of Health and Social Behavior* 9(2):146–155.
Sudnow, David
1965 "Normal Crimes: Sociological Features of the Penal Code in a Public Defender Office." *Social Problems* Winter:255–276.
Sumner, W. G.
1960 *Folkways*. New York: Mentor.
(1906)
Sutherland, Edwin
1924 *Criminology*. Philadelphia: Lippincott.
1940 "White-Collar Criminality." *American Sociological Review* 5:1–12.
1945 "Is 'White Collar Crime' Crime?" *American Sociological Review* 10:132–139.
1949 *White Collar Crime*. New York: Dryden.
1950 "The Sexual Psychopath Laws." *Journal of Criminal Law, Criminology and Police Science* 40:543–554.
1951 "The Diffusion of Sexual Psychopath Laws." *American Journal of Sociology* 56:142–148.
Sutherland, Edwin, and Donald Cressey
1966 *Principles of Criminology*. Philadelphia: Lippincott.
Suttles, Gerald
1968 *Social Order of the Slum*. Chicago: University of Chicago Press.

Swanson, Alan H.
1960   "Sexual Psychopath Statutes: Summary and Analysis." *Journal of Criminal Law, Criminology and Police Science* 51:215–227.
Swartz, Joel
1975   "Silent Killers at Work." *Crime and Social Justice.* 3:15–20.
Swigert, Victoria Lynn, and Ronald A. Farrell
1978   "Normal Homicides and the Law." *American Sociological Review* 42:16–31.
1980   "Corporate Homicide: Definitional Processes in the Creation of Deviance." *Law and Society Review* 15(1):161–182.
Sykes, Gresham
1958   *The Society of Captives.* Princeton, N.J.: Princeton University Press.
Sykes, Gresham, and John Clark
1975   "A Theory of Deference Exchange in Police-Civilian Encounters." *American Journal of Sociology* 81(3):584–600.
Sykes, Gresham, and David Matza
1957   "Techniques of Neutralization: A Theory of Delinquency." *American Sociological Review* 22:664–670.
1961   "Juvenile Delinquency and Subterranean Values." *American Sociological Review* 26:712–719.
Sykes, Gresham, and Sheldon Messinger
1960   "The Inmate Social System" In Richard Cloward (ed.), *Theoretical Studies in the Social Organization of the Prison.* New York: Social Science Research Grant.
Sylvester, Sawyer
1972   *The Heritage of Modern Criminology.* Cambridge, Mass.: Schenkman.
Tannenbaum, Franklin
1938   *Crime and the Community.* Boston: Ginn.
Tappan, Paul W.
1947   "Who Is the Criminal?" *American Sociological Review* 12:96–102.
1950   "Sexual Offender Laws and Their Administration." *Federal Probation* 33.
1960   *Crime, Justice and Corrections.* New York: McGraw-Hill.
Taylor, Ian, Paul Walton, and Jock Young
1973   *The New Criminology: For a Social Theory of Deviance.* London, Routledge & Kegan Paul.
1975   *Critical Criminology.* London: Routledge & Kegan Paul.
Teevan, J.
1976a   "Subjective Perception of Deterrence (Continued)." *Journal of Research in Crime and Delinquency* 13:155–164.
1976b   "Deterrent Effects of Punishment: Subjective Measures (Continued)." *Canadian Journal of Criminology and Corrections* 18:152–160.
Terry, Robert M.
1965   "The Screening of Juvenile Offenders: A Study in the Societal Response to Deviant Behavior." Unpublished Ph.D. dissertation. University of Wisconsin.
Thayer, James Bradley
1898   *A Preliminary Treatise on Evidence at the Common Law.* Boston: Little, Brown.

Thomas, Charles, Robin Cage, and Samuel Foster
1976 "Public Opinion on Criminal Law and Legal Sanctions: An Examination of Two Conceptual Models." *Journal of Criminal Law and Criminology* 67:110–116.
Thomas, W. I.
1909 *Source Book for Social Origins*. Chicago: University of Chicago Press.
1967 *The Unadjusted Girl*. New York: Harper & Row Torchbooks.
(1923)
Thompson, Edward Palmer
1975 *Whigs and Hunters*. London: Allen Lane.
Thompson, Hunter
1967 *Hell's Angels*. New York: Ballantine.
Thornberry, Terrence, and Margaret Farnworth
1982 "Social Correlates of Criminal Involvement: Further Evidence on the Relationship Between Social Status and Criminal Behavior." *American Sociological Review* 47:505–518.
Thrasher, Frederick M.
1937 *The Gang*. Chicago: University of Chicago Press.
Tifft, Larry L.
1979 "The Coming Redefinitions of Crime: An Anarchist Perspective."
Social Problems 26:392–402.
Timasheff, N. S.
1941a *One Hundred Years of Probation: 1841–1941*. New York: Fordham University Press.
1941b "Probation in Contemporary Law." *New York University Law Quarterly Review* 18:498–532.
Timberlake, James H.
1963 *Prohibition and the Progressive Movement: 1900–1920*. Cambridge, Mass.: Harvard.
Tittle, C. R.
1977 "Sanction Fear and the Maintenance of Social Order." *Social Forces* 55:579–596.
1980 *Sanctions and Social Deviance*. New York: Praeger.
Tittle, C. R., and C. H. Logan
1973 "Sanctions and Deviance: Evidence and Remaining Questions." *Law and Society Review* 7:371–392.
Tittle, Charles, and A. R. Rowe
1973 "Moral Appeal, Sanction Threat and Deviance: An Experimental Test."
Social Problems 20:488–498.
Tittle, C. R. and W. J. Villemez
1978 "Social Class and Criminality." *Social Forces* 56:474–502.
Tittle, C.R., W.J. Villemez and D. Smith
1978 "The Myth of Social Class and Criminality: An Empirical Assessment of the Empirical Evidence." *American Sociological Review* 43:643–656.
Toby, Jackson
1957a "Social Disorganization and Stake in Conformity: Complementary Factors

in the Predatory Behavior of Young Hoodlums" *Journal of Criminal Law, Criminology and Police Science* 48:12–17.

1957b "The Differential Impact of Family Disorganization." *American Sociological Review* 22:505–512.

Towle, Charlotte
1973 *Common Human Needs*. London: Allen & Unwin.

Traill, H. D.
1899 *Social England*. New York: Putnam & Sons.

Train, Arthur
1924 *The Prisoner at the Bar*. New York: Scribner's.

Trasler, Gordon
1962 *The Explanation of Criminality*. London: Routledge & Kegan Paul.

Turk, Austin
1969 *Criminality and the Legal Order*. Chicago: Rand McNally.
1975 "Prospects and Pitfalls for Radical Criminalogy: A Critical Response to Platt." *Crime and Social Justice* 4:41–42.
1976a "Law as a Weapon in Social Conflict." *Social Problems* 23:276–291.
1976b "Law, Conflict, and Order: From Theorizing Toward Theories." *Canadian Review of Sociology and Anthropology* 13(3):282–294.

Turner, George Kibbe
1907 "The City of Chicago: A Study of Great Immoralities." *McClure's Magazine* April 575.

Udry, J. R.
1974 *The Social Context of Marriage*. Philadelphia: Lippincott.

Uhlman, Thomas and Darlene Walker
1979 "A Plea is no Bargain: The Impact of Case Disposition on Sentencing." *Social Science Quarterly* 60:218–224.
1980 "He Takes Some of My Time; I take some of His: An Analysis of Judicial Sentencing Patterns in Jury Cases." *Law and Society·Review* 14:323–341.

U.S. Department of Justice
1975 Criminal Victimization Surveys in 13 American Cities. U.S. Goverment Printing Office.

Vallee, F. G.
1962 *Kabloona and Eskimo in the Central Keewatin*. Ottawa: Northern Coordination and Research Centre, Department of Northern Affairs and National Resources.

Vaz, Edward
1962 "Juvenile Gang Delinquency in Paris." *Social Problems* 10:23–31.
1965 "Middle-Class Adolescents: Self-Reported Delinquency and Youth Culture Activities." *Canadian Review of Sociology and Anthropology* 2(1):52–70.
1966 "Self Reported Delinquency and Socio-Economic Status." *Canadian Journal of Criminology and Corrections* 8:20–27.
1967 *Middle Class Juvenile Delinquency*. New York: Harper & Row.

Veblen, Thorsten
1967 *The Theory of the Leisure Class*. New York: Viking Press. (1899)

Velez-Diaz, A., and E. I. Megargee
1970 "An Investigation of Differences in Value Judgements Between Youthful Offenders and Non-Offenders in Puerto Rico." *Journal of Criminal Law, Criminology and Police Science* 61:549–553.
Vold, George
1958 *Theoretical Criminology*. New York: Oxford University Press.
Von Hoffman, Nicholas
1970 "Sociological Snoopers." *Transaction* 7(7):4.
Wahl, Albert, and Daniel Glaser
1963 "Pilot Time Study of the Federal Probation Officer's Job." *Federal Probation* 27:20–25.
Waldo, Gordon P., and T. G. Chiricos
1972 "Perceived Penal Sanction and Self-Reported Criminality: A Neglected Approach to Deterrence Research." *Social Problems* 19:522–540.
Wallace, John
1974 "Probation Administration." In Daniel Glaser (ed.), *Handbook of Criminology*, Chicago: Rand McNally.
Wallerstein, J. S., and C. J. Wyle
1947 "Our Law-Abiding Law-Breakers." *Probation* 25:107–112.
Ward, David, Maurice Jackson, and Renee Ward
1969 *Crimes of Violence by Women. Crimes of Violence* V.3, Appendix 17. Washington: President's Commission on Law Enforcement and Administration of Justice.
Waterman, Willoughby
1932 *Prostitution and Its Repression in New York City, 1900–1931*. New York: Columbia.
Webster's Collegiate Dictionary
1959 Springfield, Mass.: G. & C. Merriam.
Weeks, H. Ashley
1958 *Youthful Offenders at Highfields*. Ann Arbor: University of Michigan Press.
Weick, K.
1976 "Educational Organizations as Loosely Coupled Systems." *Administrative Science Quarterly* 21:1–18.
Weinberg, Martin, and Colin Williams
1975 "Gay Baths and tha Social Organization of Impersonal Sex." *Social Problems* 23:124–136.
Wellford Charles
1975 "Labelling Theory and Criminology: An Assessment." *Social Problems* 22:332–345.
Westin, Allan F.
1962 "Bookies and 'Bugs' in California." In Allan Westin (ed.), *The Uses of Power: Seven Case Studies in American Politics*. New York: Harcourt, Brace.
Westley, William
1953 "Violence and the Police." *American Journal of Sociology* 59:34–41.

1970 *Violence and the Police: A Sociological Study of Law, Custom, and Morality.* Cambridge, Mass.: MIT Press.

Wheeler, Stanton
1968 *Controlling Delinquents.* New York: Wiley.
1976 "Trends and Problems in the Sociological Study of Crime." *Social Problems* 23:525–534.

Wheeler, Stanton, Edna Bonacich, Richard Cramer, and Irving K. Zola
1968 "Agents of Delinquency Control." In Stanton Wheeler (ed.), *Controlling Delinquents.* New York: Wiley.

Wheeler, Stanton, and Mitchell Lewis Rothman
1982 "The Organization as Weapon in White-Collar Crime." *Michigan Law Review* 80(7):1403–1426.

Wheeler, Stanton, David Weisbord, and Nancy Bode
1982 "Sentencing the White Collar Offender: Rhetoric and Reality." *American Sociological Review* 47:641–659.

Whitelock, Dorothy
1952 *The Beginnings of English Society.* Harmondsworth, England: Penguin.

Whyte, William F.
1955 *Street Corner Society.* 2d ed. Chicago: University of Chicago Press.

Wiatrowski, Michael, David Griswold, and Mary Roberts
1981 "Social Control Theory and Delinquency." *American Sociological Review* 46:525–541.

Wiatrowski, Michael, Stephen Hansell, Charles Massey, and David Wilson
1982 "Curriculum Tracking and Delinquency." *American Sociological Review* 47:151–160.

Wilkins, Leslie
1964 *Social Deviance.* London: Tavistock.

Wilkinson, Karen
1974 "The Broken Family and Juvenile Delinquency: Scientific Explanation or Ideology." *Social Problems* 21(5):726–739.

Wilson, James Q.
1968a "The Police and the Delinquent in Two Cities." In Stanton Wheeler (ed.), *Controlling Delinquents.* New York: Wiley.
1968b *Varieties of Police Behavior.* Cambridge, Mass.: Harvard.
1975 *Thinking About Crime.* New York: Basic Books.
1978 *The Investigators.* New York: Basic Books.
1980 "'What Works' Revisited: New Findings on Criminal Rehabilitation." *Public Interest* 61:3–17.

Wise, Nancy
1967 "Juvenile Delinquency among Middle Class Girls." In Edmund Vaz (ed.), *Middle Class Delinquency.* New York: Harper & Row.

Wolfgang, Marvin
1958 *Patterns in Criminal Homicide.* Philadelphia: University of Pennsylvania Press.
1960 "Cesare Lombroso." In H. Mannheim (ed.), *Pioneers in Criminology.* London: Stevens.

1963 "Criminology and the Criminologist." *Journal of Criminal Law, Criminology and Police Science* 54:155–162.

Wolfgang, Marvin, and Franco Ferracuti
1967 *The Subculture of Violence*. London: Tavistock.

Wolfgang, Marvin, and Mark Riedel
1973 "Race, Judicial Discretion, and the Death Penalty." *The Annals of the American Academy of Political and Social Science*. 407:119.

Woodmansee, John
1975 *The World of a Grant Corporation: A Report from the G.E. Project*. Seattle: North Country.

Wrong, D.
1961 "The Oversocialized Conception of Man in Modern Sociology." *American Sociological Review* 26:183–93.

Yablonsky, Lewis
1959 *The Violent Gang*. New York: Macmillan.

Yinger, J. M.
1960 "Contraculture and Subculture." *American Sociological Review* 25:625–635.

Young, Paul
1976 "A Sociological Analysis of the Early History of Probation." *British Journal of Law and Society* 3:44–58.

Zatz, Marjorie and John Hagan
1984 "Crime, Time and Punishment." In James Fox (ed.), *Criminological Research*. New York: Plenum.

Zeisel, H.
1976 "The Deterrent Effect of the Death Penalty: Facts v. Faiths." In P. Kurland (ed.), *The Supreme Court Review*. Chicago: University of Chicago Press.

Ziegenhagan, Eduard A.
1977 *Victims, Crime and Social Control*. New York: Praeger.

Znaniecki, Florian
1934 *The Method of Sociology*. New York: Rinehart.

NAME INDEX

SUBJECT INDEX